The Eighth Connecticut
Volunteer Infantry
in the Civil War

Camp of the 8th Rgt: C.V. Annapolis Decbr 8th 1861.

The Eighth Connecticut Volunteer Infantry in the Civil War

WILLIAM A. LISKA *and*
KIM L. PERLOTTO

Foreword by Matthew Warshauer

McFarland & Company, Inc., Publishers
Jefferson, North Carolina

Frontispiece: Camp of the 8th Regiment Connecticut Volunteers—Annapolis, Maryland, December 8, 1861 (Joseph E. Shadek Civil War Sketchbook. Courtesy Bridgeport History Center, Bridgeport Public Library).

LIBRARY OF CONGRESS CATALOGUING-IN-PUBLICATION DATA

Names: Liska, William A., 1950– author. | Perlotto, Kim, author.
Title: The Eighth Connecticut Volunteer Infantry in the Civil War / William A. Liska, and Kim L. Perlotto.
Description: Jefferson, North Carolina : McFarland & Company, Inc., Publishers, 2023. | Includes bibliographical references and index.
Identifiers: LCCN 2022052130 | ISBN 9781476690414 (paperback : acid free paper) ∞
ISBN 9781476648231 (ebook)
Subjects: LCSH: United States. Army. Connecticut Infantry Regiment, 8th (1861–1865)—History. | United States—History—Civil war, 1861–1865—Regimental histories. | BISAC: HISTORY / Military / United States | HISTORY / United States / Civil War Period (1850–1877)
Classification: LCC E499.5 8th L6 2022 | DDC 973.7/446—dc23/eng/20221028
LC record available at https://lccn.loc.gov/2022052130

BRITISH LIBRARY CATALOGUING DATA ARE AVAILABLE

ISBN (print) 978-1-4766-9041-4
ISBN (ebook) 978-1-4766-4823-1

© 2023 William A. Liska and Kim L. Perlotto. All rights reserved

No part of this book may be reproduced or transmitted in any form or by any means, electronic or mechanical, including photocopying or recording, or by any information storage and retrieval system, without permission in writing from the publisher.

Front cover image: Monument Dedication, Eighth Conn. Vols., October 11, 1894, in Walter J. Yates, *Souvenir of Excursion to Antietam.* (Photograph by Tad Sattler)

Printed in the United States of America

McFarland & Company, Inc., Publishers
Box 611, Jefferson, North Carolina 28640
www.mcfarlandpub.com

To the soldiers
of the Eighth Regiment,
Connecticut Volunteer Infantry,
1861–1865

Table of Contents

Maps	viii
Acknowledgments	xi
Foreword by Matthew Warshauer	1
Preface	3
Introduction	5
Chapter 1. Hartford to Annapolis	9
Chapter 2. Hatteras to New Bern	24
Chapter 3. Fort Macon to Washington, D.C.	48
Chapter 4. Frederick, South Mountain, and Antietam	68
Chapter 5. Fredericksburg to Newport News	88
Chapter 6. Suffolk, Portsmouth, Deep Creek, Home	107
Chapter 7. Deep Creek to Drewry's Bluff	137
Chapter 8. Cold Harbor, Petersburg, Fort Harrison	156
Chapter 9. Richmond, Lynchburg, and Home	186
Conclusion: After the War	192
Appendix A. Record of Service	201
Appendix B. Biographies of Narrators and Notables	209
Appendix C. Flags of the Eighth	233
Appendix D. Arms and Equipment of the Eighth	241
Appendix E. The Modern Eighth Connecticut Volunteers	248
Appendix F. Map Notes	250
Chapter Notes	255
Bibliography	281
Index	285

Maps

Map 1. Burnside Expedition, North Carolina, January–June 1862 — 28
Map 2. Battle of Roanoke Island, North Carolina, February 8, 1862 — 33
Map 3. Battle of New Bern, North Carolina, March 14, 1862 — 42
Map 4. Siege of Fort Macon, North Carolina, April 1862 — 49
Map 5. Route of March to Sharpsburg, Maryland, September 1862 — 69
Map 6. Positions of the Eighth, Battle of Antietam, Maryland, September 17, 1862 — 76
Map 7. Final Attack of the Eighth, Antietam, Maryland, September 17, 1862 — 80
Map 8. Route of March to Fredericksburg, Virginia, November 1862 — 90
Map 9. Vicinity of Fredericksburg and Falmouth, Virginia, December 1862 — 93
Map 10. Positions of the Eighth, Battle of Fredericksburg, Virginia, December 13, 1862 — 100
Map 11. Vicinity of Hampton Roads, Virginia, Spring 1863 — 109
Map 12. Vicinity of Fort Huger and Suffolk, Virginia, April 1863 — 113
Map 13. Route of March on "The Blackberry Raid," July 1863 — 123
Map 14. Vicinity of Richmond and Petersburg, Virginia, May 1864 — 139
Map 15. Second Battle of Port Walthall Junction, Virginia, May 7, 1864, a.m. — 143
Map 16. Second Battle of Port Walthall Junction, Virginia, May 7, 1864, p.m. — 144
Map 17. Battle of Swift Creek, Virginia, May 9, 1864 — 148
Map 18. Battle of Drewry's Bluff, Virginia, May 16, 1864 — 150
Map 19. Battle of Cold Harbor, Virginia, June 1, 1864, 6:00 p.m. — 158
Map 20. Second Battle of Petersburg, Virginia, June 15, 1864, 7:00 p.m. — 167
Map 21. Battle of Fort Harrison, Virginia, September 29, 1864, 6:00 a.m. — 177

	Abatis		Plowed Field
	Boat		Ship
	Building		Earthworks
	Church		Camp
	Cornfield		Woods
	Lighthouse		Artillery
	Marsh		Pickets/Skirmishers
	Orchard		Confederate Forces
	Pasture		Union Forces
	Road		Ravine/Cliff
	Lane		Railroad

Map symbols.

Acknowledgments

We would not have been able to complete this book without the support and assistance of many people over the years it took to bring it to fruition. We would like to express our heartfelt thanks to a few of them who helped us put this book together.

Without the letters and diaries of the soldiers themselves, this story could not have been told. The following people were essential in making those sources available. A grateful thanks to Frederick Plumb, family friend and mentor, for sharing his family history and the story of Seth Plumb, and to Fred's son, Rick Plumb, for his continued support; Sandra and Jerry Mercer for sharing their family history of Wolcott Marsh with us; Stephen Bartkus of the Gunn Museum for providing Jay Nettleton's story; Edward Thompson for the Albion Brooks letters and diary; Joy Veronneau for donating the Roger Ford diary, and to Matt Reardon of the New England Civil War Museum for giving us access to it; Barry Fox, and to Dan Hayden and Hank Cullinane, also of the Museum, for use of the Lucius Fox diary; Donald Pfanz, NPS, and Barbara Strong, of the Simsbury Historical Society, for bringing our attention to the Oliver Case letters; Sandra Trenholm and Tristan Fangman of the Gilder-Lehrman Institute for access to the Charles Coit letters and for allowing us to transcribe the originals; Mark Radeleff and Nathan Gonzales of the Lincoln Memorial Shrine for calling our attention to the John Merriam letters and allowing us to transcribe them; Tasha Caswell of the Connecticut Historical Society for access to the Andrew Byrne diary; Lizette Pelletier of the Connecticut State Library for permission to use the papers and images from the Andrew M. Morgan Collection and the Hilliard Ferris letters; Linda Hocking of the Litchfield Historical Society for access to Plumb family correspondence; Jennifer Baker of Duke University for assistance with the Henry Hall and Fitz Hollister letters; and James Capobianco of Harvard University for help with the William Huntington letters.

Images and photographs were also important to us, and in that department, we thank Matt Reardon and Tad Sattler for use of their private collections of CDVs and other images; Elizabeth Boucher of the Mystic River Historical Society for providing us with a Hiram Appelman CDV; Scott Hann for a CDV of John Ward; Tom Laporte, Carol Denehy, and Mike Thompson, of the Memorial Military Museum, Bristol, Connecticut, for access to the rare camp lithograph of the Eighth; Carol Highsmith for her State Capitol Hall of Flags photograph; Elizabeth Van Tuyl of the Bridgeport History Center for providing images of the Joseph E. Shadek paintings; and Bill

Caughman, Steve Hill, and Eric Connery for images and information on the Connecticut state battle flags.

And for other research and assistance, we appreciate John Hennessy, former chief historian at Fredericksburg and Spotsylvania National Military Park, for the information he provided us on the Eighth at Fredericksburg; Chris Darling for his help in identifying the arms and equipment of the Eighth; Skip Riddle of the New Bern Historical Society for friendship and historical support in North Carolina; Bill Hoelzel for his professional copy editing work; and Charlie Perdue, our McFarland editor, for having the trust in us to publish our book.

And we must also thank the past and present members of the Eighth Regiment Connecticut Volunteer Infantry, Company A, Inc., the "new Eighth," for their interest, passion, and participation over the past thirty years in researching, recording and portraying the history of the original Eighth and its soldiers.

Last, but certainly not least, we thank Matt Warshauer for his friendship, knowledge and guidance in reviewing our manuscript and helping us through the book publishing process.

* * *

A particular thanks also goes to all our friends and family for indulging us with the many hours we spent following our passion. On a more personal level:

From Bill Liska: Thanks to my wife, Nicole, for her encouragement and support in helping me see this project through.

From Kim Perlotto: My heartfelt gratitude to my wife, Jane, for her continuous and unconditional support of my lifelong pursuit of history.

While we have not named every person who had some hand in this project, we give our humble thanks to each and every one who helped along the way to making this book a reality.

Foreword
by Matthew Warshauer

Unlike so many of the truly important Connecticut regiments in Civil War history, the Eighth Regiment Connecticut Volunteer Infantry has long been denied a written history of its own. Regiments such as the Fourteenth and Sixteenth boast histories penned by the very men who had served for years under their regimental banners and on the bloody fields of the South. The Eighth's history was never completed. There was talk of such an endeavor in the years following the war, but for whatever reason it never came to fruition. Until now.

William Liska and Kim Perlotto, longtime Eighth Connecticut reenactors and devotees, have done an immeasurable service by faithfully chronicling the longest serving Civil War infantry regiment in the state's history. This is no small undertaking. The history of the Eighth has been years in the making. Years to comb through archives and letter collections. Years to transcribe the many letters and other documents. Years to actually sit down and place everything in order and write. The final product will be of interest to many historians and countless Civil War afficionados.

Their book is written in the traditional, narrative style of late nineteenth and early twentieth century regimental histories. Here is not the parsing and pontificating of academic historians. Rather, it is a minute, chronological account of the regiment's service to the Union during four years of struggle. The men of the Eighth's words are foremost in the readers' minds, as Liska and Perlotto map the regiment's experiences through the narrative voices of the men themselves. As one of those pontificating historians, it is not often—except in letters—that I get to see the war directly and so extensively through the soldiers' eyes.

In this sense, this book is like a window in time. The authors have a flair for drawing out the often dire circumstances and emotions that these men faced. The reader cannot help but get to know the soldiers of the Eighth. That knowing is felt keenly when one of those narrative voices is lost through the devastation that was the American Civil War.

Anyone who picks up this book will also get to know the Eighth Regiment Connecticut Volunteer Infantry. They will know the soldiers' devotion to one another and the Union, and they will know William Liska's and Kim Perlotto's devotion to the Eighth.

Matthew Warshauer is a professor of history at Central Connecticut State University and was the co-chair of the Connecticut Civil War Commemoration Commission from 2009 to 2015.

Preface

In the Civil War that gripped the nation more than a century ago, well over seventeen hundred volunteer regiments fought as part of the Union army in the epic cause to save the nation. Men from all walks of life volunteered for the fight. Living the lives of soldiers left lifelong memories in their minds as veterans. They knew the horrors of war from their time on the battlefields together, but they also developed friendships and a sense of camaraderie that became a fundamental part of their lives.

After the war, many of the regiments, perhaps most, had members who put their stories into print, recording for posterity the experiences of the men and the significance of what they did to preserve the union.

But in the aftermath of the war, not all Civil War regiments had the will or the talent to write their own history. The Eighth Regiment Connecticut Volunteer Infantry was one of the few Connecticut regiments that did not prepare and publish a regimental history. We do not know why this was the case. The Eighth certainly had members with the intelligence, ability and wherewithal to produce such a record, and their attendance at annual regimental reunions held well into the twentieth century proved their devotion to the Eighth. Yet the story of the Eighth has not been told.

It is our goal to rectify that omission with this book. While our story cannot be an actual, contemporary account of the Eighth's experiences, it is intended to reflect the spirit of those original regimental histories, which were written by the soldiers themselves. To that end, we have relied largely on primary sources and first-person accounts of the events of those days.

As members of a Civil War reenactment group portraying, studying and honoring the Eighth Regiment, we have spent over twenty-five years researching and gathering original letters and diaries from universities, libraries, government sources, archives, and, most fortunately, from descendants of the original members of the Eighth. We have transcribed many of these documents from the handwritten originals, making them accessible for the first time since the Civil War. We amassed more than a thousand documents written by the members of the regiment during the war. As we collected the puzzle pieces and the stories fell into place, we began to hear the voices of these men telling us the history of the Eighth Regiment in their own words. We have also drawn from other contemporary records and modern secondary histories to help set the stage and give context to the soldiers' stories so we can better understand what the men themselves had written.

These sources were the preferred threads we used to weave the history of the Eighth Regiment. To be true to their voices, we have included their writings in their original form, without alteration. As a result, the materials here include opinions and language from that period that may raise eyebrows today. We believe that it was essential to use their language in order to accurately convey the character and tenor of their times. Occasionally we have used square brackets to insert editorial detail to help readers understand these primary sources.

A regimental history is not complete without a full roster of the members who served. After the war was over, the State of Connecticut compiled such a record of all men who served. We made good use of it and point interested readers to it for further research. The book is called the *Record of Service of Connecticut Men in the Army and Navy of the United States During the War of the Rebellion*, compiled by authority of the General Assembly under the direction of the Adjutants-General Smith, Camp, Barbour, and White. It was published by Case, Lockwood, and Brainard Co., Hartford, Conn., 1889. It is available on the Internet as a PDF. The URL for the Connecticut State Library download is https://cdm15019.contentdm.oclc.org/digital/collection/p128501coll2/id/177208. The book includes rosters for all the Connecticut infantry regiments, artillery batteries, and cavalry troops. The rosters contain valuable information such as name, town, rank, company, and dates of enlistments, promotions, wounds, deaths, transfers, and discharges. It is a wealth of details for historic research, family genealogy, or general interest.

While we know that our story will never take the place of an original, contemporary history, we believe that telling the story of this regiment in this way is the right thing to do. These heroes and patriots who were known as the Eighth surely deserve to have their story told. What better way to honor and preserve their legacy than with this book?

Introduction

The basic organizational unit of the Civil War army was the regiment. At its formation, the regiment comprised about one thousand men, divided equally into ten companies. However, when disease, battle and normal attrition reduced that number, no new men were sent to replace them. It was simply more politically advantageous to politicians to create new regiments—and to hand out new leadership positions—than it was to fill openings in existing units. Thus, most Civil War regiments by the middle of the war were operating at less than 50 percent strength. This practice changed later in the war when substitutes and draftees became available as replacements.

Civil War regiments were overwhelmingly *state* regiments. They were formed by the states, made up of men almost entirely from their state, and were identified with the name of their state (e.g., the Eighth Connecticut Volunteers). When President Abraham Lincoln called for volunteers, his administration in Washington asked the states for regiments, not for men. The United States Army (that is, the regular army) was relatively small at the start of the Civil War, and it remained that way. State volunteer regiments fought the bulk of war.

The nucleus for the first state regiments was the "active militia" units operating in many states at the time. Active militia meant uniformed companies or regiments of volunteers who uniformed themselves at their own expense and organized into quasi-military bodies for the purpose of discipline, training and drill. Connecticut was exceptional in that it had created an organized regimental system of active militia in each county. Two of these active militias, in Hartford County and New Haven County, formed the core for the first two volunteer regiments formed when the Civil War began.[1]

The ten companies that made up a Civil War regiment were identified by the letters A through K (there was no J). They were called "Company" first, then the letter designating their specific unit—for example, Company A—rather than by the modern term "A Company" (or Able Company).

Companies were commanded by captains. When the early regiments were first formed, many captains owed their commissions to the fact that they had recruited the bulk of the men in their company. As prominent men in their area (and often commanders of the local militia company), they were natural leaders. Thus, the companies that were formed and that became part of a specific regiment were made up mostly of men from a local town or neighboring areas in the state.

Once formed, the companies of about one hundred men each assembled locally and then traveled to a central rendezvous point where they were joined together into a ten-company unit called a regiment, and the regiment was mustered into service. The task of the officers of the regiment was to train and drill the men and turn them into soldiers and ultimately to mold the regiment into an effective fighting unit of about one thousand men.

The formation of a Civil War army usually combined four regiments into a brigade, commanded by a brigadier general. Brigades were often composed of regiments from a certain state or area. Brigades would then be combined into divisions, divisions into corps, and corps into armies. Thus, at the Battle of Antietam in 1862, the Eighth Regiment Connecticut Volunteer Infantry was part of the Second Brigade of the Third Division of the Ninth Corps of the Army of the Potomac.

The method of battle employed by Civil War armies dated back to the American Revolution and before. The armies, and therefore the regiments, fought each other by standing their infantry in long lines of battle in open fields, firing volleys at each other, and then charging the opposing line with bayonets and swords. Artillery and cavalry joined the battle, but the lines of opposing troops were the basis for engagement. It was a very formal style of warfare.

Moving these large numbers of troops from one place to another, and then forming and maneuvering them in battle, required a complex set of commands, formations and evolutions. To teach these skills, military manuals had been written: the two most prominent at the time were *Hardee's Rifle and Infantry Tactics* by William Hardee and *Infantry Tactics* by Silas Casey. Drill in these procedures took a very large portion of the soldier's time. Success or failure in battle often came down to the ability of the regiment to execute commands immediately and effectively, frequently while under fire.

The soldier's training began with the "School of the Soldier," which included instruction in the manual of arms, that is, the positions and firing of the war's primary infantry weapon, the .58 caliber rifled musket. Next was the "School of the Company," which taught the men the basics of field maneuvering. The soldiers learned the many variations on how to go from a line of march (or "by the flank") into a line of battle two ranks deep and back again. From there drill evolved to the "School of the Battalion" and "Evolutions of a Brigade"—more complex movements involving larger bodies of troops.

While training usually began immediately in the town or city where the regiment was formed, it often continued elsewhere at a "Camp of Instruction," the Civil War version of basic training. From there the regiment would be sent wherever the U.S. War Department and the generals decided they were needed. Sometimes it might take months for a regiment to see action for the first time. Other times, especially if there was a major campaign underway, they could see fighting very soon.

For example, the Sixteenth Connecticut was mustered into service on August 24, 1862. However, as a result of the Confederate invasion of Maryland just a few weeks later, the Sixteenth was rushed to the Army of the Potomac, arriving the day before the Battle of Antietam. It was put into the same brigade as that of the Eighth Connecticut. With little training and no experience, the Sixteenth found itself in the middle of a cornfield, on the far left of the entire Federal line, when it was suddenly struck by the flank attack of Confederate General A.P. Hill's division arriving from Harpers Ferry. The Sixteenth suffered greatly and was forced to retire from the battlefield.

The Eighth Connecticut was one of the longest serving regiments in the Civil War, serving from September 21, 1861, until December 12, 1865. During that time, the unit saw a wide range of duty and experience. Their wartime service began with the amphibious campaign of Burnside's Expedition to North Carolina. They marched with the Army of the Potomac from Washington, D.C., to Sharpsburg, Maryland, where they had their finest hour on the hills of Antietam in 1862. The regiment fought at Fredericksburg, Suffolk, and at battles outside Richmond. The men of the Eighth watched the Crater explode at Petersburg, Virginia, and endured the trench warfare there. Even after the surrender of Confederate General Robert E. Lee on April 9, 1865, at Appomattox, Virginia, the Eighth Regiment stayed on in Virginia to serve the Union.

The letters and diaries of the soldiers of the Eighth weave a fascinating tale of their life during this time. Their service was not just at battles. They traveled often, usually marching on foot, but sometimes moving by railroad or transporting by boat over the rivers and inland waterways of Virginia and North Carolina. They were jammed onto steamers, gunboats, converted ferry boats, sailing ships and even barges. When not on the move, they made camps in locations as varied as their modes of transportation.

Camp life involved all of the basics. They were usually housed in tents, fine tents at first, but smaller as the war progressed. Officers received better accommodations, of course. At Fredericksburg, Virginia, in December 1862, enlisted men slept outdoors in small dog tents while the officers (and their servants) stayed in a Southern mansion they had appropriated. Food was a major interest, as would be expected. The spartan rations issued by the army were supplemented by food sent from home in express boxes, treats purchased from sutlers (merchants who travelled with each unit), and whatever could be scrounged locally.

Then, of course, there was the fighting. Battles ranged from a line of battle in an open field, which the Eighth Connecticut experienced at Antietam, to assaults on forts and breastworks, often with vicious hand-to-hand fighting, to trench warfare where the wrong move or a moment's indiscretion could mean death from a sniper's bullet.

Battles (and disease, which was ever present) often meant death. It was on the battlefield where one can see the tragedy of war and the depth of character of these men. For example, the field on which the Eighth fought at Antietam was under Confederate control for two days after the battle. It was not until the enemy left that the surviving men from the Eighth could search for their wounded and dead to see to their treatment and burial.

Sergeant Seth Plumb of Company E was the first member of the Eighth to reach the field after the Confederates retreated. He was looking for his friend, George Booth, a member of the Eighth's color guard. Seth had been told that Booth had been shot so he was hoping to find him alive. But that was not to be; instead, he found

George's body. As Seth wrote later, "I cannot tell you how much I miss George. Ed [another friend], George, and I have been more than brothers since we enlisted, what was joy to one was joy to the others, and what was grief to one was grief to the rest, now it seems very hard to give him up."[2]

The story of the Eighth is contained in the letters and diaries of its soldiers. It is their voices that help us years later to understand what these men did and how they felt about their comrades, their cause, and their service to the nation.

Chapter 1

Hartford to Annapolis

Connecticut responded quickly to the crisis that gripped the nation when South Carolina attacked Fort Sumter on April 12–13, 1861. Three regiments, the 1st, 2nd, and 3rd Connecticut Volunteer Infantry, were recruited under the proclamation of President Abraham Lincoln issued Monday, April 15, 1861, and under the call of Connecticut Governor William A. Buckingham issued the next day. Only one regiment had been called for, but the eagerness of the state's men to enlist prompted the governor to intercede with the president to ask him to accept at least three regiments, and his request was granted. These regiments were recruited to serve for three months, and each fought at the first battle of Bull Run or Manassas in July of 1861.[1]

The Union defeat at that battle was a wake-up call for the Northern people. "It swept away our 'ninety-days' optimism, and showed us that what we had mistaken for an April shower was to be a long storm, and a hard one." Congress, the day after Bull Run, authorized the president to call out 500,000 men for three years.[2]

Since the first three Connecticut regiments which had fought at Bull Run were "three-months regiments," they were mustered out upon their return to Connecticut after the battle. However, most of the men in these regiments soon re-enlisted in the new units being formed, and many were either immediately promoted or subsequently rose to higher ranks there.[3] These veterans would figure prominently in the leadership of these later regiments, including the Eighth.

The 4th and 5th Connecticut Volunteer Infantry regiments were formed prior to Bull Run but did not see action there. The 4th, the first three-year regiment from Connecticut and later to become the 1st Regiment C.V. Heavy Artillery, was in Maryland at the time of the battle, while the 5th was not mustered in until the days following the battle.[4] It was on August 15, 1861, in response to the recent call for more volunteers, that Governor Buckingham issued general orders directing that volunteers be accepted for the 6th, 7th, 8th and 9th Connecticut Volunteer Infantry, three-year regiments, as part of the state's quota. In those orders, the Eighth was directed to rendezvous at Hartford.[5]

A Regiment Is Formed

The 8th Connecticut was formed from men hailing from all corners of the state, but as we said in the introduction, many of the captains owed their commission to the fact that they had recruited the bulk of the men in their company. As a result, companies were made up mostly of men from a single town or several nearby towns, as we can see by the hometowns of the men in the ten companies in the Eighth.

- Company A, Captain Henry M. Hoyt—men from Hartford and Bridgeport, with others from East Windsor, Manchester, Naugatuck and other towns;
- Company B, Captain Patrick K. Ruth—the bulk of the men from Enfield, with a few from Suffield, Simsbury and East Windsor;
- Company C, Captain Charles W. Nash—mainly men from New Hartford, with others from nearby Granby, Colebrook, Enfield, Torrington and Canton;

Governor William A. Buckingham (in W.A. Croffut and J.M. Morris, *The Military and Civil History of Connecticut During the War of 1861–1865*).

- Company D, Captain John E. Ward—men from Norwich, Lebanon and Windham;
- Company E, Captain Martin B. Smith—men from Waterbury and Litchfield, with the remainder from Rocky Hill, Woodbury and Cornwall;
- Company F, Captain Elijah Y. Smith—half of the men from Plainfield and the rest from Canterbury, Griswold, Brooklyn and Sterling;
- Company G, Captain Hiram Appelman—the vast majority of men from Stonington with the balance from Groton;
- Company H, Captain Douglas Fowler—mainly men from Norwalk, with some from Danbury, Ridgefield, Wilton and Redding;

- Company I, Captain Frederick W. Jackson—most men from New Milford and Brookfield and the rest from Newtown, Washington, and Danbury;
- Company K, Captain Charles L. Upham—men primarily from Meriden.[6]

Two interesting sidenotes deserve attention. First, Captain Ruth's Company B had initially been part of the 10th Connecticut. However, when Charles L. Russell of Danbury, who had helped recruit a company for the Eighth, was offered the lieutenant-colonelcy of the 10th Connecticut Regiment, he agreed to accept the position only on the condition that his company be transferred with him to his new regiment. This proposition was accepted by the governor, and Captain Russell's company moved to the 10th Connecticut, and Captain Ruth's Enfield company joined the Eighth.[7]

Second, some of the recruits for Company G were actually men from nearby Westerly, Rhode Island, many of whom were veterans of three-months service with the Westerly Rifles. The *Narragansett Weekly* reported that in Connecticut volunteers received not only the regular pay of $13 per month, but those with families also received up to $10 a month from the state. Moreover, when they were honorably discharged, each volunteer, married or single, received $30 from Connecticut and a $100 bounty from the United States.[8]

By September 15, the Eighth was full, and it was mustered into service beginning on September 21. The commander was Colonel Edward Harland of Norwich, who had been a captain with the three-month 3rd Connecticut Regiment.[9]

Camp Buckingham

Recruits for the Eighth were initially barracked at the "Fair Grounds" on Albany Avenue in Hartford, north of the center of the city. This is where the 3rd Connecticut Volunteer Infantry had been camped in May.[10] In early September, though, "the first fractional companies of the Eighth began to move to a camp,—the grounds that the Fifth [Connecticut] had vacated—just outside Hartford. Drilling, which had generally begun at the places of original enlistment, was continued vigorously in the camps."[11] This camp, which would be known as Camp Buckingham in honor of the governor, was located in a field at the southeast corner of Bond and Webster Streets[12] in what is now the Barry Square area of the south end of Hartford.

A portion of the camp site, what would have been its northwest corner, is now a small city park bordered on three sides by an iron fence. In the center of the park is a statue to Colonel Griffin A. Stedman of the 11th Connecticut. He was a lieutenant colonel at Antietam, promoted to colonel after the battle and the death of Colonel Henry W. Kingsbury. He was later killed at Petersburg, and is identified on the monument as a "typical volunteer soldier."

On the south side of the statue's granite base is a bronze plaque which reads:

THIS MONUMENT MARKS THE FIELD EXTENDING FROM THIS POINT SIXTY RODS EAST AND ONE-HUNDRED RODS SOUTH ON WHICH SEVEN REGIMENTS OF CONNECTICUT VOLUNTEERS ENCAMPED AND WERE MUSTERED INTO THE SERVICE OF THE UNITED STATES DURING THE CIVIL WAR. / 1861–1865. / ERECTED BY THE VETERAN SURVIVORS OF THE WAR.

Since a rod is sixteen and a half feet long, the field was about 990 feet wide along the south side of Bond Street, and about 1,650 feet deep along the east side of Webster Street. On the opposite side of the monument, another plaque identifies those seven regiments: the 5th, 8th, 10th, 14th, 16th, 22nd, and 25th Connecticut Volunteers. As a result of Camp Buckingham, that portion of Webster Street south of the intersection of Webster and Bond was renamed Camp Field Avenue, which later became Campfield Avenue.[13]

One recruit, Private Hilliard B. Ferris of Company I, described what is surely the transfer from the fairgrounds barracks to the new camp: "We are now in camp, where we arrived last night, marching down from the barracks about 1 mile north of the city and some 3 miles from camp. We were all very glad to get from there as we had to sleep on the floor. We are now quartered in nice clean tents of 8 in a mess whom we selected ourselves.... We were sworn in yesterday—no one backing out—all in good spirits. We have a smooth camping ground and we are the eighth company in. I find things a good deal better than I expected—plenty to eat and good order in camp."[14]

Ferris wrote a few days later,

> At times it is almost a Bable here—talking, hooting, singing, fiddling, drumming is all going on at the same time. Many of the soldiers here are inveterate swearers who swear more from habit than anything else, while some are as good steady fellows as are found anywhere. We were inspected last Friday, and sworn into US service Saturday [September 21].... We had 3 rejected and 2 from Sandy Hook ran away. The 8th Reg't has got her full number of companies but lacks her complement of men some 200.... I wish you could be here to see the squads drilled. There is sometimes 3 and 400 in bands of 20 to 40 men under different commands, wheeling, marching in a mixed up mix.[15]

The Eighth remained in camp in Hartford while the regiment was prepared and equipped for the anticipated trip south. Private Ferris wrote on October 3, "The knapsacks were distributed yesterday. They are well made of enameled cloth—weigh 4 or 5 lbs. I don't know as we shall get our coat & pants under a week or so—want of them and the baggage—wagons, ambulances etc is all that probably keep the 8th from being sent on. We drill but little now and have a pretty lazy time of it."[16]

Also, on October 3 the Eighth received its pair of flags. Adjutant Charles M. Coit wrote, "[W]e have just this p.m. rec'd our colors—one state, the other U.S.—they are said to be the finest given to any regiment thus far, the men say they can 'stand by them.'"[17]

Training progressed gradually. On October 11, Coit wrote, "We have had no battalion drills or dress parade as yet, we are to commence regular Guard Mounting tomorrow."[18] It was on October 16, 1861, that the regiment had a regimental drill for the first time. Governor Buckingham came to the camp to observe the drill. The Eighth was armed primarily with rifled muskets, but the companies at each end of the regiment in the line of battle, the flank companies, were armed with breech-loading Sharps rifles and saber bayonets. These flank companies were Company K from Meriden and Company G from Mystic.[19]

A few days before, the Eighth had gone to church together as a group. Coit wrote, "The regiment went together to church at South Congl this p.m. we filled the body of the church entirely, the Colonel + Staff sat in the front seat in the middle isle, the galleries, sides + platform in front of the pulpit was jammed full with the congregation, principally women. The discourse was prepared especially for the regiment, subject, maliciousness, very good + practical.... We have in our ... regiment two parsons, one Congl + the other Methodist, so we are well supplied."[20]

The Journey Begins

On Thursday, October 17, 1861, the regiment left Camp Buckingham. Samuel Jay Nettleton, a corporal in Company I, described their departure: "We were ordered to pack our knapsacks & be in readiness to form into line at two o'clock. We dined at 11 o'clock & at 12 were to strike our tents. At the beat of the drum the tents all dropped with but a few exceptions through the Regiment. One minute all that could be seen was the tents, the next the tent field was a living mass of blue."

Nettleton explained how the changeover was accomplished. "The way that is done is by pulling all but four pins previously & then four men are stationed by these pins so that when the drum taps down come the tents into the street." Then the troops began their march southward. "We marched directly to the beat but our knapsacks felt like lead a long time before we got there.... We started from Hartford at 4 o'clock."[21]

Private Ferris, also in Company I, wrote,

> We received our arms Tuesday [October 15]. They are the Springfield Minni—rifled musket[s].... Our knapsacks weigh from 30 to 35 pounds; guns, canteens, cartridge boxes, haversacks etc some 30 pounds more certain. So. you see we had a tolerable good load to carry our first march of 3 or 4 miles. After standing some half an hour the whole regiment fell in line and was ordered to march for our unknown destination. We found it rather warm in our tight coats as Thursday [October 17] was a very warm day for the season, if you remember. As we marched up the city the streets and windows were filled with spectators. Six companies took passage on the Granite State and 4 on the Mary Benton. As soon as we were put out in the river amid cheers from the wharves and vessels. As we passed Colt's [The Colt Armory, the firearms factory] we were saluted with cannon, and all the way down we were cheered from the banks as we passed.[22]

The regiment had marched from their camp to the Connecticut River, where they were to travel by boat down the river and through Long Island Sound to New York. They had been assigned to join General Ambrose Burnside's expedition to North Carolina.[23] On that day, Governor Buckingham wrote a letter to Simon Cameron, the secretary of war, which stated:

> SIR: I have the honor to report that the Eighth Regiment Connecticut Volunteers, Colonel Harland, with over 1,000 men, rank and file, sailed this afternoon for Staten Island, their destiny having been given by General A.E. Burnside, to whom the colonel will report.[24]

Oliver C. Case of Simsbury, a private in Company A, also indicated that the trip down the Connecticut River by steamboat was pleasant. The men cheered and were cheered continually. However, although they had just embarked on a great new adventure, Case indicated that they did not know their destination. On the steamboat, Company A was quartered in a gangway, forward of the shaft. Some men were in water "shoe deep," but Case was able to find a dry place and get some sleep before being called for guard duty at about 11:30 p.m.

Around 4 a.m. the next morning, New York came into view through the fog. Their ship passed New York and Brooklyn and arrived at Staten Island at 6 o'clock. They landed but did not disembark and waited there until resuming their journey sometime after nine. They passed by New York again, finally landing at about 3 p.m. at Hunter's Point, Long Island, which is located in Queens County, across the East River from Manhattan. Some companies of the regiment immediately boarded trains and left for Jamaica, Long Island, while other companies had to wait two or three hours for their cars.

The men arrived at their new camp before their baggage did, and they had to sleep that night on the open ground without tents. They awoke to a heavy dew and fog, with their blankets wet and their guns covered with rust. They had to work diligently that morning to clean their guns. Private Case reported that on Saturday, they pitched their tents "towards night," but it rained hard before they were through.[25] Corporal Nettleton, however, wrote that they had their tents erected in less than two hours, and they just got their luggage and guns into the tents when it began to rain.[26]

Jamaica

Oliver Case praised their new camp. "We are very pleasantly situated, much more so than at Hartford, the ground being slightly sloping to the south making it quite dry and pleasant with the exception that it is a very windy location outside the camp streets so there is not much danger of getting asleep on guard although we have a large camp fire burning continually." Their new camp was near the town of Jamaica, New York, and Case described the town this way: "Jamaica is one of the pleasantest places I ever saw. It is situated ½ mile from camp. The people are very familiar (much more so than Conn. people & I should also say generous and hospitable). They gave our Regt. over a thousand loaves of bread last week besides giving us many apples and welcoming to their houses all who are fortunate as to get out side the guard."

As for their new soldier's experiences, Case said: "The Regt. are now undergoing a thorough examination. The men are not troubled with clothes while undergoing this examination. Our company will probably be examined tomorrow or the next day and there is no knowing how many will be thrown out."[27] Three days later he wrote, "The whole regiment has been examined, we had to march in before the Dr. and our Capt. minus all our clothes and be subject to a thorough examination."[28]

The men were new to soldiering and had not yet developed the efficiency of the veteran. One new member of the regiment, Henry C. Hall of Newtown, a sergeant in Company I, described "a small inventory" of what he carried and its weight: "First the clothing we wear consisting of pants, dress coat, drawers ... shoes, and stockings, about 15 lbs. Knapsack with all our other clothes, blanket, and overcoat, 25, Minie musket with bayonet ... &c, 15, haversack, canteen, cartridge box, belt, &c, 10, making a sum total of at least 65 lbs."[29]

Chapter 1. Hartford to Annapolis

The camp at Jamaica was a camp of instruction.[30] Corporal Nettleton of Company I described a day there this way: "up at 6—drill from ½ past 7—breakfast & reg. drill from 9 to 11—Dinner 12—drill 1 to 2—Reg. 2 ½ to 4 ½—parade 5 & then comes supper." He also reported that they received their arms two days before leaving Hartford (Tuesday, October 15). The men would be armed with "a Rifle similar to Enfield or Minnie & use the Enfield cartridges. It is the same of the Minie. They are light & nice, but are not bronzed [browned] so we have something to do to keep them bright."[31] As for drill, Charles Coit wrote, "It takes Harland to drill the whole regiment, and he drills it every afternoon + I tell you it is done 'up to the handle.'"[32]

On September 25, 1861, a group of Connecticut citizens living in New York met to organize the "Sons of Connecticut," a group formed for the purpose of receiving and entertaining Connecticut regiments passing through New York City. One of their first acts was to visit the Eighth Connecticut, and formally present them with their regimental flag. General Prosper M. Wetmore, a Connecticut native and noted author and poet, made the presentation speech, and Colonel Harland briefly responded.[33] In a letter dated Thursday noon, October 24, 1861, Charles Coit wrote, "Our state banner is to be presented this afternoon by the Sons of Conn." The letter continued, "Between 4 + 5 p.m. Banner has been presented.... John Almy made a speech introducing Genl Wetmore who was quite lengthy. Harland was very short, he was wise enough to know his men had already stood with hats off too long in the cold west wind."[34]

The Eighth's stay at Jamaica was brief. They had arrived on October 18, and they departed fifteen days later on November 2, 1861. Sergeant Henry Hall wrote,

> Saturday morning we struck camp and made preparations to take our departure, and of all the journeys we ever go on I hope this will be the worst for it was a complete series of blunders from beginning to end. After we had all our baggage packed we marched to the railroad and stood in the cold and rain for two hours waiting for the cars and we were 12 hours on a journey of only 10 miles. When we arrived at Hunters Point there was no boat ready for us to go upon and we waited until 10 o'clock at night for our Colonel to go over to New York and get one when he returned, he brought a boat just big enough for us to go upon by standing packed as close together as we could get.[35]

Corporal Jay Nettleton wrote that

> the steamer was not a large one. It was a skeleton—seemingly made for the freight or cattle—only one deck. The whole Reg. stowed in our feet were muddy, added to the dirt [which] was on the floor before, made it anything but a neat place for us. The officers supposed we should not be on board only 2 or 3 hours & that we could stand it that time. But the storm was so hard that the Boat Captain thought best to put into a slip in New York where we staid till some after midnight. But to cut in short a little, we got into Amboy some time in the morning—not in the best humor. All the rest we could get was to put our knapsacks down in the dirt and sit on them.[36]

Adjutant Charles Coit wrote, "The passage by boat from Hunters Point to Amboy was bad enough, lasted all night the officers had a large room to sleep in with a good fire, but I don't believe many of them slept very much.... A large part of the men must have stood up all night or else sat in the water on deck. The boat was only intended for a few hours sail on a fair day."[37] In his letter, Henry Hall wrote,

> [A]bout daylight we arrived at Amboy, New Jersey. Here for a wonder the cars were ready for us to go on board and in a few minutes, we were rapidly traversing the Pine barrens and slough holes of New Jersey for that state seems to consist of nothing else. We arrived at Philadelphia at noon and our reception there was a perfect Ovation. Men, Women, and Children came out by the thousands to greet us they conducted us to a long hall where there were tables loaded with all kinds of nice things to eat and warm coffee to drink.[38]

Private Oliver Case of Company A described the scene:

> [W]e had a huge dinner and if anyone ever did justice to a dinner, we did to that. I think I never tasted anything so good in my life. We stayed there until nearly five talking and shaking hands with everyone. After we were aboard of the cars while they were passing through the city (they did not go faster than a person could walk) we were upon the platform, or with our arms out the window shaking hands and bidding everyone Goodbye. We were 27 cars in all, 19 with passengers, the rest with horses and baggage.

Case went on to report that seven of the couplings on the train cars broke at different places on their journey before their train reached their next stop at Perryville, Maryland. They arrived just before midnight, disembarked, and spent the night in and about the train depot. Case said, "This place is situated upon the NE bank of the Susquehanna, upon the Baltimore, Wilmington and Philadelphia RR about thirty miles from the former place. There is a huge ferry boat which carries over a whole train of cars at once so there is no change of cars at this place for the south."[39]

Wolcott P. Marsh of Hartford was mustered into Company A of the Eighth Connecticut as a first lieutenant on October 2, 1861. He had previously served in Rifle Company A of the 1st Connecticut Volunteer Infantry as a private, having been mustered out on July 31, 1861.[40] His new bride Anna (they were married May 8, 1861) had visited him at the camp at Jamaica. She was there when the Eighth left Jamaica, so he stayed behind in order to help his wife return to Connecticut. Thereafter, he left to catch up to his unit.

Marsh took a ferry to Staten Island and then a train to the tip of the island at Tottenville, where he paid a man $1 to row him across to Amboy. From there he took a freight train to Camden, a ferry to Philadelphia and finally a train to Baltimore, disembarking at Perryville. It was there that he found the regiment, waiting for boats.

That day, Marsh wrote to his wife,

> We have laid here all day waiting for steamboats to take us down the river to Annapolis. To night one steamboat has been loaded, taking 6 company's & gone[.] when the remaining 4 will go I do not know.... This is a small nasty village but very lively just now with troops as there are portions of 2 regts. encamped here & it is the grand depot for all the horses, mules, wagons, teamsters &c. &c. of the U.S. Army.... I saw in one pen today over 6000 mules in another 3000 horses.... There are altogether here now about 15000 Mules, with waggons belonging to Uncle Sam.[41]

Annapolis

Annapolis had been chosen by General Burnside as the assembly point of his expedition. Twenty miles from Washington, D.C., it was already an important supply depot. It was the original capital of Maryland; in the state house there, peace had been ratified to end the Revolution and George Washington had resigned as commander-in-chief. The United States Naval Academy was now vacant, its students having been transferred to Newport, Rhode Island, at the outbreak of war.[42]

The first six companies of the Eighth left Perryville aboard a small steamer. It was crowded but a little cleaner than where they had been. They arrived at their destination sometime during the night of November 4, and then marched into Annapolis in the morning of Tuesday, November 5. Corporal Nettleton was in this first group because he was a member of the color guard, and as such the only member of his Company I to be with the advanced group. The day that they arrived, he took a side trip to the State House, which is situated on the highest point of the peninsula that makes up Annapolis. He visited the room in which Washington resigned his commission and where the Secessionists tried to pass their Secession Bill.

Writing about the city of 5,000, he said, "There are a few nice buildings but most of them are small & old fashioned & a good many old shanties. Most of the streets are short. Yet there are some grounds about some of the places that in life of summer would make the city pleasant." The remaining companies of the Eighth stayed in Perryville until noon that next day (Tuesday, November 5) and then left, arriving at Annapolis that evening.[43]

The trip down the Chesapeake was reported to have been enjoyable. The weather was very pleasant, and the scenery fine. After disembarking, the men were marched to St. John's College where they were to be temporarily boarded, four rooms to a company. The officers were billeted in nearby buildings. It rained the next day, Wednesday, November 6, so they did not go into camp, although the tents had all been put up "in a fine location." The camp was located about one and a half miles from the college.[44] Adjutant Charles Coit described the arrival: "We are now nicely quartered—in this exceedingly one horse city ... in two fine new brick buildings with very spacious grounds formally used as the Recruits College. We should have been in camp if the weather had been pleasant, we have a fine dry lot for the Camp with the 10 Reg. C.V. There are about 6000 troops in town + soldiers are very plenty."[45]

Sergeant Seth Plumb of Company E also described their new base:

> Our Camp is about one mile west of Annapolis on the north side of the highway that runs in the direction of Washington, between that and the Rail Road which is about 25 rods [412.5 feet] back of us. The 10[th Connecticut] is about 70 rods [1,155 feet] to our right. On the other side of the road towards Annapolis is the 51 NY, the 25th and 27th Mass. [A]t the Naval School Building is ... the head quarters of the 21st Mass who guard the rail road and country about here.... The 25th has a very fine band which makes music enough for all of us. The 10[th Connecticut] had a band come to day from Connecticut. Our regiment has sent to Merrils to get his terms, and his band if not to high, these bands are paid by the Regiments not by the government.[46]

Charles Coit had this opinion on the issue of a band for the Eighth: "The band for the 10th (they are encamped in the lot with us) came to day + it made our boys quite mad to think White had cheated us out of ours. There were several wishing to gain bands for us but Harland gave preference to White + the result is our band is minus. I believe all the other Regiments have them I should think the state of Connecticut might pay for ours if the U.S. will not but of course they will not."[47]

Sergeant Henry Hall of Company I wrote, "Camp life here is not much different from what it was in Conn except that we do not live quite as well and we have more company. There are about 11,000 men encamped within a mile of us and still they come. One week ago, today [Sunday, November 17, 1861] we were reviewed in presence of Gen Burnside and Secretary's Seward and Cameron and other distinguished gents from Washington."[48]

In addition to these dignitaries, Seth Plumb, in a letter, added the names of Secretary of the Interior Caleb Smith, Governor Andrew of Massachusetts, and Governor Thomas Hicks of Maryland,[49] while Wolcott Marsh mentioned that Quartermaster General Montgomery Meigs attended. General Burnside was in camp, Marsh added, but he was not present at the review.[50] The letters from the soldiers in the Eighth refer to this camp as Camp Hicks or Camp Buckingham (after the respective governors of Maryland and Connecticut), or as Camp Burnside.

One of the duties that the men of the Eighth had to perform in Annapolis was provost duty, that is, police duty. Oliver Case of Company A was one of the men chosen. On Friday, November 8, he was told by Corporal Cornelius Elwood, on instructions from Lieutenant Henry Hoyt, to pack his knapsack and report for special duty, where he would be gone "perhaps one day or perhaps three weeks." Case wrote,

> There were nine privates and one corporal from each Company and three Sergeants and three Lieutenants making by and all one hundred and six men.... We marched to the city, halted before an old brick building and were marched in and told that those were to be our quarters. The duty assigned to us was to patrol the city in squads of ten, arresting all soldiers without a pass or any drunk or disorderly ones....
>
> We are on duty 4 hours and off 8. The relief that I am in is on from 11 to 3 night and day. If we are not on duty we go when and where we have a mind to![51] The 51st N.Y. ... are the hardest set of boys that are encamped here (not excepting the zouaves which are bad enough ...) Nine tenths of the arrests we make are of that 51st regiment....
>
> We are treated with much respect by the citizens and they often send some shortcakes, gingersnaps, cookies, etc.; of course, only a bite for each but enough to know that we have their good will.[52]

The patrol guard spent three weeks in the city returning to camp on November 29. First Lieutenant Henry Hoyt of Company A was among those in the detachment.[53]

Adjutant Charles Coit wrote of an incident that was told to him while he and Colonel Harland were visiting the "Assembly Rooms" where the one hundred men of the Eighth were quartered while serving as Provost Guard. They met with Captain John E. Ward, who was in charge of the detachment, and the other officers of the detail.

Coit wrote about the challenges of policing these new recruits.

> [The Provost Guard] enter drinking saloons + pour out the brandy whiskey +c, they are doing grand service in keeping the city quiet + are continually arresting drunken + disorderly soldiers of whom there are very many of course out of 10,000 encamped within two miles + 2000 of them from New York City. They had quite a time with a squad of cavalry a few days since, the cavalry drew swords + pistols + it was necessary to bleed their leader with a bayonet before they would surrender. There were six of the Cavalry + ten of our men, they were going to charge on + ride over our ten, but our men made the charge + took them prisoner after pricking their leader a little.[54]

The daily routine for the men of the Eighth was very structured.
As Corporal Nettleton wrote,

> Last night an order was read at Dress Parade (as all orders are) changing the time of our labor. I'll give it to you: Reveille at 6½ a.m., Breakfast 7, Surgeon's call 7½, guard mounting 8, Non-commissioned officers drill from 8½ to 9½, squad drill (which is that the Sergeants & Corporals have to take squads of 4–6 men & drill them as much for their own improvement as the men as it gives confidence & practice to command) from 9:45 to 11:45, Dinner 12, Company drill 12½ till 2, Battalion drill from 2½ till 4, Dress Parade 4½ , Supper 5, Tattoo beats at 8 PM, Taps for lights, all to disappear 9½.[55]

As adjutant of the regiment, Charles Coit was in charge of distributing the countersigns for the guards. These were the passwords which enabled a person to identify himself to the army's perimeter guard so that he would be allowed to pass through the lines. Coit wrote to his mother, "I shall enclose an exact copy of the countersign which I delivered to the officer of the day, to day all sealed + directed it is folded in this particular way so that the lines cannot by any possibility read it without breaking the seal. They are sent to us from Head Quarters with countersigns for the week + I make one out each day for our officers of the day, so I always know the countersign + could pass anywhere over the whole Division at night."[56]

The adjutant was also intimately involved in the day-to-day routine of the regiment. The fife and drum were used to communicate to the troops the various daily events, such as reveille. The musicians played these calls at the adjutant's tent. Coit wrote, "Rap tap goes the Tattoo at my door a dozen drummers + fifers playing + as it will continue for ten minutes + again in the morning at 6 o'clock Reveille…. All the calls during the day are made at my door + I usually like to hear them we have some fine drummers they roll it out grandly."[57] However, when Coit "moved in" with the lieutenant colonel, Coit said that the only reason the lieutenant colonel had for not wanting him in his tent was that "the drums follow me. All the Calls are sounded at my tent you know so a man can't sleep near me after 6½ AM or before 8 PM."[58]

There was an atmosphere of preparation at the camp. Discipline was strict.[59] Seth Plumb said, "Our regulations are very strict it is difficult for even sergeants to get out side of the guard, every soldier is arrested in the city if he cannot show a pass."[60] Corporal Nettleton wrote, "Usually our passes are limited not to exceed three hours & not generally over 2. So, it spoils all the relaxation by the constant hurry and anxiety to be on time."[61]

Oliver Case affirmed that punishments were severe:

> There has been several court martials held since we have been here and the sentences are very severe for running the guard, insulting officers, committing nuisances, etc. One man has to forfeit ½ months pay and go in the guard house for fifteen days, another has had 30 lbs. of dirt put in his knapsack and made to do regular duty. The punishment of going in the guard tent is more severe than you might think this season of the year, for they have no fire nor any chance to exercise and their food and drink consists of bread and water…. There is a fellow in our company close to our tent standing upon a barrel with a guard around him for insulting his corporal.[62]

However, when men were not on duty, their time was their own, and they often spent their off-time in their tents. Corporal Nettleton described their furnishings as follows:

> There are six of us writing tonight; five are sitting at a table made out of the first box that was sent to us—two of the boards were used for the platform & the other for legs & braces &c. The candle is set in our 25 cents candlesticks that we carry with us. The guns are standing on one side & the boys are sitting two on 2 benches & one on 1. These benches are split & hewed out of our firewood—with legs put in with an augur. Some of the cooks' tables are made of the split & hewed slabs....
>
> Well, this doesn't account for the Sixth person. I happened to be out when the dishes were cleaned away & feeling the necessity of writing & no change at the table I stirred about and got another candle, made a candlestick out of a hard cracker & set it on the stove and myself beside it with a knapsack & part of a bed for seat. Our stove is a Patent one that we bought last week. Cost $4.00—is make of sheet iron & to take to pieces so that we can carry it, takes into 7 pieces besides about four feet of 3 inch pipe with two elbow. It's a cute little thing. Our major says there will be a way provided to carry them.[63]

Food is always a popular subject with soldiers, and these men were no different. On November 13, Sergeant Seth Plumb stated, "Our food is very good now, we began to have soft bread yesterday again, which is the best I ever ate I believe there is some thing in it that makes it sweet. The water is miserable, and comes from a muddy slough you cannot see the bottom of the cup you drink it in, yet the Colonel drinks it and says it is good, as for us we contrive to get off every day and get a supply of good."[64] Prime supplements to the army fare were the treats and "goodies" sent to the soldiers from friends and family at home. These were usually shipped in wooden boxes through express companies, and in addition to food, included many other useful or requested items. Lieutenant Wolcott Marsh wrote to his wife on December 9:

> I received the box Saturday. I thank you & all the friends a thousand times for all your kindness & attention. Every thing was in good order & suited exactly. The coat & pants are just right. The shoes fit to a charm. The cake is excellent, the dried beef is splendid. The walnuts & chestnuts & apples will be attended to. The shirt, hose & autograph book are right every way. The comfortable is very heavy & warm. And the magazines I assure will receive every attention & be read by a great many. They were all out among the company yesterday & the boys seemed very thankful for them. Please to thank Mr. Clark for the medicine.[65]

Not everything arrived exactly as planned, but it was still appreciated. On December 16, Private Oliver Case wrote to his sister: "I received the long expected Thanksgiving dinner Saturday. The chicken looked rather old although I tasted a few pieces near the inside and [found] that [they] were good. The walnuts, chestnuts and some of the apples were nice and we have been having quite a feast. A.H. Thomas, a tent mate that opened the box, says 'tell your folks that I tasted of everything that there was in the box and found it very nice only getting rather old.' The pudding and chicken pie looked as if they were good in their day but their flavor was rather strong when they opened the box."[66]

Notwithstanding delays in shipping, the soldiers still enjoyed their gift and continued to do so. Private John L. Merriam of Company K wrote on December 7, 1861, "[W]e have just got comfortably situated. We have a stove in our tent by the fire in which we toast bread make tea and warm over turkeys and chickens sent to us by our friends from home for a thanksgiving dinner. This we enjoy finely and you can well understand how we do."[67]

In addition to be being trained at drill, the men of the Eighth also did target practice with their weapons. Jay Nettleton described one such session on December 18:

> Today, or this afternoon we went out target shooting. None of us did anything worthy of mention. My 2nd shot was next best made in our Co. today & that was 4 or 5 inches from the bull's-eye. Shot 3 times, hit the target twice.... [T]he target is set & a greater distance paced off, then marked on the sight, & then our names are called & we draw & shoot; sometimes rest & some of the time not. Each time we go out the distance varies so I can't profit by my guessing on the previous trial.[68]

Seth Plumb of Company E had target practice the next day, and also hit the target several times, one the nearest to the bullseye of any.[69] Oliver Case wrote that Company A had been out target shooting four times, and "shot the board pretty much to pieces the last time out." He added, "I suppose before many weeks we shall be trying our shooting irons upon some of the traitors between Galveston Bay and Fortress Monroe."[70] But in anticipation of their departure, Seth Plumb wrote, "I hope they will give us some new guns as many of ours are poor."[71]

On December 19, 1861, there was a grand review of all the troops at the Annapolis camp. The review was conducted by General John G. Foster of the First Brigade, other military officers, Governor Hicks, and members of the Maryland legislature. First in the review were Foster and Hicks on horseback, then the military officers, and finally the Maryland legislature on foot.[72] On the following day, General Burnside reviewed the entire division. In anticipation of an inspection of their camp by General Burnside on the third day, the men of the Eighth collected evergreens to trim their company streets.[73] The soldiers constructed arches over the company streets incorporating the company's letter designation, shields, stars and other devices, all trimmed with red berries.[74] The result was surprising. "[V]iewed at a little distance the contrast of the evergreens & the white tents rising up out of them makes a sight really charming. Wreaths & arches at the Head of the street & the street sides lined with evergreens with doorways, &c."[75]

These grand reviews of the troops contributed to the feelings that the troops would be leaving in the near future. Oliver Case wrote, "[B]y all appearances we shall leave for 'Dixie' before many weeks.... The transports and steamers are lying in the bay ready to carry us at any time that we get the orders."[76]

Seth Plumb wrote on December 29,

> We have just had a delightful Sunday, probably the last that we shall have spent here in Annapolis.... This afternoon the Sacrament was administered for the first time, about 40 communed. The Chaplain used part of the Episcopal service. It was an impressive sight. There were Methodists, Baptists, Congregationalists, Episcopalians, and probably other denominations represented, about 40 or 50 persons in all. [I]t took place in the open air.... Our sick have all been removed aboard the boat to day. This looks very much about movement soon. There was an order read to night, to be ready to leave here any time at 12 hours notice to the Colonel, with 3 days rations. Troops have been coming in every day for the last week, how many there are here I don't know. We have been put into the 3d Brigade with the 11th [Connecticut] and the Zouaves ... under Gen Parks.[77]

Oliver Case on December 29 wrote that "all of the sick were removed from camp; those liable to be sick some time to the general hospital, the others on board

Camp Burnside, Annapolis, Md., 8th Regt Connecticut Vol. Col. Harland, Lieut. Col. Terry Christmas Day, 1861 (courtesy Memorial Military Museum, Bristol, CT).

a hospital transport."[78] Case had been ill with the ague (or fever) and sent to the hospital ship *Recruit*. His condition improved, and he was ordered to report to the schooner *Scout*, along with about another 120 men, who had also gotten better. After two days a doctor came and examined them, and those who were found fit for duty were then given orders. Case, along with nineteen others, was ordered back upon the *Recruit* for guard duty.[79]

Case reported from the *Recruit* that there were six cases of measles in the regiment, and "too much sick" from his company. Among these was Private Duane Brown, who had been sick for some time when on Sunday, December 29, he broke out "very thick" with measles. Typhus fever set in, and he died a week later. Another member of Company A, Charles Arnold, age 19, of Bridgeport. died of "camp fever" on December 28. Private Henry D. Sexton, a friend of Oliver Case, was also there, "quite sick with the jaundice." He came on board the same time as Case and was in the bunk beneath him. When his condition worsened, Case tried to get the doctor to transfer him to the hospital, but to no avail. At one point, Sexton had a fit, and "it took five of us to hold him and keep him from tearing his face with his hands. He would bite at us … making a horrid noise all the time." Case stayed with him the last twenty four hours before his death. "Sexton died easy but unconscious" on January 7, 1862.[80]

Adjutant Charles Coit wrote, "Every thing now like a speedy departure. We received orders this afternoon to hold ourselves in readiness to march at twelve hours notice…. We are in Genl John Parke's Brigade, that is the third, with the 11th Conn + 53d (Zouaves) New York. We have the right, the post of honor, though no more a post of danger than the others. I suppose we are considered one of the 3 best regiments in the division."[81]

Chapter 1. Hartford to Annapolis 23

Evening Amusements—Camp Annapolis, December 24, 1861 (Joseph E. Shadek Civil War Sketchbook. Courtesy Bridgeport History Center, Bridgeport Public Library).

Regarding Colonel Harland, Coit said he was tough, but the men respected his leadership:

> Harland is a strict disciplinarian so much so that he is not a favorite with a large portion of the enlisted men. I believe this is necessarily the case with a good Colonel, they have to exercise all the real authority + must bear all the "curses" whether deserved or not. [But the men] all want Harland at their head if anything is to be done. I have heard it expressed a hundred times in different ways that they want Harland with them when they go into action for they say any one can take them into a fight but comparatively few can bring them out + they believe Harland can. I know all have the most entire confidence in him + very much respect him. Even in drilling the Battalion several of the Captains have told me that if the men see Harland out on the field + think he is to command, then men are out in full strength, every one ready + no holding back.[82]

Chapter 2

Hatteras to New Bern

General George B. McClellan and General Ambrose E. Burnside were personal friends since their days at West Point together in the early 1840s. In the fall of 1861, the two men conceived a plan to assemble an amphibious army division, composed of New Englanders and other northern men familiar with the coastal trade. The division was to move south in a fleet of light-draft steamers, sailing vessels and barges, strike the southern coastland, and then move inland.

The Burnside Expedition

There were three objectives to the North Carolina expedition. First, it was to control the navigation of the sounds on the North Carolina coast, thus cutting off supplies to Norfolk by water. Second, it was to cover the left flank of the main army when it attacked Richmond by the line of the James River. Finally, it was to neutralize the towns of New Bern, Beaufort and Wilmington, which would prevent blockade-running to those points and threaten the coastal railroads which supplied Richmond.[1]

Burnside was authorized to raise fifteen regiments and was given funds to equip them. While the troops were being gathered at Annapolis, Burnside was in New York assembling the fleet of transports to carry them south. Having to compete with the Navy for ships, Burnside settled for what he termed a "motley fleet"—barges, sailing vessels, steamers, tugs and ferry boats were acquired, improved and strengthened. The ships were ordered to Annapolis, Maryland, to take on board the troops there and then proceed to Fortress Monroe in Hampton Roads, Virginia, to rendezvous with ships from the U.S. Navy.[2]

The U.S. Navy ships supporting the expedition were part of the North Atlantic Blockading Squadron, commanded by Rear Admiral Louis M. Goldsborough. This force was composed of twenty ships mounting sixty-two guns, including fifteen of the new, nine-inch rifled cannons. Burnside's flotilla of gunboats and floating batteries added another 108 pieces of artillery.[3]

Burnside's force, called the Coast Division, was made up of three brigades, all commanded by regular army officers whom Burnside called "three of my most trusted friends."[4] The First Brigade was led by Brigadier General John G. Foster and was composed of the 10th Connecticut along with the 23rd Massachusetts, 24th Massachusetts, 25th Massachusetts, and the 27th Massachusetts.

The Second Brigade under Brigadier General Jesse Reno was made up of the 21st Massachusetts, 51st Pennsylvania, 9th New Jersey, 51st New York, and the 6th New Hampshire. The Third Brigade, commanded by Brigadier General John G. Parke, consisted of the 53rd New York, 89th New York, 8th Connecticut, 11th Connecticut, 4th Rhode Island, and the 5th Rhode Island.

In all, the Coast Division totaled some 12,000 men and eighty ships.[5]

John G. Parke, the Eighth's brigade commander, was a Pennsylvania native and a topographical engineer. He had worked on the Iowa-Minnesota boundary, on two railroad surveys, served on the U.S. Lighthouse Board and on the Northwest Boundary Commission. He became a captain of topographical engineers in September 1861, and then brigadier general of volunteers in November.[6]

Major General Ambrose E. Burnside. Matthew Brady, photographer, 1863 (Library of Congress, Prints and Photographs Division, Civil War Photographs, LOT 14043-2, no. 90).

Delays in launching the expedition caused great frustration. As General Burnside wrote, "after most mortifying and vexatious delays, they [the transports] arrived by the fourth of January, 1862, and on this day, orders were promulgated for embarkation, which were received from one end of the camp to the other with most enthusiastic cheers."[7]

McClellan first issued orders to Burnside on January 7, 1862. "[A]fter uniting with Flag-Officer Goldsborough at Fort Monroe," he ordered Burnside to "proceed under his convoy to Hatteras inlet, where you will, in connection with him, take the most prompt measures for crossing the fleet over the Bulkhead into the waters of the sound.... [Y]ou will assume command of the garrison at Hatteras inlet.... Your first point of attack will be Roanoke Island and its dependencies."[8]

Two days earlier, on January 5, 1862, Corporal Jay Nettleton could sense that the troops would soon move out.

> Our Cooks are cooking 3 or 4 days Rations tonight—putting 3 days in to barrels and the other we take in our Haversacks. The supposition is that we strike tents tomorrow and go on board.... The Harbor is full of "Sail Craft" and some of them are big looking fellows. From what I learn the boats are to rendezvous at Fortress Monroe—and I will say the general impression is that the 'fleet' is bound for a trip up the James River. I hope it not be a less

place—or to strike a lighter blow than it would be to take Richmond.... We shall be glad to leave our present camp grounds as they are in a bleak and cold place.[9]

According to Adjutant Charles Coit, the regiment broke camp that day (January 5) "in a snow storm about 2 inches deep tents all frozen down + every thing as bad as possible + very cold. Marched down to the wharf + found that our vessels were not ready for us + we must lie until to day [the 6th]. So the Regt went into Quarters in the Navy Yard buildings." Coit, Colonel Edward Harland and Lieutenant Colonel Andrew Terry, unable to get a room at the hotel, hired a small boat and sailed out to a ship and spent the night there. They found a "nice snug cabin just about large enough to hold us + a good hot fire with supper." The ship was the *H.J. Brookman*, which Coit described as a "first rate bark"; he said that "if we are going far nothing could be safer + more comfortable."[10]

When the regiment finally did go onboard ship, the companies of the Eighth were divided—six companies went aboard the *J.P. Brookman*, and four were put on the steam-transport *Chasseur*.[11] (There seems to be some confusion as to the exact name of the bark. The first two letters of the name are given by different sources as "H.D.," "H.J." and "J.P."[12]) Two of the six companies on the bark were later moved to a schooner so the troops were now sailing on three ships. "The Colonel & Major, Doctor & Chaplain & 4 companies were put on a Bark, two companies on a Schooner, & the other 4 with Lt. Colonel on the Gun Boat."[13] Adjutant Coit and the quartermaster were also on the *Brookman*. Coit identified Dr. Melancthon Storrs as the doctor on the *Brookman*, and Dr. DeWitt C. Lathrop as the doctor on the *Chasseur*.

The accommodations were not good on many of the boats in the fleet, and the *Brookman* offered terrible quarters for most of the troops who came aboard. While the field officers and staff enjoyed comfortable state rooms, the soldiers and line officers did not fare so well.[14] There were no berths on the ship, so the men were forced to sleep in their blankets on the deck or in the hold, where the air was foul with the smell of bilge water.[15] The "men were packed in like pieces of salt pork in a barrel," Coit wrote. As the last companies came on board, there was no space left on the ship so the new men could not lie down after taking off their knapsacks and equipment. "One soldier said the next day that he had a first rate bed as he slept on soldiers three deep," Coit wrote. The conditions were so bad that Colonel Harland finally went ashore and procured a schooner to take some of the men off the *Brookman*.[16]

By the night of January 7, nearly all the troops were on board the fleet. As Burnside wrote, "The scene in the harbor was inspiring beyond description. The vessels, as they passed each other from time to time, saluted each other with their steam whistles, while the bands played and the troops cheered, the decks being covered with blue-coats.... The whole fleet seemed to be under a mixed influence of excitement and contentment." The ships set sail on the morning of January 9 under orders to rendezvous at Fortress Monroe.[17]

Prior to sailing, General Burnside came around to each ship to see that all were ready. "Each ship cheered him as he approached + he would take off his hat, it was really a very interesting sight to us just about sailing we knew now when + he our commander," Coit wrote.[18]

The *Brookman* left about 11 a.m., towed by the *Chasseur*, which also towed a schooner. "[I]t was a fine sight to see the vessels sailing off crowded with men + the bands playing. The steamers towing the sail vessels," Coit wrote. About 8 p.m. the *Chasseur*, not having a regular pilot on board, towed its ships into shoal water and lead another steamer that was following it into the same waters. That steamer was also towing two ships, and one of these ran aground and the other ran into her. The first ship was carrying the 53rd New York Zouave Regiment, and the second was carrying the 11th Connecticut. The next day, Friday, January 10, the two steamers tried to free the ship carrying the 53rd New York, but to no avail. After an unsuccessful try again on Saturday morning, the steamers left with their ships in tow, minus the one carrying the 53rd New York. As the wind picked up, the *Brookman* let go and set sail.[19]

The rendezvous at Fortress Monroe near Hampton Roads, Virginia, was brief. The combined fleet set sail on the night of January 11. General Burnside made his headquarters on the *Picket*, the smallest vessel in the fleet. "I was moved to do this," he said, "because of the great criticism which had been made as to the unseaworthiness of the vessels of the fleet, and because of a desire to show to the men my faith in their adaptability to the service." No one knew the destination of the fleet except for Burnside, his brigade commanders, and two or three staff officers. Sealed orders were given to the commanders of each vessel, not to be opened until they were at sea.[20]

Hatteras Inlet

As for the 8th Connecticut, Sergeant Seth Plumb of Company E wrote that their ship, the *Brookman*, left at about noon on Sunday, January 12, and it was "one of the last ships of the fleet" to leave. There was a good wind, and they went by sail. They arrived outside Hatteras Inlet about sundown on Monday, January 13.[21]

Lieutenant Wolcott Marsh of Company A, on board the gunboat *Chasseur*, said that they left at 11 a.m. on Sunday and arrived at Hatteras Inlet at noon on Monday. He described the trip there as being rough some of the time, with a squall that tossed their vessel severely. However, their ship was able to pass through the outer bar and into Hatteras Inlet on arrival, where they anchored. Marsh wrote that the captain of their boat said that they could not have stood out to sea more than six hours or it would have "gone to pieces." Marsh described their ship as a "weak miserable boat," which was "nothing but a North river barge built over & no more fit to go to sea than an old tub."[22]

As he surveyed their new location, Marsh saw a dismal sight.

Of all the dreary bleak, Lonesome places I was ever at this is the most miserable. Fort Hatteras & Ft. Clark which the rebels built & that were taken by our forces last August lie within sight of us & that is about all there is here excepting the sand bars & the briny deep But now [Monday, January 13] (4:P.M) there is a large steam ship & a schooner lying off the bar with their flag at half mast signals of distress showing that they have not been as fortunate. The wind is blowing a gale, it will be a terrible night out. I hope all our fleet will succeed in getting

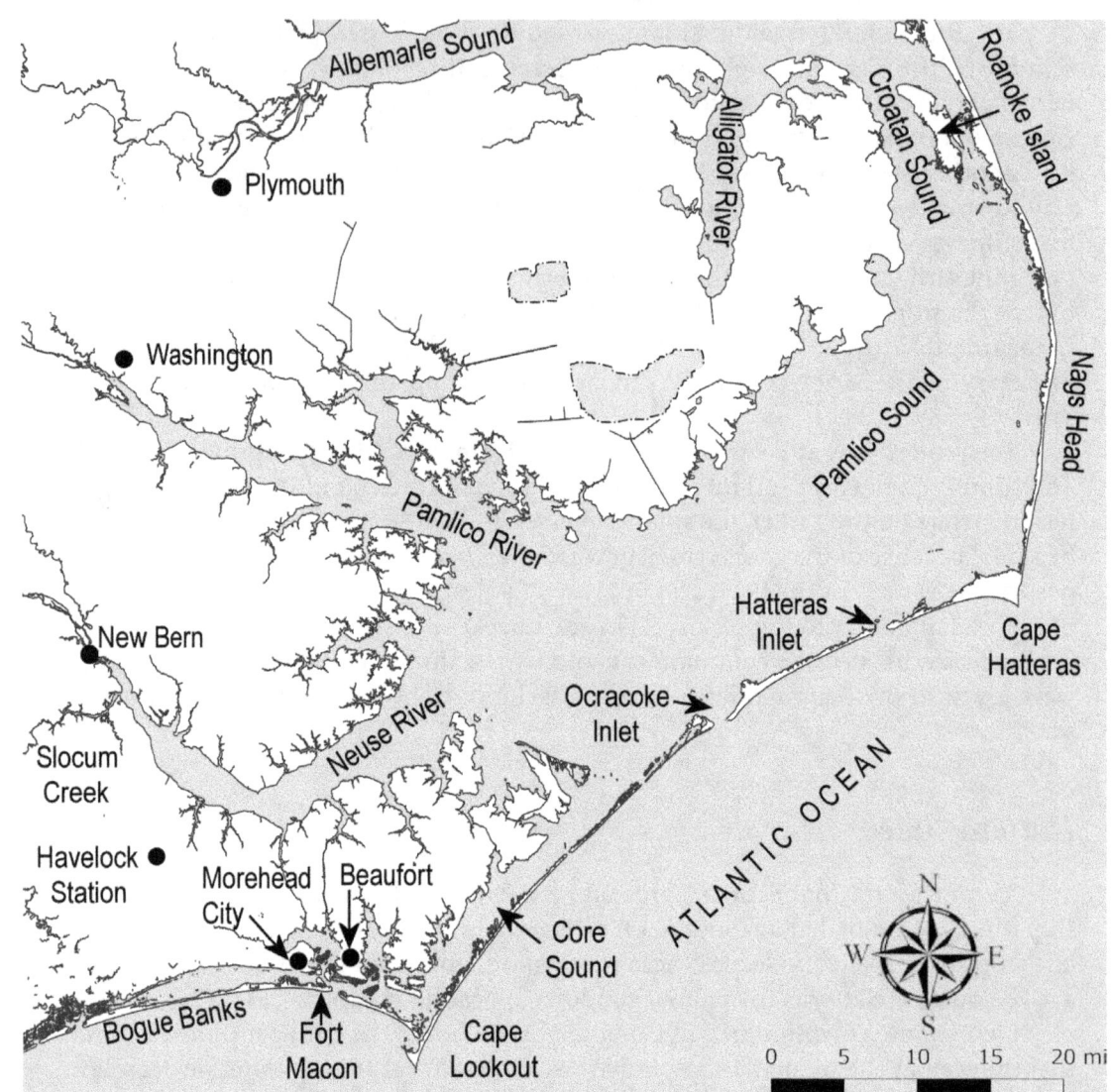

Map 1. Burnside Expedition, North Carolina, January–June 1862.

in somehow. It made a good many of us sea sick coming & your husband was not wholey exempt.[23]

The gale, a Hatteras nor'easter, raked the ships from Monday, January 13 to Wednesday, January 15. It prevented any ships from crossing over the bar from the open sea; instead, they were forced to ride out the storm at anchor. Virtually all the ships suffered damage from collisions with nearby vessels. Five ships were grounded or battered to pieces by the seas.[24] Marsh told of a "large propeller [propeller-driven ship] which went ashore yesterday [January 13]." On January 16, he reported, "The Ocean propeller that I spoke about being ashore has gone to pieces & all the crew lost but two men who staid by the ship & were saved. The others 16 in number got into their surf boats & were driven out to sea & lost."[25]

The troops aboard another ship that grounded were more fortunate. "The propeller, *The City of New York*, which was laden with supplies and ordnance stores, grounded on the bar, and proved to be a total loss. Her officers and crew clung to the rigging until the next day, when they were rescued by surf-boats sent to their assistance."[26]

On Friday, January 17, Sergeant Seth Plumb of Company E wrote that the weather was terrible, and that life aboard the ship had been difficult.

> We arrived here [at Hatteras] on Monday [January 13] about sundown and anchored about 2 miles out side the Inlet where we now are. We have been here now about 4 days a rocking and tumbling as it has stormed most of the time. I know what it is now to be sea sick from experience…. The quarters here on this ship are worse than they would be in your hog pen. The hold is dark and the straw that was put in is used up, and here are 400 men who by great exertion can find room to ly down if they ly on their sides it is against the rule to ly on the back as it takes up to much room. Why is it that the 8th is treated so?[27]

Adjutant Coit wrote that men suffered from great boredom during their time on the *Brookman*, lying outside the sandbar, waiting to enter the inlet:

> [T]his lying at anchor + pitching + rolling + tumbling is beyond comparison worse than sailing…. How long we are to lie here outside I do not know all the light draught vessels went directly into the sound + we have been expecting to be towed in each day, there are other ships outside with us the great fleet inside are in sight + we long to join them + wonder something is not done if the expedition is intended to surprise the enemy…. Certainly nothing can be worse for troops to be placed as we are, all they can do is to gamble + that they keep up from morning to night. I will tell you how the officers are employed…. The Col. Is in his bunk flat on his back, the Major is on the sofa, the Qmaster in bed…. Captains on deck + half a dozen other officers piled round them, and others asleep or trying to sleep on the quarter deck…. This is a pretty fair sample of each day, nothing doing, nothing to do.[28]

Unlike the men on the *Brookman*, the companies on board the *Chasseur* were anchored snugly in the Inlet. During their stay there, Wolcott Marsh found an opportunity to go ashore. On January 17, he wrote: "To day 7 of us officers were rowed ashore & took a stroll on the Island & had an opportunity to see the famous forts which the rebels built & lost. They are in sight of each other about ¾ of mile apart with a about 6 heavy siege guns mounted of each & are made of sods which the rebels luged about 2 miles…. Our fleet continues to increase its numbers each day there are now here about 100 vesills of all kinds." But often unseen trouble plagued the soldiers were forced to wait out the conditions. "Accidents still continue…. Night before last the Colonel of the 9th N.J. Regt. (O.N. Allen) & all the field officers also company officers & men to the number 25 got into a row boat belonging to the ship on which they were & came in to the Harbor (they being anchored out side the Inlet) to report to the Comd. General & while returning were turned over & The colonel, Doctor, & Mate of the vessel drowned…. It was a sad affair."[29]

The *Brookman* finally made it into the Inlet on Tuesday, January 21, and the *Chasseur* steamed over to see them. Marsh wrote that "the other Companies they were glad to see us & when our boat came along side they gave us three hearty cheers…. We found that all of them most had been sea sick ever since they came to anchor out side & in fact some of them ever since leaving Annapolis (two weeks)….

U.S. Gunboat *Chasseur* passing Hatteras Lights, Cape Hatteras, North Carolina—January 12, 1862 (Joseph E. Shadek Civil War Sketchbook. Courtesy Bridgeport History Center, Bridgeport Public Library).

Lt. Ives (Co. K) was so sick that he vomited his teeth overboard." Marsh also recognized that the living conditions on the *Brookman* were not as good as on his own ship. "The men living on the lower deck altogether with out any bed where as our men have separate bunks a kind of cot. But their ship is far safer at sea being a very staunch boat.... After staying about an hour we rowed back to our boat well satisfied with our quarters when compared with theirs."[30]

On January 23, Coit wrote that he was glad that they were now inside the Inlet, but the tide and wind were so strong and the fleet so closely packed that collisions were continually occurring. The day before, one ship ran into them and "tore off some of the stern works" of the *Brookman*. Later that night, the hospital ship came around and "struck us forward, our bowsprit running between her masts, the jib boom being carried away, and there she laid on our anchor chains the last part of the night, we were so entangled and the wind was driving her on all the time, that we were perfectly helpless."[31]

One diversion the men had during this time was a visit to the division sutler, the civilian merchant who followed the troops and sold them provisions. One afternoon, groups were ferried back and forth from the *Brookman* to the sutler's schooner. The men bought food and then resold some of it or all of it at a profit back at the ship. Of the others, Coit wrote, "The men were offering five dollar treasury notes for little jars of grape jelly, they were paid just before leaving Annapolis + could not spend the money there and keeping it so long seems to have burnt their fingers, but spending it so is certainly better than gambling it away as the greater part of them seem to be doing." The Eighth's sutler, George Moore, arrived a few days later on January 27.[32]

After getting his fleet into the Inlet, Burnside's next challenge was to pass his ships over the "Swash," the narrow, winding channel connecting Hatteras Inlet with Pamlico Sound. On January 16, when Burnside began trying to move his transports across, he found that many of his vessels drew more water than anyone expected, and the Swash was shallower than anyone believed.[33] As Burnside said,

> We had been led to believe that there were eight feet of water upon the swash, but when we arrived we discovered to our sorrow that there were but six feet; and as most of our vessels ... drew more water than that, it was necessary to deepen the channel by some process. The current was very swift upon the swash, which circumstance proved to be much in our favor. Large vessels were used in going ahead, under full steam, on the bar when the tide was running out, and then anchors were carried out by boats in advance, so as to hold the vessels in position. The swift current would wash the sand from under them and allow them to float, after which they were driven further on by steam and anchored again, when the sand would again wash out from under them, and so on the process was continued for days, until a broad channel of over eight feet was made, deep enough to allow the passage of the fleet into the sound.[34]

A second gale battered the fleet from January 22 to January 24. This bad weather hampered the fleet's efforts and caused several collisions (such as those Coit described on the *Brookman*), but it also refloated some of the vessels that had been grounded. The gale ended on the morning of January 24, and the work of crossing the Swash continued. Many of the ships had been lightened to aid in their passing. By February 1, the last of the transports had entered the sound.[35]

It was on Wednesday, January 29, that the *Chasseur* made it over the Swash and into Pamlico Sound. Marsh described the success. "We got over finally not being over ½ hour where as a good many others that draws less water stuck on bar for two or 3 tides. It is a lovely day as warm as June in CT." The next day, he wrote that the 11th Connecticut was landed on [Hatteras] Island, and that they were sent there to relieve a Pennsylvania regiment which is to go on the expedition because that unit was much better drilled. The upshot of this was that the four companies of the Eighth that were on the bark were now transferred to one of the ships that the 11th Connecticut had just vacated. This ship was the *Sentinel*, a gunboat similar to the *Chasseur*.[36]

Charles Coit wrote that "we were transferred yesterday [January 30] from the *Brookman* to this steamer [the *Sentinel*] the B[rookman] drawing too much water to cross the Swash. We are quite comfortable here though not as pleasant for Field + Staff as the bark.... The men are more comfortable here than on bark, they all have a kind of cot here."[37] The transfer was actually a two-step process. The troops and stores were first transferred from the *Brookman* to the tug boat *Union*, and it carried them across the Swash. Then the troops and stores were moved to the *Sentinel*.[38]

Departing the *Brookman* was not without problems. The field and staff officers, who occupied the cabins, were presented with a bill for $25 from the ship's captain, Captain Cheney, for the use of the cabin, a servant, and "privy accommodation." Colonel Harland responded by doubling their bill to the ship's captain for foodstuffs that they had bought from the commissary and then sold to Cheney. The ship's captain had also been charging men a dollar each to be ferried over to the sutler. Harland replied that he was the commander of the boat, not Captain Cheney. After such negotiations, each side lowered its bill and the matter was resolved.[39]

Life on the new ship, the *Sentinel*, was still arduous, Coit wrote.

> We are down to real soldiers rations also salt junk, fat bacon, mackerel, hominy, rice + boiled beans.... Our water is sea water distilled + tastes quite strongly of machinery + is real warm, so warm that it steams as it is pumped from the tank. We hang our canteens outside to cool it. The vessel makes a large part of water for the fleet ... the tank that receives the water after being distilled is in the hold where two of our companies are quartered and it is always leaking + a large part of the time steam rising from it, so the bunks are wet + it is really hot down there ... one of the privates told me this morning that the bed bugs down there were large enough to carry knapsacks.[40]

Roanoke Island

Once the fleet had passed through the Inlet, crossed the Swash and was anchored safely in Pamlico Sound, the ships were readied for the next advance—the attack on Roanoke Island. The Burnside Expedition got underway on the morning of Wednesday, February 5, 1862. As Burnside wrote, "The naval vessels, under Commodore Goldsborough, were in advance and on the flanks. The sailing vessels containing troops were taken in tow by the steamers. There were in all sixty-five vessels."[41]

The troops knew they were about to see action. Wolcott Marsh wrote later,

> At last we are moving towards the enemy. At sunrise the Union Jack from the top mast of the flag ship gave the welcome signal for the fleet to get underway & soon one after another left its anchorage bound for Rebeldom till the whole fleet stretching out for miles showed that finally we were all off. We are still in ignorance as to our destination but shall know in two or three hours by the direction we take.... We have been ordered to leave our Knapsacks behind & to take 3 days rations with us. We are to be landed in small boats & will have to wade in the water some ways before reaching shore.[42]

Coit said the sight of their fleet was almost inspiring. "[T]his has been a magnificent day perfectly clear sky.... The '*Sentinel*' is among the last vessels in the fleet of sixty sails + it is a fine sight indeed looking ahead as far as the eye can reach extend the vessels of the expedition + every little while one or another band will strike up 'Hail Columbia' or some other patriotic air + the wind wafts the strains back to us."[43]

Roanoke Island is about eight miles long by two miles wide, separated from Bodie Island (the Outer Banks) to its east by Roanoke Sound, and from the North Carolina mainland to its west by Croatan Sound. It was low, swampy and covered with brush, and there was just a single road, running north and south, almost the length of the island. The Confederates had constructed three earthen forts on the northern portion of the island: Fort Huger at the northern tip of the Island, Fort Blanchard to its south and Fort Bartow below that. Only the southernmost, Fort Bartow, would be involved in the upcoming battle. The others were located too far north to be involved.[44] In addition to the forts, the Confederates had installed obstructions in Croatan Sound—a double line of sixteen sunken vessels and a system of pilings in

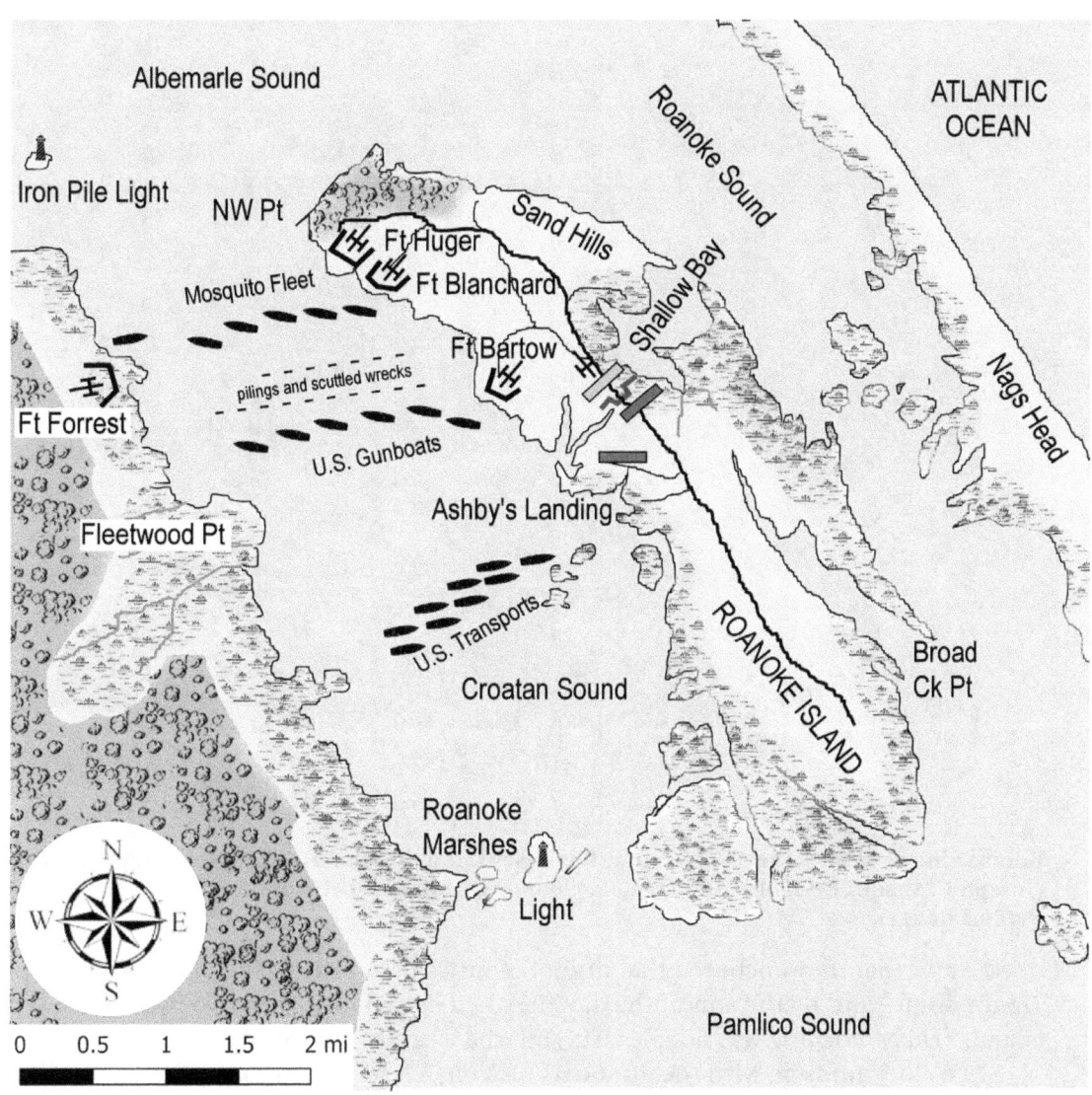

Map 2. Battle of Roanoke Island, North Carolina, February 8, 1862.

the water. Behind this barrier the Confederates also had a group of small gunboats, which they nicknamed the "Mosquito Fleet."[45]

On the morning of Friday, February 7, the fleet, with the naval ships in the lead, moved into Croatan Sound. As the Federals advanced north, the Confederate gunboats became visible behind the pilings. Goldsborough signaled for an attack on the Confederate ships and on Fort Bartow. The army gunboats would assist in the bombardment. At 11 a.m., the flagship hoisted a message based on Nelson's famous Trafalgar signal: "This country expects every man to do his duty." By 11:30 a.m., the Federal fleet had opened fire.[46]

Jay Nettleton of Company I was on the *Chasseur*, the same boat as Marsh. He wrote that Wednesday (February 5) was a beautiful day ("they could ride on the

Bombardment of the Rebel Fort Bartow, Roanoke Island, North Carolina—February 7, 1862 (Joseph E. Shadek Civil War Sketchbook. Courtesy Bridgeport History Center, Bridgeport Public Library).

deck") and that they anchored that night ten miles below the island. Thursday was "foggy some" and by the end of the day they had closed to within two miles of the island. Friday morning was not pleasant, but the weather improved during the day.

"9 o'clock finds us with the gunboats moving," Nettleton wrote. "The boats all pass a narrow channel into the Sound between the Island & main land—I forgot what it is called; & the boats turn off towards a Fort on the Island. About 11 o'clock our boats commenced firing to gauge the guns."[47] The narrow channel that Nettleton is referring to is through the "Roanoke Marshes," a series of low islands between the southern tip of Roanoke Island and the mainland, all of which have since been virtually washed away.[48] Burnside referred to the channel as the "Roanoke Inlet."[49]

Wolcott Marsh described the attack on the fort: "The first gun was fired from the rebel fort at ¼ after 11 a.m. & from that time till 6 p.m. shot & shell was fired into it from our fleet at the rate of from 1000 to 1500 an hour. But at dark they had not entirely abandoned it as they occasionally replied though it must be badly shattered & their barracks & building have been burning all the afternoon…. [T]hey say that it was one of our shots that fired their buildings."[50]

Nettleton continued, "Our boat finally opened her guns at 2½ miles distance or so. Most of the others went nearer, & this was kept up at intervals until dark…. Our guns made the best shots of any. There were also 5 or 6 Rebel gunboats to cope with at the same time. They had driven spikes & sunk vessels clear across the Sound 5 or 6 miles. The night stopped the firing. We only knew that we hit most of the buildings in the Fort & shot down their flag. The report now is that <u>our</u> boats' first two shots dislodged 8 guns."[51]

In another letter, Nettleton wrote, "About eleven a.m. the first shot was fired from one [of] the leading boats for the purpose of drawing their fire, but more to range & try our own guns. About twelve the firing became general & quite rapid—the gunboats moving up within a mile & and a half or so—firing the bow guns & then swinging a little & firing the stern ones or giving a side fire according to the shape of the vessel; yet all the while on the move so as to prevent the rebels getting good site on them."[52]

Nettleton noted that one incident aboard the *Chasseur* drew the attention of newspaper reporters—an accident involving one of the ship's larger guns: "[O]ne of her 30 lb. guns blew off the muzzle without any one hurt & the gun not spoilt. I was sitting within 12 feet of the muzzle in my bunk & Lucius Fox standing close beside me when it was shot. Lucius has two small particles hit on one cheek to break the skin & the rim of one ear pierced through by something else. It was thought best to put the gun one side & one of the guns from the boat 'Zouave' was brought to use in its place."[53] (The gunboat *Zouave* had sunk earlier in Hatteras Inlet after crossing the bar; it was a total loss.[54]) Nettleton reported that the *Chasseur* fired some "80-odd" shells from the two Parrott guns and "30-odd" from the six-pound Wiard gun on deck.[55] Marsh gave specific numbers: 81 from the large Parrotts, and 31 from the "small howitzer."[56]

The Wiard guns were the invention of Canadian-born inventor Norman Wiard, who devised both six-pounder (2.6-inch) and twelve-pounder (3.4-inch) rifled boat howitzers for use in Burnside's Expedition. The guns were designed so that the barrels could be mounted on sliding carriages aboard ships and then removed and mounted on light fieldpiece carriages for duty on land. Wiard worked in cooperation with Colonel William A. Howard of the 1st New York Marine Artillery, whose men would serve both as marines and as naval gunners for the fleet. Their crossed cannon and anchors design was later adopted by the Ninth Army Corps as its corps badge.[57]

In planning for the landing on Roanoke Island, Burnside had learned of the local conditions from several former slaves, including a young man named Tom, who described to Burnside the excellent harbor at Ashby's Landing. This was located at a point on the western shore of Roanoke, midway up the island, and about two miles south of Fort Bartow. After studying all other available information on the geography of the Island, Burnside decided to land his entire division at Ashby's Landing.[58]

At 1 p.m., after ordering preparations to be made for a landing, Burnside sent a small boat under the command of Lieutenant William S. Andrews of the 9th New York Volunteers to make soundings and examine the landing sites. Andrews' report supported Burnside's earlier decision to land at Ashby's Harbor, and Burnside ordered the landings. Each brigadier had a light-draught steamer to which were attached some twenty surf-boats, in a long line to the rear. As the steamers approached the shore at a rapid speed, each surf-boat, densely filled with soldiers, was let go and continued on to the shore. The men of the 8th Connecticut were brought into shore in boats towed behind the steamer *Phoenix*.[59] By midnight on February 7, the entire division had been landed, except for the 24th Massachusetts.[60]

But actually, there were other troops that had not been landed. Four companies of the Eighth were still on the *Chasseur*. As Marsh wrote,

> We have also learned that all our Brigade & the rest of our regt. Are on land & we should have been [landed] had not [someone] mistaken the orders. But we have had the opportunity of being right in one naval engagement where [we] was right among them. While the rest of the troop could only see it at long distance. We have had orders to also land early in the morning.... At 11 O'clock at night we were all awakened & ordered to get ready to go ashore immediately a small boat having come for us. We were soon ready & at 1 O'clock we were landed in a swamp through which we had to wade mud & water up knee near a mile before reaching dry land. Here we found our whole force but one regt. Already landed & shivering in the rain & cold around camp fires.... [I]t rained perfect torrents all night.[61]

Corporal Nettleton found that his comrades had already set up camp. "We were the last. The troops were bivouacked on a clearing of 40 acres or so & a dim light rising over all from the hundreds of fires exhibiting a mass of life.... As I passed around a little way from our own fires a great obstruction constantly attended from the heaps every few steps and care must be taken or somebody's toes will be stepped on. Men stop for the night, drop down their rubber blankets ... & woolen blankets over & soon sounds are heard that indicated the man is lost in slumber."[62]

Wolcott Marsh recalled the start of the attack on Saturday, March 8.

> Saturday morning in a drizzeling rain our small army were led forth to the attack, the 1st Brigade in advance composing 25th 27th Mass. & 10th CT. Then came the 2nd Brigade units 51st NY 53 Penn. 24th & 9th N.J. Then 3rd Brigade 4th & 5th R.I. 9th NY (Hawkins Zouaves). As soon as the army was put in motion the 8th CT. were ordered to throw out 4 companys namely Co. K, A, F & G forming a line from the coast to the swamp where the rebels with their battery were posted to prevent them from flanking us while the other 6 companies were held as a reserve.
>
> The road led through a swamp winding around in almost every direction for about 2 miles or so from the beach (or swamp where we landed) when came to a cleared place where on either side of the path the trees had been chopped down & lay as felled by the Rebels at about 200 yds. Distance the Rebels had an earth work thrown up & crossing the road & so arranged that all three guns could be brought to bare on the road....
>
> By 11 O'clock the engagement became general & every regt. was on the field excepting ours which was held as a reserve & for Gen. Burnsides body guard & also to keep the enemy back should they attempt to flank us. Our troops tried to get around to their rear but could not. The 10th CT. was led out into the clearing by their Brave Colonel when they were cut off very fast by the Rebels cannon, just then Colonel Hawkins asked his Zouaves if they would follow him when they gave one of their unearthly yells & started forward double quick & in a few moments, were in the fort. The Rebels flying in every direction. They were taken completely by surprise & did not even spike their guns.[63]

Nettleton described the action as follows:

> Here [at the clearing] the advance paused and a constant string of muskets was kept up on our part until near 12 o'clock. Our troops supposed they couldn't get around to flank the battery—certainly without meeting the enemy & the rebels thought we couldn't flank them on

account of the brush & water. But they gradually felt their way around when the "Hawkins Zouaves," the last to leave the ground, 11 o'clock, came up in the edge of the woods on the right of the road. Some of them fired 2 volleys & a charge was ordered—through a ditch in front of battery waist deep. And at the same time troops on each flank poured in. When our troops got there all but the gunners were in the distance. Some give credit to one & some to other Regts.[64]

It wasn't clear which regiment had driven the Confederates away. Coit wrote, "At the first reports we heard the Hawkins Zouaves had all the glory for charging the battery + taking it but it was the other Regiments flanking it that caused the evacuation."[65]

Colonel Isaac P. Rodman, in command of the 4th Rhode Island Infantry, wrote this in his report of the battle:

> When we had nearly succeeded in turning their flank on the left and right General Parke ordered the Ninth New York to charge in front, when the enemy, finding that they were flanked, fled up the island, followed by regiments of Foster and Reno in pursuit, General Parke ordering the Ninth New York to cut off their retreat by the Nag's Head, which they did, taking O. Jennings Wise prisoner, and capturing the battery at that point, with three heavy columbiads.[66]

General Burnside, in his report of the battle, stated: "Soon after the attack was commenced, I ordered General Parke to place a regiment in the woods to the north of Hammond's house and extending up to the main road, to prevent the possibility of the enemy's turning our left. The Eighth Connecticut, Colonel Harland, was detailed for this service."[67]

Corporal Nettleton said his unit was told to block the Confederates from flanking the Union troops. "The 8th were ordered to stay on our bivouacking ground to prevent a flank movement of the Rebels on our troops in action—supposing they might come down on the sea border, & to hold the ground as a chance to retreat. Burnside told our Col. To hold it as long as a man would stand by him."[68]

Marsh pointed out that the Eighth played a key role in the operation. "Although we were not in the engagement we held a very important post & had we been defeated should have had to bare the brunt of the battle in covering our retreat. Though of course would rather have been in the fight."[69] As Coit noted, "The fight was so near our position that part of the time musket balls flew over our heads."[70]

After their redoubt was taken, the Confederates retreated north up the island with the Federals in pursuit. Orders were sent to the other Confederate commands to spike their guns, and a white flag flew over the tent of the Confederate commander, Colonel H.M. Shaw. He later surrendered to General Foster, and at 9 o'clock on the night of March 8, the Federal fleet signaled that Roanoke Island had fallen. The Federal fleet then set sail in search of the "Mosquito Fleet"; they caught up with them and destroyed them on February 10 near Elizabeth City.[71]

Meanwhile, a pressing problem for Burnside was the disposition of over 2,000 Confederate prisoners. Unable to spare transports to take them north, he decided to parole them and on February 20 the prisoners were transported to Elizabeth City and released.[72] In a parole, a prisoner of war is released based on the soldier's pledge not to bear arms until exchanged.[73]

The Confederate losses at the battle of Roanoke were twenty-four killed, sixty-eight wounded and 154 missing, and a total of 2,488 officers and men had surrendered. The Federal losses were forty-one killed, 227 wounded and fifteen missing. There were no casualties in the 8th Connecticut. The Union victory was largely due to the Federal superiority in the number of their troops and in their training and weapons. In addition, the Federals made good use of local information in their plan of attack, and Burnside's three brigade commanders performed well.[74]

The days and weeks following the battle were spent organizing their occupation of the island. Initial foraging for food was stopped. Improvements and repairs were made to the roads and the forts. The forts were renamed, Fort Bartow becoming Fort Foster. A military cemetery was dedicated, a wharf was built at the location of Fort Bartow on Pork Point, and telegraph wires strung.[75]

Wolcott Marsh wrote that on "Sunday [February 9] we spent burying the dead & providing for the wounded. We the 8th, still kept our position [as] on Saturday one company guarding Hospital another picking up things left by rebels &c &c.... Remember that all this time it was disagreeable weather & nights we were sleeping in the open air with a single blanket over us."[76]

On Thursday, February 13, the regiment was ordered to leave the bivouac that it had occupied since the battle and establish a new camp to the north, near Fort Bartow. Under the command of Major Hiram Appelman, the regiment marched out that morning. The day before, the wounded who had occupied the house that the Eighth was guarding were removed to a hospital. However, there were still sick men and hospital stores to be evacuated. Colonel Harland, Dr. Storrs, Adjutant Coit, and a squad of men remained to accomplish that task. The boat that was sent to evacuate these men, wounded and sick, did not arrive until later that night, too late to move them, so Colonel Harland decided to use this boat and his available resources to bring the regiment's baggage, tents and quartermaster's stores ashore from the *Sentinel*, *Chasseur* and their schooner. This was accomplished overnight, and on Friday, February 14, the new camp was established and the tents set up in a grove of large pines about a half mile from Fort Bartow.[77]

Corporal Jay Nettleton wrote that the week after the battle he went to the upper end of the Island and saw the Forts and the prisoners and talked to some of them.

> They had previously signed a paper of "Paroll Exchange." This letting men go in this way has a very bad influence on our men. The mass will I dare say keep their word and as the[y] say "never will catch them fighting again"; yet we can't but feel that some will prove traitorous to their pledge. They seemed to've been misinformed about our intentions and said we treated them as well as they could ask. They thought we came to fight & abolish slavery. Who wonders that they shouldn't know: out of 460 only 16 could write their names.[78]

On February 18, Marsh witnessed 900 prisoners being marched past under guard of the 25th Massachusetts.

> If these are the flowers of their army I never care to see the more common soldiery of C.S.A. You cannot begin to imagine what a dirty, ragged, slovenish, long haired, lean lank, woebegone, sallow, ill shaped, ignorant awkward set most of them are. The most of them had a piece of carpet for blanket occasionally one with a Buffalo robe scarcely any with knapsacks. No two with coats, pants, or hats alike. To see them march aboard the boat two by two (each one

being obliged to go under the American flag which was suspended over the gang way so that it would almost touch their heads) the band playing ... was worth going a long way to witness.

In the afternoon, he watched as about 900 more were marched down, including men of the Wise Legion and a company of the Richmond Blues. "Most of the Wise Legion had on overcoats alike but their hats & pants were of every shape, size & color imaginable.... But they were well off in one respect, most all of them had good shoes or boots. Nearly all had canteens."[79]

On Monday evening, March 3, the Eighth received orders to be ready to march at 8 a.m. the next day. This prompted much preparation to break camp and be ready to move. The next morning, March 4, the men gathered their traps, and rations and ammunition were dealt out, but then orders came that the departure was delayed. At one point, the companies that came on the *Sentinel*—Companies C, E, H and K— were ordered to get ready to strike tents in thirty-five minutes, yet the call did not come. Coit wrote that it was the fourth time since they arrived that orders to move had been countermanded. It was not until the next day, Wednesday, March 5, that the regiment finally broke camp and boarded ship.[80]

New Bern

The next part of Burnside's orders directed him to seize the city of New Bern,[81] the headquarters of the Confederate District of Pamlico. Situated at the confluence of the Neuse River and Trent River, New Bern was strategically located so that Burnside could then move against the railroad inland, or attack Fort Macon, which guarded Beaufort harbor. After the defeat of the Rebel fleet at Elizabeth City, the Federal fleet had complete supremacy over the inland waters, which allowed Burnside to station a garrison on Roanoke and continue the expedition. Roanoke Island was left in the hands of Colonel Hawkins' Fourth Brigade, which consisted of the 9th New York, 89th New York and the 6th New Hampshire. The weather once again came into play, delaying the loading of the troops and equipment of the expedition, so that the fleet did not depart Roanoke until March 11.[82]

"At 6 a.m. of the present day," Wolcott Marsh wrote on March 11, "the signal was given from the flagship for the fleet to get under way.... We being in the third brigade it was 10 o'clock before our brigade signal was hoisted telling us to 'up & away.' Soon we were following in the wake of the 1st & 2nd brigade southward as you see back the way we come into Pamlico Sound."[83]

The *Chasseur* passed through the channel connecting Croatan and Pamlico Sounds without incident, but then grounded on a shoal. The *Chasseur* had been towing a schooner, which was then cut loose, but the line tangled her propeller, disabling the engine. Also grounded on shoals nearby were the steamers *New York* and *Northerner*. It was early evening before anything could be done.

Between the assistance of some tugboats and the rising tide, these ships were freed and moved on. The high tide also released the *Chasseur*, which set sail to try and follow, its propeller still fouled. A passing ferry boat which was towing a schooner and a canal boat picked up the *Chasseur* as well, which Marsh remarked was "a pretty good load for one of those little NY ferry boats." They continued on in the "clear moon light night" until about midnight when they finally reached the rest of the fleet at Hatteras and anchored.[84]

The *Chasseur*'s propeller was freed first thing the next morning so that it "could go on [its] own hook," and by 7 a.m. on March 12 the fleet was again moving up the sound towards the Neuse River. The men could see large signal fires along the shore, which had been set to alert the Confederates of the fleet's approach. They arrived at the mouth of the Neuse River about 4 p.m. and moved slowly up the river until coming to anchor about 9 p.m.

When the ship anchored, an officer left the boat to retrieve the mail—a significant moment in the lives of the soldiers. As soon as the ship anchored, "a boat was lowered & Colonel went in it to flag boat (*Alice Price*) for the mail which we understood she had taken aboard at Hatteras. It was an hour or more before he came back bringing in large mail & it was another hour before it was distributed…. It had been a lovely day as warm as summer & tonight nearly full moon & light enough to read by it."[85] As Oliver Case of Company A wrote, "You ought to have seen that boat about eleven o'clock, every light occupied by at least a dozen different persons each anxious to read the news from home."[86]

General Burnside held a council that night with his brigade commanders, and they made the decision to land the next morning, under cover of the naval guns, at the mouth of Slocum's Creek, some sixteen miles from New Bern. The plan was to advance up the road to New Bern, with support from the navy and the armed transport vessels. At 6:30 the next morning, March 13, the naval vessels shelled the woods in advance of the landings, and then, when the signal was given, the surf boats and light draught steamers moved in and landed three regiments within twenty minutes. The process was repeated until the entire force was landed. Six naval boat howitzers, under the command of Lieutenant McCook, were also landed, and the 51st Pennsylvania was detailed to assist in hauling these guns along the road.[87]

In his report on the battle, Brigadier General John G. Parke, commanding the Third Brigade (the brigade to which the Eighth belonged), wrote that as the regiments landed, they were formed on their colors and then took up their line of march. The regiments followed the bank of the Neuse River for some distance until coming to a point where a company of Confederate cavalry had been posted as an advance guard. Here the road turned away from the river and passed through some pine woods until joining the main county road from Beaufort to New Bern.

Parke wrote, "This we followed for a short distance, and soon came to an extensive line of intrenchments crossing the road and extending to the railroad. This was entirely abandoned by the enemy." It was here that the railroad crossed the county road, and from this point the Federal force divided: Parke's brigade followed Foster's brigade on the county road, while Reno's troops marched up the railroad. They marched on until after dark, when orders were received to halt and bivouac for the night.[88] The abandoned intrenchments were at Otter Creek, about six miles up from Slocum's Creek.[89]

"The landing commenced about half past 8 AM Thursday," Adjutant Coit wrote, "Col Harland went ashore with the first boat load from *Sentinel*, I went with him.

About 3000 troops landed at once, the small boats being towed by small steamers loaded also with soldiers. Our Regt commenced the march at 12½ M + did not bivouac until after dark. The afternoon had been rainy + very muddy. We had marched nine or ten miles + we had to lie down in the wet our clothes soaked thru' with rain + perspiration."[90]

Oliver Case also described their journey:

> We landed Friday a.m. in a small cove and immediately commenced marching up the river. We followed the beach for about two miles through the sand over shoes and then struck off across the fields. In a short time we came up to an encampment of cavalry which had been evacuated but a short time. Some of the boys fell out and helped themselves to chickens, ham, biscuits, etc. We travelled till after sundown over the muddiest road (if a road it could be called) that I ever saw.... About the middle of the afternoon we came to the first battery, which had just been evacuated and the barracks set on fire, which were still burning as we passed ... the fortification is a mile long with a large ditch in front protected in the rear by breast works of huge trees felled top of one another. It would have been almost impossible to have flanked them.[91]

It was a horrible time to march. "Through mud & rain over shoes it was perfectly awful walking," Marsh wrote. "We lay down for night in a drenching rain which continued throughout the night within about 2 miles of the enemy works."[92]

"We were allowed fires which, thanks to the pitch of the pine wood, could burn as well wet as dry," Oliver Case wrote. "I can tell you that after 12 o'clock very little sleeping was done by the soldiers in this division. About 6 a.m. we started, wet as rats, but due to the southern climate, not cold."[93]

By that next morning, March 14, the rain had stopped only to have been replaced by a dense fog. The Third Brigade was under arms and ready to march shortly after daylight. Under orders of General Burnside, the 11th Connecticut was detailed to relieve the 51st Pennsylvania in helping to bring up the boat howitzers, which had arrived during the night. These guns were placed directly behind Foster's brigade in the advance, with Parke's brigade behind them.

It was not long before the advance units engaged the Confederates. In his report on the battle, General Parke wrote, "[I]n the attack we would be exposed to a flank fire from heavy artillery [Fort Thompson anchored the Confederate left on the banks of the Neuse] as well as from field artillery and musketry in our front." The country in this area was generally level with growths of pine trees and occasional underbrush; it was generally described as "open piney woods." The trees in front of the Confederate line had all been felled.[94]

Burnside's plan was to have Foster's brigade attack the Confederate left and center, to have Reno advance along the railroad and attempt to turn the enemy's right, and to have Parke follow up the road as a reserve. As Foster's advance came within range of the Confederate artillery, the brigade deployed in a line on both sides of the road, with the howitzers in the center, positioned on the road. The enemy opened fire with both artillery and musketry. Meanwhile, General Reno advanced along the railroad and ordered a charge of the right wing of his lead regiment, the 21st Massachusetts, which succeeded in advancing through the railroad cut and into the brickyard beyond. The left wing of the 21st Massachusetts and Reno's remaining

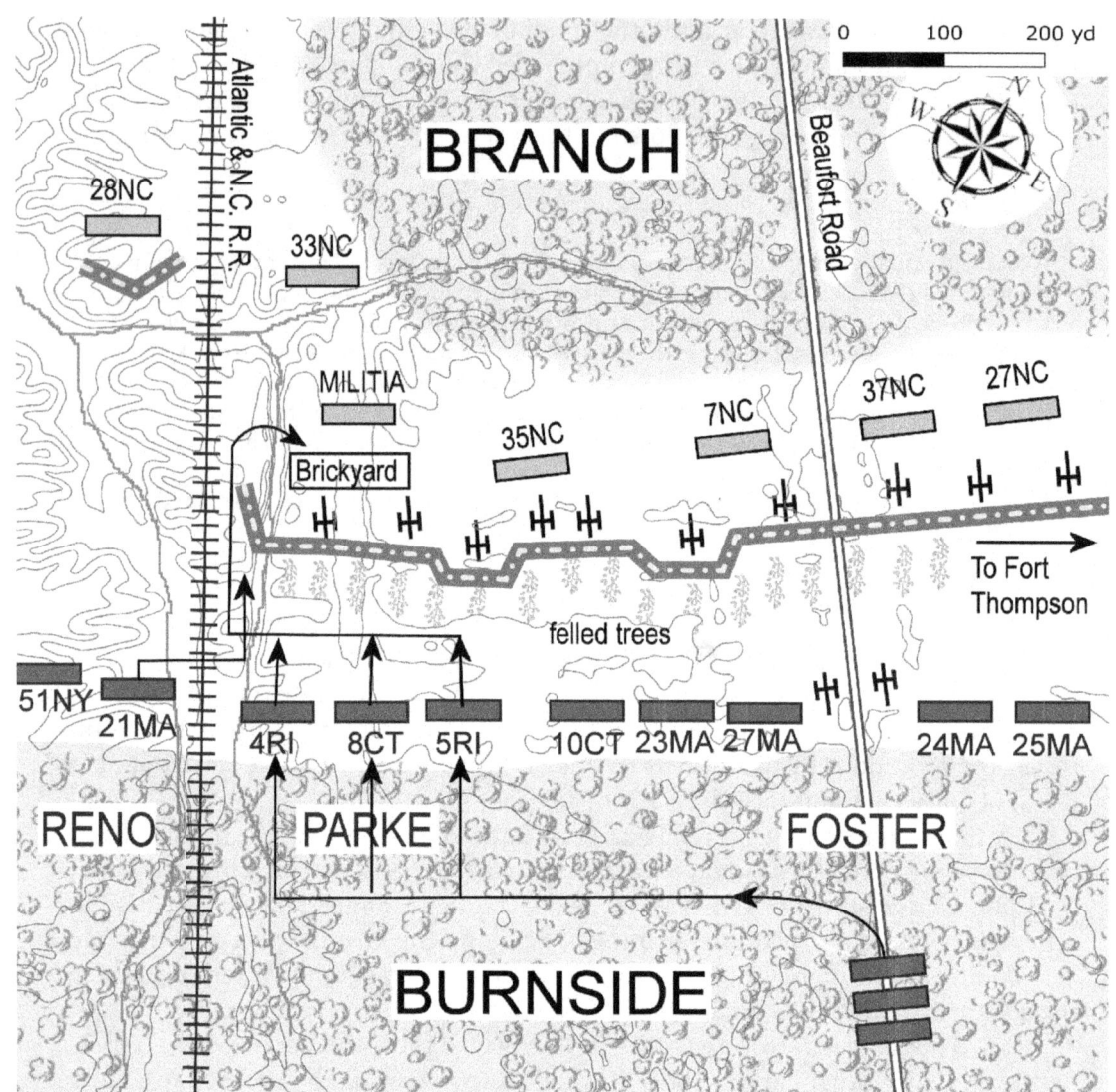

Map 3. Battle of New Bern, North Carolina, March 14, 1862.

regiments went into a line of battle to the left. However, instead of the Confederate right resting on the railroad, as originally thought, it actually extended three quarters of a mile further in a series of redans, that is, V-shaped salient angles projecting toward an expected attack. Those redans were separated from the Federals by felled trees and swamp. Now engaged with this line, Reno was unable to support the right wing of the 21st Massachusetts, and they were compelled to return.

With both wings engaged, Burnside ordered Parke to take a position between Foster on the right and Reno on the left, and to support whichever brigade required it. Parke's brigade formed with the 4th Rhode Island on the left, the 8th Connecticut in the center, and the 5th Rhode Island on the right. The 11th Connecticut, initially to be held in reserve, was sent to General Foster to assist his brigade after

General Burnside learned that the 27th Massachusetts had exhausted its ammunition.[95]

"I directed the brigade through the timber, and guided by the fire of the enemy kept a course nearly parallel to his lines," Parke wrote later. "After passing General Foster's left and when the head of the column had approached within a short distance of the railroad I halted the brigade, and being exposed to a fire of both artillery and musketry, the regiments were placed in the hollow under as good cover as the ground furnished, and skirmishers were deployed just on the edge of the plateau to observe the enemy."[96]

Colonel Harland, commanding the 8th Connecticut, wrote in his report of the battle,

> In accordance with the orders from General Parke I conducted the regiment along the road in the direction of the rebel battery, following the Fourth Rhode Island Regiment. After proceeding for about a mile in this direction we turned to the left and approached through the woods the right of the principal battery. On approaching the edge of the woods in front of the intrenchments of the enemy I received orders from General Parke to remain there with the regiment until further orders. Afterward, being ordered to engage the enemy, I threw forward skirmishers preparatory to advancing in line. Our skirmishers being driven in and it being impossible to advance in this direction, I joined the Fourth Rhode Island, who were then on the railroad and endeavored, if possible, to turn the enemy's right.[97]

It was during this advance directly towards the battery and the Confederate entrenchments that the regiment came under heavy fire and suffered casualties. Private Oliver Case of Company A described a scene that contained elements of comedy and tragedy.

> As we advanced toward the battery, the balls rung tunes over our heads and occasionally played a little nearer our heads than we cared for. Philo Matson ... was in the rank ahead of me and was much frightened; he could have fell out if possible. The orders were given to fall down, sight up, fix bayonets, fire. As soon as I had fired I heard Philo say "Oh, I am killed," turned and saw a slight flesh wound on the top of his head. I certainly could not help laughing to see him. He turned to the orderly and asked him if he thought he was killed and, when he found out that he was still in the land of the living, took his gun and made himself missing as soon as possible. Companies G and [K] were sent out as skirmishers while we lay there upon the ground. Capt. Upham of Co. [K] was wounded in the shoulder at this time; it is feared mortally. Howes Phelps of Co. B was killed.[98]

Adjutant Coit wrote that the Rebels offered strong resistance. "[The] skirmishers sent forward from Cos. G + K—they were almost immediately driven back + a volley of musketry poured into our midst. [M]en were lying down or many must have been killed." He later wrote that the Eighth was stuck in the woods in front of the "long straight battery" for quite a while, and exposed to the Confederate fire between two and three hours. He said they "fired but one volley, the enemy being so concealed that it was useless to return their fire." He credits their small loss to Colonel Harland's choice of ground while marching and to his ordering the men to lie down once they halted.[99]

Colonel Isaac P. Rodman, commanding the 4th Rhode Island on the left of the brigade line and feeling that his regiment was exposed, had moved it to under cover of the railroad embankment. It was there that Lieutenant Colonel Clark of the 21st Massachusetts met Colonel Rodman and urged him to retake the entrenchments. After reconnaissance by his aides, General Parke approved the attack, and he ordered the 8th Connecticut and 5th Rhode Island to support it.[100]

Afterwards, Lieutenant Colonel Clark of the 21st Massachusetts explained what he had told his colleague.

> On the railroad I found Colonel Rodman, with the Fourth Rhode Island, waiting for orders, and informed him of the situation of things in the intrenchments of the enemy, and urged him to advance at once and charge upon their flank, as I had done. Soon after Colonel Harland, with the Eighth Connecticut, came up, and then the two regiments advanced along the railroad to the brick-yard and charged by wing. As soon as the enemy saw them within their lines they instantly retired again to the ravine without firing a gun.[101]

Harland had moved the Eighth by the flank along the railroad and through the bushes to the open ground. Then he gave the command, "By company into line!" and a front advanced, forty men wide. The men moved at a rapid walk. "Fix bayonets!" "Forward into line!" and the rear companies came into line a hundred paces from the Confederate works. "Steady, guide center, forward, double quick!"[102]

Oliver Case later wrote of the attack,

> At this time, word came that the 21st Mass. had charged on the battery and were repulsed. We were ordered on double quick though in line until we reached the rail road where was high embankment where we halted to form. The balls, meanwhile, were flying thick as hailstones. The rebels fired one volley which wounded several and killed two from our regiment.
>
> We were then ordered to fall and by mistake our colors fell too, and the rebels, deceived by our gray coats, took us to be rebel reinforcements arriving by rail road and ceased firing upon us; this mistake probably saved many lives. When we started from there we went double quick to charge their battery, but as they did not like the look of cold steel they left in a hurry.

Case wrote that the noise was deafening. "I had no idea of the noise created in battle with the artillery and musketry until I heard it. It was like one continuous roll of thunder for perhaps half an hour without the least intermission, and then perhaps after a few seconds another more deafening, if possible, than before."[103]

Sergeant Henry E. Strickland, color sergeant and national flag bearer for the Eighth, was reported to be the first to plant his flag on the Rebel works at the battle of New Bern.[104]

Adjutant Charles Coit also described the assault:

> [W]e were ordered to flank this battery + we worked our way thru' woods + over fallen trees onto the railroad when were again exposed to a severe fire. Here we had to lie down by the side of the rail road, while the 4th RI passed us to charge the enemy's extreme right. [W]hen they had passed we started on again + formed battalion front + charged into the battery next to the one where the 4th RI was engaged. We found it just evacuated and raised our flags on the ramparts. This battery I think is an eighth of a mile long. The whole line of fortifications is said to be three miles and soon it was all ours. While we charged, other Regts were charging to our right + the RI was engaged at our right. Twas a lively time I assure you. According to orders we remained drawn up in line in the battery exposed to a scathing fire for a long time + then ordered forward to support another Regt that was engaged in front. But again the enemy retreated before we came up to them.[105]

Case recalled the moment the Eighth planted the colors. "The color guard immediately ran up to the battery and planted the colors which were the first upon the battery. The U.S. flag had two bullet holes shot through it while being planted."[106]

As to the raising of the flags on the ramparts, Coit further described it in a letter a few weeks later.

> As we "charged" into the battery, or rather just after we entered[,] Genl Parke, who followed us at short distance, called for our colors. The order was not understood so I ran to the color Co., to repeat it. Capt. Ward's + as the sergeants came forward with them I believe I walked a few steps with them + told them to go out to the rampart a few yards distant where Genl Parke was waiting for them. So the color Sergts raised the flags....
>
> There was very little danger in it anyway for there were very few balls flying around us just then + the battery was entirely evacuated + we were formed inside, so in fact the colors were planted on the battery back of the Regt. They were so planted that our own troops might know that the battery was ours + so that they would come straight forward to support us + not mistake us for rebels + fire upon us. We did not go straight over the battery but flanked it, that is went round + came in at the side.[107]

After the Confederates were driven from their entrenchments, the regiments of the brigade were formed in line behind the entrenchments, in the rear area between the entrenchments and the woods behind them. The formation included the 11th Connecticut, which had just rejoined the brigade after having been temporarily assigned to Foster's brigade. Responding to the heavy firing still occurring to their left on Reno's front beyond the railroad, Parke ordered the 5th Rhode Island and 8th Connecticut to advance and send out skirmishers to ascertain the situation.

In the meantime, finding the enemy still present in rifle pits alongside the railroad and behind the brickyard and in a series of redoubts beyond the railroad, Parke brought up the 4th Rhode Island and ordered them to attack this position. The 4th Rhode Island charged the Confederate flank while Reno's brigade charged the front, forcing the Confederates to withdraw.[108] The 5th Rhode Island had earlier advanced to an elevation on the line where they had fired into the Confederate line several times. When they observed the 4th Rhode Island charging on their right, the 5th Rhode Island ceased fire.[109]

Colonel Harland recounted the enemy retreat in his report of the battle.

> We entered the battery in the rear of the brick-yard and found that the enemy had just abandoned it. I formed the regiment in line between the rebel breastworks and the woods and sent skirmishers into the woods. Finding that a direct advance in that direction would bring the regiment in contact with portions of General Foster's brigade, I so reported to General Parke, who ordered me to move more to the left, to the assistance of the Fifth Rhode Island. I filed through the woods, and when we arrived at the railroad the enemy was in full retreat in the direction of New Berne. The regiment then moved toward New Berne and occupied barracks on the right bank of the Trent.[110]

Wolcott Marsh visited the battlefield several days later. He described the entrenchments on the west side of the railroad (across from the brickyard) as having "10 rifle pits or breast works each capable of holding from 1 to 3 companies & also 5 pits with logs piled up in front to protect the men. & besides these there were several pieces of cannon." On the other side was "one continual breast work thrown up for more than two miles with a ditch fronting it so wide that would be impossible to cross it without ladders & on the intrenchments they had 10 pieces [of] cannon all

Battle before New Bern, North Carolina, 8th Connecticut Volunteers charging—March 14, 1862 (Joseph E. Shadek Civil War Sketchbook. Courtesy Bridgeport History Center, Bridgeport Public Library).

brass.... At the end of this entrenchment we come to a fort which sweeps the river & land mounting 13 guns."[111]

The Eighth came across several Confederate camps as they moved towards New Bern. Oliver Case wrote that these camps were about three or four miles from New Bern and within about a quarter of a mile of each other. He reported that they had "just been left," and that the principal quartermaster and commissary tents were on fire, but the barracks and other commissary tents were still intact. There were lots of clothes and personal items left behind.[112] The regiment reached the Trent River where the Confederates had burned the railroad bridge after crossing over it to New Bern. Wolcott Marsh wrote that "it was a grand & imposing yet sad sight to see the flames reaching to the heavens & spreading from pillar to pillar while also several buildings in city were in flames."[113]

Burnside moved Foster's brigade across the river and into the city and left Reno's brigade and Parke's brigade on the south shore of the Trent.[114] The Eighth was ordered back to one of the camps they had passed earlier. There were "fires in stoves & fire places still burning & tables set while clothing of every description, shot guns, rifles, pistols, swords & c & c were strewn around every where," Marsh wrote. The next day, March 15, the men dressed up in "secesh cloths & armed with old dirk knives." ("Secesh" was the North's derisive term for secessionists.) Marsh later sent home to his wife a shotgun, cavalry sword and a muster roll from a Confederate cavalry unit that he had picked up.[115] Case wrote that they "have been living some since we came here upon what the secesh left. We have found molasses, sugar, rice, coffee, etc. which we cook ourselves. Just imagine a soldier having his griddlecakes for breakfast, fresh meat for dinner, boiled rice and coffee for supper, and you have an idea of the way we are living at present."[116]

In a few days, the Eighth would leave the New Bern area. The Official Records list their casualties in the battle as two dead and four wounded.[117] Wolcott Marsh put the numbers for the regiment as three killed and twelve wounded.[118]

Chapter 3

Fort Macon to Washington, D.C.

Once Brigadier General Ambrose E. Burnside's forces had captured the town of New Bern, the next objective in the expedition to pacify the North Carolina coast was to take Fort Macon and to secure Beaufort Harbor. Control of the harbor would give his force a base of supply and provide the Federal Navy with a coaling and repair station, and a haven from the storms of the Atlantic. Fort Macon, completed in 1834, was a brick, casemated fort constructed on the eastern tip of Bogue Banks, where it guarded the Beaufort Inlet and the approaches to the Beaufort Harbor.

Beaufort Harbor lies at the southern end of the Outer Banks, at the mouth of the Newport River. Ships enter the harbor through Beaufort Inlet, which is formed by the barrier islands—Shackleford Banks on the east and Bogue Banks on the west. There are two key towns on the harbor at the mouth of the Newport River. Beaufort, on the east bank, was the third oldest town in the state, and Morehead City, on the west bank, was the terminus of the Atlantic and North Carolina Railroad, which at that time ran down from New Bern.

In the years before the Civil War, Fort Macon had fallen into disrepair. With the coming of the war and word of the impending Burnside Expedition, the Confederates repaired the fort and armed it. By the time the Federal forces prepared to renew their advance after New Bern, Fort Macon was garrisoned by five heavy artillery companies totaling 441 officers and men. They were commanded by twenty-seven-year-old Colonel Moses J. White, an 1858 graduate of West Point. Given the size of the garrison and the lack of any other Confederate force in the area, General Burnside decided to use only a portion of his force to mount the attack on the fort. The task fell to Brigadier General John G. Parke and his Third Brigade, which included the 8th Connecticut.[1]

The Siege of Fort Macon

On March 19, the 8th Connecticut and the 4th Rhode Island broke camp and boarded transports for the journey down the Neuse River to Slocum's Creek, where six days before they had disembarked before their advance on New Bern. With them was a siege train carrying heavy ordnance that might be needed in the attack on the fort. Meanwhile, the 5th Rhode Island battalion (it consisted of only five companies) marched down the railroad to Havelock Station, where they were to rendezvous with the other units. On March 20, the waterborne expedition, along with General Parke,

Chapter 3. Fort Macon to Washington, D.C.   49

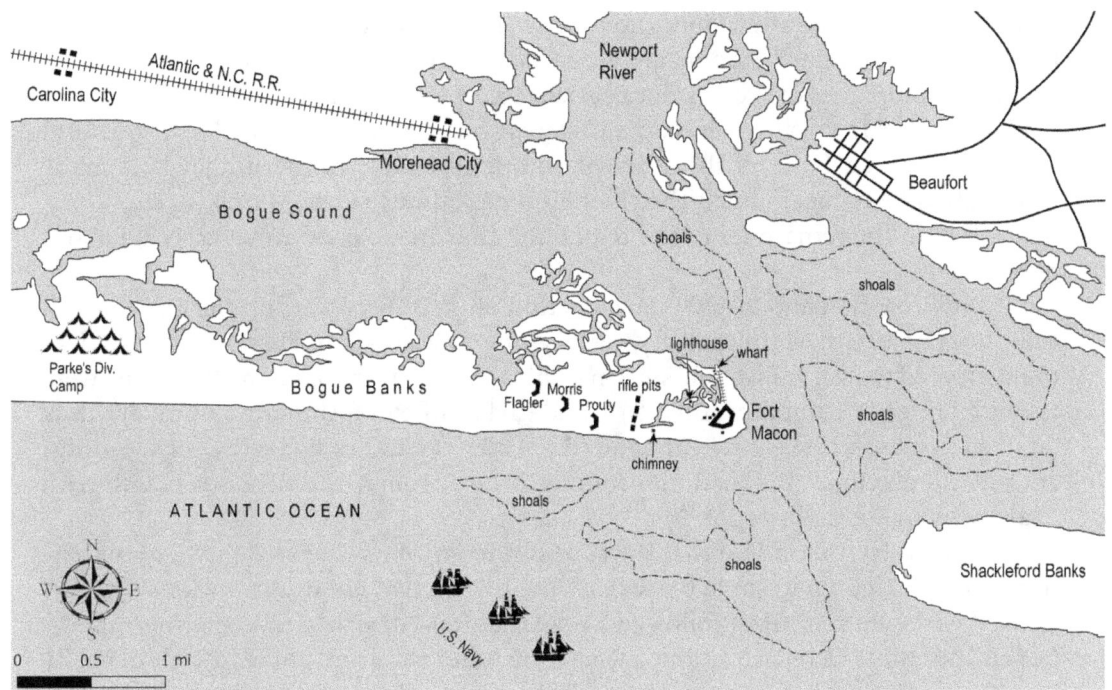

Map 4. Siege of Fort Macon, North Carolina, April 1862.

steamed down the Neuse River and up Slocum's Creek to a spot about a mile and a half from Havelock Station. It was here that they disembarked.[2]

Sergeant Jay Nettleton of Company I, who had just been promoted to sergeant a few days before, said that a swift move toward the coast was ordered, but the trip was not very fast at all.

> Last Wednesday morn [March 19] we were ordered into line all of a sudden, after a while march[ed] toward [the] railroad bridge or boat landing opposite Newbern, and in the course of the day we were put on the old "Chasseur" again. Our Regt. & the R.I. were put on the boats.... Thursday the two Regts. with our Brigade General moved down the river to the place where we landed to go up to Newberne. Some of the troops of both Regt. were taken by two light draft steam boats & disappeared up the creek. Night came & the boats didn't come for us so we put up our beds and went to sleep. Friday morn the Alice Prince [*Alice Price*] came for [us]& soon with our knapsacks we were moving up a <u>crooked</u> creek into the country. They say it was 7 miles up to where we landed.... We landed on a clearance & spent that day sunning & lazing around.[3]

Adjutant Charles Coit went aboard the *Sentinel* about 5:30 p.m. on Wednesday, March 19, after standing all day at the landing, waiting for transportation. The boat's captain did not want to make the journey down the river at night, due to "spikes +c with which the channel is obstructed." Taking advantage of the delay and having nothing to eat but hardtack, Coit and a few others (probably Colonel Edward Harland and the staff) rowed over to New Bern for supper. They had "a pretty good supper, best we have had lately but hardly up to a New England hotel meal," and then returned in a hard rain. They left the next morning on the *Sentinel*, anchored off

Slocum's Creek in the afternoon, and took small steamers up the creek to the assembly point near Havelock Station, arriving that evening.[4]

Four companies of the 8th Connecticut (of which Sergeant Nettleton had been a part) had gone down the river on the *Chasseur* on Thursday, March 20. The boat did not return to New Bern for the other six companies until that evening, which made it too late to start back down the river. The next day, Friday, March 21, the *Chasseur* left with the remainder of the regiment. They made good time, arriving about noon.[5]

Coit wrote that about 4:30 p.m. a portion of their force were on the march, with their final objective, Carolina City, twenty-one miles distant. He said that as it was to be a forced march (a fast non-stop march), and only thirty-five "picked men" were taken from each company. The 4th Rhode Island fielded the same number. They "started in fine style the 4th Regt band (the American of Providence, Green leading) at the head playing." The road they followed was through a continuous marsh with "hardly a single firm dry spot."[6]

Sergeant Nettleton said that it was at sundown when they left, in "light marching order" to "march to some barracks." The Eighth had not drawn rations that day and left without them. They followed a road that was "dryish" and sometimes sandy, he said, but there were also swamps where the water was from ankle to knee deep. By 9 or 10 o'clock, they had gone ten miles. They reached the barracks later that evening, and by midnight they were ready for bed.[7]

The next day, March 22, Nettleton wrote,

> Sat. morn. Up & made a little coffee in my cup. Finally went out onto the railroad to see a bridge the rebels had burnt. 9 o'clock orders were to fall in & we were off. Found the teams on the main road with our rations, got some crackers & a ration of whiskey in my canteen, & on we went at the rate of a mile in 20 minutes—traveling the same as last night only more sand. Met no opposition.... Reached Carolina City Sat. p.m. rather tired. We have besides our 40 or 60 cartridges our haversacks & canteens (not always very heavy), our two blankets & overcoats to carry.[8]

First Lieutenant Wolcott P. Marsh wrote in a letter to his wife that they left at 11 a.m. and that Company E was left behind to guard the barracks and the road bridge that crossed the Newport River, the railroad bridge having been burned by the Confederates. He described the march to Carolina City as "another tedious march of 10 miles through sand, mud & water."[9]

Jay Nettleton described the town that the rebels had torched a few days before.

> Carolina City is a place on Bogue Sound Creek that sets up from Beaufort—is about 3 miles above Morehead City, the terminus of the railroad. Were perhaps 10 houses there. A large Hotel & a dwelling house the rebels burnt a few days before we came. They don't mean we should have good quarters. The 8th & 4th bivouacked on a cleared plot facing southward running down to the Sound. Buildings near the water or shanties used for salt distillery & resin & turpentine works were stripped of their boards & finally the frames to make us covers to sleep under. Found a quantity of cord pitch pine wood for fires, a large number of barrels of resin that the boys took & broke on the fires & such a smoky camp & such a dirty looking set of men you never saw....
>
> This pitch wood blacks us up every day. One hardly recognizes himself. Our clean clothes are in our knapsacks & when they will come out we don't know, but we have worn clothes 3 or

4 weeks before. 3 Companies of each Regt have gone to Morehead & Beaufort cities as guard—also to cut off communication.

At nearby Fort Macon, the Confederates were not ready to give up. As Nettleton wrote, "A surrender has been demanded—with an answer that they should hold out as long as they could. The rebel flag <u>floats defiantly</u> every day over the fort."[10]

Rations became an issue for the force that had advanced. Adjutant Coit wrote that they had but six baggage wagons with them that had to bring their rations from the landing site twenty-one miles away. The wagons were loaded lightly due to the terrible road conditions; they made the trip up one day and returned the next. The nights were cold, he said, because the town was near the coast, and the men suffered from the exposure. There were only four houses in the city, and all were occupied. The Field & Staff of both the 8th Connecticut and the 4th Rhode Island were quartered in the railroad freight depot.[11]

Parke ordered Major John Wright of the 5th Rhode Island to rebuild the railroad bridge over the Newport River so that an efficient supply line could be established. The remainder of the 8th Connecticut and 4th Rhode Island that had not made the advance to Carolina City were now ordered to join Parke there.[12]

By March 31, the railroad bridge at Newport had been rebuilt, Marsh wrote, so baggage could be brought down to the troops on rail cars. It arrived that evening, except for their tents, which would have to come on a later trip. The distance and the poor quality of the roads had prevented the baggage from being brought down earlier by wagon. Having been reunited with his luggage, Marsh asked for some personal items in a letter he wrote to his wife that day. The list included a pair of boots to be made of "french calve skin double soled & sewed," "a few goodies" such as a can of preserves, a silk handkerchief, a fish line and hooks, and some old clothes to give his "Contraband," that is, a former slave that he now employed as a servant.[13]

The arrival of the Federals prompted the Confederates to destroy anything near the fort which would hinder their defense or be of use to the Federal army. At 4:15 on the afternoon of March 23, the rebels took the bark *Glenn,* which was anchored near the fort, and ran it ashore in the bulkhead channel and set it afire. It burned through the following day.[14]

As Marsh wrote of the event, "The ship which was burned was owned North & captured by the rebel privateers last fall & run in here. It was a grand sight to see that whole ship as the flames leaped from mast to mast & through the sails then it burned for hours & after night came on it was really magnificent." The men of the Eighth responded with their own blaze: "the boys to be even with them set all the remaining rosin (a good many barrels) afire & such a fire you never saw. Thus ended the rosin & in a measure the black disagreeable smutty smoke."[15]

While waiting for the railroad bridge to be rebuilt, Parke began preparations to surround Fort Macon. Men of the 8th Connecticut were ordered to begin constructing rafts and flatboats to transport troops to Beaufort. Parke wanted to occupy the town and establish communications with the blockading Federal fleet. A crossing was planned for the night of March 24, but the weather was bad so the advance was postponed. On the evening of March 25, two companies, one from the 8th Connecticut, and one from the 4th Rhode Island, both under the command of Major

John Allen, embarked in a flotilla of small boats and crossed from Morehead City to Beaufort. They reached the town about 2:00 a.m. on March 26, and soon occupied it.[16]

In order to make contact with the Federal fleet and enlist their help in the planned operations against Fort Macon, a detail of men from the 8th Connecticut crossed over to Shackleford Banks on March 28 in some small fishing boats. Then, carrying the boats on their shoulders, they marched across the island and launched them into the surf on the ocean side. They were picked up by one of the Union blockading cruisers, the *State of Georgia*, and contact was made.[17]

With troops at Morehead City, Carolina City and now Beaufort, the final step was to land troops on Bogue Banks. A potential landing site was identified near a salt works at a place called Hoop Pole Creek, directly across from Carolina City and about four miles west of the fort. On March 29, under the cover of a boat howitzer mounted on a launch and the guns of the *State of Georgia*, a detachment of the 4th Rhode Island rowed over to Hoop Pole Creek and landed. The remainder of the company followed the next day.[18]

On the afternoon of Wednesday, April 2, an order came for Company A of the Eighth to be ready in fifteen minutes in light marching order with one day's rations. From their camp at Carolina City, they were marched down to the wharf and taken in small row boats across Bogue Sound to the banks opposite—Bogue Banks. They were ordered to report to Captain Wood of the 4th Rhode Island, who was there with two companies of his regiment. Company A of the 8th Connecticut was to assist in supporting three heavy siege guns that had just been brought over.

It seemed to be a fairly safe encampment. As Wolcott Marsh wrote, "Our Pickets & the rebels are in sight of each other & occasionally exchange a shot, but thus far have done no damage on either side. The enemy had salt works here which make very comfortable quarters for us." Another Rhode Island company arrived on the night of April 3. Food was not a problem. Marsh wrote that another day's rations were sent over, and in addition "there are a plenty oysters within a stones throw also clams. Fish are being brought in over the other side plentifully large sea trout."[19]

Adjutant Charles Coit reported that the companies of the 8th Connecticut were not together at this point, but they were all in sight of the fort. "Co A is at present on duty across the Sound on the Banks. Co's D (Capt Ward's) + K (Capt Upham's) are in Morehead + have fine quarters in a good house. Co. B [E] is at Beaufort, the remaining Co's are at this encampment. So you see we are all round. The Fort is plainly visible from all these places."[20]

On April 9, the six companies of the Eighth at Carolina City received orders to break camp and move over to the Bogue Banks. Their equipment was packed and transported that day with the troops to follow the next day. Charles Coit, however, was sick, and did not accompany the remainder of the regiment to Bogue Banks. Instead, he traveled to Morehead City, where Colonel Harland had gone before when he became ill.[21]

Ever since the move down from New Bern, the Federal troops suffered from insufficient food and lack of shelter as they waited for an adequate supply line to be established. These conditions help fuel an outbreak of illness and disease. Colonel

Chapter 3. Fort Macon to Washington, D.C.

Harland and a number of other officers from the 8th Connecticut were sick. Typhoid fever sent over a hundred men to the hospitals.[22] Marsh reported that Second Lieutenant William H. Johnson of Company K died of typhoid fever in Morehead City on April 6 "after an illness of but few days."[23]

Typhoid fever and other diseases were a terrible problem in the Civil War, and disease took the lives of two soldiers for every one killed in battle. When Charles Coit was in New Bern in early April, he called on Dr. DeWitt C. Lathrop, an assistant surgeon with the Eighth. Coit recalled that the doctor told him that he was "living constantly in an atmosphere of Typhoid Fever" and that "everything he ate tasted of it + he could smell nothing else." Dr. Lathrop himself later died at the hospital on April 18.

Coit described Dr. Lathrop as much beloved and esteemed in the regiment, a man who was thought to be the best physician there because he had a kind manner and he spent time nursing the sick.[24] Dr. J.W. Page, an inspector with the United States Sanitary Commission in North Carolina, wrote of Dr. Lathrop, "His devotion to the sick and wounded was untiring day and night. His humane sympathies were too strong for the heavy responsibilities which fell upon him. His heart was too much in his work, and led him to sacrifice to the preservation of others the strength which was necessary to his own." The men of the Eighth later erected a monument to Dr. Lathrop in Windham.[25]

Inspired by the British Sanitary Commission of the Crimean War, the United States Sanitary Commission was an organization formed by northern citizens to provide relief to Union soldiers. The Commission worked to minimize the effects of rampant diseases by helping to develop better hygiene and diet for the soldiers, by caring for the sick and wounded, and by aiding in the flow of food and supplies to the soldiers.[26]

While on duty with the regiment, Dr. Lathrop had been assigned to care for the left five companies, while Dr. Melancthon Storrs, the surgeon with the Eighth, administered to the right five companies. Coit wrote that Dr. Storrs was a very able surgeon and physician, with a clear, logical mind, but he felt that the doctor was a bit selfish and looked out "sharp" for his own comfort.[27]

Since the time that the first troops arrived on Bogue Banks, General Parke continued to move troops and equipment over to the island. A total of seven companies of both the 4th Rhode Island and 8th Connecticut were transferred there, as well as the 5th Rhode Island and three artillery batteries.[28] As the Federal presence built, several skirmishes occurred between Parke's men and pickets from the Fort Macon. On April 11, General Parke, accompanied by Lieutenant Daniel Webster Flagler, his chief of ordnance, Captain Robert S. Williamson of the Corps of Topographical Engineers, and Captain Lewis O. Morris of Company C, 1st United States Artillery, made a reconnaissance of the fort to select suitable sites for the three siege batteries. They selected sites that were from less than 1,300 yards to 1,700 yards from the fort.[29]

On April 12, General Parke ordered five companies of the 8th Connecticut under the command of Major Hiram Appelman to advance and drive the Confederate pickets back into the fort. Appelman marched the battalion by the right flank along the beach until they reached a point about three miles from the fort, where they formed in line of battle across the width of the island. With Company G under Captain James L. Russell deployed as skirmishers, the Eighth continued forward.[30]

Wolcott Marsh of Company A gave this account of the mission.

> Friday night we had orders to draw & cook one days rations & be ready to move in light marching order at 8 a.m. Next morning at the hour named.... Co. A,H,G,I, & L [see note] ... were marched up the beach towards the rebel pickets the sight of whom we reached in about an ½ hour (they having fallen back from their old station) when Co. G. was thrown out as skirmishers. The rebels slowly fell back firing on our advance & they returned it for distance from hill to hill till finally they could not be driven by the skirmishers from a sand bank behind which they were securely screened from our bullets.
>
> So the advance halted when we the main body was brought up they keeping up a continual fire upon us, when pretty near the bank orders were given for the men to fix bayonets & charge double quick over the hill (that is for 3 companies we still being left behind). The order was no quicker given than performed but not so quick however but that the rebels seeing the movement out ran our men & soon disappeared over the next hill. As soon as driven from this place the companies halted & Co. A was ordered forward as skirmishers which order was quickly obeyed.

Eventually the Union forces drove the rebel skirmishers into the fort, Marsh said.

> Now it was our turn to have a chance at them & a pertly hot & tedious job was had of it too. for they resisted our advance pretty well but we gradually drove them from hill to hill 'till we were with in ¾ mile of Ft. Macon when we halted the rebels leaving pell mell for fort.
>
> And now that they were safe in side the fort commenced to shell us but could neither scare us or drive or hurt us as we were sheltered by the sand hills. We were soon relieved by Co. H. who were stationed as pickets & we fell back to near where the rest of companys were where we lay all day & night but it was not but a little ways from the pickets & hardly as well sheltered as they were for the hills were much higher. Still we were comparatively safe.[31]

After the return of their pickets, the fort kept up a continuous fire until the middle of the afternoon of the assault. Then Confederate skirmishers reappeared, believing that the Federals had retired. When they reached the Federal picket line, another skirmish occurred until the Confederates again withdrew to the fort. The night was quiet, and at 8 a.m. the next day the 8th Connecticut was relieved by the 5th Rhode Island. The Eighth's casualties were two wounded in Company H: Captain Sheffield and a private.[32] Captain Thomas Sheffield was reported as having been severely wounded in the body[33] but survived the injury. He later commanded Company E, and was promoted to lieutenant colonel on November 16, 1865.[34]

Now the heavy guns and ammunition were floated over to the banks on two-masted scows, moved across the island at night, and then slowly worked into position. Sand bags were used to create breastworks.[35] In a letter of April 21, Charles Coit described the batteries that were constructed by the Federals:

> We have built three batteries the nearest is within about 1000 yards of the fort. This is an eight-inch, mortar battery, the second farther back has three 30 pounder, Parrott rifled guns, the third is back further still its armament consists of ten or a dozen mortars, some very heavy. In front of the first battery + within rifle range of the fort, pits for sharp shooters have been dug + it will be the duty of those in the pits to keep the rebels away from the guns....
> Then our men have had to build a magazine large enough to hold the immense quantity of shot + shell needed for the siege and all this work has to be done in the night, so you can see

that there is good reason for our delay here when the deficient transportation +c is taken into account, but I believe all is ready now.[36]

The rifle pits were dug at night within 2,000 feet of the fort and were continuously occupied. The 8th Connecticut and 4th Rhode Island were alternately on duty. On the evening of April 21, General Parke ordered that the rifle pits be dug closer to the fort, so that sharpshooters could try to silence the Confederate guns. A volunteer force commanded by Major Appelman and under the direction of First Lieutenant Henry E. Morgan began to dig these pits near the chimney of a ruined house. However, as First Sergeant Amos Clift of Company G was positioning the pickets, the Confederates discovered the attempt to move closer, and they opened fire on the men with canister, wounding Major Appelman in the thigh and Private J.H. Alexander in the body.[37]

Wolcott Marsh wrote that about 10 a.m. on the morning of April 22, a litter was brought into their camp on Bogue Island on which lay Major Appelman, wounded by grape shot. "The Doctors examined it immediately & found it a very bad contusion on the back of the fleshy part of leg above [the] knee. Although skin was not broken it was a terrible bruise. The leg being black clear around it." Marsh thought that perhaps the ball that had struck Appelman was spent, possibly hitting the ground first.[38] The major was moved to the hospital at Morehead City. There Dr. Storrs concluded that the wound was bad, but not dangerous if it was properly treated, and he said Appelman could not return to duty for two to three months. To replace Appelman, Captain John E. Ward was ordered to Bogue Banks to take command of the seven companies of the Eighth there. Colonel Harland, still not well, acted as military governor of Morehead and vicinity.[39]

The men of the Eighth suffered from the conditions of the siege. At one time, sixty men lay sick at Morehead City, and almost forty died of typhoid fever. On April 21, only two captains were present for duty, and Dr. Melancthon Storrs was the only healthy member of the field and staff.[40] The Eighth had worked hard since their arrival in building entrenchments for both the artillery and infantry.[41] It had taken its toll.

The siege continued as the batteries were being finished. On April 22, Burnside's flagship, the *Alice Price*, left New Bern with a schooner full of ammunition and two floating batteries, *Grenade* and *Shrapnel,* arriving in Back Sound off Shackleford Banks on April 23. That day Burnside sent another surrender demand to Colonel Moses J. White in Fort Macon. The *Alice Price* delivered the message under a flag of truce. Colonel White again refused to surrender. At a meeting arranged between General Burnside and Colonel White early on the morning of April 24 on Shackleford Banks, Burnside renewed his demand for surrender. Colonel White's final decision was to fight.

Burnside was now determined to commence the attack and ordered Parke to have his batteries commence firing as soon as possible. It was decided that they would open fire early on the morning of April 25.[42] In accordance with the procedure of alternating twenty-four hour shifts with the Rhode Island troops, the 8th Connecticut went on duty at the batteries at 9 p.m. on the evening of Thursday, April 24. Lieutenant Wolcott Marsh with Company A realized that the bombardment

Siege Guns Battery—Bogue Banks, North Carolina, 1862 (Joseph E. Shadek Civil War Sketchbook. Courtesy Bridgeport History Center, Bridgeport Public Library).

would commence the next day because he saw the artillery men busy opening the embrasures of the battery and exposing their guns to the enemy. Seeing this happen, Marsh ordered his men to dig a trench parallel to the battery to provide them with as much protection as possible.

On Friday, April 25, Marsh watched as the bombardment finally began.

[A]fter daylight the sun came & yet all was quiet. Then [a]t six o'clock they run up the "bared rag" for the last time & no sooner had it reached the top of the pole than the very earth under our feet quaked as the guns beside us belched forth in deafening tones fire & smoke &sent after the traitors & their contemptible flag as solid shot which must have made their hair stand on end. No sooner had our siege guns sent this challenge than the morter battery to our left & the one to our right gave warning to the rebels of their doom by tossing 8 shell nearly at once into & around the fort sending as the bursting fragments flew in every direction death & consternation to its traitorous occupants.

It was not long before their guns were manned & the shot & shell flew around our heads in every direction & now the Battle Waged Hotter & Hotter ere long 4 gun boats came up & tossed into the fort their deadly missels. It now became to hot for the enemy & the firing on their side seaced altogether exception on one side toward the boats. They succeeded in sending daylight through one of the boats when they all returned out of range.[43]

But then the Confederates began firing once again.

They now again directed their whole attention once more at us & there it continued till afternoon when their guns fired less often & more wild…. On our side everything progressed finely not a man had been Killed & only two wounded their shot had done very little damage to the works & as their fire lessened ours increased. Thus the afternoon passed & it seemed probable that they would stand anothers days bombarding. When at 5 o'clock a white flag appeared on the parapets.

The firing at once seaced on both sides & all was excitement to know what it meant.... A white flag was immediately sent forward from our side & the two met mid way between us & the fort.[44]

The Confederates agreed to surrender provided they would be released on parole. General Parke was sent for and after another meeting it was decided to have an armistice for the night and leave the decision to General Burnside.

The 8th Connecticut was relieved at about 9 p.m. and returned to camp. Marsh wrote that they had been under fire for eleven hours and had to sit doubled up in trenches where the sand would cover them either in a shower or in a cave in.

> [A] shot would strike the bank & in 4 instances 32 pd. shot came completely through the bank & dropped twice on to the men's necks. One buried a man completely up & pass over his head & dropped at his feet once without hitting anyone in the trench.... The bank where we lay was completely riddled with shot & beyond us the ground was plowed in every direction & shot & shell might be found in every direction....
>
> During the whole day we had but two men wounded they were serving the guns at the time & but slightly hurt. But the very last shot Killed one man.... He was at the morter battery & was on top of the bank driving a stake to take range from & saw the shot fired & hollered to the men saying, 'down men,' There comes a shot but did not get down himself, had hardly got the words out of his mouth when he was struck side ways & the whole of his breast was completely carried away exposing his heart & the whole of his insides & knocking him down 10 to 15 feet to where the men were under the hill out of danger.[45]

No one in Marsh's Company A suffered more than very slight injuries. Marsh himself narrowly missed being hit. "One of the first shells fired struck in the bank close to myself (where I was looking at the fun) & burst covering me entirely up with sand filling my face so full of powder that [I] could not breath at first but none of the fragments hit me, still it was near enough to be unpleasant."[46]

Parke met with Burnside on the *Alice Price* about 4 a.m. on the morning of Saturday, April 26. The two discussed surrender terms, and they decided to allow the Confederates to be released on their parole of honor, that is, to not take arms up against the United States until properly exchanged. This was in keeping with Burnside's policy of paroling the Confederates earlier in the campaign, largely because he did not have the means to send them back to Northern prison camps. The *Alice Price* arrived off the fort under a flag of truce about 6 a.m. A party was sent to the fort and Colonel White agreed to the proposed terms. At 9 a.m. the Confederates marched out of the fort, stacked arms, and waited for the Federal troops to arrive.[47]

It was then that one of the more controversial events for the 8th Connecticut occurred. While the Confederates were preparing to surrender their fort, General Burnside and General Parke had gone ashore and walked down the beach to the trenches to notify their men of the surrender. It was the 5th Rhode Island that had relieved the Eighth the night before, and Burnside ordered them out of the trenches. They formed on the beach where Burnside personally unfurled their new set of colors, which had just arrived from Providence. With the generals in front, the unit marched in column to the fort. Orders were also sent for the 4th Rhode Island

Interior of Fort Macon, North Carolina—April 26, 1862 (Joseph E. Shadek Civil War Sketchbook. Courtesy Bridgeport History Center, Bridgeport Public Library).

Regiment to come up. At 10:10 a.m. the Confederate flag was lowered from the flagstaff and an American flag that the rebels once captured was run up in its place. Major Wright of the 5th Rhode Island requested the Confederate flag, and Burnside agreed.[48]

The 8th Connecticut was deprived of honors they richly deserved. They had the most arduous service and they alone were in the rifle pits during the long and final cannonade. It was by chance that they were not present at the surrender, having endured the hardships of the actual battle. In fact, they had not even been summoned to the surrender. General Parke's explanation for why the Rhode Islanders were given preference was that there was no field officer of the 8th Connecticut present to receive the surrender.[49]

The men of the Eighth were not satisfied with the outcome of the surrender. Marsh wrote,

> [T]he 5th R.I. who relieved us the night before had marched into it & taken the secesh flag. We felt pretty bad over this for we felt that we had had the hardest of the work all through & were entitled both to plant our colors on the fort first & take the stars & bars down & the men have not got over it yet. They think we are misused.... But what made our regt. feel still worse, in the afternoon 5 companies of the 4th R.I. were marched up with band & fling colors & the 5th sent back. As before we thought we should have gone. But, the 4th comes from R.I. & so does Gen. Burnside. We expect to have in the papers how the colors of the 4th & 5th R.I. were the first to be planted in Ft. Macon. As at Newbern we did the work & they won the glory.[50]

Charles Coit also said the Eighth felt shortchanged. "There is a great deal of feeling in the Regt at the manner in which we have been slighted by Genl Parke. I fear

+ believe he is influenced more by soft speeches + compliments than by real service. The 8th does not play the first part but when called for the latter it has never been found wanting."[51]

Return to New Bern

Once Fort Macon was captured, the Eighth was again on the move. Wolcott Marsh wrote that orders came on the morning of Wednesday, April 30, to be ready to leave on fifteen minutes' notice. Three of the seven companies on Bogue Banks left that day on two small, flat-bottomed schooners called lighters; they landed at Morehead City. The remaining companies were transported the next day. Company A was the last to leave and had to take charge of a large scow containing most of the regiment's baggage. The scow became grounded several times and the men had to go overboard to help free it. The company spent that night at the railroad depot.

On the morning of Friday, May 2, four companies—Company A, F, H and E—boarded the *Highland Light*, a small Hudson River steamer, and traveled through Core Sound and Pamlico Sound and up the Neuse River, reaching New Bern at 5:30 p.m., a distance of 100 miles. They spent the night on the boat. The next day, May 3, they landed and set up camp. The other six companies of the 8th Connecticut also landed that day.[52] Sergeant Seth Plumb of Company E described the camp.

> [It is] very pleasantly situated close by the river, and we have access to its waters, there is also a good spring in camp.... The Gun Boats, transports, and craft of every description ly here in the river close by us.... Our boats seem like old friends and we know the names of most of them. The [tug boat] *Union* or *Wheel Barrow* is a noted boat with us, it is a long narrow boat with the wheel in the stern and will run in 2 feet of water and carry 800 men if necessary, it has landed many times, and is considered one of the institutions.[53]

Plumb said that the plantation where they were camped was about 50 acres, bounded by woods on two sides and the river and the railroad on the other two. There were two small houses and a barn, with a great deal of fruit, including blackberries, mulberries, peaches, plums and apricots. The owner of the plantation was in the Confederate army.[54] The Eighth's camp was about a mile below the city, on the west bank of the Neuse River.[55]

On May 7, the Eighth received new Sibley tents. "They are perfectly round with a center pole about twelve feet high and a ventilator at the top," Private Oliver Case wrote. "The diameter of the tents at the bottom is about twelve feet and they accommodate when full twenty, although at present they will have to accommodate only twelve."[56] The officers fared even better. Charles Coit, now the captain of Company B, wrote of the new Sibley tents, "Only one tent is allowed to the three Officers of a Co. but we are permitted to keep one of our old wall tents, so the Capts. take the new Sibley's + give their Lieuts the old wall tents. I am just sending a detail of men down to the rebel barracks half a mile below here for boards for a floor +c + I expect soon to be fixed up in apple pie order."[57]

The men recorded events that happened off the battlefield, too. For example, Sergeant Seth Plumb wrote to his friends about the death of a comrade.

[A]nother of our Litchfield boys has been taken from us by death. Franklin A. Newcomb died this morning at 2 o'clock. We have just got word of his death this afternoon and are going over to bury him soon. A guard of 8 men and a corporal is allowed to bury a private. Booth is a corporal, and I am going as one of the men ... a volley of three guns will be fired over the grave. We shall write to his friends as soon as we get the particulars of his death.[58]

In a letter, Oliver Case told his sister about the continuing harassment from the rebels.

Every few days our pickets are driven in (about twelve miles below here) by some secesh cavalry. Several have been killed and some taken prisoners. To prevent this in the future, Gen. Burnside has ordered several thousand cavalry to be sent on to scour the country and look up the scattering rebels.... The troops are busily engaged in building a railroad bridge over the Trent (where the rebels burnt the old one) and in a short time R.R. communications will be open throughout the whole extent of the road.[59]

Charles Coit wrote his family that he had hired a servant, a common practice among officers. "I have persuaded Napolean Bonaparte to accept a command under me + he will hereafter preside over frying pan + coffee pot for which I am to pay him eight dollars per month. He has done very well thus far. Says he is a good cook, can make bread, biscuits, pies, +c besides cooking meat."[60]

On May 28, Wolcott Marsh wrote in his daily log about promotions that had been awarded. "At dress parade this evening, the following appointments were announced—Major Appelman from Lt. [Major] to Lt. Col., Capt. Ward to Major... [Lieutenant] W.P. Marsh Co. A to Capt. Co. F. ... Co. A cheered me in eve. & also Co. F came to my quarters & cheered me." A few days later, Marsh wrote about daily life: "Thursday, 12 June—Drilled company morning & afternoon. played chess in evening with Capt. Hoyt. Weather cool & pleasant. Friday, June 13—A hot sultry day, Chess in morning with Sergeant Major. Brigade drill afternoon at 4 p.m. Steamer Neasje came bringing in mail."[61]

When the weather was unbearably hot, those in command changed the schedule to keep the men safe. Captain Coit wrote, "There is no drilling from 9 AM to 4 PM, all the middle of the day being devoted to sleeping + trying to keep cool, it is not considered safe to drill it is so warm. Five of my men fainted last evening at Dress Parade."[62] Oliver Case confirmed that reduced schedule: "Reveille at 5 o'clock a.m. Drill 7.30 to 9 a.m., Battalion drill 4 to 6.30 p.m., Taps 8.25."[63]

The 8th Connecticut had been seriously worn down by the siege of Fort Macon, and suffered from fever, especially during the month of June.[64] Seth Plumb wrote that the Eighth probably suffered the most of any regiment in the division: at one point, it reported fewer than 500 men active for duty. He said that his company, Company E, was the healthiest of the regiment, owing to its stay in Beaufort during the siege. About seventy men were reporting active for duty, which was about twenty above the average.[65]

Efforts were made to improve on the men's health while in camp. Charles Coit wrote on June 1 that the troops worked hard on sanitation.

Every one gives the 8th credit for having the cleanest + handsomest camp in the Department ... the streets are all regularly laid out, graded + drained. [T]he cess pools for the reception of the cook's slop are dug very large + deep+ covered over a foot or more below the level of the ground ... and then dirt filled in to the level, so the sun has no action upon the contents and there is no smell rising from them.... Dr. S[torrs] is round often inspecting the conditions of the tents + is very particular about men bathing so much that we now have an order from Col. that men must bath at the drum call at 5 PM + out at second call at 20 minutes past 5.[66]

In late June, Colonel Harland was ordered to assume command of a brigade consisting of the 8th Connecticut, 11th Connecticut and the 4th Rhode Island. Charles Coit felt that while the men of the Eighth had reason to be proud that their commander would now lead a brigade, many felt that Harland could not be replaced. "Lt. Coln. Appelman is a fine officer + will do grandly I doubt not but he cannot fill Col. H's shoes by a long shot." Yet, Coit wrote, "we have lately had a stronger + more competent Field, (Col. H. Lt Col A + Major Ward) than any Regt in the Division. The line officers only yesterday presented Lt. Co. A with an elegant sword with belt + sash. There is the best of feeling among all our officers."[67]

While the 8th Connecticut remained camped at New Bern, the Confederate army under General Robert E. Lee fought General George B. McClellan and the Army of the Potomac in the Seven Days' Battles—a series of seven battles fought over seven days from June 25 to July 1, 1862, near Richmond, Virginia. In the midst of these battles, McClellan directed Burnside to create a diversion by advancing his force immediately upon Goldsborough, North Carolina. Three days later, unaware of McClellan's directive, President Abraham Lincoln ordered Burnside to instead move north to support the Army of the Potomac. Confusion arose as to which orders to follow until finally Secretary of War Edwin M. Stanton made it clear to Burnside that he should follow Lincoln's orders, not McClellan's.[68] (Lincoln officially removed McClellan from command on November 5, 1862, and replaced him with Burnside.)

A Return North

For the Eighth, their move began on Wednesday morning, July 2, 1862. At 6 a.m. tents were struck and baggage was loaded into railroad cars, while the men were placed on the top of the cars. The train got under way at 11 a.m. and arrived at Morehead City two and a quarter hours later.[69] The Eighth was to depart on the steamer *Guide* (formerly called the *Admiral*), but they found that it had not been unloaded. Men were detailed to work throughout the night and into the morning unloading the boat, coaling it, and then loading on the Eighth's baggage. The regiment was quartered in nearby houses and sheds for the night.

The next morning, July 3, the men of the Eighth marched to the wharf, and stood in the depot ready to depart, when an engine from New Bern rolled in at full speed, bringing dispatches from General Burnside. Richmond had been taken, they said, and their orders to depart were now countermanded. The Eighth was ordered back to their temporary quarters, and there they remained for the next few days.

On the night of Saturday, July 5, they received further dispatches informing them that McClellan was repulsed outside Richmond, and they were now ordered to cook three days' rations and board their boat the next day. Charles Coit felt that they were headed for the James River.[70] On the next day, July 6, at noon they left

Morehead City on the *Guide*, bound for Fort Monroe in Hampton, Virginia. Coit described the voyage as "delightful" and "our 4th of July excursion": he wrote that "if you could look at us all on board you would hardly imagine we were on our way to join a repulsed army." They arrived at Fort Monroe about 2:30 p.m. on Monday, July 7.[71] Fort Monroe, also known as Fortress Monroe, is an antebellum fort located on the tip of the Virginia Peninsula on Hampton Roads. Never captured by the Confederacy, it served as a strategic base and staging area for Union troops throughout the Civil War.[72]

The 8th Connecticut was the first regiment of Burnside's army to arrive at Fort Monroe. They waited as more transports arrived. Wolcott Marsh wrote that General Burnside was seen "flying among us in his shirt sleeves on the *Alice Price*," and that the harbor was "full of crafts of all kinds sizes & shapes." Companies A and F of the Eighth were ordered to move to the steamer *New York* because the *Guide* was so heavily loaded. They moved to the new ship, but on July 9 they moved again to the steamer *Donelson* when the *New York* was ordered north.[73]

Newport News

Waiting for orders, the regiment stayed at anchor. On the evening of July 8, a party of officers went ashore to Fort Monroe. It was too late to go inside, but they had a bath outside, just under its walls. Coit remarked on the vast number of cannon, shot and shell stored there.[74] The next day orders came to proceed to Norfolk to coal. The Eighth left that morning, sailing southward through Hampton Roads and up the Elizabeth River, reaching Norfolk about 3 p.m. They were under weigh early the next morning (July 10) and proceeded to their new camp at Newport News.

Coit wrote that the camp "over looks the fighting ground of the Merrimac + Monitor + in plain sight are the wrecks of the Cumberland + Congress."[75] Sgt. Seth Plumb described it as follows: "The Congress was burnt, but what is left is stuck fast where she was burnt. All that can be seen of the noble Cumberland is her three masts sticking out of the water her sails still fastened to the yards. We pitched our tents yesterday and are now in a good camp, there are about 10 or 12 regiments here now, all from Burnside's Division."[76]

Meanwhile, Companies A and F were on the steamer *Donelson*. On July 10, Wolcott Marsh wrote that all the other transports carrying Burnsides' troops had left to head up the James River, and that they "were the only men left behind."[77] They did eventually reach Newport News.

Charles Coit said that heat was "infernal" at their new camp, so their duties were limited to the cooler periods of the day, before 8:30 a.m. and after 4 p.m. The 11th Connecticut, now under the command of Colonel Henry Kingsbury, was camped next to the Eighth.[78] On July 30, Coit wrote that "Charley Breed died that morning." Breed had been very sick for some time, and during his illness, he stayed at Colonel Harland's headquarters, serving on Harland's staff as a signal officer. Breed had asked that no one alert his family to his illness.[79] Breed was a native of Norwich and a first lieutenant in Company D of the 8th Connecticut. He died of typhoid fever.[80]

When General Burnside was ordered north to support General McClellan, he left Brigadier General John G. Foster's division in North Carolina to garrison the occupied towns, and since his mission was urgent, he also left his artillery and cavalry there. By the time Burnside and his troops reached Fort Monroe, McClellan's position had become more secure and the crisis was over, so Burnside directed his men to the camp site at Newport News. There the divisions of General Parke and Major General Jesse L. Reno were joined by another division which had just come up from the South Carolina coast. This new division was commanded by Major General Isaac Ingalls Stevens. These forces—Parke, Reno and Stevens—would soon be formally consolidated into the new Ninth Corps.

While the troops waited at Newport News, the Lincoln administration was trying to decide its next move. Lincoln offered the command of the Army of the Potomac to General Burnside, who declined. At this time, Lincoln named a new general-in-chief of the armies of the United States, Major General Henry Halleck. On July 24, Halleck and Burnside (at Halleck's invitation) traveled south to meet with McClellan at Harrison's Landing, Virginia. In the initial plan that Lincoln approved, McClellan's forces would attack Richmond from the southeast, while Major General John Pope's Army of Virginia would attack from the north. However, this plan was never implemented. Instead, the advance by McClellan was abandoned, and he was ordered back to Aquia Creek to support Pope. Burnside, rather than reinforcing McClellan with his troops, was now ordered to precede him in the move to Aquia Creek.[81]

The 8th Connecticut's stay at Newport News lasted just over three weeks. On Saturday night, August 2, the Eighth embarked on the steamer *Columbia*. Oliver Case was part of a group of seventy-five men that had been detailed to load the baggage on board. They worked from 4 p.m. until 3 a.m. the next morning. Everything was put on one small steamer, he wrote—baggage, horses and all; the weather was "hot, hotter, hottest." He said he was lucky to get a place on the hurricane deck when the ship sailed so that he got all the breezes that there were.[82]

The steamer sailed from Newport News at noon on Sunday. It stopped at Fortress Monroe, departing about 4 p.m. The trip took the regiment up the Chesapeake Bay and the Potomac River, arriving at Aquia Creek on Monday afternoon, August 4. The troops landed the next day and took the train south towards Fredericksburg.[83]

Falmouth and Fredericksburg

The regiment went on one train, while their baggage followed on the next. It took an hour and a half for the train to travel about the twelve miles to its destination, although another writer put the distance at more like fifteen miles. The train stopped at a station about a half a mile from Fredericksburg, which lay to the south, across the river. The Eighth was directed to meet up with Reno's division, and they marched east, up a hill, stopping at a table land overlooking the landscape. There the men had a splendid view of Falmouth and Fredericksburg.

The day was very hot, and on their march many men had fallen by the wayside due to the heat. After they had gone a mile or so, they stopped and rested in some woods. Here they waited until about 6 p.m. when they were ordered back down the hill. They marched back and across the railroad to a place where they bivouacked for the night. Sergeant Jay Nettleton described it as "a nice level plot of meadow land, the turf worn out with horses and not far from the bank of the river."[84]

Nettleton wrote that a little village called Falmouth lay a mile above Fredericksburg, on their side of the river. There were shops there where the men could obtain pies and other food ("all they want"), and there was also a "Government Bakery" that produced many loaves of bread. "We have got soft bread today, the first, & the same may be said with fresh meat," he said. "Our diet is altogether too much confined to salt food. Vegetables we haven't seen from Government worth mentioning in a long time." As for water, a constant concern, he reported springs in the region that provided wholesome water, although they had to carry it 40 rods (220 yards).[85]

Unlike previous campaigns, the men were now limited on what they could bring with them. Wolcott Marsh wrote that orders were received on August 9 to have all the men's overcoats and dress coats packed and ready to send back to Aquia Creek. Officers were limited to thirty pounds of baggage.[86] Charles Coit related that he had to pack up his extra clothing, bedding and trunk, which he would either send to Aquia Creek for storage or ship home. "We carry the clothing we have on + a change or two of underclothing with woolen + rubber blanket. That's about all. We three Co. officers carry one trunk (my old one) have also had all the men's dress coats +c packed in a box which goes to the Creek also. We are getting down to our fighting rig, blouses + light blue pants, just like the privates."[87]

Nettleton wrote that first the dress coats were boxed up. Then the boys from Washington, Connecticut, fixed up a cracker box and put their overcoats and some other things in it and sent it home by express, rather throw those things away later on the march.[88] In a fitting comment to these changes, Seth Plumb wrote, "Officers can have only 30 lbs carried for them here after, they have generally had a cart load a piece, the men all rejoice over this as they have had to lug themselves to death for the officers."[89]

On August 12, Halleck instructed Burnside to send troops to Pope's Army of Virginia, which was north of the Rappahannock. By that evening, two divisions, Reno's and Stevens', were on their way. The regiments remaining all belonged to Parke's division.[90] Charles Coit wrote on August 13,

> Troops have been marching last night + this morning to reinforce Pope. Stephen's division Reno's + part of Parke's. I think no infantry Regts are remaining except Col. H's brigade + I think we are to remain for the present at least. I do not particularly desire to be engaged again but it is very unpleasant to see so many other Regts moving + be left behind yourself. About twenty officers of the 4th RI Regt have resigned which leaves the Regt in rather a disorganized state perhaps that's why we are left. They are always in our way.[91]

Charles Coit noted in a letter of August 26 that General McClellan had arrived at their camp the night of August 24, and had been in consultation with General Burnside since. (The Eighth's camp was on the grounds of the Lacy house, a mansion named Chatham, in Falmouth, which also served as Burnside's headquarters.) McClellan was serenaded the night before by the band from the 4th Rhode Island

and a glee club from the 8th Connecticut. Coit was able to see "Little Mac" while the band was playing. He wrote that McClellan was in full dress, "even to patent leather boots," while Burnside wore "a kind of rough + ready suit, his favorite knit shirt over everything." He described McClellan as "quite small + trim while Genl B is fast assuming the goodly proportions of a N Yk alderman."[92]

While Pope and the Army of Virginia dealt with their own problems, the 8th Connecticut and the remaining regiments of Burnside's force held their position near Fredericksburg. Sergeant Jay Nettleton had a good sense of the overall military situation.

> The 3d Division of the "9th Army Corps" was left here serving as guard to the place & protect the railroad from Acquia Creek. This road seemed to be used as a general thoroughfare for reinforcements to the army that was higher up in this valley. Large supplies of provisions & stores of all kinds have been gathered here—ammunition &c. to supply troops. It appears from what we can learn that "Pope" has withdrawn his forces so far to the north that the rebels have crossed the Rappahannock & thus stepped in between them & us—or left us open to any flank movement the rebels may feel disposed to make. Thus, cutting off all sure communication with Pope. I understand we have already lost a large supply train of provision & ammunition sent for Pope. Today everything is shaping towards the earliest evacuation of this place.[93]

A false alarm occurred on August 29. Wolcott Marsh wrote that at 4 o'clock drums played "the long roll beat," and the men were immediately formed in line and sent to the river to guard a foot bridge there. Two batteries were unlimbered on the ground above them. Burnside, who had galloped with his staff across the river to reconnoiter, returned and rode by the men "when such cheers as only Burnside could receive were given by all hands." The men slept on their arms that night, but when morning arrived with no further disturbance, they returned to camp.[94]

On Sunday, August 31, the 8th Connecticut went out on picket duty. It was a rainy, cold day with the mud deep and slippery. The men built fires and stood around with rubber blankets and coats on to keep out the rain. At noon they were told to keep themselves in readiness to march upon further orders, which finally came at 5 p.m. The men marched back the five miles to the city to find the bridge burning and fires blazing all around.[95]

Company E of the Eighth had been detached from the regiment on Saturday, August 30, to guard the depot across the river from Fredericksburg. Company E replaced a company from the 4th Rhode Island that had been there several weeks. The depot was filled with extensive supplies of commissary stores inside and out. Trains had been running day and night to evacuate as many stores as possible to Aquia Creek. On Sunday morning, August 31, the last train was loaded with stores and left about noon. The depot was then made ready for the torch. Sergeant Seth Plumb wrote that the depot was strewn with hay and tar, which were also used to cover the lumber and stores, along with barrels of beef, pork, sugar, flour, vinegar and salt (although much of this was condemned stores and hence not a loss). About 4 p.m. orders were given to Company E to set it on fire.

The remainder of the 8th Connecticut and the 11th Connecticut came in about dark. The three bridges to the city were then set on fire. The 4th Rhode Island left with the train of wagons, cavalry and artillery along the road, and at 9 p.m. the 8th Connecticut and 11th Connecticut marched out on the railroad, the Eighth bringing up the rear. Thus, Fredericksburg was evacuated.

The force reached Potomac Creek at 1 a.m., slept for two hours, and then marched to Brooks Station, arriving about 10 a.m. on September 1. Many of the former slaves had left Fredericksburg, too. Seth Plumb described the situation as multitudes fled from plantations. "In the throng were ox carts piled full of little young ones, and old women, women carrying their babes in their arms, and nearly all had bundles on their heads. Till the last bridge was set afire, they kept coming, old and young of all shades and in every description of dress. The trains of cars were always free to them after all the baggage was on that could be piled, yet for all that, hundreds of little children had to walk to the Creek."[96]

Washington, D.C.

The 8th Connecticut and 11th Connecticut, along with two field pieces and some cavalry, had formed the rear guard on the retreat from Fredericksburg. They bivouacked the night of Monday, September 1, and much of the next day, and then marched to Aquia Creek, arriving on the night of Tuesday, September 2.[97] On Thursday, September 4, their baggage was loaded, and the regiment left for Washington, D.C., in the early afternoon. They arrived that night and bivouacked near the landing.[98]

The next day, September 5, the 8th Connecticut marched up Pennsylvania Avenue and received compliments on their fine marching. They were taken to be the 8th U.S. Regulars.[99] The Washington Star reported that "the Eighth Regiment of United-States Regulars marched in splendid order to join the forces of McClellan."[100] The Eighth later marched up 7th Street and went into camp on the same ground, Meridian Hill, where the 1st, 2nd, and 3rd Connecticut Voluntary Infantry had camped in May of the year before.[101]

On the same day that the Eighth marched up Pennsylvania Avenue, General Burnside arrived in Washington from Aquia Creek. Reports began reaching Washington that the Confederates were crossing the Potomac into Maryland. Burnside was again summoned by Lincoln and again declined command of the army. After the loss at the second battle of Bull Run, Pope had been relieved of command and his troops were assimilated into the Army of the Potomac, so the command went again to McClellan.

At this point, the Army of the Potomac was reorganized into three wings, with Burnside commanding the right wing. Burnside's wing was made up of the First and Ninth Corps. Major General Jesse L. Reno was now in charge of the Ninth Corps, with Division commands as follows: Brigadier General Orlando Bolivar Willcox commanded the First Division. Brigadier General Samuel D. Sturgis was now leading Reno's old Second Division. Brigadier General Isaac P. Rodman, the original commander of the 4th Rhode Island, took over Parke's Third Division. Parke remained as Burnside's Chief of Staff. These divisions were joined by a fourth, the

Kanawha Division, commanded by Brigadier General Jacob D. Cox and largely made up of Ohio troops.[102]

The 8th Connecticut was part of the Second Brigade of Rodman's Third Division, the brigade commanded by the Eighth's own Colonel Edward Harland. With Harland's promotion, command of the Eighth went to Lieutenant Colonel Hiram Appelman.

The three other regiments that made up the Second Brigade were the 11th Connecticut, the 4th Rhode Island, and a brand new unit, the 16th Connecticut. The remaining brigade of the Third Division, the First Brigade, was commanded by Colonel Harrison S. Fairchild. It consisted of three New York regiments—the 9th, the 89th and the 103rd.[103]

While the commanders and soldiers of the reorganized Army of the Potomac adjusted to their new roles and positions, the Army of Northern Virginia was already crossing the Potomac into Maryland in its first invasion of the North. The 8th Connecticut and scores of other Federal regiments would soon be on the march to stop them.

CHAPTER 4

Frederick, South Mountain, and Antietam

The March from Washington, D.C.

It was on Sunday, September 7, that Major General George B. McClellan put the Army of the Potomac in motion to move against the Confederates in Maryland. The Army of Northern Virginia, under General Robert E. Lee, had crossed the Potomac into western Maryland three days earlier on September 4. Lee believed that a Confederate invasion of the north would serve several purposes—it would harass the enemy on its own soil, it would permit his own army to resupply from the bounty of the northern farms while allowing time for Virginia farmers to bring in their crops, and it would shift the focus of the war north and away from Richmond before winter set in.[1] McClellan felt that an active campaign against the Confederates was now necessary to protect Baltimore, prevent an invasion of Pennsylvania, and to clear Maryland.[2]

The four divisions of McClellan's Ninth Corps marched north from Washington, D.C., to rendezvous at a staging area at Leesborough, Maryland, six miles north of the city.[3] The 8th Connecticut, part of Colonel Edward Harland's Second Brigade, of Brigadier General Isaac P. Rodman's Third Division, of Major General Jesse L. Reno's Ninth Corps, joined the march that day. "We left ... Sunday September 7th early in the morning but on account of the roads being blocked up with troops & baggage wagons it was 10 a.m. ere we got under way & then we had [to] pick our way among waggons, artillery, cavalry & c & c. Which raised such a cloud of dust as to almost smother us," Captain Wolcott Marsh wrote. "But we lived through & halted for night at Leesboro 10 miles from Washington."[4]

The Eighth stayed in Leesborough the following day. First Lieutenant Roger M. Ford of Company K noted in his diary that the men were issued shelter tents that day, with each man receiving one half of a tent each.[5] The two halves could then be buttoned together to form one shelter tent. Captain Charles Coit had bought himself a shelter tent three days before at a cost of two dollars. He described it as "open at both ends, simply canvas stretched over a pole [I] can just sit up in the center."[6]

As for their one-day layover, Sergeant Jay Nettleton commented, "Stopped on the Rockville road for the night, and for some cause were allowed to spend Monday & Monday night. Why couldn't [we] have lain still Sunday & marched Monday?"[7]

Wolcott Marsh spent the extra time well. The 16th Connecticut, a new regiment which had just joined their brigade, was camped a short distance back. Oliver Case's brothers, Ariel and Alonzo, who had recently enlisted, were now members of the 16th Connecticut, and they came to the Eighth's camp to visit. The three Case brothers and Marsh "went off in woods & roasted corn, potatoes, picked & eat grapes, peaches apples &c."[8]

On Tuesday, September 9, the march resumed. Roger Ford wrote in his diary that reveille was at 3:30 a.m. and that they were off at 4:30 a.m. At 10 a.m. they halted for a rest and did not resume the march until 2 p.m., with troops passing by all the time. Jay Nettleton reported that the rest stop was near Brookville, about ten miles out. The wait at Brookville was to allow these other troops—infantry, artillery,

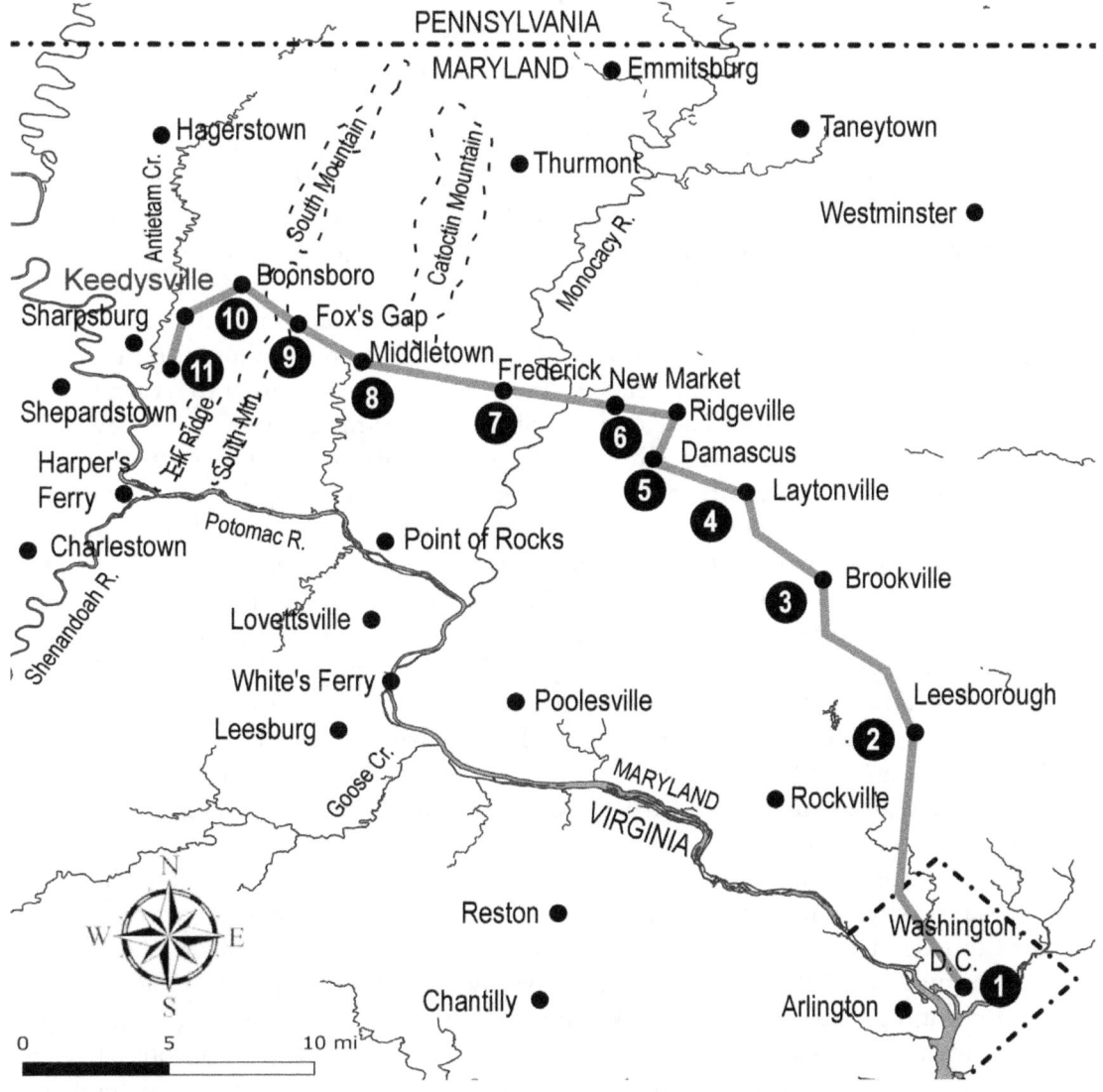

Map 5. Route of March to Sharpsburg, Maryland, September 1862.

September 7–September 16, 1862—103 miles in 10 days

1.	Sep 7	Camp at Washington, D.C.	–
2.	Sep 7	Marched to Leesborough (Wheaton)	10 miles
3.	Sep 9	Marched to Brookville	10 miles
4.	Sep 9	Marched thru Laytonville	10 miles
	Sep 10	Marched only to return to bivouac	8 miles
5.	Sep 11	Marched to Damascus, then to Ridgeville	15 miles
6.	Sep 12	Marched across B & O R.R.	5 miles
7.	Sep 12	Marched through New Market to Frederick	9 miles
8.	Sep 13	Marched over Catoctin Mtn. to Middletown	10 miles
9.	Sep 14	Marched to Fox's Gap, South Mountain	9 miles
10.	Sep 15	Marched thru Boonsboro to Keedysville	12 miles
11.	Sep 16	Marched to Sharpsburg, Left Flank of Army	5 miles

cavalry, and their baggage—to pass. These troops took roads to the right and left, while the Eighth's division followed the center road. When the march resumed, it was start and stop and they only made about five or six miles by 8 p.m. Roger Ford reported that at 5 p.m. they passed through Laytonsville and at 9:30 p.m. halted for the night. They marched twenty miles that day.[9]

The Eighth remained at their bivouac on Wednesday, September 10, until about 3 p.m. when they moved out. Marsh wrote that they had marched about three or four miles when a mounted orderly rushed in. They soon received an order to return from where they had come. They ended up camping on the same ground as the previous night. When Marsh later asked why that happened, he was told that they were too far ahead and that the other parts of the army were unable to keep up.[10]

After several pleasant days, the next day, Thursday, September 11, was cloudy and rainy. The 8th Connecticut moved out early, between 7 a.m. and 9 a.m. After a march of about ten miles, they reached at midday what Marsh called the "little dirty village of Damascus." After a rest, they continued on until they arrived at the town of Ridgeville, Maryland, which lay just off the Baltimore & Ohio Railroad and the National Road, both of which ran from Baltimore to Frederick and beyond. The Eighth bivouacked there for the night, suffering through some heavy rainstorms. Friday, September 12, was foggy after the rain, and the Eighth started out about 9 a.m. They crossed the B&O Railroad and then continued westward on the "Baltimore & Frederick Pike."[11]

Roger Ford wrote that at 1 p.m. they passed through the town of New Market, Maryland, which the Confederates had left the night before.[12] Jay Nettleton reported the Confederates as being "a large force of Stuart's Cavalry," and Wolcott Marsh put their number at 2,500. Marsh said that following a rest, the Eighth continued on and after climbing a mountain came to a spot with a beautiful view of the Monocacy River, the city of Frederick beyond it, and farther on, the Blue Ridge mountains.[13]

The Confederates had occupied Frederick for about a week, but by September 12, the infantry had left, leaving only some cavalry under Confederate General Wade

Hampton. These troops resisted the Federal advance, which was led by Brigadier General Jacob D. Cox's Kanawha Division. The commander of Cox's Second Brigade, Colonel Augustus Moor, deployed his three Ohio regiments across the National Road and then led an attack on the town with a troop of Chicago dragoons. Moor was captured in that attack, but not long after, the Confederates withdrew.[14]

Jay Nettleton wrote that the Eighth and its brigade passed Reno's division [see note] in New Market, and then heard cannons firing ahead of them as they approached Frederick. However, as they neared the Monocacy River, they saw that the fight was over, and that the Confederates had left. They reached Cox's line outside Frederick where the Ohio troops had deployed skirmishers and had formed a line of battle on either side of the road. The Eighth's division marched by the flank over the fields to the left, careful not to get ahead of Cox's line. After crossing the railroad, the division deployed into a line of battle, and skirmishers advanced forward in one line as they approached the outskirts of Frederick. After passing through some corn fields and over some fences, the Eighth happened onto a hospital, which Nettleton said was well "into the suburbs."[15]

Frederick

Wolcott Marsh reported that there were "demonstrations of joy" upon their arrival there. "Women came rushing up to us screaming & clapping hands & acting if crazy," he wrote. "The yard & hospital were full of sick rebels 600 of them & 150 of ours left when [the] city was evacuated. The Surgeon came up to our colors & kissed them in tears of joy dropping from his eyes." The Eighth bivouacked in the hospital yard for the night.[16]

The next day, Saturday, September 13, the Eighth moved into the city of Frederick where they were "cheered every where in [the] city."[17] Roger Ford wrote that the day was pleasant, with a number of flags out, and the people were "fairly crazy," and gave the boys "wine, cake and everything nice." He reported that "the people cheered us on and most every home had the Stars and Stripes flying."[18]

Meanwhile, the cavalry commander, Brigadier General Alfred Pleasonton, had asked Burnside for infantry to support his troops heading west in advance of the army. Burnside gave him Rodman's division.[19]

The Eighth's Company H was detailed to stay behind to guard the trains left in Frederick as the army moved rapidly to engage the Confederates. As it turned out, Company H would not rejoin the regiment until after the battle of Antietam. When the rest of the Eighth moved out of Frederick with Rodman's division, it was with but nine companies, with a total effective strength of about 400 men.[20]

As part of Rodman's division, the 8th Connecticut continued through the town and beyond until they reached a point on the main road near the base of the mountains. The city of Frederick lies in a valley. A mountainous ridge known as the Catoctin Mountain lies about four miles to the west. This is where they halted. Artillery fire had been going on in this area since daybreak. The Confederates had the high ground with full command of the road. The Eighth's brigade began the ascent of the mountain, marching for some distance until halting for further orders.

It was at this time that one of Confederate's solid shots landed in the brigade, injuring three men in the 11th Connecticut, two badly. At 1 p.m. the Eighth was ordered to flank the Confederate battery, and they marched by the flank to the right along the base of the mountain for about a mile and a half until they reached another road that went up the mountain. They took this road, but by the time they arrived, the Confederates and their battery had fled. The Eighth continued on over the mountain and marched another ten miles or so to reach the town of Middletown. The Confederates had recently fled there, too.[21]

Once again, the people in Middletown cheered the arrival of the Union troops. As Marsh wrote, "We were received with joy by citizens & before rebels were out the Stars & Stripes were flying.... We had not rested more than hour before were marched out side town & formed in line of battle not knowing but enemy intended to attack us as they had driven in our cavalry but the night pass[ed] without an alarm."[22]

South Mountain

At daylight the next morning, Sunday, September 14, the 8th Connecticut watched as the battle began with an artillery barrage on South Mountain, about four miles ahead of them. They lay quiet until about noon when they were ordered to move out.[23]

As the battle for South Mountain developed, Pleasonton of the cavalry made another request for infantry support. In response, Burnside ordered Cox to send forward a brigade. Cox led three regiments of Colonel Eliakim Scammon's brigade forward, and then followed up with another brigade. He led these six regiments of Ohio troops up the mountain, then off the National Road to the left and towards Fox's Gap. There Cox's men fought the North Carolina troops defending the Gap and swept them off the ridge, only to have a second line of North Carolina troops attack. Reno sent support.

Brigadier General Orlando B. Willcox's Division was the first to arrive, and then two other divisions—those led by Brigadier General Samuel D. Sturgis and Brigadier General Isaac P. Rodman—came up, until the Ninth Corps was reunited. Sturgis's division was deployed between those of Cox and Willcox, and Rodman's division was split to cover the flanks. The Ninth Corps did not attack until late in the day on Sunday, but when they did, they pushed the smaller Confederate force back over the crest of the mountain. The Federals advanced until a Confederate counterattack at dusk resulted in the death of Reno, who was shot out of the saddle as he rode near the enemy's lines. Fighting continued into the night, until the Confederates finally withdrew towards Boonsboro and Sharpsburg.[24]

The Eighth had been ordered forward around noon on that Sunday. Wolcott Marsh wrote:

> [T]he boys hurried forward in high glee at the prospect of an engagement. We soon crossed a little stream then began to climb the mountain we had not proceeded far ere shells burst

around us but our Fort Macon experience had learned us to care but little for them in short time we reached a battery which was shelling the rebels & were ordered to lie down & support it the battle was now at its height. the roar of artillery & musketry was terrific as the sound reverberated through the deep mountain gorges. The wounded the dieing & dead lay around in every direction.[25]

Their division reached the top of the mountain around 5 p.m. The Second Brigade, of which the Eighth was a part, was then ordered down the mountain to guard against a flank attack. Marsh wrote,

> We had been in present position but a short time before ordered forward in line of battle through a thick piece of woods but no enemy appeared. we went down a steep hill or mountain towards main pike till finally it was impossible to proceed farther but we were near enough to support another battery which had been posted near road. Night was coming on but no abatement of the battle. Bullets were dropping quite fast around us but doing no damage as were spent. Darkness came & with it, it seemed as if the struggle was only the more terrible.[26]

Jay Nettleton wrote, "Such volleys of musketry as were given at dark & a short time after we never before heard." The battle subsided by 9 o'clock and all was quiet.[27]

On Monday morning, September 15, the 8th Connecticut marched across the road to the left and into a patch of woods where it waited for an attack that did not come. They then marched back and over the mountain. Marsh noted, "[S]uch sights I never saw. Hundreds of dead rebels laid piled up in a small narrow lane & behind on … [a] stone wall. The victory was ours."[28] Jay Nettleton wrote that "morning revealed a sorry picture for humanity" and that "our own dead & the rebel dead [lay] by the score." He stated they started again about 5 p.m., passed through Boonsboro and "one or two other little 'valleys,'" until they finally stopped around 11 o'clock at night in the Antietam valley.[29] Marsh wrote that they halted for the night around midnight at the little village of Keedysville.[30] Keedysville lies on the Shepherdstown Pike, halfway between Boonsboro (on the National Pike) and the town of Sharpsburg.

On Tuesday, September 16, the action began early with artillery fire from both sides, with some shells bursting near the 8th Connecticut. Many of the baggage wagons that had come up during the night were fired on, forcing them to flee to the rear. The artillery fire was kept up most of the day, with the two armies "in plain sight of each other." The Eighth remained in readiness throughout the day, but didn't move until about sundown when the division was ordered out. They took up an advanced position on the extreme left of the Union army, along a line of hills where artillery was posted. The pickets were firing all that night.[31]

The Battle of Antietam

The advanced position that Harland's Second Brigade had taken up on the evening of September 16 was a line of battle facing northwest and formed along a road that ran past the house and prominent barn of Henry R. Rohrbach to a crossroads called Porterstown. A new regiment, the 16th Connecticut, joined the brigade that evening, after having made forced marches from Washington to do so.[32] The brigade line was behind a range of hills running roughly parallel to Antietam Creek, which lay to the northwest. The brigade was positioned between Colonel George Crook's Ohio Brigade on its right front, and Rodman's First Brigade under Colonel Harrison S. Fairchild on its left. Fairchild's men occupied the northeastern portion of a cornfield that extended downhill to a road leading to the Lower Bridge or Rohrbach's Bridge (which thereafter became famous as "Burnside's Bridge"). Harland's line of battle consisted of the 4th Rhode Island on the left, the 16th Connecticut to its right, then the 8th Connecticut, and the 11th Connecticut on the far right. The left flank of the brigade was located opposite Rohrbach's orchard, with the Rohrbach house and outbuildings lying just on the other side of the orchard.[33]

In the area near Burnside's Bridge, Antietam Creek flows generally south along the left or west flank of Harland's line. At daylight on September 17, Captain John Eubank's Virginia battery, which was positioned across the Antietam from the Federals on the heights to the southwest, began shelling the Federal position. This Confederate cannon fire apparently came as a surprise to the Union troops, and Harland reported that "as they had obtained the exact range our loss was considerable."[34]

The Eighth was among the regiments that suffered casualties. Wolcott Marsh wrote,

> Ere it was light on Wednesday we were aroused blankets rolled up & every man in his accustomed place. Objects had scarcely become distant around us. Before the flash of a gun was seen a short distance in front of us on a little hill & in a moment a shell burst over our heads then another & another now they came thick & fast but not a man stirred, but there was no reply from our side we wondered at this thus it went on they using their artillery on us continually sometimes throwing shell then solid shot & railroad iron. In a little while they had succeeded in getting excellent range on us one of my men was wounded in head & sent to rear, & in a few moments later a solid shot struck in the ranks of Co. A. & killed Srgt. [George H.] Marsh & 3 privates of Co. K. & wounded two others. Yet not a man in regit. stirred excepting ambulance corps who attended to wounded.[35]

At 7 o'clock, upon Rodman's orders, Harland moved his brigade to a new position behind a ridge and to the rear and left of their starting position. They were now in a line of battle facing to the left, or southwest, at right angles to their former line. They remained there about an hour or two and then moved again, changing front on first battalion, and forming a new line of battle parallel to their original line but to its left and rear. They were now in a ravine, sheltered from the Confederate artillery. Shortly thereafter, Harland received orders from Rodman to move the brigade again, this time to a point farther to the left. The 11th Connecticut, however, was detached from the brigade at this point and remained in support of a battery. The remainder of the brigade marched to its left and formed a new line of battle on a high ridge overlooking the Antietam.[36]

The ridge was located just east of where Antietam Creek makes a 90 degree turn to the west and this location had a grand view of the surrounding countryside and of the battle which was now progressing in full fury. Wolcott Marsh wrote,

> While our skirmishers were advancing & we lay quiet on this high hill I had the privilege of witnessing the Grandest sight of my life. [It was] [a] great battle all around me almost with out for [a] moment being personally engaged. All along to the right for miles the cannon & musketry kept up a deafening roar while the air was thick with great clouds of smoke & almost in fact exactly in front of us was a rebel battery on [a] hill across creek shelling our troops at

[the] bridge & [with] one of our battery's replying the rebel battery was after [a] short time compelled to leave.[37]

As the morning passed and the attack at the bridge bogged down, Burnside needed to push his assault forward. It was time for a flanking maneuver. He ordered Rodman to cross his division at a ford located downstream from the bridge. The reconnaissance of the fords of Antietam Creek in this vicinity had been performed by McClellan's engineers the day before, and Captain James Duane, McClellan's senior engineer on the general staff, had personally posted the locations of Burnside's divisions that day.[38]

Fairchild's First Brigade was formed to the left of Harland's on these heights. Attached to Fairfield's Brigade and to its left was a battery of naval howitzers under the command of Captain James R. Whiting of the 9th New York Zouave regiment. The battery was put into position to shell the wooded bluff opposite the ford that Rodman proposed to use to cross the Antietam. While the fire of this battery did do some damage to the Georgians defending the west bank of the Antietam, it did not achieve its primary function since the ford proved unusable.[39] It was not until Rodman's skirmishers reached the creek that it was discovered that the ford was useless—it was located at the foot of a steep bluff rising some 160 feet on the west side of the Antietam, and impossible for the troops to overcome. Learning of this, Rodman directed Harland to make further reconnaissance in search of a crossing. In response, Harland sent out two companies from the 8th Connecticut under the command of Captain Charles L. Upham to locate a new ford. Upham soon reported that a practicable ford was found, Snavely's Ford, a few hundred yards downstream. The column, with Fairchild's Brigade in advance, headed there. It was now shortly after noon.

As the division marched to the ford, Rodman ordered Harland to detach one regiment to support Whiting's New York battery which was positioned on a hill just downstream from the ford. It was placed there in order to cover the crossing. Harland detached the 8th Connecticut for this task and placed them in what he considered to be the strongest position to defend the battery. He then accompanied the remainder of his brigade as it moved by the left flank and followed the First Brigade across the Antietam. The creek at the ford was about seventy-five feet wide, with a swift current and the water about hip deep.[40]

As the First Brigade crossed Snavely's Ford, they encountered fire from skirmishers but ignored it and turned to the right under the shelter of a high bluff rising up from the creek. Facing to the left, the brigade, led by the 9th New York, scaled the steep bluff to its summit 185 feet above the Antietam. The brigade then moved north by the right flank along the top of the bluff, eventually meeting up with the Federal troops, which had forced their way over the Burnside's Bridge.

Harland's Second Brigade also ran into resistance at the ford. In crossing the creek, the 4th Rhode Island took fire from Confederate skirmishers positioned behind a stone wall which ran parallel to the creek and about 165 yards from it. After crossing, the regiment filed to the left and then advanced on the wall, driving off the Confederates. They came under more musketry from their left, which was quickly silenced by Whiting's battery. The 16th Connecticut, which had crossed the creek

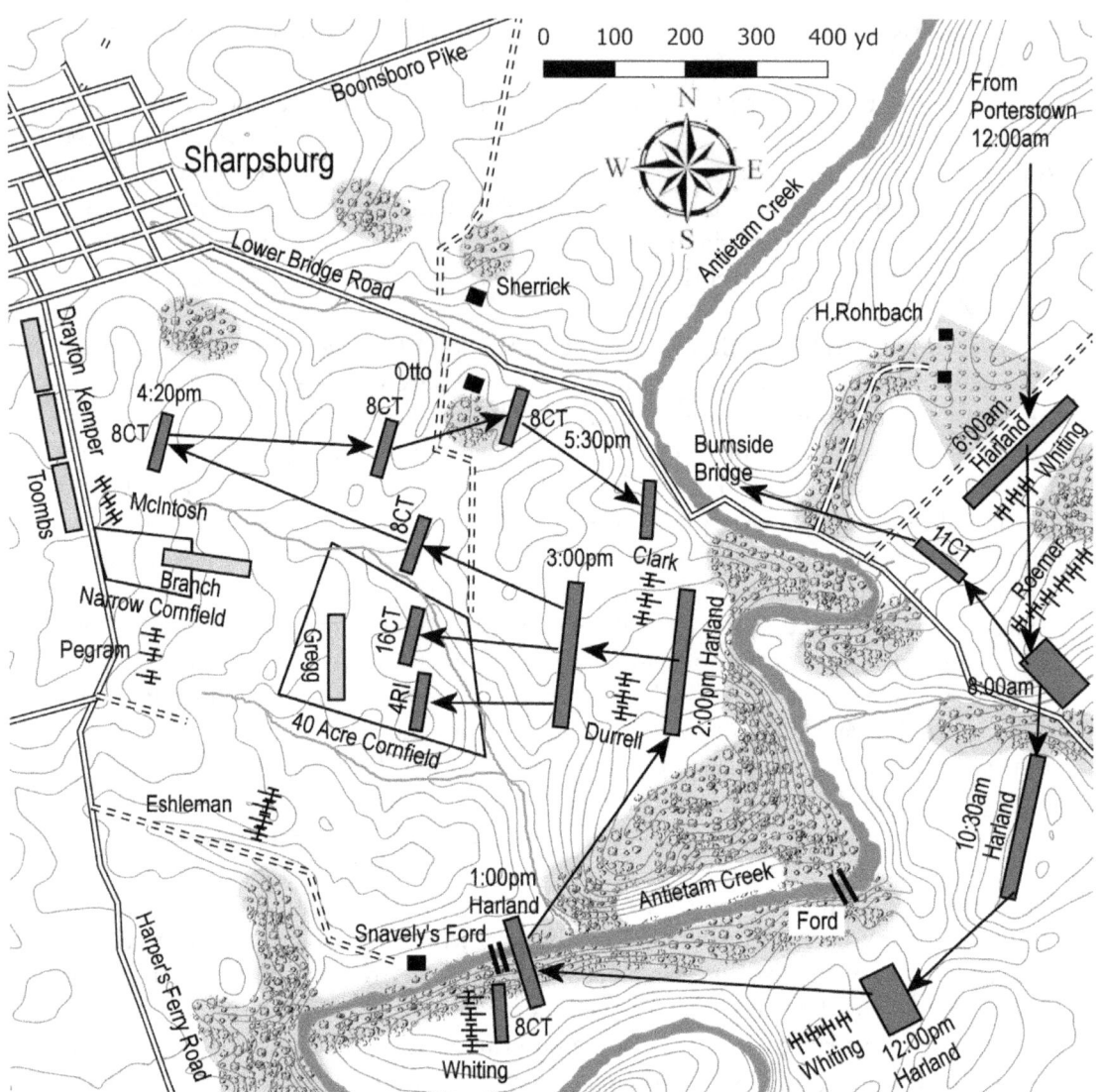

Map 6. Positions of the Eighth, Battle of Antietam, Maryland, September 17, 1862.

behind the 4th Rhode Island, moved past the Rhode Islanders in an effort to support the Fourth's left flank. Skirmishers from the 16th Connecticut were sent further to the left, but they were soon driven in by Confederate cavalry and artillery. The regiment then retraced its steps and retired to the right of the 4th Rhode Island. When the Rhode Islanders came under artillery fire from the left, they followed the 16th Connecticut to a more sheltered position.[41]

Back with Whiting's battery, the 8th Connecticut received artillery fire as well when Captain Benjamin F. Eshleman's battery (Washington Artillery, Louisiana) opened fire on the battery. Wolcott Marsh wrote, "The rebels replied with guns of much longer range their shot & shell again flieing all around us. Our battery seeing they could do nothing against such long range guns drew their pieces to the ford &

we followed crossing in water up to [our] knees."⁴² After crossing, Whiting found the ground too rough to allow his battery to follow the infantry so he moved upstream along the creek, recrossed at the ford above Snavely's Ford, and then joined the Federal troops at the bridge.

When the 8th Connecticut rejoined the brigade, the advance resumed. Harland reported that he was conducted by one of Rodman's aides, who deployed them in position to the rear of the First Brigade. The three regiments marched up a wooded ravine spreading out to the right and up the steep slope beside them. The 4th Rhode Island remained on the left in the woods near a small creek which ran through the ravine. The two Connecticut regiments were on their right.⁴³ Wolcott Marsh wrote that they filed to the right along the steep banks and up to the top of the hill, where they rested briefly and then pushed on again to the front.⁴⁴

Moving west from Antietam Creek in the area of Burnside's Bridge, the land rises almost continuously until it reaches the first of a series of ridges which culminate at the Harpers Ferry Road. The First Brigade of Rodman's division had formed to the immediate left of Willcox's First Division in a north-south line just behind the crest of this first ridge. On the ridge in this vicinity were located the battery of Joseph C. Clark, Jr., (Battery E, Fourth U.S. Artillery), and, to the left of Clark, the battery of Captain George W. Durell (Battery D, Pennsylvania Light Artillery). Just on the other side of this ridgeline was Otto's Lane, a farm lane which ran north to the Otto farmhouse located on the Lower Bridge Road. Beyond this lane the land dropped down into a little valley and then rose again for the long climb to the heights beyond.

As Harland's Second Brigade came into position with the other Federal troops in this area of the battlefield, it became the extreme left of the Union line. The 8th Connecticut took up a position on the ridgeline to the left and a little behind the 89th New York, the regiment on the far left of Fairchild's First Brigade. The 89th New York was in the rear of Durell's Battery. The 16th Connecticut was further left but forward of the Eighth, down in the little valley, in the northeast corner of a 40-acre cornfield which continued up the far slope of the valley. The 4th Rhode Island was to the left of the 16th Connecticut, just outside the cornfield.

The entire Federal line in this area had been under Confederate artillery fire since it crossed the Antietam and began the climb up. On the ridgeline, the First Brigade, along with the batteries of Clark and Durell, were receiving artillery fire from the Confederates on the heights above them. Primarily this fire came from Captain James S. Brown's battery (Wise Artillery, Virginia) of Brigadier General D.R. Jones's Division and Captain James Reilly's battery (Rowan Artillery, North Carolina) of Brigadier General John B. Hood's Division, which were located far up on the heights, almost to the point where the Harpers Ferry Road enters Sharpsburg. Shelling came, too, from Captain John B. Richardson's battery (Washington Artillery, Louisiana) which was posted on the far side of Harpers Ferry Road.⁴⁵

The 8th Connecticut had been under artillery fire throughout the day, and their position on the ridgeline next to the First Brigade provided no relief. Wolcott Marsh remarked that they had come within range of the enemy's cannon here as well, and as they "tossed shell at us again," the regiment "lay down & let them work." He wrote, "Finally our battery's got into position & replied when shot & shell flew like hail around us & among us wounding & killing some of different regit."[46]

By about 3 p.m., the Ninth Corps battle line was in position, stretched out along the ridge and across the Lower Bridge Road. Note that Brigadier General Jacob C. Cox was in immediate command of the Ninth Corps during the battle at Antietam, having succeeded to command following the death of General Jesse Reno on September 14. Colonel Eliakim P. Scammon assumed command of the Kanawha Division.

In accordance with McClellan's instructions, Burnside directed Cox to move forward with the entire command, with the exception of Sturgis's division, which was to be held in reserve. The line was to advance in the order in which it was formed. Willcox's division on the right was to move against Sharpsburg, and Rodman's division on its left was to go forward, then incline to the right and attack in echelon with Willcox. Cox gave the order to advance at 3:15 p.m.[47]

Willcox's division, with Crook's brigade of Scammon's division in support, moved forward on both sides of the Lower Bridge Road. General Rodman first sent forward skirmishers from Fairchild's brigade, but then seeing Willcox's division go forward ordered the entire brigade to advance. Under heavy artillery fire, the brigade went over the ridge and the fences of Otto's lane, down and across the valley, and then attacked the Confederates waiting behind stone and rail fences on the slope beyond.[48]

When Rodman gave Harland the order to advance and Harland passed it on to his brigade, the 8th Connecticut stepped off promptly. They wheeled slightly to their right and passed to the right of the cornfield, with their right flank to the rear of Fairchild's left. First Lieutenant Henry C. Hall of Company I wrote, "As soon as the line was formed the order was given to move forward and away we went. As we went over the brow of the first hill we had a fine view of the rebel position and rushed on with a cheer over fences and through plowed fields to gain it."[49]

The 16th Connecticut and the 4th Rhode Island, down in the cornfield below the ridge, did not hear Harland's order. Seeing this, Harland sent an aide-de-camp to order these regiments forward. This delay caused the Eighth to advance ahead of the rest of the brigade. Harland asked Rodman if he should halt the Eighth and have them wait until the 16th Connecticut and 4th Rhode Island could come up. At this point, the Eighth was at the foot of the next hill and sheltered from the incoming Confederate artillery. Instead of holding the Eighth where they were, Rodman ordered Harland to advance the Eighth, saying that he would hurry up the other regiments.

Harland moved forward with the Eighth, and they commenced firing. Then, in looking back to see if the other regiments were moving forward, Harland noticed enemy infantry advancing on the brigade's left flank. These Confederate troops were the 7th and 37th North Carolina regiments. The presence of enemy infantry on the left had been reported earlier to Harland by an aide-de-camp, Major Thomas W. Lion, who was assisting in the deployment of the troops. Lion had told Harland that he and officers of Scammon's division had seen Confederate infantry forming on the left. Harland had reported this to Rodman, but nothing apparently was done.

Now, seeing Confederates on the flank, and without waiting for orders, Harland immediately wheeled his horse around to rush to the 16th Connecticut to hasten their advance. He knew that if these Confederate troops were not checked, it would be impossible to hold this part of the field. Harland no sooner started when his horse was shot out from under him. This "delayed my arrival," he later reported, but he was able to reach the 16th Connecticut.

Under Rodman's orders, the 16th Connecticut had changed front to the left, which was accomplished. When Harland arrived, he found the 16th Connecticut heavily engaged, but he saw that the right of the 12th South Carolina was exposed, so he ordered the Connecticut regiment to change front again to the right and attack, which was done. This change and the appearance of the 4th Rhode Island caused the South Carolinians to retreat, but the two New England regiments were then flanked on their left by other oncoming Confederates and driven from the field.[50]

The 8th Connecticut came under fire from skirmishers as it continued to move forward up the hill before them. That fire came from the two North Carolina regiments spotted earlier. The 7th and 37th North Carolina, of Brigadier General Lawrence Branch's Brigade, Major General A.P. Hill's division, had come up the road past Blackford's house, crossed the Harpers Ferry Road, and marched east. When they saw the 8th Connecticut moving to the northwest, they sent out skirmishers which opened fire on the Eighth, and then the remainder of these regiments followed by the flank.

Jay Nettleton wrote that the 8th Connecticut moved straight forward to the top of the ridge, though exposed to grape and canister fire.[51] Some of this fire came from a newly arrived battery—Captain David G. McIntosh's battery (Pee Dee Artillery, South Carolina) of A.P. Hill's division. The battery had preceded the Confederate infantry up the road from Blackford's Ford over the Potomac and first took a position near Blackford's house. From there they were ordered by A.P. Hill to report to Brigadier James L. Kemper, to help support the right of Brigadier General David R. Jones' division.

Accordingly, McIntosh moved up and crossed the Harpers Ferry Road at the northwest corner of what the Confederates referred to as the "narrow cornfield." There the battery reached a gate in a plank fence bordering the road on the east. McIntosh waited until Brown's battery left the field through this gate, then he moved the battery into the field. They took up a position a hundred feet north of the narrow cornfield and a hundred feet or so east of the road, a short distance back from the crest of the ridge. Their battery consisted of two rifled cannon and a Napoleon.[52]

While helping to man one of the guns himself, McIntosh observed the colors of the 8th Connecticut, and occasionally the tops of the men's heads, as the Eighth moved behind the ridge. From McIntosh's viewpoint, the Eighth was moving diagonally from right to left. McIntosh opened fire on them, but then the advancing men appeared to halt and lie down for a few minutes before beginning to advance again.

Perhaps this was what Henry Hall was referring to when he wrote, "When we were in the field next to the one that contained the rebel batteries we stopped for a moment to breathe and then started on again with only one fence and a few rods

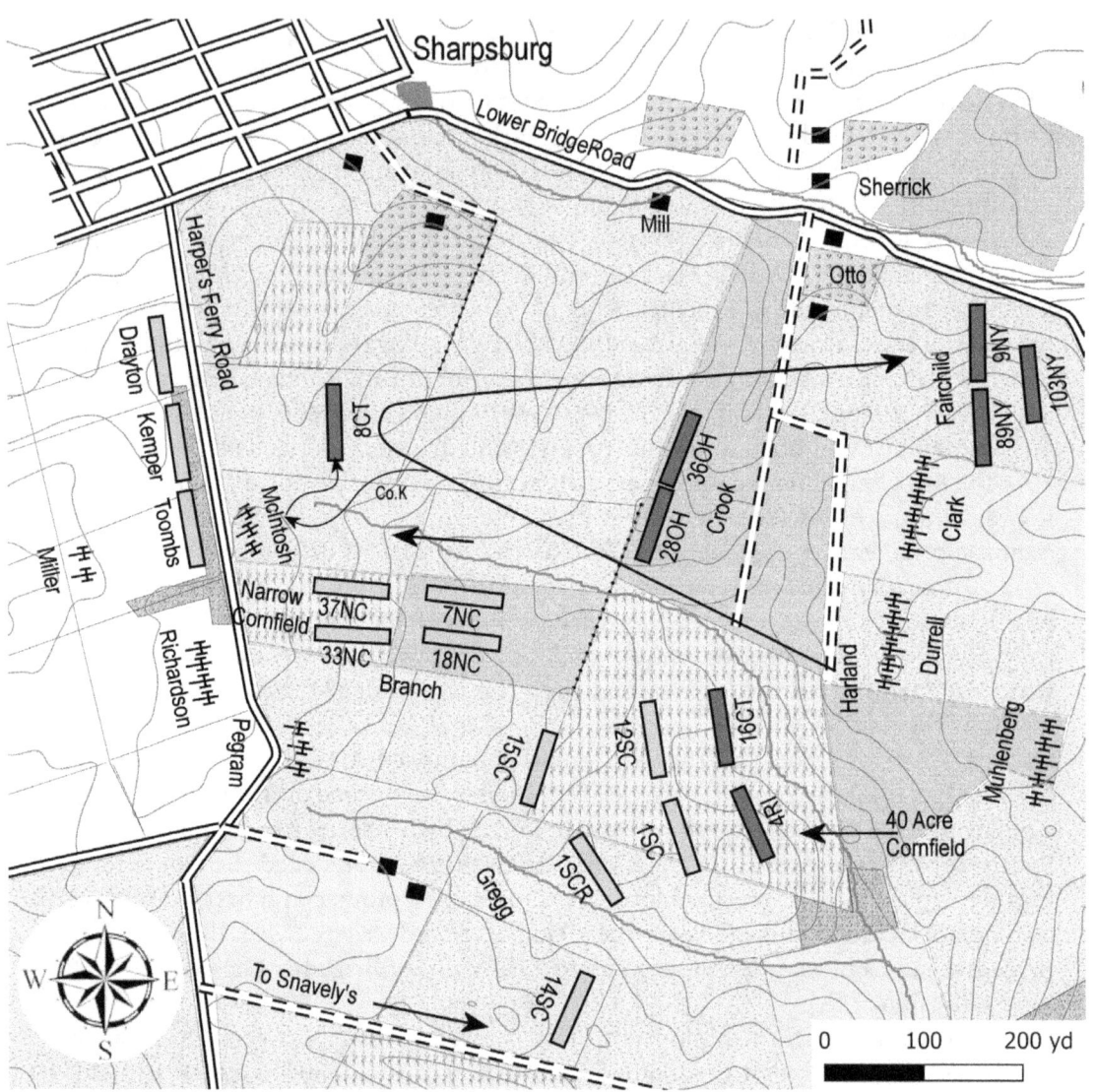

Map 7. Final Attack of the Eighth, Antietam, Maryland, September 17, 1862.

of uneven ground between us and victory. As we rose the Hill to the fence, a terrible burst of every description of missile from the Battery was showered upon us."[53]

As the Eighth approached his guns, and with all but two of his horses shot, McIntosh ordered the guns abandoned. It was at this time that Captain Charles L. Upham's Company K, the left flank company of the Eighth, was detached to take the battery. Roger Ford described the scene in his diary.

> [A]s we got to the top of the hill or most to the top there was a man came & told Major Lyon [Lion] that there was a battery of 3 guns on the hill abandoned. My comp[any] was then detached to take the battery we started with a cheer we got within 6 or 7 rods [about 35 yards] of the battery when we saw the Rebs were lying down behind their guns. we opened on them before they had time to open on us….

Chapter 4. Frederick, South Mountain, and Antietam   81

[W]e played on them until we heard a yelling on our left & there came up a Rebel Brigade. We then commenced on them we were firing brisk when we heard them shout we were surrounded on three sides. still the men fought bravely. The Captain finally ordered us back to the Regt. they had been deployed into line. They were cutting us right & left & also in the front but with all to discourage [us] ... the men fought like Tigeres we started for the Regt & all the while the men were falling around us ... the Regt was being cut bad as we were.[54]

Charles Upham said, "They [the Confederates] came up company or division front and deployed on reaching the fence at the edge of the field, each division opening fire as soon as it came into line. We fell back to our regiment which changed front and engaged them." The Confederates that he described were the 7th and 37th North Carolina, the same regiments whose skirmishers had been harassing the Eighth as it advanced up the slope. When Upham and his company rejoined the regiment, the 8th Connecticut had reached the high ground to the left and forward of where Fairchild's Brigade had fought.[55]

To reach this ground, the Eighth had climbed steadily from the point where they had left their sister regiments. They were under fire most of the way. About three hundred and fifty yards from the Harpers Ferry Road the rising land crests in a long ridgeline running parallel to the road. Past this crest, the land levels out and is relatively flat as it extends to the Harpers Ferry Road. It was behind this ridgeline that McIntosh first observed the 8th Connecticut moving across his front. As the Eighth came over the ridge and advanced, they suddenly found themselves exposed to the fire of the waiting Confederates. As noted above, Henry Hall described the fire when they crested the ridge as a "terrible burst" and it was then that "the Hawkins Zouaves and 103rd N.Y. broke and ran back down the Hill while the 8th Conn alone closed up the gaps in her ranks and moved on over the Hill and Fence." As the regiment advanced up the hill, Hall was a file closer in the rear of the line. With Major John E. Ward and Lieutenant Colonel Hiram Appelman, he was "punching up the laggards and keeping the alignment as correct as possible."

When they reached the top of the hill, an order was given to lie down and to load and fire. Henry Hall "lay down behind the dead body of a rebel and looked over his back to see the proceedings. A cannon ball drove me away from there just as Lt. Col. Appelman was wounded and then I was all around after that, doing all I could to encourage the men and keep them steady."[56] Jay Nettleton, in the same company as Henry Hall, wrote that "exposed to grape & canister we moved rapidly to the top of [the ridge] & were met with a volley from a Brigade behind a board fence 100 yards ahead. We used our muskets as well as possible & dropt down & loaded & fired 5 or 10 minutes when we were ordered to retire."[57]

Fairchild's Brigade, which included the 9th New York (Hawkins Zouaves) and the 103rd New York, had moved up the hills to the right of Harland's brigade. They first drove back the 7th Virginia and then, like the Eighth, came under artillery fire in their advance up the hills. One of the batteries shelling them was McIntosh's, which at the time was still positioned at the Blackford house. Moving up the final slope, Fairchild attacked the Confederate brigades of Brigadier General Thomas Drayton and Brigadier General James Kemper (part of Brigadier General D.R. Jones' Division of Major General James Longstreet's Corps). These brigades were deployed behind a stone wall and a post-and-rail fence on high ground just to the north of the spot where the Eighth crested the ridge. Fairchild's men overcame these troops, suffering considerable losses, and drove the Confederates back towards Sharpsburg. The brigade then pursued some of the Confederates down the hill to the north, until it was finally ordered to fall back.

As the Eighth came over the ridge and moved onto the flat ground beyond, the Harpers Ferry Road lay directly before them. The fence that Henry Hall referred to was the continuation of the same fence that Kemper's men had deployed behind and which Fairchild overcame. As it went forward, the Eighth soon found itself under attack from three directions.

To their left in the narrow cornfield were the 7th and 37th North Carolina regiments of Branch's Brigade, A.P. Hill's Division. On the Eighth's right front, in the road, were remnants of the brigades of Drayton and Kemper, which had retreated to the Harpers Ferry Road after their fight with Fairchild. On the Eighth's left front was Brigadier General Robert Toombs' Brigade, consisting of three regiments of Georgia infantry (the 15th, the 17th, and 20th) under Colonel Henry L. Benning together with five companies of the 11th Georgia of Colonel George T. Anderson's Brigade.

Toombs had been engaged in the area of the 40-acre cornfield, but upon the arrival of A.P. Hill's Division, Toombs had been ordered back to the Harpers Ferry Road to help its own division (D.R. Jones) against the Federal assault. The rebel brigade double quick marched down the Harpers Ferry Road, past the narrow cornfield and McIntosh's abandoned guns, and then halted opposite the 8th Connecticut and opened fire. Colonel Benning of Georgia later said of the fight, "The fire soon became general. It was hot and rapid. The enemy returned it with vigor, and showed a determination to hold their position stubbornly."

At the same time, the fire from the North Carolina regiments in the narrow cornfield to the left of the Eighth caused it to change the front of its left in defense. If that was not enough, Richardson's battery of the Washington Artillery also opened up on the Eighth from across the Harpers Ferry Road.[58]

It was now about 4:40 in the afternoon. The Eighth found itself in a very difficult position. It was a regiment alone, under fire from three fronts.[59] Charles Coit noted,

> For quite a time the bullets took us on three sides + it was evident to all that we could not hold our own but not a man stirred except to load + fire + fall wounded. It was very affecting to have the men as they fell wounded turn to me as they did + say "Capt I have got it" or "Capt what shall I do I am wounded." I think hardly a man left the ranks of my Co. when wounded without asking permission in some way.[60]

Captain Wolcott Marsh of Company F wrote later about the hopelessness of the situation.

> We now returned their fire & the men went to their work as cooly as if on drill. But we were trapped on our left flank was a large corn field & it was full of rebels on our right was a high hill where they were pouring in a gauling [fire] upon us & all this beside those in our front. Where was our support. Where was the first brigade none of them to be seen on the right where they had gone. Where was the 16th and 4th who were on left....
>
> Alas! They had been repulsed. It was death to remain in this advanced position longer. The Lt. Colonel [Appelman] was wounded & taken to the rear.... Capt. Hoyts company was as bad

Chapter 4. Frederick, South Mountain, and Antietam

off & on right they were suffering terribly but not a man faltered a steady & continual fire was returned against 6 times or more of our numbers but a few minutes had gone & it seemed as if the regit. must be entirely annihilated.

The Major [Ward] seeing that it was more than folly to remain ordered us to fall back. But many of the men seemed determined not to leave & would yell you to each other "Boys Lets Never Retreat. No Never." The major yelled at top of his voice in a pleading tone "Boys will you follow your colors" rally around them & follow me The word "Colors" brought the men to their senses & the devoted little band rallied around them down the hill we continually facing about & firing....[61]

In his diary, First Lieutenant Roger M. Ford of Company K concurred that the situation was terrible, but the men fought hard.

We joined the Regt. [after returning from the foray against McIntosh's Battery] the order was to change front to rear on first company which was done in good order. We then gave it to them again we gave as well as they but our position was terrible we now had orders to fall back we done so but we halted & formed & commenced on them gave them lead & we sent some of them to their homes. we were ordered to move back again we done so & rallied the third time & the men were as fast for fighting as they were at first. We had lost about half of the men that went into the fight.[62]

In a letter to his sister, First Lieutenant Henry C. Hall of Company I described the ferocious fighting by the Eighth even after the order to retreat:

The rebels soon saw our situation and commenced a move to flank us and take us Prisoners before our support could reach us. Just then Col [A]ppleman fell.... The red flag of the rebs was now coming steadily upon us from three sides and in a few moments the open space between us and our friends would have been filled with foes, while our Major gave the command to retreat. But not until the order had been three times repeated did our gallant fellows obey, so busy were they with their fighting. Meanwhile the gallant Zouaves were doing nothing safely sheltered behind a protecting hill.[63]

When Lieutenant Colonel Appelman was wounded (remember that Appelman commanded the regiment while Harland commanded the brigade), Major John E. Ward assumed command of the 8th Connecticut. Brigadier General Rodman (commanding the division) had gone forward with the Eighth, then rode ahead to Fairchild's Brigade, and then had started back to the Eighth when he was shot through the breast and fell from his horse. Two men from Captain Upham's Company K—Private Seth D. Bingham and Private Timothy E. Hawley—were falling back from the advance against McIntosh's battery when they heard Rodman's cries for help. They moved him first to a sheltered position under the hill and later to the Roulette house, where he died several days later.[64]

Both Toombs and Benning alleged that the Eighth had retreated in confusion, but officers of the 37th North Carolina disagreed. They reported that the Eighth "held ground quite stubbornly, fought splendidly, and went off very deliberately, firing back at the 37th and waving its flag." The 37th North Carolina men also admitted that while some of the Connecticut men retreated without stopping to fire, the greater part of the Eighth stopped several times to fire at them. As the Eighth withdrew, Toombs ordered pursuit and his men, along with what was left of troops of Kemper and Drayton, advanced to where the Eighth had stood. General Toombs ordered a charge over the hill, but Colonel Benning, wary of Federal reinforcements, convinced him otherwise.[65]

The Eighth moved back down the hills. Still, even in retreat, the regiment would stop and fire back at the Confederates. When the men reached a ravine which screened them from the enemy, they "halted & blazed away at them again." Upon reaching some haystacks, the regiment moved to the rear of them and reformed. Then they marched down to Antietam Creek, and with fresh troops coming across to relieve them, they crossed and encamped on the other side. Colonel Harland came by and the men were glad to see him, not knowing if he had been killed or wounded since leaving the regiment. He ordered up rations but the men were so exhausted that they did not wait for them and ate nothing until morning.[66] Jay Nettleton wrote that in two days they had been given only five crackers in addition to coffee.[67]

William A. Croffut and John M. Morris, in their comprehensive 1868 work, *The Military and Civil History Connecticut During the War of 1861–65*, gave this stirring account of the 8th Connecticut's gallant stand at Antietam.

> The Eighth is now alone clinging to the crest. Three batteries are turned on them, and the enemy's infantry close in around.
> Col. Appelman tells the standard-bearer never to leave the colors. He responds firmly. One of the color-guard falls; two; three; four; the last, and the standard goes to the ground with him. Private Charles H. Walker (of Norwich) springs forward, and seizes it amid the storm of death; strikes the staff firmly in the ground; and shakes out the flag defiantly towards the advancing foe.
> No re-enforcements come. Twenty men are falling every minute. Col. Appelman is borne to the rear. John McCall falls bleeding. Eaton totters, wounded, down the hill. Wait, bullet-riddled, staggers a few rods, and sinks. Ripley stands with a shattered arm. Russell lies white and still. Morgan and Maine have fallen. Whitney Wilcox is dead. Men grow frantic. The wounded prop themselves behind the rude stone fence, and hurl leaden vengeance at the foe. Even the chaplain snatches the rifle and cartridge-box of a dead man, and fights for life.
> "We must fall back," says Major John E. Ward, now in command. Some protest against what they feel is inevitable; and the hundred men still unscathed are faced to the rear, and marched back in unbroken and still formidable column down the hill. No regiment of the 9th Corps has advanced so far, or held out so long, or retired in formation so good. By their stubborn fight they have saved many others from death or capture, and by their orderly retreat they save themselves.[68]

A Very Costly Battle

The Eighth's casualties in the fight had been considerable. Of the 400 men who entered the battle, the regiment suffered thirty-four killed, 139 wounded and twenty-one missing for a total of 194—almost 50 percent casualties. The sergeants and every corporal of the color guard had either been killed or wounded.

Looking behind the statistics, the story becomes more personal.

From Charles Coit: "Lt. Col. Appelman is wounded he will lose his leg.... Marvin Wait is wounded in three places one is we greatly fear mortal. He showed true pluck. Capt Ripley looses an arm; Capt Russell of So. Norwalk is supposed mortally wounded. He was married just before we left Hartford."[69] Coit also told of the bravery of the men bearing their colors. "Our Flags are safe but full of holes. All but one of the color guards were shot + the colors were down several times but up they would go again."[70]

Chapter 4. Frederick, South Mountain, and Antietam

From Seth Plumb:

Thomas Mason ... was shot through the head and died instantly.... Brave little James Peters was wounded in the back badly but not dangerously, I think.... Beeman and Nichols were slightly wounded in their legs, a ball grazed my head above my right ear but did not break the skin, another went through my blanket which was swung acrost my shoulders and a piece of shell clicked the stock of my gun.... George [Booth] was shot through the right arm and into his side, probably reaching his lungs, as he bled from the mouth, he died about 3 am, so the wounded say that lay by him, perfectly calm and in his right mind to the last.... Corp. Ferris, Co. I, was shot and died within 4 feet of George.[71]

One of the notable casualties of the Eighth at Antietam was First Lieutenant Marvin Wait of Company A. He was the son of a prominent Norwich attorney and the grandson of a judge for whom he was named, so he had a promising future. He had enlisted as a private in the Eighth and soon rose to the rank of first lieutenant. In the climactic battle on the hills before Sharpsburg, Lieutenant Wait was urging his men forward when his right arm was shattered by a ball. He was advised to leave but would not; instead, he transferred his sword to his left arm only to be hit in the left arm, the leg and the abdomen. Chaplain John M. Morris helped conduct him to a sheltered spot by a fence. It was believed that his mortal wound was inflicted as he was being taken to the rear.[72]

The morning after the battle, Wolcott Marsh reported that the men were up at daylight with plenty of hot coffee meat and hard bread. Colonel Harland had ordered the food brought forward the night before, and the cooks had been busy all night preparing the rations. Marsh then went about the neighboring houses and barns looking for the wounded and missing of his company and reported that he was able to find quite a few of them. On return to the regiment, the brigade was marched down to the stone bridge and then formed in line on the banks overlooking it, and there allowed to stand and rest in place.[73]

Throughout the night of September 17 and all the next day, the Confederates remained on the field. Neither side attempted an offensive action. The field on which the Eighth had fought lay behind Confederate lines after the battle. The men of the Eighth wanted to tend to their wounded still on the field and recover the bodies of their comrades killed in the battle. But they were unable to reach them until the Confederates finally withdrew.

Seth Plumb of Company E wrote, "There was no chance to get onto the field till yesterday morning [Friday, September 19th] without being shot. I got away from the regiment then and was the first man of our regiment to visit the dead, I found that every thing had been taken from the pockets of our men and much of their clothing stripped from them. We gathered our dead and brought them away to bury yesterday morning but were ordered away before we could do it ... we left names of all on a piece of paper tied to their clothes."[74]

Seth Plumb also recounted his search for his friend, Corporal George Booth. Booth had been the representative of Company E in the color guard and had not returned from the battle. Plumb wrote,

In every regiment there are 2 sergeants to carry the colors and 8 corporals with guns as guard, that march to the left of the 5th company, and are a part of it on a march, one from each company. ... When we came from the exposed part of the field the first thing I looked for was Ed and George. I immediately saw Ed but not George. I knew that he must be hurt, I went right to the Colors and asked the only one left of the color guard, [Corporal Lemuel B. Clark of Company A] he told me they were all shot ... but we could not go back.... That night one of the color guards, slightly wounded, told me George was badly wounded and thought he would die.

When Plumb was finally able to go to the scene of the battle, he found the body of his friend, George Booth. "I found George where he fell lying on his back slightly turned to the right side, his cap and shoes had been taken and his pockets picked, his right arm I think was broken, and the ball entered his side to his lungs as there was blood in his mouth. I then went to a barn [Otto's] nearby where the rebels had carried our wounded, and learnt from Sergeant Strickland, the Color Sergeant that George died calmly in the course of the night."[75] Sergeant Strickland, too, died of his wounds a month after the battle.[76]

Wolcott Marsh related that on Friday morning the men were ordered across the bridge and onto the field where Wednesday's battle had taken place. The men stacked arms, and details were sent to pick up the dead so that they could be buried together. Marsh wrote,

> I went up where our regit. was engaged & there what a sight. 30 men from our regit. alone lay dead in a little field & nearby was 42 Zouaves (9th N.Y.).... The first man I came to of my company was Charles E. Lewis my acting orderly. Then Corp. Trask my color corporal & close by them lay Dwight Carey, Herbert Neff, Horace Rouse & Mr. Sweet all of my company then passing on to Co. A. were the body's of Oliver Case, Orton Lord, Martin Wadhams & Lucius Wheeler, then to Co. K saw Jack Simons body.... I saw many more body's from companys on our right & we followed on where the regit. fell back over fence & formed & gave it to them again. Saw Lt. Waits body then Sergt. Wilcoxs body Co. A. (the tall big whiskered segt.) a little way below Harvy Elmores body of Co. C.[77]

Sergeant Jay Nettleton described the experience of collecting the bodies of the dead:

> To go over the field & see the dead that had lain 36 hours or more, exposed to the weather, & see the bloated bodies—some that are putrid, others that are shockingly mangled, is revolting rather than touching to the sympathies. We feel that the man is not there & that what remains is unfeeling clay. The necessary duties of gathering the dead, although unpleasant & laborious, is set about with energy—yet handling them carefully as if we thought they had been men & not animals. It is not pleasant to go over such a field.[78]

* * *

So what happened on the ridge? The one recurrent theme that appears in the letters and writings of members of the 8th Connecticut who were at the Battle of Antietam is that the Eighth could have succeeded in its assault on the ridge if they had received support from other Federal troops. While the 16th Connecticut and the 4th Rhode Island were caught up in the 40-acre cornfield, the Eighth was ordered on alone by General Rodman, while he stayed back to "hurry up" the other regiments. Shortly thereafter, seeing Confederate infantry approaching the left flank of the Federal assault, Colonel Harland likewise returned to these regiments, leaving the Eighth to continue on alone. General Rodman later joined the Eighth, but then rode ahead to Fairchild's Brigade. All this time, without support, the Eighth marched on under constant artillery fire.

Perhaps General Rodman was trying to link the Eighth up with Fairchild's Brigade and continue the assault, or maybe he rode on to Fairchild's Brigade to warn them of the Confederate threat on their left. We'll never know, since Rodman was shot as he was returning to the Eighth. If the plan was to link up with Fairchild's Brigade, it probably would have been too late to help the Connecticut regiment. The First Brigade had suffered many casualties in their assault up the hills, had pushed the Confederates back from the ridge, and had begun chasing down the rebels when Fairchild's men were ordered back.

In retrospect, the best course may have been for Rodman to have held the Eighth until the other regiments of their brigade could advance with them (though that may never have happened), or to have waited to coordinate an assault with Ewing's Ohio Brigade in reserve behind them. But instead, Rodman said to Harland, in effect, "Forward the Eighth," and the rest, as they say, is history. In any event, it may not have mattered in the overall outcome, because the deciding factor in this phase of the battle was A.P. Hill's timely attack on the Federal left.

In its assault, the Eighth was totally unsupported yet they continued on a full half mile beyond the Federal line, and engaged a force several times their size. Under fire from three sides, they retained their composure and returned fire. Even in retreat, the Eighth did not panic, but stopped several times to return fire. They never ran. As Charles Coit wrote, "The Regt. acted as books say Regts. will at times. The men stood + fired until they were ordered away + then walked deliberately away to another position all the way under fire + so we changed our position with perfect coolness. This conduct is beyond all praise."[79] No more need be said.

Chapter 5

Fredericksburg to Newport News

Only days after the battle of Antietam, the 8th Connecticut, along with the rest of the Ninth Corps, moved south along Antietam Creek to a new camp at the Antietam Iron Works, an iron forge that had been built a century before. They were camped a short distance from the point where Antietam Creek emptied into the Potomac River, and just a few miles from the battlefield.

On October 3, Sergeant Seth Plumb reported that the regiment was staying "near the mouth of Antietam Creek, encamped in our shelter tents." He said that the Eighth now numbered about 250 men; those who were slightly wounded and those who had been separated from the regiment had now rejoined it. On that day, the division was reviewed by President Abraham Lincoln, Major General George B. McClellan, and "a host of others." Plumb wrote that "the review was like all reviews, and the President looks some like his pictures but much better. He is very popular with the army, as is McClellan and Burnside."[1]

In early October, the Ninth Corps moved away from the Antietam Iron Works, crossed over Elk Ridge, and settled into camp in a large area known as Pleasant Valley, for rest and reorganization after the battle. The valley lies north of the Potomac River between Elk Ridge on the west and South Mountain on the east.

Colonel Edward Harland returned to command the brigade, now made up of four Connecticut regiments—the 8th, 11th, 16th and 21st.[2] The Eighth had left the Antietam Iron Works on October 7 for the six-mile journey to Pleasant Valley. Sergeant Jay Nettleton described the passage.

> Yesterday [October 7] at 10:00 a.m., or thereabouts, we did up our things and made our Haversacks heavy ... with little things we thought we might want in camp.... But instead of the easy road down the river towards Harpers Ferry we went to the mountain & up its side. A steeper ascent I don't think I ever went up.... It was very warm, and the labor of getting up a steep mountain side 4 or 5 miles in ascent caused almost every thread in our clothes or whatever was in one's pockets to be saturated in sweat. Thus envelopes & a little paper I counted on sending you was spoilt.[3]

On October 10, Captain Charles Coit said the men could now see how great the company's losses had been, but they were glad to be in their new camp. "The Co.[s] are now generally well ... as we are now issuing clothing + shoes, will again ... present a decent appearance but the thinned rank will long remind us of the battle of the 17th.... Peter Mann + John A. Dixon have since died of wounds received.... While we were camped at Antietam the lime water so effected us that at one time we had hardly a man fit for duty.... The change of our camp ground has proved most beneficial."[4]

On Tuesday, October 21, Captain Coit, with a detachment of ten men, traveled to Washington, D.C., to recover knapsacks and baggage that the regiment had left there before the battle of Antietam. During their journey, he noted that "Genl Marcy + lady + Mrs McClellan + baby came on in the train with us. Genl McC was at the depot to see them off. Had a fine opportunity to see them all. They had a car to themselves—the car that the President + the other common people ride in. The Genl (McC) sat in the car trotting the baby until the train came + then mounted his stud + galloped off."[5]

Coit and his men arrived in Washington, D.C., late that evening, and after finding quarters at the depot for his men, Coit took a room at the National Hotel. The next day, he bought a complete new suit of clothes before making arrangements to ship the Eighth's baggage from Alexandria. He wrote, "[A]t the expense of about $40. Dollars purchased a complete suit, from head to foot, cap (blouse coat) vest pants + boots, also paper color + neck tie."[6]

Collecting the Eighth's baggage and bringing it back was no easy task because of all the red tape in moving things. Coit had to obtain passes for himself and his men, he needed orders for wagons to transport the baggage, in some cases to travel from Alexandria across the Potomac, so that required orders for boats as well. And then he needed to requisition more wagons to take things to the railroad depot. But he and his men finished the job and left Washington on Thursday night, "packed in [an] old freight car," and they returned to camp on Saturday morning, October 25.[7]

The March to Fredericksburg

The weather was excellent during the latter part of September and throughout most of October. But on October 25, when Major General Ambrose Burnside received orders to begin moving troops across the Potomac, the weather turned foul. Still, Burnside moved his units over the pontoon bridge at Berlin, Maryland (now known as Brunswick) and encamped around Lovettsville, Virginia. The storm abated on October 27, and the rest of the Ninth Corps crossed over. The full Army of the Potomac then followed Burnside's advance corps. On October 29, Burnside marched his troops ahead to Wheatland and Waterford, making his headquarters at Lovettsville. On Sunday, November 2, Burnside began to move his troops south, down the eastern side of the Blue Ridge Mountains.[8]

The men of the 8th Connecticut were packed and waiting to move out for two days before they finally left Pleasant Valley on Tuesday, October 28, and marched seven miles to Lovettsville, Virginia. They spent Wednesday night at Lovettsville, and the next day marched another six miles to Wheatland, Virginia, bivouacking in a beautiful oak and walnut grove.

Captain Coit and three other officers were camped in a wall tent that Coit had found among the baggage in Washington, D.C. He remarked that he had one rubber

90 The Eighth Connecticut Volunteer Infantry in the Civil War

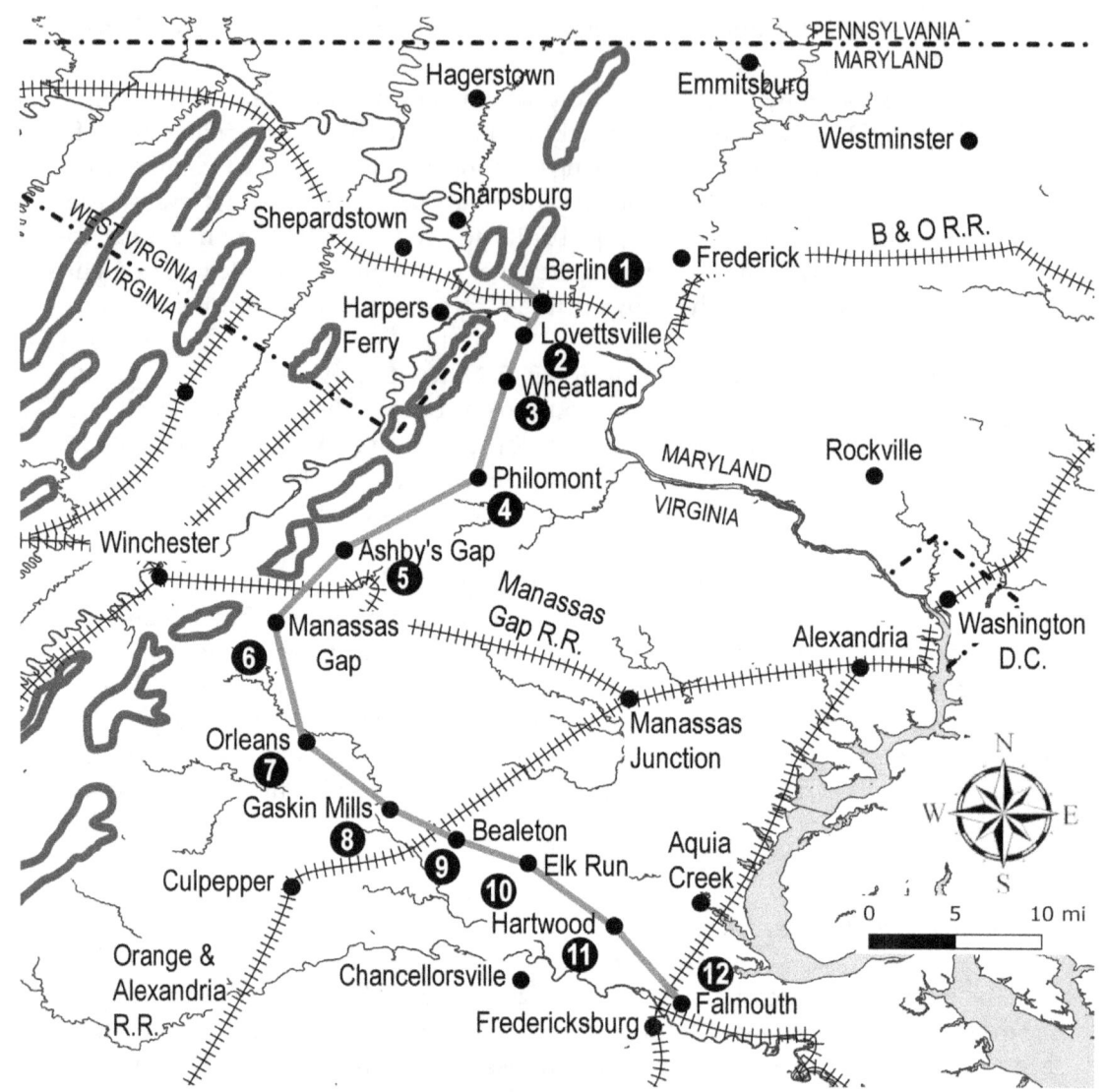

Map 8. Route of March to Fredericksburg, Virginia, November 1862.

October 27–November 19, 1862—165 miles in 22 days

1.	Oct 27	Camp at Pleasant Valley near Berlin	-
2.	Oct 28	Cross Potomac at Berlin, Marched to Lovettsville	7 miles
3.	Oct 30	Marched to Wheatland	8 miles
4.	Nov 2	Marched to Philomont	19 miles
5.	Nov 3	Marched to Ashby's Gap	17 miles
6.	Nov 5	Marched to Manassas Gap	19 miles
7.	Nov 6	Marched to Orleans	24 miles
8.	Nov 7	Marched to Gaskin's Mill	13 miles
9.	Nov 16	Marched to Bealeton	23 miles

10.	Nov 17	Marched to Elk Run	9 miles
11.	Nov 18	Marched to 7 miles from Fredericksburg	19 miles
12.	Nov 19	Marched to Falmouth	7 miles

blanket plus three good woolen ones, whereas the men had only shelter tents with one rubber blanket and one woolen one apiece. The regiment was so small at the time that they were divided into only eight companies on the march, not ten. Still, Coit commented, "How glad I am that I am with the bully [E]ighth."[9]

The 8th Connecticut camped at Wheatland until early Sunday, November 2, when they moved out with the Ninth Corps. Sergeant Jay Nettleton reported that they marched all day, finally stopping near Philomont, Virginia.[10] First Lieutenant Roger M. Ford wrote in his diary for that day, "[We] started at 9 a.m. ... we went on 4 miles and went through a place by the name of Goose Creek we marched on until sunset and camped opposite Snicker's Gap. we have marched 16 miles to day."[11] The next day, November 3, they were ordered to the front and passed through a place called Union (also known as Unison). At 4 p.m. they came in sight of the Federal advance troops, and witnessed a cavalry charge by the Federal cavalry, driving off the Confederate rear guard. The Eighth marched until 8:30 p.m. that day and camped opposite Ashby's Gap. Tuesday was a day of rest.[12]

On Wednesday, November 5, the Eighth proceeded south along the Blue Ridge, crossing the Manassas Gap Railroad at 5 p.m. and going into camp opposite Manassas Gap at 8:30 p.m. Jay Nettleton wrote that they were on the move again on Thursday, November 6, marching between fifteen and eighteen miles to Orleans, Virginia, and making camp a half mile beyond. On Friday, November 7, it snowed in the morning, and the Eighth marched about five miles to a camp on Carter's Run, a stream which runs south to the Rappahannock River. Roger Ford reported that on their way there they passed through a place called Watterloo [Waterloo] before finally going into camp in the woods at a location named Gaskins Mill. He said it was very cold and there were two inches of snow on the ground. Nettleton stated that this camp was about eight miles west of Warrenton, Virginia, and that "the whole 'Corps' is in this region."[13] Charles Coit also confirmed this camp as being at Gaskins Mills, and wrote that the Eighth remained there one week.[14] Since crossing the Potomac, the Eighth had traveled across major portions of Virginia's Loudon and Fauquier counties.

On November 7, General McClellan received an order (No. 186) relieving him of command of the Army of the Potomac, and replacing him with General Burnside.[15]

With a reorganization of the Army of the Potomac and its command structure after Antietam, it may be helpful to look at the Eighth Connecticut's position in the army at this point.

The Ninth Corps was part of the First (Right) Grand Division (composed of the Second and Ninth Corps), which was commanded by Major General Edwin V. Sumner. The Ninth Corps was commanded by Brigadier General Orlando B. Willcox. Its Third Division was commanded by Brigadier General George W. Getty, and the Third Division's Second Brigade by Colonel Edward Harland.[16] The 8th Connecticut was part of the Second Brigade.

The week that the Eighth spent at Gaskins Mills saw pleasant weather but it was generally uneventful, according to Roger Ford. One event he did mention in his diary was a two-day shortage of Hard Bread (hardtack), resulting in crackers selling for 20 cents apiece. A shipment of the staple finally arrived on Wednesday morning. The Eighth left camp on Sunday, November 16, at 8 a.m. and headed southeasterly towards Fredericksburg. They passed through a place called Liberty and "Beal Town" (Bealeton), and camped two miles further near the "Fredericksburg R. Road" (Orange & Alexandria Railroad). Two more days of marching brought them to within seven miles of Fredericksburg, and at about 2 p.m. on Wednesday, November 19, they arrived in Falmouth.[17]

Falmouth, Opposite Fredericksburg

The Eighth's first camp was on the east side of the Rappahannock River (the "Falmouth side"), about a mile below Fredericksburg, and somewhat back from the river. According to Charles Coit, on the evening of their arrival, the soldiers of both sides were talking across the river. "The Secesh were decidedly saucy," he said, and "asked how we liked Sharpsburg +c but our boys were good for them generally. ... They said they thought Genl Burnside a 'pretty shrewd old cuss.'"[18]

The weather was miserable; it rained heavily for the first few days after the Eighth arrived. The shelter tents the men had been given were hardly better than paper tents, Charles Coit wrote, and the men lay in the mud with blankets and clothes soaked. Shelter tents were the original dog tent. They were two-man tents: each man carried a cloth half that was about five and one-quarter feet square and made of cotton drill or duck. Each tent half had buttons and holes so that the two halves could be buttoned together and strung over a pole or rope to form the tent. There were no end caps, poles or stakes issued. Coit was thankful for his quarters in a much larger, enclosed tent known as a wall tent, which he shared with other officers.[19]

Soldiers have always been concerned that their unit gets the recognition it deserves. The men of the Eighth were no exception. On Wednesday, November 26, there was a Grand Review by General Sumner, who commanded the First (Right) Grand Division of the Army. Captain Wolcott Marsh described the moments when Sumner and his entourage reached the Eighth:

> Yesterday there was a grand review of the command of Gen. Sumner by that general composed of the 2nd & 9th Corps. As the old general rode past our colors he suddenly wheeled his horse around & riding up close to them stopped & sat gazing at them some moments then rode on whether he was reading the names of the different battles in which we have been on them inscribed or counting the bullet holes I do not know. But it was a proud moment for the noble old 8th, & every heart swelled with pride & satisfaction.
> As the General & Staff approached the regit. (8th) our Division General Getty was heard to say to General Sumner thus, "This General is the 8th Conn." And as the General was looking at the colors one of his staff a Lieut. Col. read the names of the battles on our flag out loud. "Roanoke Is., Newbern, Ft. Macon, South Mountain, Antietam (The two last are not on the flag but he repeated them over as though they were) Well no wonder they are a small regit." So, you see we are not entirely over looked out here. If we are at home.[20]

Chapter 5. Fredericksburg to Newport News 93

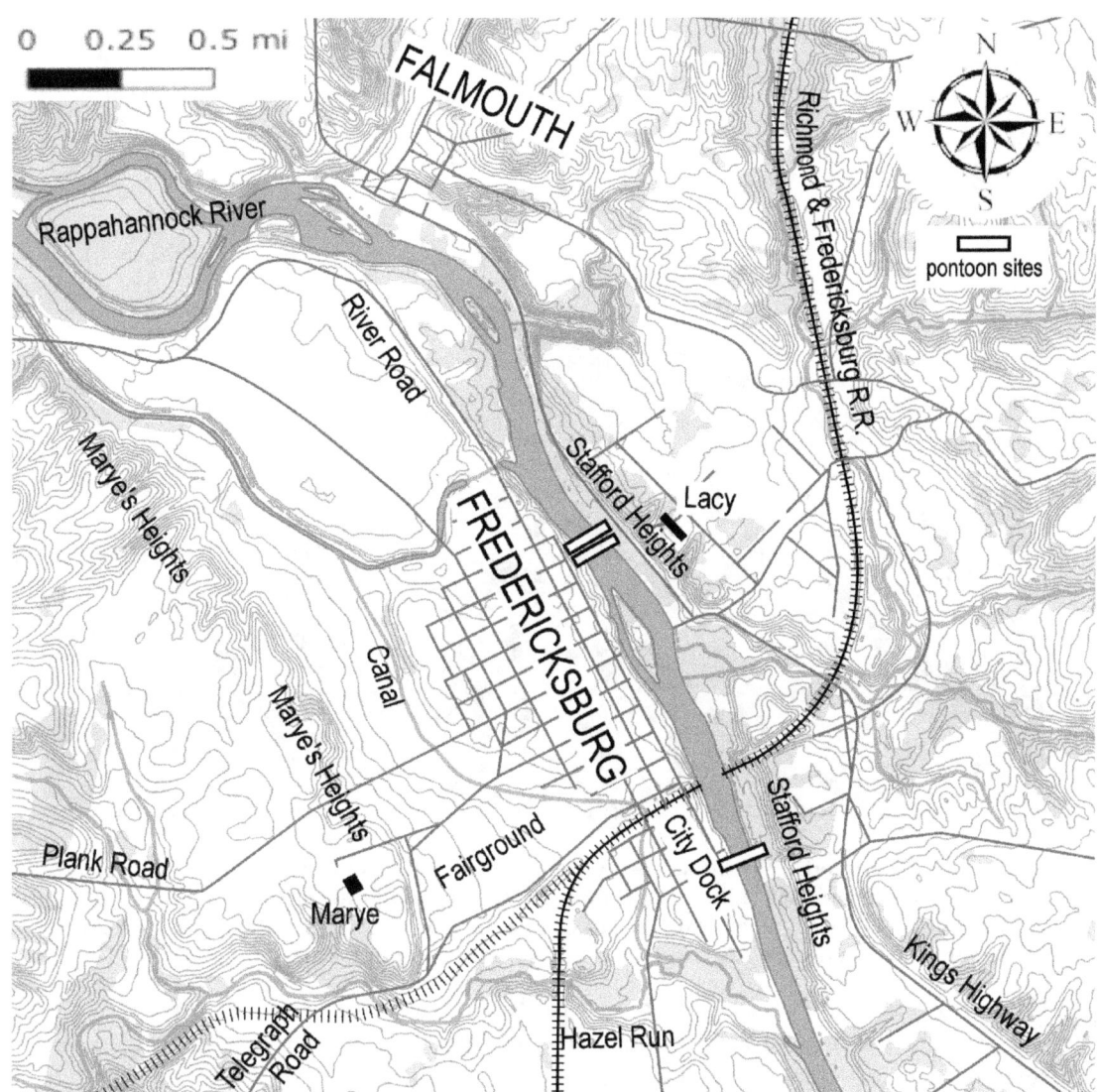

Map 9. Vicinity of Fredericksburg and Falmouth, Virginia, December 1862.

On Thanksgiving Day, November 27, the Eighth moved their camp back about a quarter mile to a place that was drier and nearer to some woods. However, a few days later, on Saturday November 29, they moved their camp again, this time a mile and a half upriver to a far better location—the grounds of the Lacy House, an antebellum mansion.[21] This change of camp had a special significance for the members of the Eighth, because the grounds of the Lacy House were the site of their camp that summer, before the Antietam campaign.

The Lacy House, also known as Chatham Manor, is located on the bluffs of the Rappahannock River, known as Stafford Heights, and overlooks Fredericksburg. Dating to the late eighteenth century, Chatham Manor was a large and thriving plantation. Washington and Jefferson both visited Chatham, as did Abraham

Lacy's House, Falmouth, Virginia, Headquarters of Gen. Burnside, Alexander Gardner, photographer, December 1862 (Library of Congress, Prints and Photographs Division, Civil War Photographs, LOT 4165-G, no. 23). The 8th Connecticut Volunteers were camped in the front garden of the house first in August 1862, then again in December 1862.

Lincoln when he met with Major General Irwin McDowell there in early 1862. At the time of the Civil War, the plantation was owned by James Horace Lacy, who was serving the Confederacy as a staff officer.[22]

The camp for the 8th Connecticut occupied the verdant area in front of the Lacy House (the front was the side away from the river). First Lieutenant Henry C. Hall wrote, "Our little regiment (numbering 300 men present) have spread their shelter tents in the front yard of a splendid residence (the property of Major Lacy of the Secesh Army) while the Officers have taken quarters inside."[23] When the Eighth had been there during the summer, General Burnside's headquarters occupied this area in front of the house, while the Eighth's camp was about 20 rods (330 feet) further away, and across a road.[24]

The officers enjoyed the privilege of quartering inside the mansion. As Henry Hall wrote, "We have gay times here as we have plenty of Furniture for housekeeping purposes[,] beds to sleep on and an organ to make music for us." He did jokingly recognize that the mansion was a rebel target, though. "What adds still more to our enjoyment is the fact that there are no less than 19 rebel cannon bearing directly on the House within a distance of half a mile and we rather expect to be disturbed by pieces of flying bricks when the impending conflict commences."[25] But apparently the benefits outweighed the risks.

It was a good time to be an officer. As Charles Coit wrote, "So here I sit in a real chair, + my paper rests on a handsome black walnut table. A good fire is burning in the fireplace at the right of which sits Capt Smith reading my 'Eugene Aram,' on the sofa ... on which I expect to dream to night, sits the Major reading 'Old Curiosity Shop.'" Coit recognized that the privileges were the result of his rank: "While the officers, all of whom are nearly as pleasantly located as we, are so comfortable I am sorry the men must still be in the little shelter tents exposed to the weather as much as ever though they occupy good ground."[26] In a letter home, Sergeant Seth Plumb noticed the disparity. "The health of the regiment is very good considering the tents we have, there is room enough in the Lacy buildings for the whole regiment to quarter without using half the rooms, but none but officers and servants can occupy them."[27]

The Eighth had been moved to Lacy House to relieve the 48th Pennsylvania, and their job was to support a nearby artillery battery. The battery was located on a hill to the left of the Lacy House (looking toward the river). On Friday night, November 28, the night before the Eighth's early morning march to Lacy House (reveille was at 4:00 a.m.), details from each regiment in the division were ordered to build entrenchments near that artillery battery. When they finished their work, Captain Wolcott Marsh said that the grounds looked a good deal like a fort. Marsh told his family that the role of the Eighth was to defend the battery in case the Confederates crossed the river and attempted to take the guns or spike them. But he believed that "they [the Confederates] will do no such thing" in that the rebels had built extended earthworks on the hills behind the town.[28]

Henry Hall wrote that the battery consisted of 10-pound Parrott guns, "planted so as to sweep some of the streets in the city."[29] Marsh said that the battery was composed of 20-pound Parrotts, but he had heard that they were going to be replaced by 30-pound guns.[30] As it turned out, Marsh was right, at least with regards to the final posting. On or about December 8, two companies of the 1st Connecticut Heavy Artillery arrived with "a Battery of 8 32 pound rifled cannon." Hall reported that they were being put into position on the night of December 9 "under cover of darkness."[31]

The two companies were Company B and Company M of the 1st Connecticut Heavy Artillery, under the overall command of Major Thomas S. Trumbull. They fielded seven 4½-inch rifled guns, also called 4.5-inch siege rifles, (four in Company B and three in Company M). Their stay at the Lacy House was short lived, however. At dusk on December 10 the 1st Connecticut moved to a position farther to the south, on "a high bluff opposite the left of the town [Fredericksburg]." It was still on Stafford Heights, but now it was across from the lower part of Fredericksburg, rather than the upper part, which was the case at the Lacy House. During the course of the battle, these two Connecticut batteries fired 357 rounds.[32]

In his letter of December 19, 1862, Captain Coit expressed the resentment that some of the infantry felt toward the artillery. "One of you write 'that this Country is safe because two companies of the 1st Connt Arty. has joined us—so says PBS [unknown source].' If I was about to go to war again+ desired to join a Regt where they would never be in danger of being shot, I would enlist in the First. I think any boy at home is in as much danger [at] any 4th of July celebration as a man in the 1st Conn during a raging battle."[33]

The Pontoon Bridges

On the night of December 10, the Union and Confederate armies stood opposite each other across the Rappahannock River. It puzzles historians why Burnside decided to continue with his original plan to cross the river on pontoon bridges and surprise the rebel forces, when the element of surprise had long since been lost. Even the soldiers could see that it was now too late to implement the idea, as Jay Nettleton wrote. "I suppose Burnside's plans have been defeated—by government itself—in not meeting their promise to have the railroad in readiness & pontoons ready.... The Pontoons have come but the favorable opportunity has passed. They (the rebels) have been reinforced; earth works have been thrown up. A 'labor' now stares us in the face."[34] It should be noted that the 15th New York Engineers and the 50th New York Engineers had arrived and bivouacked in the rear of the Lacy House on the afternoon of November 27, bringing with them two full trains of boats and materials—enough to build two pontoon bridges across the Rappahannock. They could have constructed the bridges that night without opposition, had they been allowed to do so.[35]

The pontoon bridge trains were in the charge of Major Ira Spaulding of the 50th New York Volunteer Engineers. Three bridges were to be built by this regiment: one across to the lower end of Fredericksburg, and two across the upper end, about opposite the center of town.[36] On the morning of December 9, Major Spaulding and Captains Wesley Brainerd, George Ford and James McDonald, all of the 50th New York Engineers, were ordered to meet with Brigadier General Daniel P. Woodbury, commander of the Engineer Brigade, at the Lacy House. They were amazed when they were told that General Woodbury had decided to force a crossing directly across from the town.

Captain Wesley Brainerd, who was in charge of one of the upper bridges, wrote in his memoirs, "Well, we went down to look at the position ... and after we had pondered the situation well we all came to the conclusion that we might now return to our quarters and with great propriety execute our last Wills & Testaments. With the enemy so strongly posted on the opposite side of a river 400 ft. wide and for us to lay a Pontoon Bridge right in their very faces seemed like madness."[37]

Nevertheless, that was the order. At 1 a.m. on December 11, the 50th New York began moving their pontoons down the long hill and into the water. The men of the regiment, who had left their arms stacked at the Lacy House, quickly began to lay the bridge. By 3 a.m., the bridge was out 200 feet, halfway across the river. But movement on the far shore was detected, and at 4 a.m. there came "a perfect storm of bulletts." Federal artillery, assembled on the hill behind them, responded in kind and fired at the Confederates over the heads of the New Yorkers. Captain Brainerd wrote

Chapter 5. Fredericksburg to Newport News

that "his men did not require any command to fall back in good order," and everyone started for the shore. Many of the men were shot and fell into the boats or in the water, or lay on the bridge.[38]

Back on shore, with no earthworks or protection, the men dropped onto the ground. The regiment of infantry, sent for support, was rapidly melting away. "It was simple murder, that was all," Brainerd said. They lay on the ground for an hour; then a second attempt was tried, and it failed. It was now 7 a.m. When General Woodbury arrived, he told them that Burnside said the bridge must be completed at all costs, and that the whole Army was waiting on them. "After great difficulty" another detail was formed, and a third attempt was made.

The seventy pieces of artillery that had been firing, and which had not been able to silence the Confederates so far, opened up again. Brainerd led the first team of ten men to the end of the bridge. Half his men were killed or wounded before they reached the end, and the rest soon suffered the same fate. Then Brainerd, the last man standing, was wounded, too. He made it back to shore and was taken to the Lacy House.[39]

The Lacy House and the camp of the 8th Connecticut were about 500 feet downriver from the upper bridge being constructed by the 50th New York Engineers. Sergeant Seth Plumb was up most of the night with all that was going on. The men of the Eighth could hear everything from their vantage point. The Engineers had the bridge halfway across when it began to get light enough for the Rebels to see the activity and commence firing.

The batteries on each side of the Lacy House responded. Plumb wrote that reveille that morning was more animated than usual. Bullets passed over the men of the Eighth as they cooked their breakfast, and one man in Plumb's company was wounded standing by the fire. General Woodbury of the Engineer Corps came to the Eighth's camp and called for a hundred volunteers to help lay the bridge. Major Ward ordered each of the Eighth's eight companies to furnish twelve men and called for volunteers. Plumb reported that his company produced nine volunteers, all the Litchfield boys except one.[40]

Now, Plumb wrote, the Eighth's detachment was marched down to the bridge without arms. "I need not tell you that as we marched down to that bridge it seemed as if we were going to certain death," Plumb wrote, "and that our only hope was in getting wounded, but duty called us, and the path of duty is always right." At the bridge, the detachment was divided into two work squads (with Plumb in the second squad). The first squad went to work while the second lay flat to protect themselves from the Confederate fire. "[I]t was all of no use[,] it was almost certain death to go onto the bridge, and the job had to be given up, and we got back to our camp as best we could with the loss of one killed and one or two wounded, this ended the attempt to lay the bridge under fire of the enemy."[41]

The soldier killed was Robert Rice of Company C, from New Hartford. The wounded man was Sylvester Godfrey of Company H, from Ridgefield. Godfrey was later captured by the Confederates in 1864, and died at Andersonville.[42]

In a letter dated December 11, 1862, to the Editors of *The* [New Haven] *Daily Palladium,* Chaplain John M. Morris wrote,

[W]hen opportunity was offered, 100 men of the 8th C.V. volunteered to go down and try to finish the work on the bridge.... I could not help going with them.... [T]he men divided into squads, marched down without arms and halted in positions as much sheltered as they could be.... When all was ready, a fire really terrific was opened from our batteries.... In a few moments we were ordered to shoulder boards, &c., and advance upon the bridge. With what anxiety I looked as I saw *friends* stepping bravely along the narrow wooden pathway. Hardly had the foremost man reached the end when the rebels fired on us. Two were quickly wounded. The officer superintending ordered the men back at once, for he saw that our artillery had not driven the rebels out of their hiding places.... We lay, however, behind the pontoon boats at the river's bank till nearly 12 o'clock.... The chief engineer then told us that at present no further attempts would be made, and we climbed up the banks and back to our camp, conscious that we had done a gallant thing, even though we accomplished little, and really suffered less than we expected. Failure was not our fault.[43]

Other accounts of the Eighth's determined service at the bridge are similar. Captain Charles Coit wrote, "These volunteers made three unsuccessful attempts + the Major of the Engineers then ordered them off."[44] Roger M. Ford, in his diary, said that after the volunteers were obtained "[T]here was a call then for their officers to Volunteer to take charge of the detail. Capt. Marsh, [Wolcott P. Marsh] myself and Lieut A.M. Morgan [Andrew M. Morgan] volunteered to go we went down and went to work but the fire was so severe that the commander of the Engineer corps ordered us to return with our men to our Regt."[45] There is no account of the battle by Wolcott Marsh. He was ill from a chronic medical condition contracted while in service, and shortly after the battle he resigned and returned to his home and wife.[46]

In a report dated December 17, 1862, Captain Henry M. Hoyt, who was then the regiment's commander, summarized the day's events:

On the morning of December 11, our regiment was encamped near the Lacy house, and at daylight was under arms awaiting orders. About 10 a.m. General Getty came to our camp and called for volunteers to assist the engineers, under General Woodbury, in completing the pontoon bridge which was being thrown across the river near the center of the city. About 90 men immediately offered their services, and, under command of Captain Marsh and Lieutenants Ford and Morgan, proceeded to the river bank and commenced their work; but, after laying one length of the bridge, they were ordered to retire by Major Spaulding, of the engineers, having suffered a loss of 2 men wounded.[47]

The Reports of Brigadier General George W. Getty, commanding the Third Division, and of Brigadier General Willcox, commanding the Ninth Corps, acknowledge the Eighth's valiant efforts on the bridge until they were ordered to retire by Major Spaulding.[48]

It should be noted that the Reports of Brigadier General Woodbury and Spaulding differ from these other reports.

General Woodbury wrote, "About 10 o'clock I led 80 volunteers from the Eighth Connecticut, under Captain Marsh, Lieutenant Ford, and Lieutenant Morgan, to the scene of operations, placing one-half of them under cover as a reserve. Before the other half touched the bridge, several of them were shot down, and the remainder refused to work."[49]

Major Spaulding wrote, "During one of the intermissions between these several attempts [by the 50th New York Engineers] to complete the bridge, a detachment of

80 men, volunteers, as I understood, from infantry regiments, came down to assist us in completing the bridge, but upon their arrival near the shore they could not be induced to enter the boats or go out on the bridge."[50]

However, two of the non-commissioned officers of the 50th New York Engineers tell a different story. Sergeant Arthur T. Williams of Company H wrote in a letter to the *Elmira* [NY] *Weekly Advertiser and Chemung County Republican,*

> At about 11 A.M. our battalion again rallied, and were joined by about sixty infantry from the 8th Connecticut, who volunteered for the occasion, and again attempted to finish the bridge, and again failed, after losing several men. Our men were most discouraged. It seemed almost like murder to ask them to go out on the bridge, within thirty yards of the enemy's sharpshooters, where every man was sure to get killed or wound-ed within one moment after taking his place there....[51]

First Sergeant Daniel M. Hulse of Company A, in a letter to *The Pen-Yan* [NY] *Democrat*, wrote,

> Finally about 100 men from the (I think) 8th Conn. Regiment, volunteered to finish the bridge, or assist us. Before Co. A [of the 50th NY Engineers] got together and could get to the bridge, the men who had volunteered were just going on the bridge, when the enemy opened on them driving them off, killing I think 3 and wounding 12. They had got enough of pontooning and went back to their encampment, satisfied with their short service as Pontooners.[52]

According to Captain Brainerd, there were no further attempts by the men of the 50th New York Engineers to complete the bridge after the attempt in which he was wounded, shortly after 7 a.m. (although remember that Brainerd had been taken immediately to the Lacy House because of his wound, so he was not present at the pontoons after that). The men remained on shore "protecting themselves as best they could behind the tree and one solitary tool wagon.... Here they were with no chance of service or escape until Spaulding managed to get word to General Woodbury suggesting some infantry be sent across in our boats to drive the enemy away."[53] It was not until 3 p.m. that the attack by troops in pontoon boats was begun.[54] This amphibious attack was ultimately successful, and the bridge was completed. It seems clear that the attempts to lay the bridge while under fire, though perhaps heroic, were costly and futile.

While a few units of the Second and Ninth Corps crossed the Rappahannock on the evening of December 11, and occupied the town, the majority of the Right Grand Division crossed the next day, Friday, December 12.[55] At 10 a.m. on Friday, the 8th Connecticut received orders to join the brigade. The Eighth marched to where the brigade was positioned, a little above the middle pontoon bridge, which lay just down river from a railroad bridge. They arrived at 11 a.m. At 2:30 p.m. Confederate batteries, which could be clearly seen across the river, opened up on the troops, causing them to move back into a ravine. Seth Plumb wrote that the shelling killed and wounded some men in the brigade, but none in the Eighth.[56]

The Battle of Fredericksburg

At 5 p.m. on Friday, December 12, Harland's brigade, having crossed over the middle pontoon bridge, formed in line on Caroline Street with its right resting on

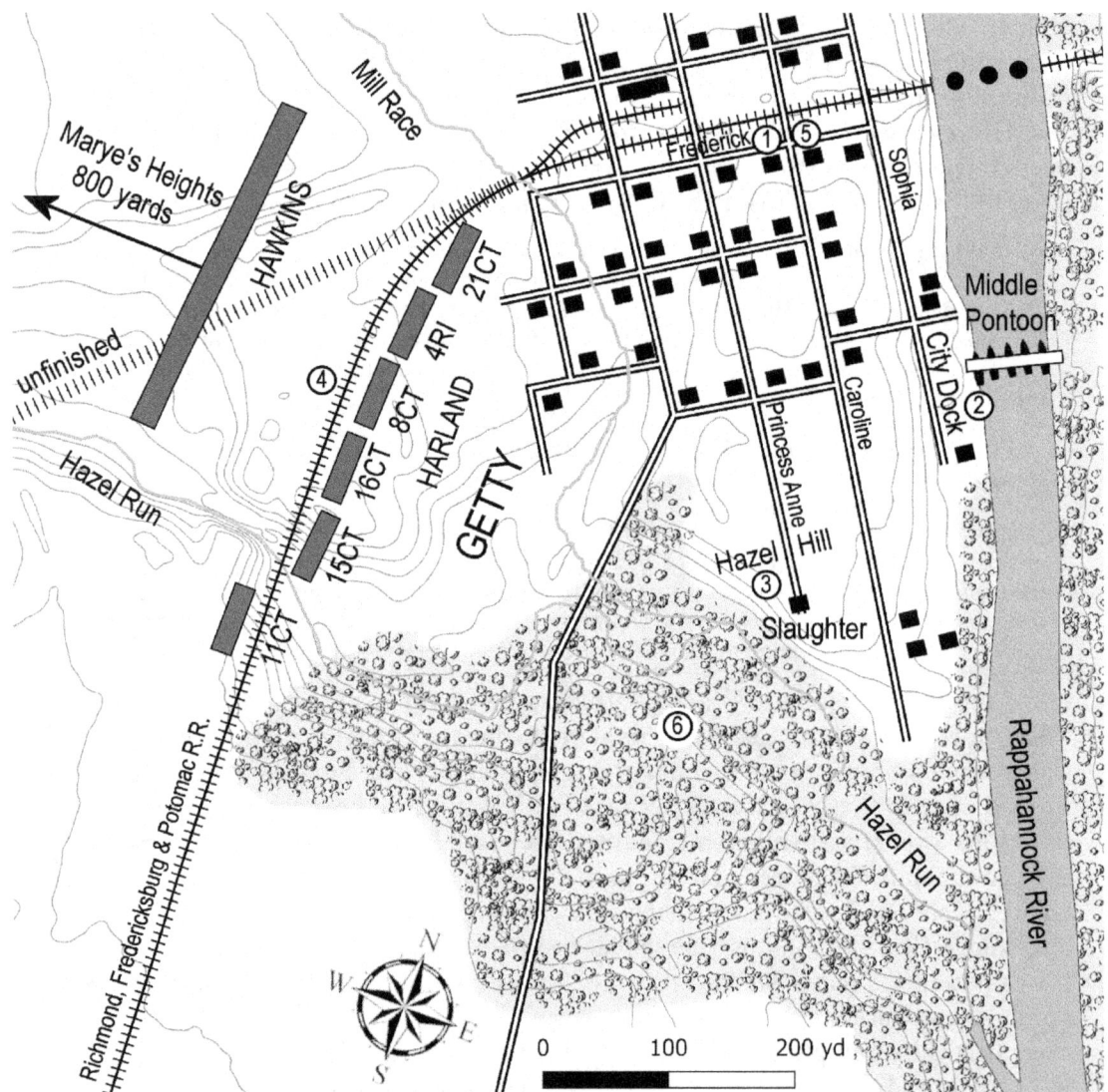

Map 10. Positions of the Eighth, Battle of Fredericksburg, Virginia, December 13, 1862.

1. Friday, Dec. 12, 5:00 p.m.–Saturday Dec. 13, a.m.
2. Saturday, Dec. 13, a.m.–Saturday, Dec. 13, 5:00 p.m.
3. Saturday, Dec. 13, evening
4. Saturday, Dec. 13, evening–Sunday Dec. 14, predawn a.m.
5. Sunday. Dec. 14, predawn a.m.–Monday, Dec. 15, a.m.
6. Monday, Dec. 15, morning–Monday Dec. 15, evening, return to Lacy House

the railroad. Here they stacked arms and occupied houses and enclosures on the east side of the street (the river side).⁵⁷ Seth Plumb, however, reported that the men lay in the open in one of the streets of the city that night.⁵⁸

Early the next morning, Saturday, December 13, the division was moved to the extreme lower end of the town, near Hazel Creek, where it was massed under cover of the bank of the Rappahannock River. However, it was there that the troops were hit by friendly fire—the premature bursting of shells from a Federal battery back across the river—Captain Otto Diederichs' Battery A of the 1st Battalion New York Light Artillery.[59]

The Eighth's position was close to the banks of the river, a little below the middle pontoon bridge. Seth Plumb reported that five or six men in the division were killed and many were wounded from this friendly fire, and that his Company E "seemed to be right in range of one of the guns which scattered iron among us a number of times, and several of us had very narrow escapes." He said his company's position was very near a hill from which the whole of the battle in front of the city could be seen. "[O]ur men pressed up the [farther] hill to their works in long lines, but every time were driven back before they reached them, sometimes in great disorder."[60] It is likely that the nearby hill from which they watched was Hazel Hill, located a short distance to the west, and which is still known by that name today. The farther hill, no doubt, would be Marye's Heights and the Confederate breastworks below it.

As the day wore on, Getty's Third Division, of which the Eighth was a part, had been so far held as a reserve and used to guard the left side of the town. At 4 p.m., with the battle still raging, General Willcox, commanding the Ninth Corps, decided to advance Getty's division to draw off some of the pressure being put on the Federal troops advancing from its right, and possibly find a weak point in the Confederate lines.[61]

Getty received orders from Willcox at 5 p.m. to advance by brigade front and charge the enemy. The First Brigade, under Colonel Rush Hawkins, led the way followed by the Second Brigade, under Colonel Harland. They marched by the flank through the streets of Fredericksburg and then formed in two brigade lines behind the railroad. Both brigades met with a continual artillery fire. Lieutenant Colonel Curtis of the 4th Rhode Island was killed while leading his men. While the Second Brigade, including the Eighth, remained behind the line of the railroad, the First Brigade advanced towards the Confederate line in the dark. When they had almost reached the enemy's line, they were met by a devastating front and enfilade fire that forced them to withdraw.[62]

The path of the Eighth had taken them through the southern part of Fredericksburg. Upon receiving the order to move forward in support of the First Brigade, Colonel Harland advanced the Second Brigade in two columns—the right column consisted of the 21st Connecticut and the 4th Rhode Island, and the left column was made up of the 8th Connecticut, 16th Connecticut, and 15th Connecticut. Harland reported that "on the street in front of the slaughter-house, I reformed the line, and advanced until the right of my line was nearly up with the Ninth New York [of the First Brigade], and the left had arrived at the foot of a steep hill, about 10 rods [165 feet] in the rear of the railroad, where the Eleventh Connecticut had been stationed during the day as a reserve for the pickets of the First Brigade." It was here that the Second Brigade was ordered to halt, and they remained there until the morning.[63] Seth Plumb wrote that they lay that night on the battlefield, just a little way from the enemy, and at times the firing would commence and "the bullets fly thick but to little effect."⁶⁴ Just before daylight, the brigade returned to the city, to the same location as Friday night, the Caroline Street area.⁶⁵

The authors believe that the term "slaughter-house" used by Harland in his official report actually meant the house owned or occupied by Montgomery Slaughter, who was the mayor of Fredericksburg at the time of the battle, and not to a butcher shop or meat processing building. The house, known as Hazel Hill, was built in 1793 by John Minor. It was located on Princess Anne Street, south of Dixon Street, and was presumably named for the prominence on which it stood. Severely damaged in the battle, it was restored, but was later torn down. A historical marker currently marks its location.⁶⁶

Despite the clear defeat of the Union efforts of the day, Burnside was not accepting the outcome as final; instead, he planned a grand bayonet charge for the next morning, Monday, December 15, to be led by his favorite Ninth Corps, which he would lead personally.⁶⁷ Seth Plumb wrote in a letter home that on Sunday morning the leadership decided that the Ninth Corps should charge the Confederate works, and that the officers were to so inform the men. Captain William J. Roberts of Company I encouraged his men to do their very best and said it would be the work of but a few minutes.

Plumb outlined the battle formation of the Ninth Corps: the Eighth's division, the Third, would be in the center with the First on its right and the Second on its left. The Eighth's brigade, Harland's Second Brigade, would take the lead, with the 21st Connecticut in front and followed by the 15th, the 16th, the 8th, and the 4th Rhode Island. The 11th Connecticut would not be with the Brigade. But then, Plumb wrote, things changed. "This plan was countermanded by Gen Burnside he considering it too risky to be undertaken but the men all suppose[d] that it was to take place till we left the city which kept us all in dreadful suspense and anxiety."⁶⁸

On Monday, December 15, General Getty, anticipating an advance by Confederate skirmishers on the division's left flank, took steps to bolster that line. The Eighth was ordered to report to Captain Charles L. Upham, temporarily in command of the 16th Connecticut, for the purpose of extending the line of pickets along the brow of the hill on the south side of Hazel Creek. Other troops, including 200 of (Colonel Hiram) Berdan's Sharpshooters, were also called onto strengthen the position.

Enemy skirmishers did advance in a line of skirmishers, perhaps with a view of gaining the crest of the bank of Hazel Run, but they were prevented by the increased number of Federal troops in place. That night, the Eighth and the 16th Connecticut were relieved from their picket duty and rejoined their brigade. The Ninth Corps, numbering about 16,000 troops, recrossed the Rappahannock in less than two hours in a well-organized, orderly, and noiseless procedure. The Eighth then returned to its camp at the Lacy House.⁶⁹

The Lacy House was used as a hospital during and after the battle. Clara Barton was there providing assistance to the doctors. Walt Whitman, who came to Fredericksburg to visit a brother wounded in the battle, also visited the Lacy House.⁷⁰ Charles Coit, who, along with other officers of the Eighth that had been billeted in the house, were now "crowded in two small rooms of an outhouse [i.e., out building]." Once the wounded were removed, Coit expected they would return to their old rooms "if it is possible to purify them sufficiently."[71]

The duty of the 8th Connecticut while it was posted at the Lacy House was to support the nearby batteries and pickets. The pickets of both sides took up their old positions on the banks of the river.[72] The pontoon bridges were taken up soon after the army crossed, and communications with the rebels were then carried on by means of a ferry. In the next two days details crossed under flags of truce to bury about a thousand Federal dead who had been left on the field when the army evacuated the city. Nearly every day men of the Eighth would cross over to bring wounded back that the rebels brought down to the river.[73]

On Monday, December 22, the Eighth struck camp at the Lacy House and returned to the brigade camp on the hill about a mile back from the river. One notable event there was the arrival of eighty to ninety barrels of apples and vegetables as a gift to the Connecticut regiments from the good people of the state of Connecticut. The Eighth received ten of the barrels: Company E got about half a barrel, and Seth Plumb happily got six big Rhode Island greens.[74]

Despite the defeat at Fredericksburg, or perhaps as a result of it, General Burnside still wanted to resume the offensive against the Confederates. His plan was to move up the Rappahannock, cross the river, and then swing around to the south and turn the Confederate left. But politics got in the way of his plans. A Burnside offensive planned for just before New Year's was halted because President Lincoln was not informed of it (he learned of the plan from two of Burnside's less than loyal subordinates).

Despite serious disagreements with his generals, a complete lack of concurrence on his plan, and less than ringing support from Lincoln and Halleck, Burnside proceeded with his proposed offensive in the new year. On January 20, 1863, Burnside announced his plan to his troops. At the Eighth's dress parade that evening, Burnside's order was read. Seth Plumb reported that the order was to the effect that the troops were once more to meet the enemy, that the opportune moment had arrived, and under the providence of God, Burnside and his troops hoped to strike a blow that should crush the rebellion.[75]

The Mud March

Rain began to fall that night, and grew worse the next day, January 21. Roads turned to mud, and pontoon and artillery trains stalled as wagons sank deep in the mud. The rain continued four days, and when it ended, there was no choice but to return to camp. Thus ended the "Mud March."

The troops that suffered through this disastrous march were the troops of the Left Grand Division. The 8th Connecticut, part of the Right Grand Division, had not yet departed camp, so they stayed in camp as the weather worsened. Roger Ford made three entries in his diary that captured the frustrations of those days for the Left Grand Division:

On January 21, he wrote, "Cloudy rained all night and all day the wind blows very hard the Left Grand Division marched last night some of the men died of exposure we have orders to be ready to march at a moments notice."

On January 22, he wrote: "[T]he Left Grand Division is returning to camp there is no use of trying to get through the mud let alone fighting it is one to two feet deep."

And on January 23: "[T]he troops are passing by our camp returning to their camps ... there is no chance to make a forward movement the mud is so deep."[76]

The political backlash in Washington only increased when the capital heard of this ignominious end to Burnside's offensive, and the president finally ordered that Burnside be replaced. Brigadier General Joseph Hooker was named the new commander of the Army of the Potomac.[77]

The 8th Connecticut's next move came about on very short notice. At 4:30 a.m. on Friday, February 6, 1863, the Eighth received orders to move at daylight, proceed to the train depot, and then take the cars to Acquia Creek. They arrived at the depot, Falmouth Station, at daylight, departed at 11 a.m. and arrived at Acquia Creek at 1 p.m. At 4 p.m. they boarded the steamer *John Brooks*, which Charles Coit described as a "Connecticut boat. [A Long Island] Sound steamer, nice strong new boat but no accommodations for Officers." Coit believed that the boat had been "gutted" since it had been chartered by the U.S. in order to increase its troop-carrying capabilities.

Three of the brigade's regiments were on board—the 8th, 15th and 16th. All the officers were in one room, except that Colonel Harland, staff officers and regimental commanders occupied a separate saloon at the stern of the boat. The boat laid off in the stream that night and got under weigh on Saturday, February 7, at noon. It reached Fort Monroe at 11 p.m. and anchored offshore for the night. On Sunday, February 8, the *John Brooks* left at 11 a.m. and arrived at Newport News, the brigade's destination, at 1 p.m.[78]

Newport News

Newport News is at the western extremity of Hampton Roads on the north side of the James River. From there, Seth Plumb reported that you could see Fortress Monroe and the fortified Rip Raps (artificial islands at the mouth of the harbor) about ten or eleven miles to the east, and you could see all the shipping in that direction. Just visible to the south across the bay is Norfolk, and up the James River for nineteen miles you could see any craft with the naked eye. Plumb noted that one of the monitors was lying in the Roads nearby, as well as the Union's ironclad gunboat, USS *Galena*, and other gunboats.[79]

On the afternoon of the day that the Eighth arrived at Newport News, they spent time cleaning their new barracks, which were log structures; sealing the windows and doors; and constructing bunks.[80] The left wing of the regiment occupied one of the barracks, and the right wing the other.[81] Sergeant Jay Nettleton had high praise for their new quarters:

> We Conn. men are quartered along side by side in the barracks—and it begets a pride that I like among the men because it brings about the desired effect. According to my ideas of things

we are in the best quarters we have ever had and can play the soldier with as much comfort. The ground is hard & sandy enough to be dry even in wet weather.

The barracks are on the bank of the river. First, buildings for field officers & generals; then a row of not quite so good ones for the line officers. About 150 feet from these are a continuous line of barracks for the men—a space so or good between each one, and a nice parade & drill ground in the rear. The barracks are for a row of bunks on each side. Most have them up off the ground so that they with the open space can be kept clean.... The 3rd Division of the Corps are quartered in these buildings. The other two coming after us are encamped on the ground above us....[82]

Newport News gave the Eighth the benefit of comfortable quarters and a welcome period of rest. Still, they were constantly reminded that they were soldiers. Sergeant Jay Nettleton said they had to "black up shoes & cartridge boxes" and polish the brass and clean their clothes before the daily dress parades.[83] And drills—the inevitable drills!—occupied much of the time for all the regiments at Newport News.

In a letter home, Charles Coit described what he called "the most interesting curiosity of the day"—a division guard mount. Civil War camps and armies were continually protected by a network of guards, drawn from the troops themselves. The process of posting these guards and periodically changing them is termed "guard mount." This is a precise procedure proscribed by army regulations, and is performed in a ceremonial fashion. Guard mount at the regimental level would be normal. At a division level it would be unusual and very impressive.

Coit explained that the guard details were formed at the regimental level and then combined and reformed again at the brigade level, and finally at the division level. When the final formation was assembled, there were "42 officers, all in full dress, white gloves, sashes, +c" out in front of the Guard. "The splendid 103d Band marches clear down the long line playing at the slow time with the Drum Major ahead flourishing his great baton back + forth in all manner of kingly gyrations."

Coit also described one notable feature of the Eighth's presence on the field:

> The 8th held out their tattered + bullet pierced flag. When I first saw it as they marched out, I wanted to sing out or yell or do something. I had no very clear idea what but my better judgement prevailed and I only gazed at it hard and long + thought how many brave fellows had fought—suffered + died that this flag and the principles which it represents might be protected from an enemy more savage + determined than any foreigners who have dared to attack it. The Old Eighth is sadly reduced but appeared very well. Some of the evolutions were executed remarkably well.[84]

When they weren't busy with drill or other soldierly activity, the men did have time for fun. Sergeant Jay Nettleton watched a game of whist being played by four other sergeants—Ed Wadhams and Seth Plumb, both from Litchfield and Company E, and Charles Irwin and David Baldwin, both from New Milford and Sergeant Nettleton's Company I. Nettleton explained that whist is a game that few of the card-playing boys understood, while "Bluff" is played by the gamblers, and "Euchre" and "Old Sledge" are played to kill time.

But, he said, the principal pastime that the boys enjoyed was "ball playing—mostly base," but the 16th and 11th Connecticut usually go in for "wicket." These games could be seen up and down the ground.[85] Most historians today no longer think it's true that baseball was invented by Civil War General Abner Doubleday;

instead, many believe that baseball evolved from older versions of the game brought to North America from England by immigrants.[86] There is no doubt that the knowledge and popularity of baseball spread as a result of the huge concentrations of soldiers who learned to play during the Civil War.

It's important to note again that the men of the Eighth had a great love and respect for General Ambrose Burnside, and that honor for their leader is very apparent in their letters and writings. In the period of time between Burnside's removal as commander of the Army of the Potomac and his final troop assignments, the men fully expected to follow him as members of his Ninth Corps.

Here's what Sergeant Seth Plumb wrote in early 1863.

> February 5, 1863 [W]e now think that Burnside is to join his old Corps here and then to proceed to either North or South Carolina.... I cannot say that we are sorry to get out of the Army of the Potomac, the place for the 9th Corps is under Burnside, and the government probably thinks so by moving us here.[87]
>
> March 3, 1863: All quiet at Newport News, and no signs of moving yet, but we expect Burnside along soon, then there will be a start some where....[88]
>
> March 11, 1863: Gen. Burnside is expected here soon, his horse has already arrived, when he arrives we shall expect that there is a move for us a little way ahead, as he is not the man to be idle.[89]

Captain Charles Coit voiced similar expectations.

> February 10, 1863:... [T]he idea of getting out of the Army of the Potomac + the mud + being (we hope) under Burnside again is most pleasing to us. We don't care much where we go if he only leads.[90]
>
> March 4, 1863: We are expecting Genl Burnside every day. The best informed say that he is to have command of the 5th and 9th Corps + return to New Berne, N.C.... I should think it quite probable that we move soon after Genl B. arrival.[91]
>
> Undated (written about November 9, 1862): While I write the welcome news of Genl Burnside's appointment as commander in chief of the Army of the Potomac reaches us.... Wont the old 8th give him three times three [cheers] when we meet him next.... We love to call him our General + rejoice that we have always served under him. The 8th never cheers any other but always have three round ones for him. ... I close with three cheers for Genl Burnside.[92]

When the 8th Connecticut left Newport News on the afternoon of Friday, March 13, bound for Suffolk, Virginia, they were not to be under the command of Ambrose Burnside. Changes were coming.

CHAPTER 6

Suffolk, Portsmouth, Deep Creek, Home

Winter quarters at Newport News, Virginia, gave the Army and the 8th Connecticut Volunteers a chance to rest and reorganize in late 1862 and early 1863. But as winter showed signs of receding, the Army began, once again, to prepare for the campaigns that were soon to come.

One major objective for the new year became apparent: the Union army needed to reinforce its hold on the Suffolk, Virginia, area. Soon, the 8th Connecticut would be headed to Suffolk.

Three generals would direct the Union's defense of Suffolk and the work of the Eighth there. Major General Erasmus D. Keyes commanded the military Department of Virginia. Under Keyes, Major General John J. Peck commanded the Suffolk defenses. Under Peck, Brigadier General Michael Corcoran commanded the First Division of the Seventh Corps occupying the area.

> At the same time, the Confederates were also preparing for the coming campaign season. Lieutenant General James Longstreet was in command of the Confederate Department of Virginia and North Carolina. Longstreet was given four objectives for the campaign. They were: to protect Richmond from the south, to support Lee's Army of Northern Virginia when Lee needed support, to forage the untapped region around southwest Virginia for supplies, and to capture the Union garrison at Suffolk if that were possible.[1]

Move to Suffolk

Once the North understood the Confederate's intentions, the Union Army began to bolster the Suffolk area defenses. Major General George W. Getty was ordered to move his troops there. The Third Division of the Ninth Corps, including the 8th Connecticut, was ordered there for support. Although the Eighth was still part of the Ninth Corps, there were rumors that their division (the Third) would be called back to join the rest of General Ambrose Burnside's command, which was moving to Kentucky to reinforce General William Rosecrans.

The men often questioned why the Third Division had been separated from their old corps. Then the Eighth received their official orders. On March 12, 1863, just before midnight, they were ordered to prepare two days rations and to be ready to move the next day. Sergeant William Huntington wrote that the troops were ordered to pack knapsacks for inspection with overcoats inside. So, they did. Then they were ordered to wear the overcoats for the inspection, so they repacked. Finally, they were told to pack everything immediately; there would be no inspection. Then they stood waiting to leave for several more hours.[2]

The absurdity of all this activity was not lost on the soldiers. As Sergeant Huntington wrote,

> If you was acquainted with packing Knapsacks, you could appreciate more fully what I have written about it. The amount of it was that we had to pack them three times in about an hour. From this time till 4 in the afternoon we had to wait around with our things all on. at this time, we were called into line + marched to the boat, there were three Regts on board of her when we were on. She immediately got under way for Norfolk.[3]

That Friday, March 13, 1863, around 3 p.m., the 8th Connecticut and the 16th Connecticut were the first regiments to embark. Once onboard the steamer *Georgia*, they set out for Portsmouth, where they arrived just before sundown. They took the railroad west through the Great Dismal Swamp to Suffolk, where they set up camp a half mile southwest of the village.[4] Their camp was near the South Quay road, where they did fatigue work, picket duty, and occasional reconnaissance.[5] The daily routine here was very different from what they had done on the battlefield. They were no longer focused on military tactics and drills in the manual of arms. Instead, they performed their drills in the manual of the shovel, pick, and hoe, working on the incomplete earthwork fortifications and rifle pits in and around Suffolk.[6]

Lieutenant Colonel John E. Ward was promoted to colonel of the Eighth on March 9, 1863. The Eighth was now part of the "Connecticut Brigade," or "Harland's Brigade," which consisted of the 8th Connecticut, 11th Connecticut, 15th Connecticut, and 16th Connecticut Volunteers. The brigade was commanded by the Eighth's own one-time commander, Brigadier General Edward Harland. They were the Second Brigade, of the Third Division, under Brigadier General George W. Getty, of the Ninth Corps, which was still commanded by Major General Ambrose E. Burnside. Many of the Eighth's officers were assigned to Harland's brigade staff positions, along with other Connecticut officers.

> The officers of the brigade were: Brig.-Gen. Edward Harland of Norwich, in command; Capt. H.P. Gates of the Eighth (Norwich), A.A. G; Lieut. C.J. Arms of the 16th Connecticut (Norwich), A.D. C; Lieut. Alfred M. Goddard of the Eighth (Norwich), A.D.C; Lieut. N.P. Ives, of the Eighth (Meriden), Brigade Commissary; Lieut. Stuart Barnes of the Fifteenth (Fair Haven), [and] Brigade Q. M; Surgeon Melancthon Storrs of the Eighth (Hartford), Brigade Surgeon.[7]

General Getty, with his Third Division, now reported to Major General John J. Peck, commanding the Suffolk garrison. Rear Admiral Samuel Lee of the North Atlantic Blockading Squadron with his two flotillas, under Lieutenant Roswell Lamson and Lieutenant William B. Cushing, were also attached to Major General Peck's command for naval gunboat support up the tidewater rivers and along the shores. The Eighth served under General Getty's portion of Peck's defensive plan around Suffolk.

> Peck organized the Suffolk defenses roughly into a large circle, ringing the city. The Southwest Front was led by Col. Robert Sanford Foster; the Southeast Front was led by Brig.-Gen. Charles C. Dodge; the Northwest Front led by Brig. Gen. Henry Dwight Terry; the Northeast

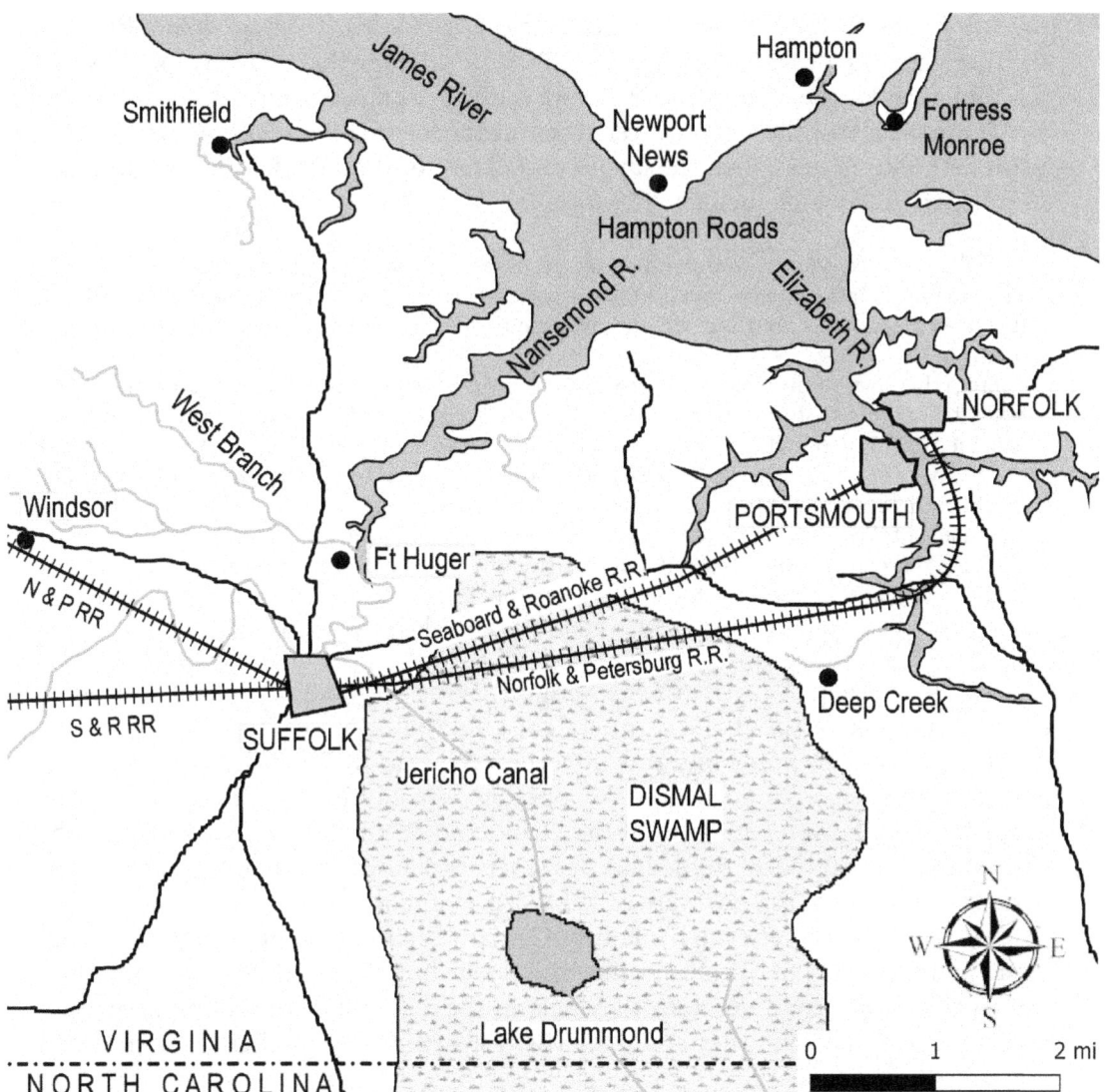

Map 11. Vicinity of Hampton Roads, Virginia, Spring 1863.

Front led by Colonel Arthur H. Dutton. Corcoran supervised the southern fronts and Getty supervised the northern fronts; river defenses were left to the navy. Peck had a good natural defensive position with the Great Dismal Swamp protecting the eastern flank and the Nansemond River protecting the western flank.[8]

At the end of March, the Army officially moved the 8th Connecticut out of Burnside's Ninth Corps. They now were part of the military Department of Virginia, in the Seventh Corps, both commanded by Major General John A. Dix. They served in General George W. Getty's Division, and General Edward Harland's Second Brigade, along with the three other Connecticut regiments. Colonel John E. Ward remained in command of the Eighth.[9]

Sergeant Albion Brooks said the men weren't happy to be assigned to the new

Seventh Corps. "We have been changed into the 7th Corps. The men do not like it at all. They groaned for Dix and cheered for Burnside. I hope that it is only for the present, though as long as we are under Dix we shall have an easy time."[10]

It was clear that the work of strengthening the fortifications was important. Sergeant Seth Plumb described the layout and extent of the fortifications around the Suffolk garrison, which included five forts.

> Suffolk is situated, you are aware, on or near, the Nansemond river, which runs from North Carolina in a north easterly direction to the James, emptying opposite Newport News. Suffolk is on the west side of this river. The river is quite narrow, but navigable for small gun boats.
>
> From this river to the Great Dismal Swamp there is a long line of earth works which protect Suffolk on the south, in this line of works there are 5 regular forts, the one nearest the Swamp is named Fort Halleck, the next Dix, the next Union, the next McClellan, and the last which is on the river is Fort Nansemond. These Forts are all connected by heavy breast works, in front of which there is a ditch which requires a smart jump to cross.
>
> Outside of these works for more than a mile the wood has been all cut off so that our guns can have fair play. Towards Norfolk and Portsmouth on the east there are other forts and breast works, and some on the north side down the river also. These forts have about 6 or 8 guns each, then all along in the breast works there are field batteries planted.[11]

While the men of the regiment were fortifying Suffolk that spring, they were talking incessantly about the Connecticut gubernatorial election coming up on April 7, 1863. The Republicans and Governor William A. Buckingham were challenged by the Peace Democrats or "Copperheads" and Thomas H. Seymour. (The Peace Democrats were a faction of the Democrats in the Union who opposed the Civil War; they wanted an immediate peace settlement with the Confederates. Democratic supporters of the war were called War Democrats.)

On April 10, in a letter to his family, Captain Charles Coit described the political attitudes of many of the men in the ranks regarding the elections back home, and the results of the mock elections they held in the field. Since the soldiers were not actually in Connecticut, they could not cast votes. But some of them took informal tallies on the battlefield.

In 1862, the General Assembly tried to pass legislation for absentee voting, but the Supreme Court ruled the law unconstitutional.[12] Connecticut added absentee voting provisions to the state constitution in 1864 so that Civil War soldiers could vote, but the amendment was effective only for the duration of the war.[13]

Captain Coit was pleased to hear that the state had reelected the Republican governor, William Buckingham. During their mock elections in Suffolk, he was surprised that some men supported the Peace Democrat candidate, Thomas Seymour.

> Genl Harland told me, just as we were coming off the field that our good Gov. had been reelected. I spread the news pretty quickly. Almost every Co. had elections here + I was much surprised at the number of Seymour votes cast. I did not suppose there would be a dozen cast in the Regt. In my Co. I wrote the votes + gave each man two ballots, one for Buckingham + one for Seymour + the boys put the one they preferred into the hat.... Thirty votes were polled. Twenty-five for Buckingham + five for Seymour. As the Co. comes from a strong

Democratic district, I was greatly pleased at the result + I really believe every man voted independently. Two or three Co's were unanimous for Buckingham + one had a majority for Seymour but 'twas not a fair vote. More votes were polled than there were voters.[14]

That same day, Sergeant Jay Nettleton also wrote home about the political opinions he heard in the regiment. "There has been considerable interest manifest in the Election through all of our Regt. The unanimous voice is 'glad that Seymour is defeated.' Our Co. did not vote, but there would not have been more than two or three votes for Seymour if every man had voted…. In some Cos. there was 1 in 30 or 36. Co. E was unanimous for Buckingham. Co. H is probably a good share Seymour men. They voted for Seymour mostly out of spite to their Capt. [Elam Goodrich]."[15]

The Siege of Suffolk Begins

The 8th Connecticut now served in the defensive fortifications around Suffolk. The enemy was not far off, so every unit practiced greater vigilance. Picket duty and long roll alarms (drum call to battle) were common, and the men often slept on their weapons. General Longstreet and the Confederates were closing in from the west.

On Saturday, April 11, General Peck rode through the town and the camp, sounding the alarm. The Eighth was called out by the long roll to defend the works around Fort McClellan against a Confederate attack from the west. About 4 p.m., the cavalry videttes came running in. (A vidette was a mounted sentinel whose duty was to watch the enemy and report any danger.) One of the officers told Captain Martin B. Smith that he had better fall back quickly. Captain Smith told him that he would do that when he received orders.[16]

When the Confederates attacked, the Eighth held their ground and repelled the attack. Only one man in the Eighth was wounded. Private George H. Tucker, Company H, was badly wounded in the neck, but survived.[17] The Confederates continued pressure on Sunday when they showed attacked again with battery and infantry. By Monday morning, April 13, the enemy had retired from the front. They were still present in force, however, holding a line along the Blackwater River road.

Thus began the Confederate siege operations on the Union garrison and their Suffolk defenses. The Union forces were not truly surrounded, however, since they could be supplied by the Navy along the shores and rivers. Suffolk itself was, at that time, accessible by boat via Hampton Roads and the Nansemond River.

On Tuesday, April 14, the Eighth was ordered to move from their post south of the city to a post north of the city to support operations along the Nansemond River. That night an artillery engagement began between the Union and Confederate batteries on opposite sides of the river. On Wednesday night, April 15, the Eighth was sent out on picket along the river to relieve the 10th New Hampshire. They settled deeper into the routine of fatigue work and picket duty.

About this time, Captain Charles M. Coit recounted a story demonstrating the mindlessness of army bureaucracy. Lieutenant Samuel S. Foss was discharged from the service, apparently because he returned to duty in Virginia. It seems that Colonel Ward was away from the regiment when the unit moved to Newport News. At the same time, Lieutenant Foss, who had recently been promoted, was also away on detached duty in North Carolina. In returning to the Eighth, both men travelled through Washington, D.C., to find out where their regiment was located.

Colonel Ward and Lieutenant Foss were both named on a single pass that the colonel held. So, when the Provost Guard picked up Lieutenant Foss in Washington, he told them that Colonel Ward was holding his pass. The Provost Guard ordered Foss to report to the Provost Marshall with the pass at 10 a.m. the next morning. But since the colonel and the lieutenant were supposed to leave Washington at 8 a.m., Colonel Ward advised Foss to ignore the order and proceed with him to join their regiment at Newport News.

That's where bureaucracy prevailed. The officers at Suffolk received orders to summarily discharge Lieutenant Foss for not appearing for the Provost Marshall as ordered. It may have been wrong, but it was understandable that Foss disobeyed the order. As Captain Charles Coit later wrote to his family at home, "Foss was certainly entirely in the wrong in not reporting as ordered + cannot complain that he is discharged but under like circumstances I think nine out of ten officers in the service would have disobeyed in like manner + I cannot blame Col. Ward more than I do Sam."[18]

Samuel Foss returned home to Norwich, a civilian once more. But with the help of Governor Buckingham and others, he was able to get his case reviewed, and he was reinstated. He returned to the regiment once more around the middle of May. He was later wounded at Ft. Harrison, Virginia, then discharged, but survived the war.[19]

One other change in the Eighth's leadership happened that spring. Captain Charles L. Upham of Company K was promoted to lieutenant colonel of the Eighth on March 9, 1863. On April 18, 1863, he was transferred and promoted to colonel of the 15th Connecticut.[20]

Hill's Point Battery or Fort Huger

At the fork in the Nansemond River, guarding the river from ascension to Suffolk, sat a Confederate fort. A branch flows in from the west, where the main channel continues north, broadens out, and empties into the James River near Hampton Roads. The fort was known by many names. Some called it the "West Branch Battery," and others called it the "Old Fort." When the 8th Connecticut painted the battle honor on their flag, they called it "Hill's Point Battery."

The old fort was originally constructed during the War of 1812 to block vessels from reaching Suffolk by the Nansemond.[21] It was an earthen fort with a 400-foot front and a 225-foot width. During the fighting around Suffolk, the old fort was seized by the Confederates, and prepared for garrison and guns. They reinforced the fort quickly, and placed guns there on the night of April 13. It was now named "Fort Huger" by the Confederates to honor the man responsible for its rehabilitation during the siege. "Captain Robert M. Stribling's Fauquier (Virginia) Battery, with its two 24-pounder howitzers and three 12-pounder Napoleans would occupy the old fort

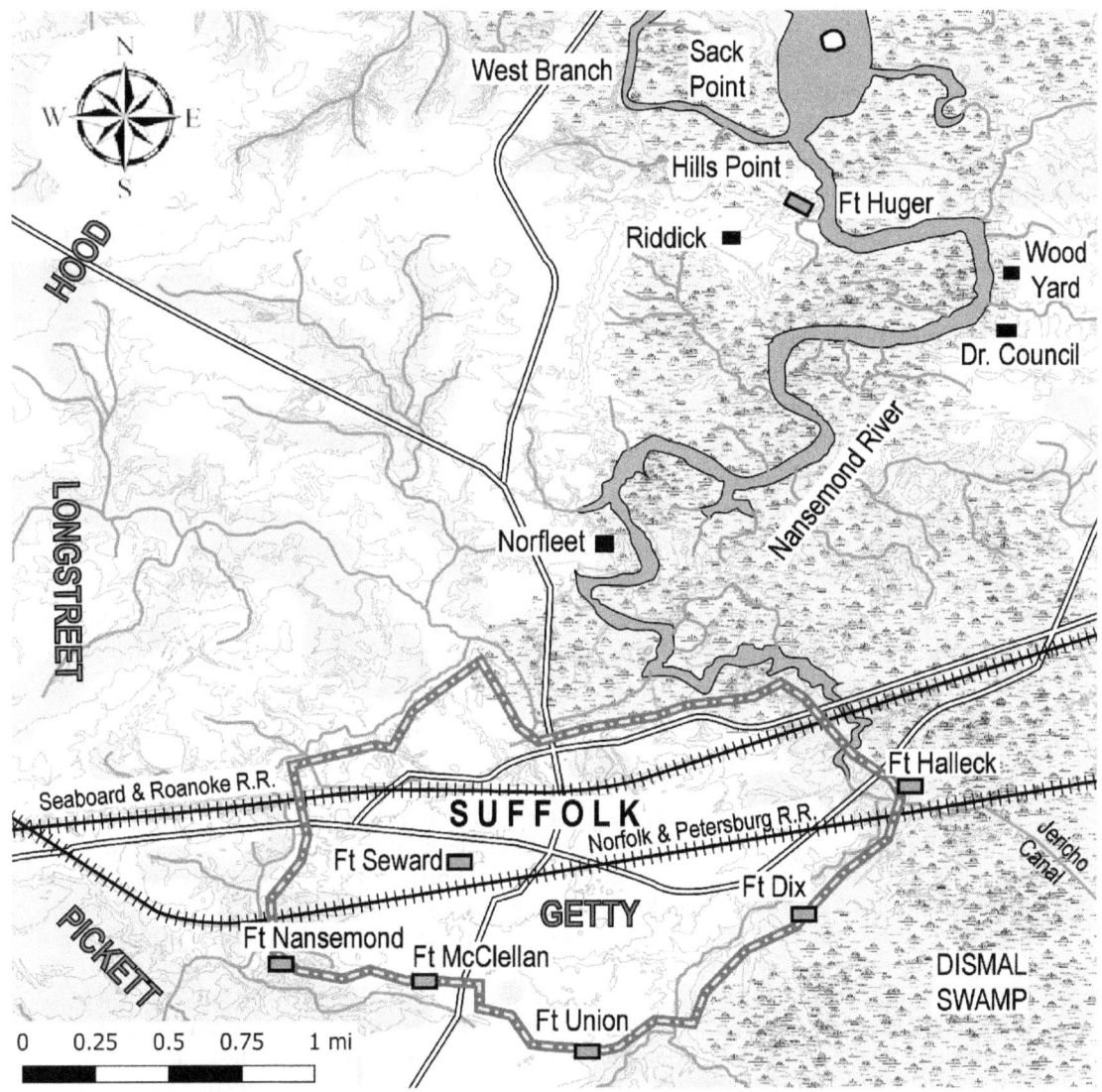

Map 12. Vicinity of Fort Huger and Suffolk, Virginia, April 1863.

after it was modified for field guns."[22] Stribling's battery consisted of 59 men. Infantry support was provided by about 150 men from Companies A and B of the 44th Alabama. They were commanded by Captain David L. Bozeman of Company A.[23]

The Union gunboats thus were now blocked from sailing up the Nansemond to Suffolk. There were, however, Union gunboats already above the fort and at Suffolk. On the night of Saturday, April 18, the 8th Connecticut and the 89th New York regiments received orders to fall in at midnight. At midnight the two units were told they would cross the river to storm the lower fort in the dark. They marched, boarded a gunboat, shoved off, but then were recalled. Lieutenant Roswell Lamson, the Navy creator of the plan, with Getty's support, determined the troops were too tardy to mount the attack before broad daylight.[24]

On Sunday morning, April 19, things were quiet. The four right wing companies of the Eighth (Companies G, B, H, and C) were ordered out on picket. About 4 o'clock, the six remaining companies of the Eighth, about 140 men under Colonel John E. Ward, and five companies of the 89th New York, about 150 men under Lieutenant Colonel Theophilus L. England, were ordered under arms.[25] They immediately marched to the gunboat *Stepping Stones*, where they were screened by a large pile of wood on shore while boarding. General Getty went aboard with them. The boat was curtained in canvas stretched around the deck. The men were ordered to keep still and quiet, as the boat started down the river. Sergeant Seth Plumb wrote that Colonel Ward gave the orders as follows. Company K with their Sharps rifles were to go first, and take a stand on the bank to cover any retreat. Company E was then to charge the rear of the fort, followed by Companies F, D, I, and A in that order. Then the 89th New York was to follow, with three companies to help get the marine howitzers into place.[26]

The gunboat *Stepping Stones* descended the stream silently, and approached the landing behind the fort, which was obscured by a small bluff there. The boat headed in, but it stopped in deep water. When the planks were thrown out, they floated away. Lieutenant Lamson maneuvered the stern back towards the banks. Colonel Ward ordered, "Every man for himself!" and they all jumped in, some up to their necks. They rushed the fort, "yelling like daemons."[27]

Sergeant Seth Plumb described the furious attack and the chaos at the fort in a letter home.

> The Fort was not 50 rods from where we landed and it was instantly surrounded by a dripping, yelling, shouting, wheezing, headless rabble. They fired grapeshot and bullets among us, but very few took effect, an instant more, and that portion of the crowd where I was, which was a little to the left of the rear of the Fort, made a rush for the parapet with fixed bayonets. Our bayonets were at the breasts of the nearest men in the Fort, and were all shouting surrender when up came a white handkerchief on a short pole, but just an instant after one of the guns at the other end of the Fort let fly a charge of grape at us, then the boys hollered "shoot them" "kill them" and charged there bayonets into their very throats, but the rebels begged for life, and strange to say not one of them was pricked with a bayonet.... The honor belongs equally to the 8th and 89th, there were not 200 men that charged on the Fort in all, and not more than 25 were on it when it gave in.[28]

The *Connecticut War Record* praised both units involved in the surprise attack. "Much as I love to praise Connecticut boys, I can say that they were only side by side with the brave boys of the 89th New York. Moved by one purpose along one path, they dashed into the works together, and the two old standards, torn and pierced by bullets in many battles, were planted on the breastworks at one moment, in triumph."[29]

Lieutenant Lamson noted in his report that the captured guns were originally Union guns the Confederates had captured earlier in Harper's Ferry and western Virginia.[30] General Getty's official report summarized the affair: "The capture of 5 guns, 7 officers, and 130 men, the liberation of the five gunboats above, and the occupation of a point of vital importance to the enemy and an admirable point of operations for us were the results of one of the most brilliant achievements of the war. Our loss was 4 killed and 10 wounded."[31]

Chapter 6. Suffolk, Portsmouth, Deep Creek, Home

The prisoners were escorted onto the *Stepping Stones* and deposited at the Wood Yard landing. The rest of the 8th Connecticut and 89th New York set to work hauling off captured guns and ammunition. They were reinforced during the night by the remaining four companies of the Eighth, two of the 9th Vermont, and a portion of the 10th New Hampshire. They also threw up banks around the guns and dug rifle pits. The picket was set out about 40 rods (220 yards). Sergeant William Huntington was on duty after the attack. "I had a pretty tough time the night we stormed Ft. Huger. Had eaten nothing since morning + they would not let us take our Haversacks, Canteens, or Blankets. I stood on my feet + watched for the approach of the Enemy all night + my teeth went so, that if anyone had come near me they would think they were near some kind of Mill Gear."[32]

Around 3 a.m. on the next morning, Monday, April 20, bullets started flying, and the pickets came rushing in, some were wounded. Confederate Captain Leigh R. Terrill, the assistant adjutant general to General Evander M. Law, was advancing to retake the fort with two companies of the 48th Alabama. Colonel John K. Connally and his 55th North Carolinians met them on the Riddick property and joined the skirmishing forward, but neither would attack the enemy of unknown strength in the dark.[33]

With the help of the gunboats lying near, the Union line was re-established. The 117th New York Regiment was added for reinforcements. The next morning, the Confederates could be seen advancing, but the attack was not made. About noon, the 8th Connecticut and 89th New York boarded the boat and returned to their camps after more than twenty-four hours of action.

Afterwards, Captain Charles Coit, who was part of the reinforcements from the Eighth, complained that the newspapers were giving all the credit for the victory to the New York regiment:

> The fort that we surprised + captured a week ago today was evacuated the next day by Genl Peck's order + nothing hinders the enemy from planting other guns on the same point + annoying the gunboats as much as ever. I see the papers as usual give all the credit of taking the battery to the [89th] New York Regt. The battery was taken by both Regts + I have not yet seen a man who ventured to say which flag was in first. All the officers of both Regts were ordered to gather such men as they could of either Regt + not wait to form but rush on + the battery was taken by a rush from each Regt. Col. Ward commanded under Genl Getty.[34]

The Eighth's losses in this "brilliant little affair" were one killed in Company D, four wounded (one each in Companies B, C, H, and I), and one wounded twice in Company E.[35] The 89th New York losses were about the same. The Confederates had none killed or wounded.[36]

Sergeant William Huntington said he was grieving most of all, since the soldier from the Eighth who was killed had been his tentmate.

> Before this reaches you, you will probably get the news of the Gallant work of the Bloody Eighth + the 89th N York Volunteers in Charging on to a Rebel Battery It was a dangerous + exciting piece of work, but it was very quickly done. And it is myself that feels the effect of it more than anyone else in the Regt perhaps, for it has forever taken from me my tent-mate. It is very sad + I can hardly keep the tears back as I write, didn't think much about it at the time when they came + told me [Frank] Jerome was wounded but when I had got back across the

River + had time to think + consider the tears would flow in spite of me very abundantly. His body was embalmed + is going to be sent home. he was the only killed in the Regt."[37]

Sergeant Seth Plumb said making the attack with a surgeon might have prevented the death of Frank Jerome. "Through some blunder no Doctor went with us, the man that was killed from the 8th bled to death for the want of someone to stop it. His wound was not dangerous otherwise."[38]

Sergeant William Huntington also included a unique souvenir of the war in his letter home. "Am going to send a piece of our old Flag that got disengaged during the storming of Ft. Huger. It is not very good looking but is very precious must keep it safe."[39]

Francis Jerome, killed at Fort Huger (courtesy Tad Sattler Private Collection).

The official report from Colonel Ward gave stark testimony to the courage of the fighters at Fort Huger. Ward recounted the orders from General Getty to take men from the 8th Connecticut and the 89th New York, board the *Stepping Stones*, descend quietly to Hill's Point, and then rush the rear of the fort. Ward told of their quick success, and capturing the prize of five guns and 130 prisoners, including seven officers. He described the deployment of skirmishers and the positioning of the captured guns and Navy howitzers to defend the fort from counterattack from the land side. That attack was repulsed the next morning. At the end of his report, Ward listed the losses in the Eighth—one killed, four wounded, and several injuries.[40]

As Croffut and Morris wrote later in *The Military and Civil History Connecticut During the War of 1861–65*, "The coolness and fearlessness of Col. Ward won for him the admiration and abiding confidence of the veterans of his regiment."[41]

The Siege Continues

The Eighth settled once again into continued siege operations with fatigue duty on the works and rotating picket duty. Captain Charles Coit described the fatigue duty of making gabions (wicker baskets filled with earth and stones) and fascines (bundles of sticks bound together) as part of the hardening of their fortifications. It was not the kind of work that the Eighth wanted to be known for. Coit was pleased, though, that they had improved their situation by finally acquiring new tents. "After lying out, with only such shelter as we could find from day to day + in all kind of weather, for almost two weeks we have obtained a lot of A tents + have established a temporary camp near the portion of the River that we are to defend. I have a tent to myself and am quite comfortable."[42]

Skirmish on Edenton Road

On Friday, April 24, a reconnaissance in force was conducted to the south of Suffolk along the Edenton Road. The 15th and 16th Connecticut were in the advance. (A reconnaissance in force uses significant force to elicit a strong reaction by the enemy that more accurately reveals the enemy's own strength, deployment, and preparedness.) The Eighth did not go, but it moved from the north side of Suffolk to replace those two regiments in the fortifications on the south side of the village.

About four or five miles outside of Suffolk, the enemy was found strongly entrenched. The Union troops engaged them, and caused the enemy to panic and run. The 15th Connecticut and 16th Connecticut suffered a number of casualties. When the skirmish was over, they all returned to their camps. Captain Coit described the engagement this way.

> My letter of Friday closed as we were marching off with one day's rations. We marched two or three miles to Fort Dix, which commands the Edentown road + the 8th Connt, 19th Wisc + 9th Vermont all under command of Col. Ward remained as reserve, manning the fort + breastworks while Genl Corcoran + 6 or 8,000 troops proceeded out on a reconnaissance. They marched out bravely until they found a rebel battery with a few hundred men in support + then they [Union] hastily retreated. Very brilliant affair, nothing under heavens accomplished + so it is with everything here.[43]

Changes to the command structure of the Eighth were made with some officers receiving well-deserved promotions. Major John E. Ward was promoted to colonel on March 9, and Captain Martin B. Smith was promoted to lieutenant colonel on May 1.[44]

The Eighth was assigned to picket duty on May 1, on the east side of Suffolk in the Great Dismal Swamp. They were located at the point where the Norfolk and Petersburg Railroad crossed the Jericho Canal. Their goal was to keep the railroad running regularly from Portsmouth to Suffolk with supplies from Fortress Monroe, and to prevent Confederate guerrillas from destroying the tracks and bridges.

On May 2, the Eighth did fatigue work to improve defenses along the rail lines once again. Charles Coit wrote that their work wasn't very interesting:

> I think I am sorry but nothing special has taken place. Part of the time has been very stormy and our chief occupation has been building corduroy roads + gabions by day + working on the forts at night. The work goes on rain or shine. Some queer remarks are made at Genl Peck's expense—one I must write. I heard it this morning. One of the men said he hoped Genl

Peck would be killed for if he (Genl P.) went to hell before he did, he (Genl P) would have it so strongly fortified that he was sure he could not get in. I could not help writing that.[45]

On May 5, Coit wrote:

> To day we have had a heavy force across the river + the firing has been incessant. Genl Harland with the 11th, 15th, + 16th Regts has crossed + been heavily engaged with what results I have not learned. The Rebels has certainly been driven quite a distance + a number of Connt men have been wounded—this is all we yet know. We had orders from Genl H. to join him but Genl Getty countermanded. So for once we lie in Camp while the remainder of our division are out + engaged. I do not believe in this Sunday fighting.... It was mainly commanded by Getty, actually by Harland. I wish I felt at liberty to write what he told me, but perhaps it is sufficient to say that it resulted as everything has resulted in nothing gained. Genl Getty was at Genl Peck's Hd. Qts. in the city instead of being on the field. Our lofs is from 75 to 100.[46]

With the Eighth now positioned on the east side of Suffolk, Sergeant Seth Plumb said things were quiet in the Suffolk area. "The war is over at Suffolk and along the Nansemond for the present, as you probably are aware. The skirmish fighting on Sunday (May 3rd) resulted in the hasty retreat of the rebels on that night to their land of safety beyond the Blackwater."[47]

The Siege of Suffolk Ends

With the stubborn Union foothold in the Suffolk area, the Confederates ended the Siege of Suffolk on May 4. After some stiff skirmishes, Longstreet withdrew from the area to the west, safely beyond the Blackwater River. As history records, the coming summer campaign brought the Confederate invasion to the north, where General Longstreet's corps figured prominently. Meanwhile, the Eighth and the rest of the Union forces in the Virginia Tidewater area continued to press the Confederates, divert their attention, and occupy their territory.

Duty settled into a routine in the vicinity of Suffolk. The soldiers focused once again on improving the forts and fortifications, much to their disappointment. As one officer of the Eighth wrote,

> For about two weeks we were kept busy at making gabions [barrel-shaped basket—open at both ends, to hold the earth in the construction of forts] and building a corduroy road. Our works, unlike those attributed to good men, will not probably live after us. As we failed to feel the importance of building the road, and did not think that a reputation for great mechanical skill would be for our advantage while in the field, we took care not to earn such a reputation. The boys styled themselves, after the manner of sensational authors, "Peck's Avengers; or, the Basket-Makers of the Nansemond."[48]

At about this time, some of the soldiers decided to pull a prank to make light of their manual labors. "One morning a flag staff appeared in camp with a well-made gabion suspended from the peak."[49] No one admitted doing it, and the staff officers were upset. But it seemed like a good-natured prank to "celebrate" their achievements in fortification.

Overall, the Eighth was reported to be in good health, with about 350 men present for duty. That was a big improvement from the time of Fredericksburg, when the

Chapter 6. Suffolk, Portsmouth, Deep Creek, Home

ranks were reduced to fewer than 200 effectives present.[50] But keep in mind the regiment had left Connecticut in 1861 with about 1,000 men.

The boys of the Eighth were not themselves facing enemy threats, but they knew they served as a continued distraction to the Confederate efforts as General Hooker's Army of the Potomac was operating across the Rappahannock. The war news was eagerly followed by every soldier in the Army. "[L]ast night it is reported a telegraphic dispatch was received by Gen Peck stating that Hooker had been reinforced and that he was again fighting with the rebels on the south side of river.... We have been very anxious about Hooker, with great hopes of his success, and we do not like to believe he has been defeated."[51]

On May 10, Captain Charles Coit told his family that things were returning to normal.

> Sunday 6 ½ p.m. Am again comfortably settled in my wall tent, it seems spacious enough after living for several weeks in the small one.[52]
>
> I was real comfortably fixed in Camp. The boys had made me a splendid great bower + I had my hammock swing under it + I thought I was about right, but after enjoying it one day, the Adj't came to me + gave me orders to march the next morning with my Co. to Fort Jericho to act as support.... Sam Foss is back fully reinstated. We laughed at him considerably. He returned one afternoon + was sent off on picket the next morning. He came down to my tent this morning about 5 AM + destroyed my morning nap.
>
> Dr. Storrs is back + acting as Brigade Surgeon. He has been on duty at Washington Hospt since about the date of the first battle of Fredericksburg. I am glad he is with us again for he is truly able + I like him. I gave my man Jim a pass to go to Norfolk + stay one day at his home + he has not returned yet has been gone nearly a week. I hope I have not lost him for he is a real good boy.[53]
>
> The boys have had a good deal of trouble since the "Siege" commenced as the Provost Guard have caught them where ever they could + set them at work in the Forts.[54]

Toward the end of May, the Eighth found itself on duty west of Suffolk, near Windsor, Virginia. They had marched twelve miles to a place called Deserted House, then proceeded to Windsor, on the Norfolk and Petersburg Railroad. There, Colonel Ward was serving as Provost Marshall, with some companies of the Eighth serving as Provost Guard. The rest of the Eighth had been assigned Special Duty, so they were riding the railroad back and forth to Suffolk serving as guards. A large Union force was also working in the area, tearing up track west of Windsor on the Norfolk and Petersburg Railroad and on the Weldon Railroad. The rails were then taken to Suffolk, and sold off at $65 per ton for the National coffers.

Sergeant Seth Plumb said Confederate guerrillas were operating in the region, and the Union troops were responding harshly.

> It is not safe for men to go out alone on account of the bushwhackers. One of our men was shot last Thursday on the road but a little way from here. In consequence of these things nearly all the houses have been burnt in this region, and in some instances the women and children left by the ruins with not a place to lay their heads. Their husbands and brothers are Guerrillas. You don't know how this portion of Virginia suffers it is almost a perfect waste. It makes me feel bad to see little ragged boys and girls starving as they are here.[55]

At this point, the Union forces, with the Eighth, relocated their base of operations from Suffolk towards Deep Creek, Virginia, in an effort to protect Portsmouth,

Norfolk, Suffolk, and all the waters in the vicinity. The move to Deep Creek minimized the number of troops required to hold the area compared to the numbers needed to hold the vicinity from around Suffolk.

The Eighth and the rest of the old Ninth Corps, Third Division were praised for their role at Suffolk in an order written to them by General Burnside. This surely cemented the good will feelings the soldiers retained for him.

> Hd. Qts. Dept of the Ohio
> Cincinnati, O. May 26, 1863
>
> Genl. Orders No. 75
>
> Although the Third Division is temporarily severed from its brethren, the 9th A.C. looks upon its acts as its own, + the Commanding General directs that his thanks for bravery + soldier like conduct he communicated to Genl. Getty + the Officers + soldiers under his command for their behavior in their brilliant action before Suffolk, Va., where they so well sustained the historic fame of the Ninth Army Corps.
>
> By command of Major Genl. Burnside[56]

In one of his letters, Sergeant Seth Plumb wrote about changes in command for Company E. "Our Capt [Martin B. Smith] is now Lieuten Colonel and [Second Lieutenant Frank W.] Spalding is going home I believe discharged, he is not with us now, and he has been very little since the 11th of Apr."[57]

At the end of May, some members of the Eighth began work again on the fortifications around Suffolk. Private Allen Dauchy posted from "Battery Ward" about the reputation of the Eighth, and how much they cherished their honored flags. Since Dauchy could not spell or write well, this entry is a transcription of what he wrote.

> The old Eighth has got a good name that is that they would not let their flag fall for rebels to grasp it up and carry away to Richmond, or to some other state house or capital. We had our flag given to the Regiment at Jamaica, L.I., and we have had the offer of a new flag if we would send them home but the old flag that we brought out with us is a better one than any new one that can be got for the Regiment although it is cut up and torn with shot and shell, so it is not much better than a lot of Red and White and Blue ribbons.[58]

Some of the Eighth were back in camp east of Suffolk and doing picket duty once more along the Jericho Canal, the Norfolk and Petersburg Railroad, and into the Great Dismal Swamp. Sergeant Plumb wrote home about conditions in the swamp:

> The mosquitoes are not much worse than they are in Fat Swamp as I can see, but wood ticks are the greatest pest in the insect line I know of. You can hardly go into the woods without getting covered with them. They look like a bed bug. They go to work in a very quiet way, and get into the flesh as far as they can so that it is hard to pull them without leaving their heads. I much rather have half a dozen mosquito bites than one of these.[59]

Plumb praised the officers of the Eighth for the way they treated the men, and he said everyone was eager to know how the war was progressing on the major fronts.

> Col Appelman could never halt the regiment on a march, without getting them onto a rod or so of ground and putting a guard around them, but Ward is no such man, his mode of punishing is to tie the offenders up to a tree and let the innocent alone. There are many good things to be said of Col Ward if he does have some faults. The 8th regiment has more men for duty than either the 11th or 16th and the men appear to be in better spirits. I think this is owing in part to our officers treating the men more as if they were men. Our Col has never starved us

on a march as the 16th has been. I think there are some officers that will get roughly handled when they get home.

General Grant has won our admiration by his valor and we confidently except soon to here that Vicksburg is ours. I cannot tell you how greatly interested we soldiers all are in the success of our arms anywhere. It seems that portion of our old 9th Corps in Ky is to have warm work soon. I can see no prospect of our leaving here at present.[60]

Seth Plumb criticized the Peace Democrats for their active campaigning back in Connecticut, despite having lost the gubernatorial election in the spring: "It is not a little thing to stand the privation of a soldier's life, much less to stand bravely on the battlefield, and it is hard for those who have made these sacrifices, and lost their friends to be told that they are in the wrong."[61]

The daily orders became more routine as described at the time by Captain Charles Coit:

> I was Officer of the Day in Camp day before yesterday + today am in command of the Pickets. The Picket lines are quite extended—some five or six miles—but as there are Lieuts. in command of different portions of the lines it is not necessary for me to visit the whole line. My post is with the reserve, posted at a house only about a quarter of a mile from Camp. I have a large front room for my quarters for the twenty-four hours that I am on duty. There are fine large shade trees in front + altogether this duty is quite as pleasant as duty in Camp.[62]

Sergeant Jay Nettleton sent a long letter home on June 20 in which he painted a very detailed picture of the picket posts on the railroad through the swamp.

> The "picket post" is a few rods outside of the twenty-mile post from Norfolk and nearly three miles from Suffolk on the Norfolk & Weldon or "seaboard road" thus you have the location. A few railroad ties and some brush constitute the picket "shanty" and your most obedient sits on a "tie" that supports the road just a few feet one side.... We are in the "Dismal Swamp" so notorious through America, that is, on one extremity. A space about 6 rods wide has been cut away for the railroad and ditches on each side, quite large ones. And the road is as straight as a line so that in the night apparent ball of fire on the engine can be seen all of half an hour before it reaches us. Outside of the track the open space is grown up with bushes & weeds, blueberries, briers, elders, and the pokeweed and some sumac. Blackberries are half grown and look nice; elder bushes are in blossom. Outside of the ditches and open space the mass of verdure is like one great dense body of green. The eye cannot think of penetrating it even ten feet, much less the body only as a way is opened.
>
> The mass of vines exceeds what I saw in Kentucky on the Louisville Railroad. This mass begins on the ground with a thick growth of cane (fish pole material) with vines of various sort, and smaller trees. This cane grows 10 or 12 feet high, then the vines take to the trees and cover the bodies more or less forty feet high. Not least among the venerable trees is the "magnolia" and is in full bloom at this time. Don't know that I ever saw a forest that appeared as venerable as this. Trees that run up 60 or 80 feet without a limb and their tops are stub lengths towering up 20 or 30 more. Then this swamp is not Union inhabited. If not peopled by the home genus it is by the reptiles & felines. Bears are seen occasionally. They are black, used to be quite troublesome before the firing was so frequent about here.

Sergeant Nettleton described the importance of the canal, which was used to bring lumber out of the swamp.

> There is a canal that connects with the Nansemond or Jericho Creek, and the lake inside of the swamp (Drummond Lake) some ten miles. I have changed my base within a short time and am now a half a mile nearer camp waiting for the other picket to come in. and then the away for camp, and next the cars will trundle us down to Portsmouth.

> This canal was used before the war to bring shingle & lumber out of the Swamp the water is not to exceed three feet deep. In through the swamp it is said that the canal was bailed out instead of being shoveled. The boats are long, flat & narrow; are propelled by negroes &c, men hired. The shingles are made of cypress and juniper wood, are carried north to be dressed, are called worth $25.00 a thousand and will last a century. This business is carried on by the "Dismal Swamp Company" formed in George Washington's time. The present owners are heirs of the original proprietors.[63]

As both armies reduced their troop strength in the Tidewater area, the Federal forces decided to change the base for the Union occupation to Portsmouth. It was closer to Fortress Monroe, it was easier to reach, and it took fewer troops to sustain.

> About the middle of June, Gen. Getty evacuated Suffolk, and fell back north-eastward to Portsmouth, across the Elizabeth River from Norfolk, and almost within sight of Fortress Monroe, rising over the broad James River, only twelve miles distant. Here they occupied some incomplete fortifications, and worked to finish them. The Eighth lost a total of two men killed and four wounded during the siege of Suffolk.[64]

On June 21, Sergeant Seth Plumb said the evacuation was almost complete in the vicinity of Suffolk. "There are very few troops at Suffolk now and I think that there will be none there by the end of the week. I think that Suffolk should be evacuated as it is about to be, as it will take but a few troops to hold Norfolk and Portsmouth at this point, and Suffolk is not worth as much as a dime."[65]

And on June 21, Captain Charles Coit described the new stand of colors that the Eighth had received, and the pride that the regiment felt for what they represented in terms of achievements in battle. "By the way we have within a day or two recd a splendid new set of colors from the State + sent our old ones back to Hartford. If you go to H. be sure to see them—you can't know how much we love them—may our new ones be kept as free from all suspicions of dishonor as those."[66]

The Blackberry Raid

On Monday, June 22, General Getty's division, including the Eighth, started on a reconnaissance in force. They left Portsmouth on the transport *Utica*, and proceeded to Yorktown, where they arrived about noon. They made camp in their shelter tents a mile outside of the village. Croffut and Morris later explained what was happening in *The Military and Civil History Connecticut During the War of 1861–65*,

> During the last week of June, 1863, while the armies of Hooker and Lee were moving towards Gettysburg, Gen. John A. Dix [commanding Seventh Corps], conceived the idea of moving on Richmond, up the peninsula; hoping to draw off Confederate troops from the Army of Northern Virginia. Gen. Getty's division was immediately started from Getty's Station on transports, and moved to Yorktown. Here the troops remained two days, the few rebels on the peninsula giving them plenty of room.[67]

Captain Charles Coit wrote about the baggage trains that the troops used: "There are but two wagons assigned to each Regt—one of which is for Officer's blankets + shelter tents + cooking utensils—we have so few officers present that we are also able to carry a change of clothing. I carry all that I have with me in a knapsack + think I am very fortunate at that. The men carry nothing but blankets + shelters."[68]

Chapter 6. Suffolk, Portsmouth, Deep Creek, Home

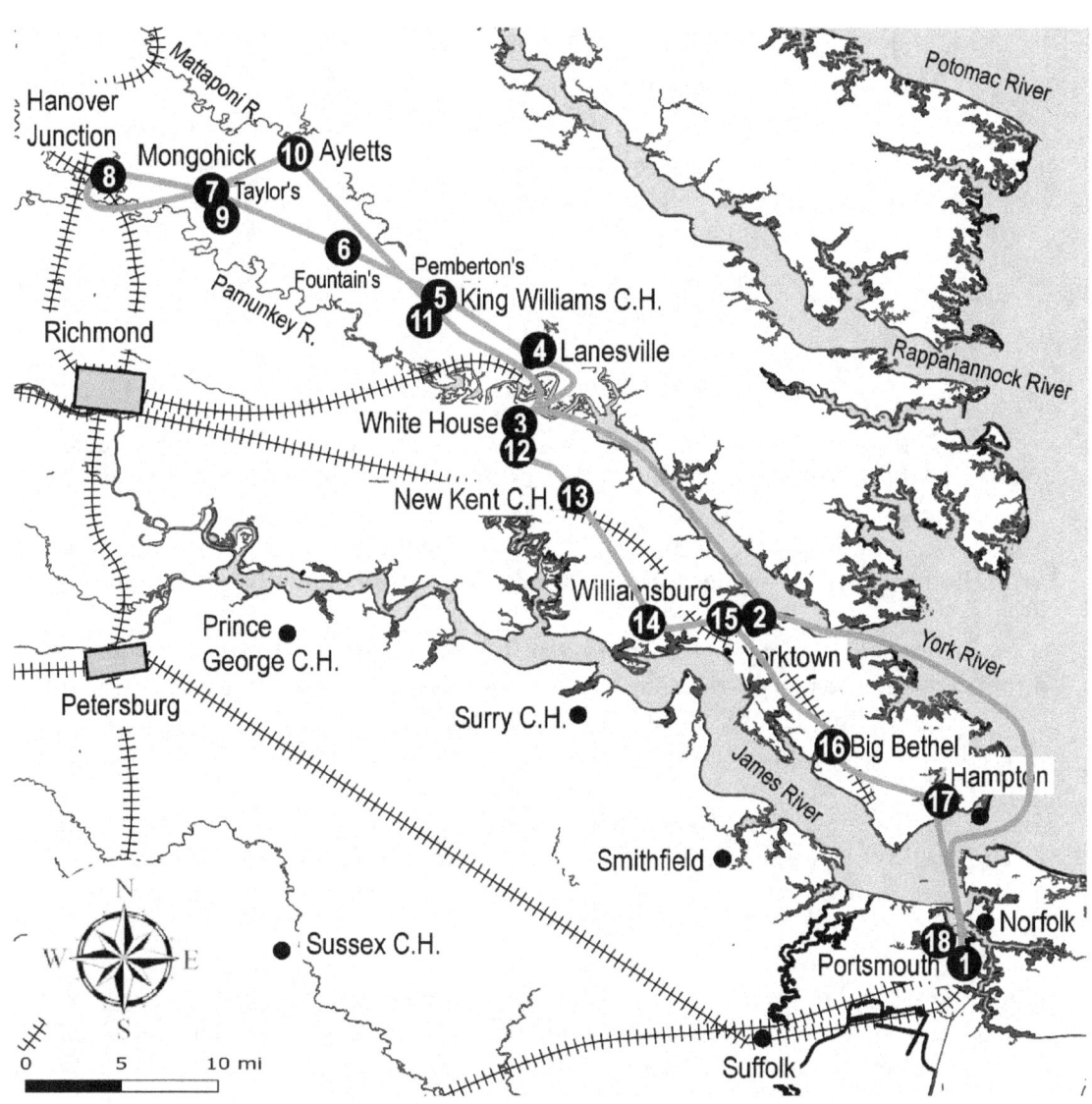

Map 13. Route of March on "The Blackberry Raid," July 1863.

June 22–July 14, 1863, 153 miles in 13 days

1.	June 21	Assembled at Portsmouth	Train
2.	June 22	Sailed to Yorktown	Boat
3.	June 26	Sailed to White House	Boat
4.	July 1	Crossed Pamunkey, Marched through Lanesville	5 miles
5.	July 1	Marched to King Williams C.H. to Pemberton's	6 miles
6.	July 2	Marched to Dr. Fountain's	8 miles
7.	July 3	Marched through Mongohick to Geo. Taylor's	15 miles
8.	July 4	8CV at Taylor's, Division to Hanover Junction	14 miles
9.	July 5	Division returned to Taylor's	16 miles

10.	July 5	Marched to Ayletts near Mattaponi River	10 miles
11.	July 6	Marched to King William's C.H.	11 miles
12.	July 7	Marched to White House	12 miles
13.	July 8	Marched to New Kent C.H.	5 miles
14.	July 9	Marched to Williamsburg	23 miles
15.	July 11	Marched to Yorktown	12 miles
16.	July 12	Marched to Big Bethel	10 miles
17.	July 13	Marched to Hampton	7 miles
18.	July 14	Sailed to Portsmouth	Boat

On Friday, June 26, troops led by General Keyes joined with troops led by General Dix at Yorktown. The two forces were consolidated, and they moved to a place called White House Landing. It is a little landing village on the railroad to Richmond, where it crosses the Pamunkey River, about twenty-one miles from Richmond. The burned ruins of the White House plantation mansion were there.

The mansion's history was significant. It was the home that Martha D. Custis inherited, and the place where she was married to George Washington on January 6, 1759.[69] The White House stayed in the Custis family for generations. General Robert E. Lee joined the family when he married Mary Anna Custis in 1831. During the 1862 Peninsula Campaign, the plantation was owned by Robert E. Lee's son, William H.F. "Rooney" Lee. His mother took refuge there from the fighting around Richmond. When General McClellan retreated from the peninsula, he ordered the plantation burned on June 27, 1862. Mrs. Lee fled and spent the rest of the war in Richmond.[70]

On Wednesday, July 1, Getty's division, including five brigades, crossed the Pamunkey River to the east via the railroad bridge and headed north for Hanover Junction. They marched eleven miles the first day and halted a little beyond King William's Court House. On Thursday, July 2, they marched eight miles more. On Friday, July 3, they marched again, another fifteen miles, with the Eighth in the advance as skirmishers. The sun was very hot, and a high number of men fell out with sun stroke. As Croffut and Morris wrote in their history,

> On July 3, the Connecticut brigade had the advance, the Eighth out as skirmishers. It was fiercely hot, and many fell sun-struck. Surgeon Sabin Stocking of the Eighth, and the chaplain, impressed from the plantations along the march all the horses, mules, carriages, and carts they could discover to transport the loads of sick and fainting men. It was a motley collection of carts and gigs, of colts, toothless nags, and broken-down mules, uniform only in leanness and worthlessness; but they served the purpose to the extent of their feeble ability, and were turned loose at the journey's end.[71]

That night, they camped at the plantation of a man named George Taylor, which was four or five miles from Hanover Court House, near the Pamunkey River. General Harland made the house his headquarters, and the Eighth was assigned

Chapter 6. Suffolk, Portsmouth, Deep Creek, Home

Headquarters Guard. During the night, the rest of the division came up. The Eighth's brigade stayed at Taylor's all day on the Fourth of July, while the rest of the forces went on towards Hanover Junction.

Sergeant Seth Plumb described the plantation's owner, who, remarkably, was an acquaintance.

> Now about George Taylor, where I spent the 4th. He has been in Litchfield [Connecticut] often in the summer, he had a seat in church behind us. Taylor is very wealthy and owns a number of plantations, there was 200 acres of wheat all stacked in a field next to his house, and any quantity of corn. This was raised by the wenches. Our men were hungry and they helped themselves to everything that was not guarded, chickens, sheep, and everything else soon were scarce. Taylor took it all like a hero. he is an open secessionist, and preached it without stint to us all. He made a 4th speech to us, and compared his niggers to those he saw in Litchfield.... By the way, Taylor is an old tyrant and his niggers are abused, they all ran away with us, but 2 white ones.[72]

Sergeant Jay Nettleton described Taylor's plantation and how the troops enjoyed foraging in the Confederate breadbasket.

> This Taylor's farm is a paradise. He has boarded on Litchfield Hill (Conn) through summer months in years past. He is a King and his estate a kingdom, and has nearly all the paraphernalia of self-sustaining, except clothing. He counts his plantations not many less than ten and his acres by the thousands, and slaves in all some 900. His home farm has on it about 200 acres of wheat in stacks and being harvested, and his corn field is about the same. His farm implements are northern invention of course, has a reaper &c, a grist mill &c &c. His house is of ancient dimensions and his rooms are profusely furnished with costly furniture and paintings.[73]

On Saturday, July 4, the Union forces, excepting the Eighth's brigade, marched for the Hanover Junction objective. On Sunday, July 5, they returned to Taylor's. Seth Plumb wrote about the results of all that effort.

> Sunday morning the 5th we marched up onto a high hill and got into position with artillery and waited for our troops to return, they soon came in. It seemed that they had been to the Junction and tore up many miles of track on both roads, but they did not destroy the bridge acrost the South Anna, as the rebels had fortified their position there and collected a large force. The firing that we heard was all done by the rebels I believe. Two men were killed on our side and a few wounded. If our object in going to the railroad was to destroy the bridge, we were not successful, but I think the whole move here was for the purpose of keeping the enemy from sending help to Lee [at Gettysburg] by scaring Richmond.[74]

The entire force started on their return to Portsmouth, marching all night and most of the next day. Captain Charles Coit described the blistering heat that slowed their progress.

> We have had the most severe marching on this tramp, that we have ever seen—we have marched farther day by day at other times but never during such excessive heat. Several received such severe sun stroke as to cause death immediately + others will not recover. A few of our troops were taken prisoners—they were straggling in rear of the column + picked up by rebel cavalry or bush whackers. We hear that Genl Meade has thus far been successful, has captured twenty thousand prisoners + has Lee in a tight place. The 8th brings back every man from our expedition. A few were sun struck—none fatally.[75]

Our marching since the 1st inst has been the most severe we have ever known because of the extreme heat—we have made no very rapid or very long march—the longest was twenty-six miles in eighteen hours. About half the troops are barefooted + a good proportion of the Officers. I marched barefooted all day before yesterday about eighteen miles—I could not get on my boots they had been so thoroughly soaked the day before.⁷⁶

Seth Plumb detailed the challenge of the return march from the reconnaissance.

Sunday night about 5 o'clock we set out on our return, marched 18 miles that night stopped for two or three hours at the village of Ayletts in the morning, then went on again.... I should have said that our route back was not the way we came, most of the way, but that we went near the Mattapony river. The night of the 6th we stayed near King William's C.H., and the nesct day we marched in at the White House.....

After resting overnight, the troops, most of them, returned for Yorktown, though a part of them took the transports. Our first day's march from the White House was through swamps and the worst mud I was ever in. It rained in torrents a portion of the day. We passed New Kent C.H. about noon. The C.H. and jail were greatly damaged by McClellan's men last year.... The next day we marched through Williamsburg and reached Yorktown, having marched every day for the last 9 days.....

We stayed at Yorktown over Saturday.... We left a great many men that had sore feet at Yorktown and they come from there here in the transports. There were a great many men bare footed in our regiment through the last of the march.... Sunday, we marched from Yorktown to Big Bethel, stopped at night on the battle field. Monday marched to the ruins of Hampton which was once quite a place. Yesterday we took the transports there, landed at Portsmouth, and marched to our camp here.⁷⁷

The operation totaled nine days of steady marching, resulting in nothing much but a way to divert the Confederates and distract them from the operations of the Gettysburg campaign. Back in Portsmouth, at the 8th Connecticut's camp, Seth Plumb wrote about possible promotions as the unit was being rebuilt. "There will be a good many promotions when the regiment is filled, but you must not be disappointed if your Litchfield friends are slighted. Col Ward will not promote plain farmers as long as there any serfs left in the regiment, that is certain. Merit is a thing that he seems to care very little about." Plumb joked that the diversionary operation had been given a nickname. "Our Rade on the Peninsula, and up to Hanover Junction is the subject of considerable joking among the boys, they all call it the 'Blackberry Rade.'"⁷⁸

In what is perhaps a more eloquent description of the adventure, John Morris, one of the authors of the *Connecticut War Record*, and the chaplain of the Eighth, recounted the events almost romantically, especially the blackberries.

Early fruits were in their prime, and the troops lived voluptuously. The soldiers from the hard hills of New England had never before seen such a wealth of berries, especially of running blackberries, as now bestrewed the route of march. A man could sit upon the ground, and, without changing his position, pick as many as he could eat. An officer recalling this time says, "I picked a water-pail three-quarters full from the vines within my tent." These promoted the health of officers and men, previously inclined to dysentery; and the column returned rapidly and in good spirits, five hundred thoughtless, careless, jolly contrabands swarming upon the flanks and rear.⁷⁹

Sergeant Jay Nettleton, too, recalled the wealth of blackberries along their march. "We have enjoyed a few dishes of blackberries—the country abounds with them. One night the Regt. Broke ranks and like a parcel of turkeys after grasshoppers we started for a rail fence and skirmished through the blackberries, both hands at work but with the eyes on the fence to see that that didn't all run off."[80]

Sergeant Plumb admitted that he had eaten too many blackberries, but now he was enjoying other fruits and vegetables.

> These southern blackberries made my mouth sore so that I have hardly touched one since the 5th of July. … You speak about my feasting on Mr. Taylor's chickens and mutton, I believe I did eat one meal of mutton that was given to me by one of the Co, I did not ask though what it was.… I am glad to say that plundering is not popular in our Co. We are having all the fine fruit and vegetables we can eat now days. It is brought to our camp for sale, peaches, figs, apples, cucumbers, tomatoes, potatoes, water melons &c &c.[81]

The return through White House, Williamsburg, and Yorktown, to Hampton, was made on foot, through a region too poor for plunder; and the division crossed the Roads next day, and again quietly encamped for rest and drill, cheering over the news from Gettysburg and Vicksburg, and resolutely subduing their feelings of pride as they rehearsed the achievements of "The Blackberry Raid."[82]

Continued Occupation

Sergeant William Huntington told of his reaction to a restful duty assignment after the Raid. "We are doing Provost Duty in Portsmouth, and live in fine style. The men have good barracks and the officers board at the Hotel or elsewhere. About a dozen of us are at the Pennsylvania Hotel just opened, where we have board and lodging for $7.00 per week. That sounds pretty steep, and so it is. But it seems to be about as well as we can do all things considered. We have good living and all the conveniences."[83]

The drawdown of troops in the Suffolk area continued, since they were needed in active operations elsewhere. Seth Plumb described the changes. "There has been quite a change in affairs in this department. Michael Corcoran and his Irish Legion have gone to help the Army of the Potomac. So has Gen Keyes and his troops, and it is said that Dix has left too, and that Foster is to take his place at the Fortress. Gen Getty is now in temporary command at Fortress Monroe and Gen Harland of everything this side of the James."[84]

Croffut and Morris were able to capture the tenor of the Eighth's condition and their duties at the time.

> The regiments were kept almost constantly busy, felling trees, digging trenches, throwing up breastworks, and doing picket duty. Their work on the fortifications reduced the fire of their patriotism, and diminished their soldierly spirit, but they sometimes did a review and dress parade with the accompaniment of a fine brigade band, when the weather was fair, which kept the military spark from extinguishing, and reminded the poor fellows, weary with chopping trees, rolling logs, and throwing shovelful after shovelful of dirt all day, that they belonged to the noble profession of arms. The men were required to be neat and clean in their persons and accouterments.[85]

When the Secretary of War issued General Order No. 262 on August 1, 1863, he dissolved the Seventh Corps, and transferred those forces to the Eighteenth Corps, under Major General John G. Foster.[86] The Eighth remained with the Third Division under General George Getty. The Connecticut troops were part of the Second

Brigade under General Edward Harland; the other regiments in his brigade were the same—the 11th, 15th, and 16th Connecticut.[87] The Eighth was still commanded by Colonel John Ward.

Picket and garrison around the Portsmouth area continued for the Eighth without relief that summer. Sergeant Seth Plumb described typical reconnaissance and fortification operations.

> Since I commenced this letter we have received "marching orders" light marching orders three days rations, to be ready to go to night, the rations are now cooking (salt pork) it is now 4 pm. I suppose that we are going out to reconnoiter to Suffolk, or there about, I do not know whether the whole of the brigade is to go or not. I have been expecting as much all day, for there was firing in that direction this morning.[88]
>
> When I closed my last letter home we were all packing up to march, well, just as we got all ready, rations in haversacks, blankets rolled, &c, the order was countermanded, which was nothing very strange to us for we are used to such things. I think some one got scart when they thought the rebels were in Suffolk.[89]
>
> The breast works that we build are 9 feet at the bottom and 5 on top, and 5 feet high. We first pile up bags to the proper height taking pains to have a good perpendicular face on the inside. We then go into the other side and bank up the earth till it reaches its required dimensions.[90]

The Eighth was in the process of building back up to regimental strength after the drafts provided more men to refill the ranks. There was a time that the Eighth feared that they would be reduced to a battalion and see reductions in staff. However, that didn't happen, and several recruiting details were detached and sent by the Eighth to Connecticut to rebuild their enrollment. Sergeant William Huntington wrote to his family back home: "Wonder how you come on in Conn with the draft. Presume a good many think it time to 'Express themselves.' There was three. Capts Coit, Ripley, + Goodrich with six enlisted men left Camp this morning for Conn to bring on recruits for this Regt."[91]

The doldrums finally turned a little lively one payday.

> The men of our regiment made bigger fools of themselves than usual this pay day. About 25 or 30 men from the 4 right Co. most of them, ran away to Portsmouth, got drunk, hired hacks with nigger drivers and had a great time generally. They came back the next day most of them, and were put into the guard tent, and punished by being made to ride the wooden horse, and work on the fort. (The wooden horse is a pole set up on two crotches, there is a span of them at our guard quarters) Friday I counted 11 riding at once.[92]

Near the end of August, the Eighth found itself in South Mills, North Carolina. It was at the southern end of the Dismal Swamp Canal. On August 17, the Eighth received orders to cook rations and be ready to march the next morning. They marched from Portsmouth about eleven miles, and bivouacked near Deep Creek, Virginia. The next day they marched along a road built through the swamp parallel to the canal about twenty miles. The men cheered as they passed a large stone on the road at the border between the states.[93] They arrived at South Mills a little before dark. It is thirteen miles north of Elizabeth City and thirty or so south from Suffolk.

Sergeant William Huntington was not thrilled with the arrangements:

Chapter 6. Suffolk, Portsmouth, Deep Creek, Home

I thought this Regt had been in as mean a place as could be found on the face of the Earth nearly but this beats the whole have got us now way down in the middle of Dismal Swamp away from everything altogether an isolated affair—are 32 miles from Portsmouth + 17 from Elizabeth City on the Dismal Swamp Canal, these are our nearest places of communication. We are not a great way from our first fighting ground (Roanoke Is.) Had a pretty tedious time getting here, had to March in Heavy Order and the last day had to go 20 miles. Had to Clear up a Pine Grove for a Camp Ground....

As far as I have seen among the Citizens a Union sentiment seems to prevail. The place is noted for Guerilla depredations + that is why we are here.[94] There has been a good many Citizens in Camp + I think some were acting as Spies as they were very curious to know how many men we have here + how near there was any troops to us. The boys will in such cases give very exaggerated accounts, will make them believe we have a 1000 men where can only muster about 200. They have all of them thus far treated the boys very well. The Col tells them if there is one hurt about here their Property will all be confiscated.[95]

Sergeant Albion Brooks wrote of their situation in South Mills: "We have been doing picket duty up and down the Canal towards Portsmouth and Elizabeth City. The greatest trouble is the North Carolina fly which bites outrageously, and which, when once they have commenced to pay attention to you, are very hard to get rid of."[96]

Captain Roger M. Ford recorded in his diary their relief from South Mills, and the return to Portsmouth for the Eighth.

September 1863

5th Saturday pleasant we are to return to Portsmouth, Va we are to be relieved by the 11th Penn. Cavalry they arrived here about 9 p.m. with 10 Rebel Prisoners

6th Sunday pleasant at 7 p.m. our Guards were relieved by the Cavalry we are to move very early in the morning

7th Monday pleasant we had reveille at 4 a.m. we are to go on Barges up the Canal we left South Mills N.C. at 10 a.m. and arrived at Deep Creek at dark we camp for the night

8th Tuesday pleasant 8 a.m. we started on again we arrived at our camping ground at 11 a.m. Capt. Ripley came here to night they have a Boat load of Substitutes for our Regt

9th Wednesday pleasant we sent a guard after the Subs this morning 9 a.m. the Subs are here they are a rugged set of fellows[97]

Back in Portsmouth, the new recruits, draftees, and substitutes all began arriving at the seat of war. Albion Brooks wrote of his assessment of their return to Portsmouth. "We left South Mills about a week ago. I should rather have stayed where we were. The only advantage here is that we receive the mail and papers daily."[98]

Chaplain John M. Morris wrote about the arrival of the recruits. He mentioned that they arrived on September 9. After that, the camp guard was expanded from just a dozen to sixty-four men, and passes were strictly enforced. Morris also mentioned the efforts of Dr. Stocking to oversee the health and welfare of the regiment in all aspects of cleanliness of person and camp.[99]

Sergeant Seth Plumb, returned from a furlough to see his brother at the U.S. Army Hospital in Washington, D.C., described their new additions:

I arrived here last Saturday safe and sound, found the 8th had been reinforced by 165 substitutes and more are expected daily. About 20 have deserted, but they will most of them return I think as they cannot get North, and they dare not go to the enemy, some came back to day.

20 were assigned to our Co. most of them Germans. 5 deserted before being assigned to the Co. They are from all parts of the earth and many of them cannot speak English, but 15 of the whole claims to be from Conn.[100]

On the first anniversary of the battle of Antietam, in a letter home, Seth Plumb remembered the dear friends that the Eighth had lost. "We talk and think of one year ago today Antietam is so impressed upon our minds that we can never forget every event of that most bloody day of the war. George is not forgotten by the men of this Co. and they often say 'we miss no man like Booth.'"[101]

Expedition to South Mills

In late September, five companies of the 15th Connecticut, under Lieutenant Colonel Samuel Tolles, took boats down the canal south and halted near South Mills, North Carolina. On October 12, six companies of the Eighth, the other five companies of the 15th Connecticut, and a Pennsylvania Cavalry unit, joined together in an operation to surprise and capture a camp of Confederate guerrillas in the area.

Two companies of the Eighth, Company G and Company K, with their Sharps rifles were transformed into mounted infantry, and skirmished right up to the breastworks surrounding the camp.[102]

> On Oct. 12, the other five companies, with six companies of the Eighth, left camp at Portsmouth, and marched to Deep Creek, being there joined by a part of a Pennsylvania cavalry regiment. They moved on to South Mills next day; were there joined by three of the other companies of the Fifteenth; and pressed on to surprise, and, if possible, capture, a camp of "conscript catchers" reported to be quartered in the swamp. Before arriving at the place, the infantry halted, while the cavalry and two mounted companies of the Eighth rode down on the camp of the bushwhackers; but they were in the woods beyond reach. The Union forces returned next day with nine prisoners, and a quantity of ducks, geese, turkeys, and other plunder. The expedition was under Col. Upham of the Fifteenth; Capt. Hoyt of the Eighth commanding the battalion of infantry.[103]

Seth Plumb was part of the affair, and wrote home to tell the story.

> A portion of our regiment has been out on an expedition into North Carolina, they got back Saturday. Two companies of the 8th were mounted at South Mills. The expedition went about 25 miles southwest of South Mills when they came on to a rebel camp and earth works. The 2 mounted Co of the 8th dismounted and skirmished into their camp without opposition, taking 2 or 3 prisoners who were on guard there. It seemed that the whole force had gone out another way to look after a force that had been sent up from Newbern, and that the move from this way were a complete surprise to them. Our men took 5 or 6 prisoners, the rest hid in the swamp and bushes. The Rebels were said to be a company of the 66th NC who were there enforcing the conscription. We are now encamped where we have been since our return from South Mills, and there is a prospect of our staying here this winter, do if we shall have good quarters and live well enough for soldiers.[104]

On September 29, 1863, the Eighth's chaplain, John M. Morris resigned his commission. He took a post in New Haven as the editor of the *Connecticut War Record*. This newspaper was full of war reports directly from the soldiers and officers themselves. The paper became widely circulated as the standard for war news reporting in Connecticut (and is an important source for this book).

Sergeant Albion Brooks wrote how disappointed he was over his chaplain's departure: "There is one thing for which I am very sorry. Our Chaplain, Mr. Morris, has resigned and gone home. I was hoping with his assistance to make considerable advance in my studies, but now, any such idea is completely knocked in the head. He resigned, I believe, to take charge of the Conn. War Journal, a paper published in New Haven, I believe."[105]

Execution of Dr. Wright

The Eighth was ordered, along with the rest of the brigade, to witness the execution of Dr. David Minton Wright, who was convicted by a military commission of the murder of Second Lieutenant Anson L. Sanborn of the First District of Columbia Colored Regiment.[106] The hanging was conducted in Norfolk on October 23, 1863. Sergeant Seth Plumb detailed the particulars of the proceedings in a letter home.

> I sent you some papers yesterday that had accounts of the execution of Dr David M Wright of Norfolk. Our regiment was over to the execution, you see by the paper. The position of our company in the square was about 6 rods from the gallows, so we could hear and see everything. It was a sad, solemn, painful sight. Our regiment, the 4th RI, and 5 companies of the 15th went over to Norfolk Thursday evening in light marching order, rigged in our best with white gloves. That night we marched to the fair ground, a mile back of Norfolk, where the gallows was erected, and bivouacked.
>
> The next morning, we formed 3 sides of the square around the gallows. The five Co of the 15th in rear, the 8th on the right, the 4th on the left, and waited for the coming of the execution. The platform of the gallows was about 9 feet from the ground, with a pair of stairs to get up, above the platform hung the rope and the noose. Between 9 and 10 AM we could hear the procession coming from Norfolk playing the death march. First came a line of 7 or 8 cavalry men followed by a large corps of music, then the 118th NY, then the carriages, with Dr. Wright and the ministers, then the 21st CV. They came into the square in front and marched up on the left of the scaffold. The 118th marched around and formed in front of us. The carriages stopped behind the gallows, the 21st in front of the 4th. A black brigade formed in front just outside the square.
>
> The Provost Marshall, Dr Wright, and the ministers ascended the scaffold. Dr Wright was a venerable looking man with white locks, almost 60 years of age. I could have taken him for a judge or minister, but never for a murderer. The parting with the ministers, their prayers commending his soul to his Creator, and his repeating the Lord's prayer, and a petition for mercy on his knees under the rope with his hands shackled, were touching beyond description. He stood composedly while the rope was being put on his neck. At the proper time the trap door on which he stood opened, and he dropped through falling about 6 feet. He died without a struggle. There were very few citizens present except the blacks. At 12 noon a delegation of citizens came and took the corpse. We stayed at the fair ground till Saturday afternoon then came to camp in the rain.[107]

Deserters

The Eighth also witnessed the execution of two Union soldiers for desertion on November 9, 1863. Sergeant William Huntington recounted the event.

A week or two ago I witnessed the Execution of Dr. Wright. Today I have been the witness of a similar sad sight; the Shooting of two Men of this Regt (one of them from this Co) for Desertion. I suppose that the retribution is just but somehow it never seemed quite in keeping with the Passage "Vengeance is mine, I will repay with the Lord." for Man to take it upon himself to deal it out—Each of them had 12 Men to fire at him. All of the troops out here had to be there + I have no doubt that effect will be good upon many who have said they will desert—as soon as they have been paid off again.[108]

Captain Henry C. Hall, in his diary, wrote this brief entry on November 9, 1863: "Privates Mitchell Vandall and Francis Wales of the 8th C.V. were executed to day for desertion. I was Officer of the Day."[109]

Principal Musician George W. Farnham reported on the execution for the *Connecticut War Record*.

> Therefor, two of them who had deserted twice, and were caught again, were sentenced to be shot, and the sentence was carried out yesterday. At 9 a.m., the regiments of the brigade were formed on their respective parade grounds and marched to an open field near Fort Reno. A hollow square was formed, and the men rested on their guns to await the arrival of the prisoners. They were made to kneel in front of their coffins, and bandages put over their eyes. Soon the fatal order was given to fire, and their souls passed into eternity.[110]

Winter Quarters

The camp of the Eighth was in the vicinity of Getty's Station,[111] which was not a town, but a military designation. Getty's Station was actually a stop on the Seaboard and Roanoke Railroad about three miles southwest of Portsmouth, adjacent to the Bunting house property. By this point in the season, it was apparent that the Eighth could be spending the winter in the Portsmouth area. To that end, they began preparing winter quarters. Sergeant Seth Plumb described the lodgings being built in camp.

> Winter quarters are being put up throughout our camp, which with other fatigue duty keeps us all quite busy. There is plenty of pine timber close to our camp, and everyone is allowed to get and build as they please. The upright part of our habitations are generally of wood and the roofs are made of tents. It would be quite interesting for you to visit our camp to see what a city we have built. The 15th is but a few rods from us on our left. The 10th NH is but a half a mile from here.[112]

The Eighth spent Thanksgiving in camp. They listened as orders were read from General Benjamin Butler, suspending all duties that could be dispensed with that day. The holiday dinner of Company K was well provided for by Lemuel Curtis of Meriden, who sent six large turkeys to thank the troops for their service. It was also noted that Captain Henry M. Hoyt was now in command of the regiment in the absence of Lieutenant Colonel Smith.[113]

Sergeant Jay Nettleton told of the activities in the process of building a winter camp. "Building is the main business in the Regt. at this time. Guard-quarters are nearly completed. Details of men are working on buildings for "Line" and field officers. Timber is hewed on three sides and blocked together at the corners with a laying of clay between each log. Capt. Hall said he had already spent $25.00 on his house the floor and door and casing costing over $12.00."[114]

Chapter 6. Suffolk, Portsmouth, Deep Creek, Home

Second Lieutenant John Merriam also discussed preparing for the coming winter.

> I am very much engaged in the building of a log house for winter quarters. I expect to have a good one when it is done. It will be 24 feet by twelve and about ten feet high. perhaps you can get some idea of its capacity. We are to have two rooms one sleeping room 10 by 12 feet and the front room 14 by 12 ft. When finished and we are once in it I think we shall be very comfortably fixed for the winter. Some of the officers are for sending home for their wives and when they are all here it will be very pleasant indeed. There is not much prospect of our moving this winter especially now as General Grant has been successful in the West. General B.F. Butler presides here puts a stop to all the rumors concerning a move, as everyone knows he is not a fighting general. In this department then we rest secure from all excitement this winter.[115]

Veteran Re-Enlistment

Late in 1863, the state of Connecticut sent recruiting officers to the regiments in the field in an effort to reenlist soldiers for another term. The state offered a veteran a bounty of $702 and a thirty-day furlough before the end of his existing enlistment. The entire effort was quite successful.[116]

On December 17, Captain Roger Ford noted in his diary that Captain Elam T. Goodrich was assigned to recruit the veteran volunteers in camp.[117]

Sergeant Jay Nettleton did not re-enlist. In a letter home in early December, he suspected some of the men would rejoin for the bounty.

> Furloughs have stopped in our Regt. and we can't account for the fact only that they want to have as many as possible reenlist and think some will do so for the sake of going home. I have only to say that when I have served three years then will be the time for me to talk with them. Money did not cause me to go; it will never cause me to reenlist. Other causes may.... What a fine chance to put $700.00 into one's purse or add so much to the private Bank: I have such a high estimation of men as to believe that more men will enlist for the mere dollars than any other cause.[118]

Sergeant Seth Plumb, who did re-enlist, thought most men wouldn't sign up again. "There is nothing new here except that Capt. Goodrich has been appointed Recruiting Agent for this Reg, but I don't know as he has opened his office yet : Any one would suppose to hear 'the Boys' talk about it that they did not intend to reenlist in 'the Old 8th' and I shall be much surprised if they get 50 but we can't always tell what they will do."[119]

Sergeant William Huntington defended his decision to take the bounty, since the war appeared to be nearly over.

> Are having a good deal of excitement here just at this time over the subject of Re-enlisting or of gaining the name of "Veteran." There is a little upward of three hundred left in the Regt left of the thousand that left Hartford about twenty-six months since. If two thirds of the old organization re-enlist we can go Home as a Regt about the middle of January + thirty or more days. They commenced yesterday morning + now they have about eighty names down. I am not a veteran yet but I expect I shall be. Now don't go to scolding +say I don't think it was necessary but just think how a man would feel to go home + leave a job almost done for I honestly believe that before our remaining two months are up, that about all the fighting will be over. + if I reenlist for the next year alone I receive over $200.00 so that it will pay to stay a few months longer.[120]

One soldier enumerated the details of the re-enlistment proposal. Once signed as re-enlisted, a soldier would receive a Connecticut bounty of $375 and a United States bounty of $100, along with a thirty-day furlough. If one did not re-enlist, the rumor was that they would be transferred to the Army of the Potomac, a disagreeable assignment. As a result of all the recruiting, almost three out of four of the Eighth's veterans stepped up for another tour of duty, and service to their state, and their country. The period for re-enlistments closed, and those who signed up were recorded with the Connecticut Adjutant General on December 24, 1863. "In December, 1863, three hundred and ten of the original members of the Eighth re-enlisted as veterans, and in January, 1864, went to Connecticut on veteran furlough. March 1st found the regiment returned to the field for duty."[121]

Sergeant William Huntington reported on the arrival of the Eighth's new chaplain, Moses Smith, who was drafted as a private in Company A on August 15, and promoted to chaplain on December 22. "Our new Chaplain arrived day before yesterday. He spoke a few words tonight on the re-enlistment subject. + I think made a very favorable impression to begin with. All were pleased which is very good. His name is Moses Smith. His wife is here with him."[122]

Those soldiers who were not eligible, or did not re-enlist, were detailed to other regiments while those who did re-enlist were on furlough. About 110 soldiers of the original Eighth stayed in camp in the Portsmouth area. They were later discharged when their terms of service expired in September 1864. But it's important to note that, out of 310 who did re-enlist, most did not stay with the regiment to the war's end, due to transfers, discharges, or deaths. In fact, only 91 of them were present at the final muster out of the Eighth on December 12, 1865.

Home on Furlough

The whole of the Eighth remained in camp in Portsmouth during the Christmas and New Year holidays. Then on January 11, the re-enlisted men of the 8th Connecticut and the 11th Connecticut boarded boats for the trip home. They were officially furloughed on the January 16 when they arrived in Connecticut.

When they reached New Haven on January 15, large crowds greeted them with gratitude and affection. People from all over the state crowded the streets to welcome their soldiers. The line of march was decorated with flags, signs, and patriotic emblems. Cannons were fired, and bells were rung. Receptions were held at the Music Hall in New Haven and at Allyn Hall in Hartford for both regiments.[123]

Gov. Buckingham made a grand speech, welcoming the veterans who were returning home:

> Gen. Harland, and officers and men of the Eighth and Eleventh regiments,—In behalf of the General Assembly and the citizens of Connecticut, I greet you with a cordial welcome,—not as long-lost prodigals who have neglected their duty to themselves and their homes, but as devoted sons who have gone in their manhood from parental roofs, and, after achieving brilliant successes through heroic deeds and sacrifices, return, crowned with glory, to receive the blessings if parents and friends.

Chapter 6. Suffolk, Portsmouth, Deep Creek, Home

I remember the time, not long in the past, when a certain race of men declared to the world, that, from the corner-stone of human bondage, they would erect a government of their own in defiance of law and constitutional obligations; and that they raised armies to carry out their bold declaration, though the land may be deluged on blood. I remember that they, in their madness, struck at the old flag of their country as it waved over Fort Sumter; and that earnest men, fired with the zeal and patriotism which should animate every true American heart, while on their way to defend the capital of the nation, were shot down in the streets of Baltimore by an infuriated mob stimulated to bloody deeds by the desire to overthrow liberty that slavery might live. Then it was that you stepped out from your workshops and fields of labor, and, bidding adieu for the time being to peaceful pursuits and the enjoyment of home, buckled on the armor of brave men, and marched to distant fields to defend the national life from the assaults of a wicked and desperate foe. I remember—and the people of Connecticut remember—your full ranks as you stood shoulder to shoulder; two thousand strong, when leaving the borders of the State; and since that time watchful eyes and prayerful hearts have not lost sight of you.

Through all the vicissitudes and dangers of the battlefield, you have been watched with eager anxiety. We remember when. with the indomitable Burnside. you landed on the sands of Roanoke Island, through the battling waves of Hatteras, to the securement of a foothold in the old North State. We remember you at Newberne, at South Mountain, and at other fields where your valor has been displayed with untold honor to yourselves and your native State. At Antietam, where your gallant Col. Kingsbury laid down his life; where the intrepid Griswold led the way across that fatal stream, and died heroically; where the brave Lieut. Wait would not leave his post, though wounded mortally,—we remember you with particular devotion.

It is in that record that we find the names of sixty-nine of your numbers who know how sweet it was to die for their country, and of over two hundred more who died in defense of liberty. And we owe you who stood at their side a debt of gratitude which we can never repay. We would have your names inscribed on the finest marble and granite; but, if that cannot be, you may rest assured, that, engraved on the brightest pages of history, the names of the nation's defenders will ever stir the gratitude of those who shall read hereafter the history of this Rebellion.

Though your flags come back tattered and torn, they are crowned with glory, and will ever stand, with the names of bloody battlefields which are inscribed upon them, as faithful witnesses of your struggles in defense of constitutional liberty.

I feel grateful to God that you are here; that you have come to us with such a noble record. Your re-enlistment is evidence that you first entered the service of your country from motives of patriotism, and are ready to fight on, giving your lives, if need be, to the maintenance of those principles which lie close to the hearts continue to beat true liberty, so long will they cherish with gratitude the services of the Eighth and Eleventh Connecticut Regiments.[124]

The newspaper concluded that "after another speech by Roland Swift, Esq., and an excellent dinner, they dispersed, to seek that tenderer reception by fathers, mothers, wives, and sisters, in many happy homes."

Captain Roger Ford described in his diary the particulars of the preparation, the travel, the furlough, the rendezvous, and the return to the war by the Veteran Volunteers of the Eighth Regiment Connecticut Volunteer Infantry. Note how he writes that "there was nothing but a routine of pleasure" once the thirty-day furlough began.

January 1864

10th Sunday pleasant I went to Camp and got paid

11th Monday pleasant expect the Regt down to go on board of Boat to go home 11th the Regt arrived at Portsmouth at 9 A.M we left there at 12 M we arrived at Fort Monroe at 1 P.M left there at 2 P.M and started for Yorktown to get the 11th CV arrived there at 8 P.M

12th Tuesday pleasant we take 125 men of the 11th Regt CV the remainder of the Regt go on the Haze we left there at 12. M.

13th Wednesday Cloudy we arrived in New York Harbor at 11 P.M

14th Thursday Pleasant we left N York at 5 ½ but before we got by the Navy Yard we run on a rock the fog was so thick we lay untill 12 M. when we had 4 Steam Tugs and they finally pulled us off and we left for New Haven we arrived in the Harbor at 7 p.m. the Harbor is frozen over the Ice is quite thick we are trying to get up the Wharf.

15th Friday Cloudy 9 A M. we have just got up to the Dock 9 ½ AM. we got off and marched up to Music Hall to take some refreshments then we marched for the train and arrived at Hartford about 3 P M. We marched around the City then went into a Hall and had a grand Supper then went up to the Union Hall and left our men &c.

16th Saturday Pleasant we got our men their furlough this noon and they have gone home.

February 1864

There was nothing but a routine of pleasure until the 16th of February when we reported to Wallingford on the 17th 1864 for duty once more

17th Wednesday Cloudy arrived in Wallingford on the first train the Regt is Quartered in the old Knife Shop I am staying at Uncle Robert Wallace's

18th Thursday pleasant I am Officer of the Day 12 PM there was a detachment of 31 Recruits arrived from Fort Trumbull Capt [William C.] Burgess of the 15th Conn Vols in Comdg of Detachment

19th Friday there came an order for us to be in readiness to move at a moment's notice

27th Saturday pleasant we left Wallingford at 2 PM arrived in New Haven at 3 PM went on board of Steamer Daniel Webster and left the Wharf at 11 ½ PM

28th Sunday Cloudy we are going very slow we are making out our Muster and pay rolls

29th Monday Cloudy and storms very hard there is a good many sea sick we were mustered to day by Capt H. Hoyt. Lieut Bingham turned over the clothing camp and Garrison Equipage to me to day

March 1864

1st Tuesday Cloudy we arrived at Portsmouth Va at 12 M left there and arrived in our old camp at 3 PM found our House all right Lieut Bingham turned over the Ordnance to me to day.[125]

On the morning of March 1, the veterans of the Eighth and the 11th Connecticut, returning from furlough, were on board a transport anchored off Fortress Monroe. The Eighth disembarked at Portsmouth, and returned to their old camp.[126]

Thus began the Eighth Regiment Connecticut Volunteer Infantry's Campaign of 1864.

Chapter 7

Deep Creek to Drewry's Bluff

Their furloughs over, the soldiers of the 8th Connecticut, now veterans, left their homes and returned to the Union army in Virginia. The Eighth, like the other Connecticut regiments, had received many new recruits, bringing their numbers almost to regulation strength. However, a large number of the recruits soon deserted, leaving the regiments not much stronger than when recruiting began.

On March 1, 1864, most of the returning veterans of the 8th Connecticut, along with those of the 11th Connecticut, were on board a crowded transport at Fortress Monroe, waiting to be reunited with their regiments. The members of the Eighth disembarked at Portsmouth, Virginia, and returned to their old camp there. Their stay was short, however, for on March 13, they were ordered to Deep Creek, where the regiment was assigned to outpost and picket duty, a type of guard duty.[1]

Deep Creek

Deep Creek, a small village about eight miles south of Portsmouth, Virginia, is located on the stream Deep Creek, a tributary of the Southern Branch Elizabeth River (see Map 11). Sergeant Jay Nettleton called it a "little cluster of houses" at the junction of the Dismal Swamp Canal and the Elizabeth River. This new camp was four miles farther from Portsmouth than their old camp, on what Nettleton called "the Picket front."[2]

Captain Charles Coit said their new camp's location was "delightful," since it was on the banks of Deep Creek where the stream bends, so that the river formed two sides of the camp. The ground was "dry + healthy." Their assigned duties, however, changed their routine from the usual. With so many men on picket, Coit said, they did hardly any drilling, so the officers had much more time to themselves.[3]

Sergeant Seth Plumb did not accompany the main group of returning veterans from the Eighth, but instead came a few days later with some other members of the regiment, and met up with the unit at Deep Creek. The day after his arrival, Seth was detailed by the adjutant to be the sergeant commanding the "Pioneer Corps" of the regiment. The Pioneer Corps was a special detail, composed of ten men, one from each company, with a sergeant in charge of this group. This unit performed a variety of labor related duties for the regiment; the primary one was to obtain firewood.

But they could also be assigned to do any odd jobs for the regiment—digging that might be needed, putting up tents for the officers, and especially taking the lead in a march and clearing the way of obstacles and repairing the road so the rest of the regiment could pass. There was no night work, so the men were on their own on nights and Sundays.

The sergeant of the Pioneer Corps received his orders from the field or regimental officers; he was independent of any line or company officers and not subject to their orders. The sergeant was not required to keep or carry a musket or accoutrements. He called the roll and reported like a first sergeant, and he could write passes for his men the way a company commander could. He also was given a pass at will, which allowed him to take his men out of the camp and past the pickets whenever he wished. Though the Pioneer Corps was clearly quite independent, Plumb still lodged with his company and took his meals with them.[4]

For an example of the Pioneers in action, consider their participation in a raid (or reconnaissance) across the Nansemond River. On April 13, the Eighth's Pioneer Corps, Seth Plumb commanding, left camp and moved by railroad and then by foot to Suffolk, where they met up with other units—the 13th New Hampshire, parts of the 27th Massachusetts and 28th Massachusetts, and a "squadron of negro cavalry." When the expedition reached the Nansemond, the Pioneers first had to construct a structure of timbers and poles so that the troops could cross. Once that was done and half of the troops had crossed this make-shift bridge, Plumb received orders from the commander of the expedition to build a full-scale bridge for the troops to cross on their return.

Plumb wrote that they built a "first rate bridge" using long timbers that they had cut and bound together with grape vines. The bridge was so strong that the cavalry crossed it; it was better than what anyone had expected. Since the bridge was completed by 11 a.m., the Pioneers took the rest of the day to rest and dry their gear. Plumb told his family that the Pioneer Corps now consisted of twenty men, and that there were no officers or noncommissioned officers except for himself. He wrote that "I get along first rate and all are satisfied. I much prefer it to any thing I have ever been in the army."[5]

On April 1, 1864, Lieutenant General Ulysses S. Grant, now general-in-chief of the armies of the United States, met with Major General Benjamin F. Butler at Butler's headquarters at Fortress Monroe. Butler was the commander of the Department of Virginia and North Carolina, and Grant wanted Butler's help in formulating the overall strategy and plan for defeating the Confederacy, which included the capture of Richmond and defeat of the Confederate armies defending it. Butler showed Grant maps of the territory in his department, described the lay of the land, and recommended that an attack against Richmond be made from the south, up the James River, where the land was good for campaigning and less strongly defended.

First, however, Butler said it was essential to the campaign that the army seize and fortify a base of operations on the Bermuda Hundred peninsula, and at City Point, located on the south side of the James River at the confluence with the Appomattox River. They could accomplish this objective by moving Butler's forces, to be

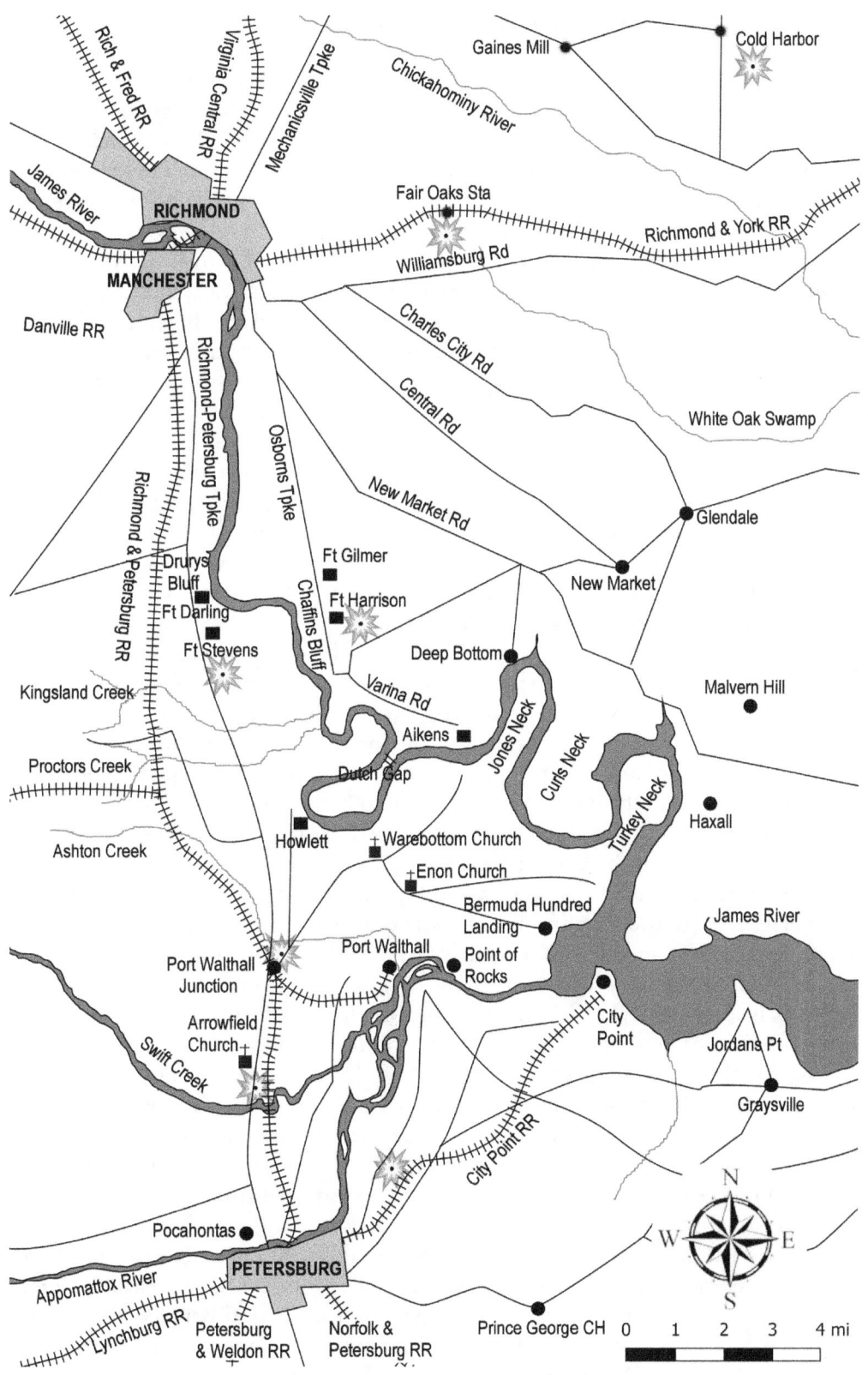

Map 14. Vicinity of Richmond and Petersburg, Virginia, May 1864.

known as the Army of the James, from its bases at Yorktown, Gloucester Point, and Fortress Monroe, up the James River by water, and then seizing Bermuda Hundred and City Point. As a diversion before that attack, a force would be dispatched up the York River to construct a base there, so that the Confederates would think that this base was the objective of Butler's combined forces—and the point where they intended to join with Grant's forces.

Grant approved of Butler's plan, but Grant would not move the Army of the Potomac down to the James River and expose Washington, D.C., to attack. Rather, the Army of the Potomac would attack Lee's army and drive it back to Richmond, while Butler's army would surround Richmond from the south. The two Federal armies would then link up and "scoop [Richmond] out of the Confederacy." Grant emphasized strongly that the objective must be Richmond.[6]

On Tuesday morning, April 19, the 8th Connecticut broke camp at Deep Creek and marched to Portsmouth, arriving about 2 p.m. There the regiment boarded the transport *Escort*, and set out for Newport News, landing there around 4 p.m. The unit then marched four or five miles toward Yorktown before stopping at 7:30 p.m. to make camp for the night. On Wednesday, the Eighth moved out at 9 a.m. and marched until about 4 p.m. On Thursday, April 21, they started out at 6 a.m. and reached their next camp at Yorktown about 11 a.m.

It was clear that something was up. Seth Plumb wrote that troops were collecting at Yorktown to "probably" go up the Peninsula to join with the Army of the Potomac. Troops were also massing across the York River at Gloucester, and they were assembling "quite rapidly" at Annapolis. The men were going to draw shelter tents soon, another sign of an upcoming movement of the army. As Captain Roger Ford wrote in his diary, "[T]he next order will be on to Richmond, I suppose."[7]

It is worth taking a moment here to review the 8th Connecticut's place in the command structure in the upcoming campaign.

The 8th Connecticut was now part of the Second Brigade. The other regiments in the brigade were the 10th and 13th New Hampshire and the 118th New York. The brigade was in the command of Brigadier General Hiram Burnham.

The Second Brigade was part of the First Division of the Eighteenth Army Corps. Brigadier General William T.H. Brooks commanded the division, and the corps was in command of Major General William F. "Baldy" Smith.[8]

On April 30, Butler received orders from Grant to begin the move. From his headquarters at Culpeper Court House on April 28, Grant had written, "If no unforseen accident prevents, I will move from here on Wednesday, the 4th of May. Start your forces the night of the 4th, so as to be as far up James River as you can get by daylight on the morning of the 5th, and push from that time with all your might for the accomplishment of the object before you."[9]

On this same day, General Butler reviewed the entire Eighteenth Corps. As brigade officer of the day, Captain Coit was standing by the general while the regiments passed in review. After the First Brigade passed, the Second Brigade approached, with the 8th Connecticut in the lead. Coit became so excited in watching them that he called out "Bully." He was later told by one of the men that General Butler asked what regiment this was, as the Eighth passed by.[10]

Bermuda Hundred

On Wednesday, May 4, major portions of the Tenth Corps and Eighteenth Corps, totaling some 25,000 men, began embarkation at Yorktown. At daylight on May 5, the entire fleet of transports was assembled at Newport News and began moving up the James River. Ironclads and other vessels led the fleet to Wilson's Wharf, and seven miles above it, to Fort Powhatan, where three regiments of black troops seized and occupied those places. The black troops were part of Brigadier General Edward W. Hink's division of United States Colored Troops of the Eighteenth Corps. The rest of that division seized and began fortifying City Point, while the remainder of the Tenth and Eighteenth Corps pushed on to Bermuda Hundred.[11]

In his diary, Roger Ford recounted the journey of the 8th Connecticut on its way to Bermuda Hundred.

> 4th Wednesday... [W]e are turning over everything we cannot carry. Regt are to have only one team to carry Hospital Stores, officers baggage. We left camp and went on board of the Steamer George Washington at 6 PM and left for Fort Monroe arrived there at 1 AM Thursday morning.
>
> 5th Thursday... [W]e arrived at Fort Monroe at 1 AM, we left there 5 AM up the James River, at 1 PM we passed a wharf where we had landed some Negro troops, 4 PM we passed Fort Powhatan a strong Rebel earth work which commanded the river for 3 miles which they had abandoned and there were more Negro Troops landed here; passed Harrisons Landing at 5 PM arrived at City Point and passed the mouth of the Appomattox River at 6½ PM; 12 Midnight we landed at a place called Bermuda Hundred and went into camp.[12]

Early in the morning on Friday, May 6, the Eighteenth Corps (which included the 8th Connecticut) and the Tenth Corps began moving up the Bermuda Hundred peninsula on Bermuda Hundred Road, as more of their troops continued to disembark. At the road's intersection with North Enon Church Road, the Eighteenth Corps turned and followed North Enon Church Road southwest towards Point of Rocks, while the Tenth Corps continued west. It was at the Cobb's Hill and Point of Rocks area that the Eighteenth Corps began digging entrenchments.

Later that afternoon, the First Brigade of the Second Division of the Eighteenth Corps, commanded by Brigadier General Charles Heckman, left its entrenchments near Point of Rocks and advanced towards a place known as Port Walthall Junction. Port Walthall was a shipping point on the Appomattox River. A railroad spur line ran from the port to the main line of the Richmond & Petersburg Railroad; the point of intersection of these rail lines was called Port Walthall Junction. As Heckman's First Brigade neared the junction, they encountered the defending Confederates, many of whom had just come in from Petersburg by train. A battle ensued, and lasted until Heckman finally withdrew his First Brigade and returned to his entrenchments. This action has come to be known as the first battle of Port Walthall Junction.[13]

After arriving at Bermuda Hundred at midnight on Thursday, May 5, the 8th Connecticut did not rest long in camp; they were up and moving again at 5 a.m. on Friday, May 6. They marched "towards Petersburg" until about noon when they halted, went into camp "in line of Battle," and began building earth works.[14] They remained there that night.

That Friday evening, May 6, while the Eighth worked and then rested, Butler met with his corps commanders, Major General William F. "Baldy" Smith of the Eighteenth Corps, and Major General Quincy Adams Gillmore of the Tenth Corps. They decided to renew the attack against Port Walthall Junction the next day, this time with a greater force. Each of the five Federal divisions would supply one brigade for the attack, for a total of 8,000 men, all under the command of Brigadier General Brooks, the Eighth's division commander.

The Eighth's Second Brigade, under Brigadier General Hiram Burnham, was the brigade selected from their division. The plan of attack was for the main force to proceed, in column, from the northeast down Old Stage Road to Port Walthall Junction. Heckman's First Brigade would provide a diversion by attacking the Confederate flank from the same route they had used the day before. Their mission was to break the railroad line of the Richmond & Petersburg Railroad.[15]

Second Battle of Port Walthall Junction

On the morning of Saturday May 7, at about 10 a.m., the Confederate brigade of Brigadier General Johnson Hagood left its position behind the railroad and headed northeastward up Old Stage Road in an attempt to locate the Federal troops. After proceeding about a mile, they ran into the vanguard of the Federal attack—eight companies of Colonel Benjamin F. Onderdonk's 1st New York Mounted Rifles. After a brief charge down the road by the New Yorkers and repelling fire from the Confederate infantry, the cavalrymen fell back to the Federal column. Burnham's brigade was the lead brigade of the Federal column. Ordered to develop their position, General Burnham instructed his lead regiment, the 8th Connecticut, to form a skirmish line and advance along the west side of the road, supported by the 13th New Hampshire. His other regiments, the 10th New Hampshire and 118th New York, were also deployed west of the road. To oppose the Federals, General Hagood positioned the 27th South Carolina east of the road and three companies of the 25th South Carolina to the west.[16]

In his report later, General Burnham described the battle:

> In the movements of the 7th instant, to cut the Richmond and Petersburg Railroad, this brigade took the advance, with the exception of a small force of cavalry. The command left camp at daybreak, and after proceeding about 4 miles in the direction of the railroad, encountered the enemy, strongly posted on rising ground, with a swamp and tangled growth of underbrush in their front. Here the cavalry was withdrawn, the Eighth Connecticut Volunteers thrown forward as skirmishers, and my other three regiments deployed in line on the right of the road. The enemy was at once engaged, and finally, after a skirmish of some duration, were pressed back upon the railroad by the skirmishers of the Eighth Connecticut, my whole line of battle moving up in support.
>
> Colonel Drake at this time moved his brigade into position on my left, and my command was moved farther to the right, the Eighth Connecticut being thrown forward in line of battle under a hot fire from the enemy's artillery, until they became warmly engaged with the enemy's line, which was posted behind the embankment of the railroad. The Thirteenth New Hampshire Volunteers, Colonel Stevens, was thrown forward to support this regiment, the remaining two regiments being held in reserve. A ravine prevented the Eighth Connecticut

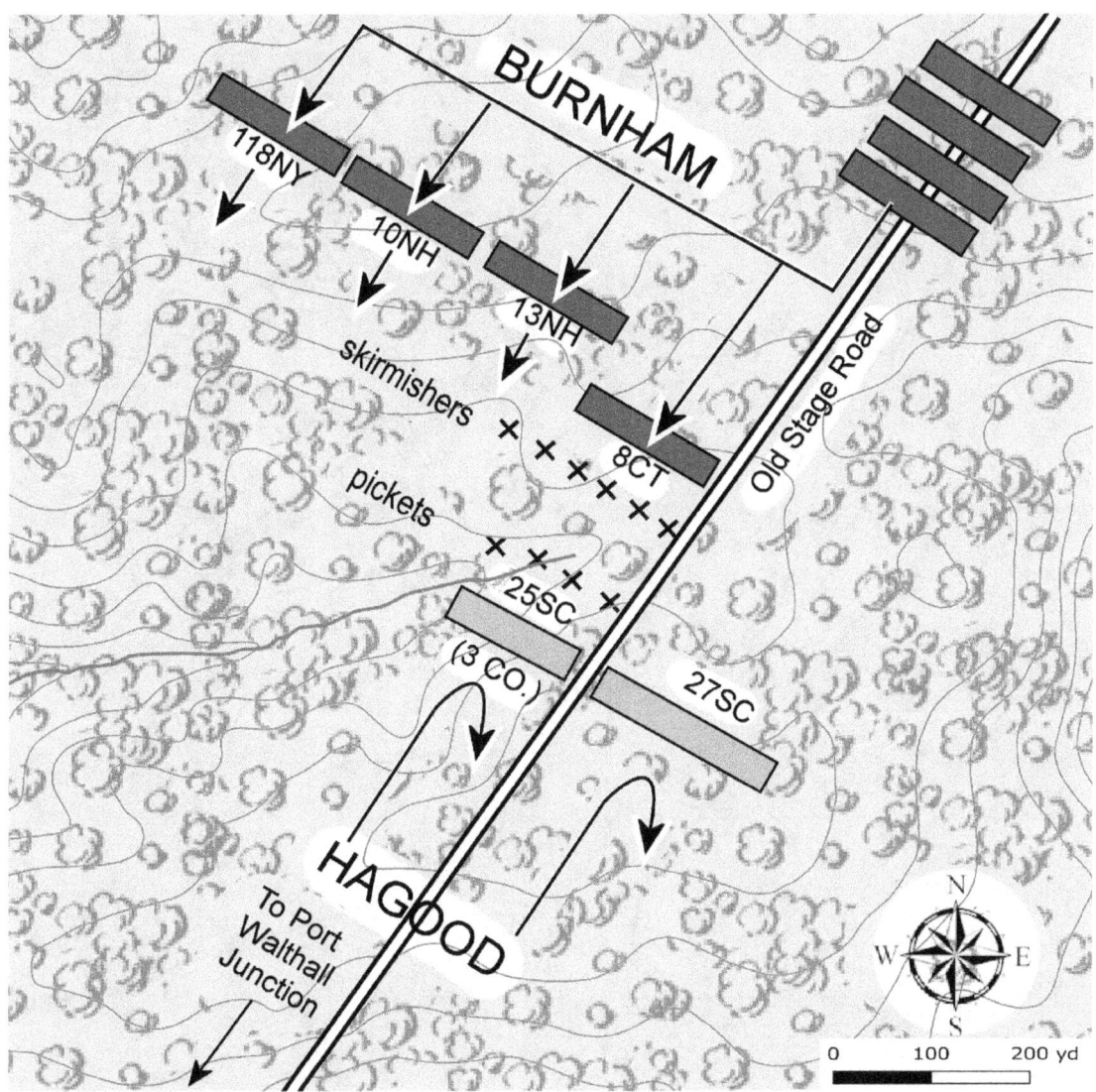

Map 15. Second Battle of Port Walthall Junction, Virginia, May 7, 1864, a.m.

from reaching the railroad, but Colonel Ward attacked the enemy with a well-sustained fire of musketry, and kept them warmly engaged for a considerable time, while the forces on our right reached and destroyed the railroad track.

Burnham said he withdrew his forces once the tracks were destroyed, and he praised the Eighth for its courage.

This object having been accomplished, the Eighth Connecticut was withdrawn without molestation from the enemy, upon whom it must have inflicted a severe loss, and with my brigade I covered the withdrawal of our forces from the railroad, holding an advanced position with the Tenth and Thirteenth New Hampshire until 6 p.m., when my whole force was withdrawn and returned to camp. The fighting of the day fell mostly upon the Eighth Connecticut, which sustained considerable loss, but behaved handsomely, driving the enemy in spirited manner wherever it met them.

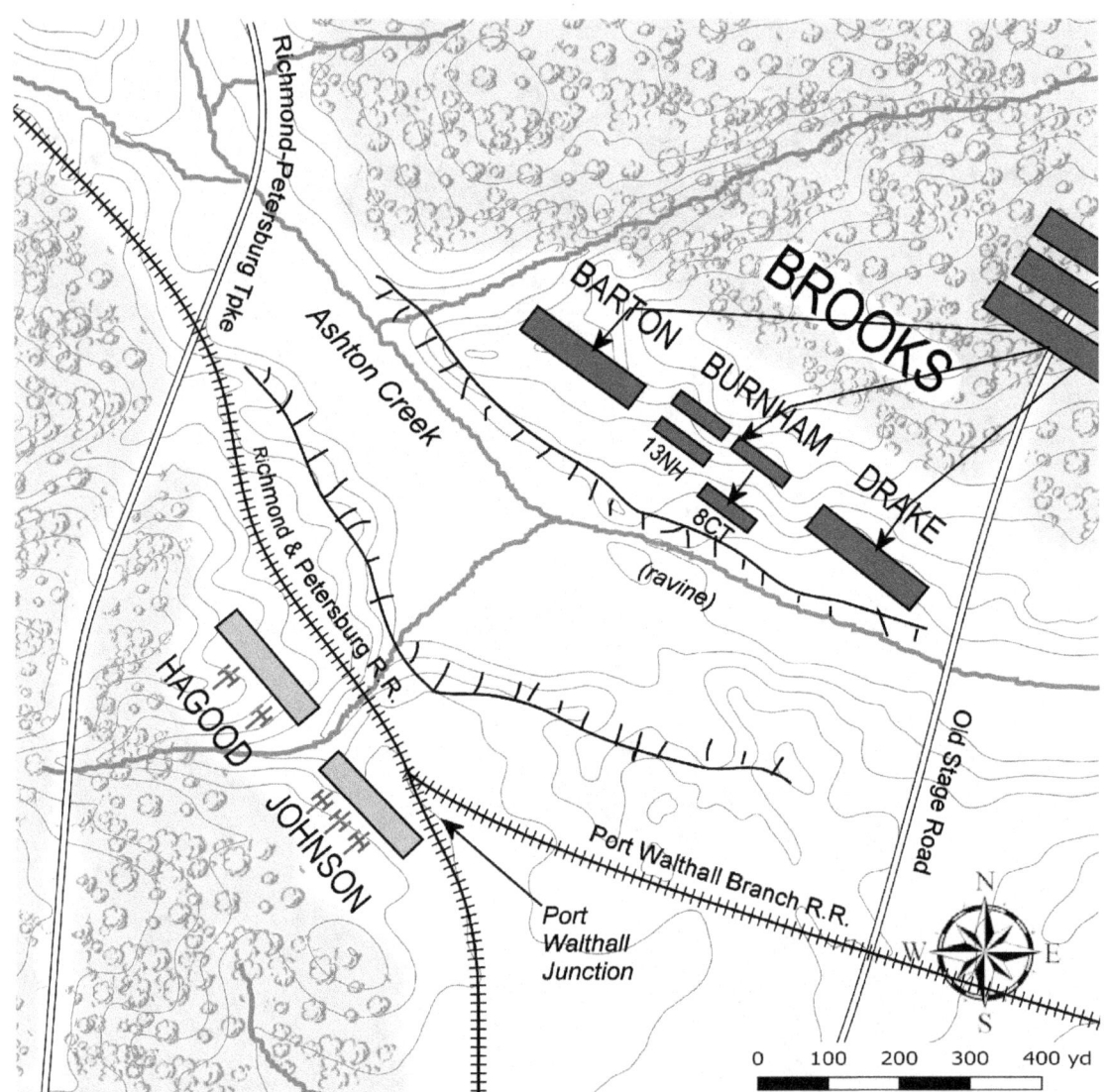

Map 16. Second Battle of Port Walthall Junction, Virginia, May 7, 1864, p.m.

My thanks are especially due to Col. J.E. Ward, commanding that regiment, both for his coolness and gallantry and the able manner in which he handled his regiment. I regret to say that he was wounded in the engagement, his injuries being sufficiently serious to deprive me of his services for the present.[17]

The men who did the fighting also described the engagement in their diaries and in letters home. Here are excerpts from some of their writings.

Captain Henry C. Hall, Company F of the 8th Connecticut:

> [O]n the morning of the seventh leaving our baggage in camp we started for the railroad that runs from Richmond to Petersburg our brigade in the advance and the old 8th leading the brigade. We had proceeded but a short distance when we came upon the enemy's pickets posted in a dense forest which skirted both sides of the road and stretched away on our front as far as we could see.

Four of our companies were deployed as skirmishers the other six being in reserve and away we started battling back the rebel pickets step by step, our reserve companies charging upon them whenever they made a stand in any force to check our skirmishers. The rebel picket was composed of the 25th South Carolina regiment and they fought long and well laying many numbers of the old 8th bleeding upon the ground before we succeeded in driving them back upon their main force.

After driving the rebs from the woods we came out upon an open field fronting the railroad, formed our regiment in line and advanced upon the rebels who were posted in large numbers behind the track and upon the slope of a hill opposite. When we were within about 100 yards of the track they opened upon us with musketry and artillery and we lay down upon the ground and replied. A Brigade of South Carolinians were on the slope of the hill opposite and upon them and the artillery we directed the most of our fire with terrible effect. In vain their officers tried to rally them for a charge upon us, they would start and then break and fall back in disorder under our fire.

The Shrapnel, Shell, and bullets were also making music all around us but we held our position until we had expended sixty rounds of ammunition and all our guns were so dirty that it was almost impossible to ram a bullet down in them, and then Gen. Brooks ordered us to retire and let another regiment take our place which we did after being under fire for four hours and twenty minutes and losing seventy-two men killed and wounded....[18]

Captain Roger Ford, Company G of the 8th Connecticut:

I had a Sergt in command of the extreme left, the left was attacked and the Sergt in command fell back and took the left of the company with him. I then had the center fall back so as to save my company. I fell back about ten rods when I halted and faced about and established a new line. I was then ordered to move by the right flank so that Capt. Coit could deploy his company on my left. I then advanced my line but soon halted because Capt. Coit's Company did not keep up on the line....

Then came the tug of war. We charged and drove them, but we lost quite heavily. Lieut. Bingham had come up and was on the left, when we had orders to move on as fast as possibly. He got excited and exposed himself and the men also. The Enemy then opened on us when Lieut. Bingham was mortally wounded....

We were then ordered to advance in line of Battle, the Enemy were posted on a hill with a ravine between us and them we advanced our line of Skirmishers and line of Battle, the Skirmish Line advanced to within about five or six hundred yards when they halted until the Regiment came up when we opened on them. They brought two pieces of artillery to bear on us. They advanced two lines of skirmishers, they posted behind the rail road which gave them good protection there was a strong line of Battle about one hundred yards in the rear of this line was another Line of Battle, they opened a galling fire of musketry but we advanced about 50 yards and took our position when we gave shot for shot until we expended all our ammunition we were then ordered to fall back there were fresh troops took our place we tore up the rail road for about two miles....[19]

Sgt. Seth Plumb, Company E of the 8th Connecticut:

Yesterday our noble regiment fought its way from 2 miles this side of the Richmond and Petersburg rail road to that road, and our loss has been heavy. 72 is the number killed and wounded of the regiment. Of this E lost 2 killed ... and 5 wounded, Sergt Keeler skull broken dangerously. Hotchkiss lost right arm. H. Garrigus hit in the head, not dangerous but bad. Corporals Cook and Evans flesh wounds in the arm and shoulder....

The regiment never fought more bravely, and it is now the admiration of all the troops around. It seems that it was a reconnaissance to the railroad and the 8th was the point of the plow to reach it. Long lines of troops lay in our rear and rear flanks but few of them even fired their pieces, the 8th was in for hours and fired nearly all its ammunition.

I am not with the company in a fight but help carry and take care of the wounded. Yesterday I worked very hard and followed the regiment into the hardest of the fight. The Pioneer Corps done good work. It is a great satisfaction to me to know that we could help so many of our poor wounded yesterday. We had to carry many of them nearly a mile through the brush.[20]

In his *History of Battle Flag Day,* published in 1880, General Joseph R. Hawley, who served as Connecticut's governor in 1866–1867, reported on the courage of the color bearers at the battle: "Sergeant Thomas J. Hubbard of Torrington was appointed color-sergeant, and carried the national color until the battle of Walthall, Va., May 1 [May 7], 1864, where his elbow was shattered by a minnie ball. Although the arm was completely crushed, Hubbard still clung to his color for a considerable distance, advancing with the line of battle. Finally, he was relieved by Sergeant Orlow J. Root, ... who carried the flag through the remainder of the engagement."[21]

In several of his letters home, Charles Coit told his family about a new lieutenant, Alfred Mitchel Goddard, who had joined the Eighth and was assigned to Coit's company. Like Coit, Goddard was from Norwich, so there was most likely a connection between the two men from back home. Coit said that Goddard was a "real clever fellow" and was liked by his fellow officers, but in learning drill, Goddard was Coit's "most awkward + troublesome" recruit. Coit also didn't like Goddard's penmanship, so he didn't let Goddard help him with the company's paperwork. But Coit apparently did enjoy the lieutenant's company as he told of playing chess with him on several occasions, and mentioned him often in his letters home. In one letter, after describing Goddard's awkward attempts at keeping step to music, he wrote that Goddard was a real pleasant fellow and "I really like him."[22]

On Sunday, May 8, Charles Coit wrote home about the battle the day before (the second battle of Port Walthall Junction). He told his family how he had been spared when many others were cut down beside him. He then wrote, somewhat matter-of-factly, that Alfred Goddard was seriously wounded in the abdomen and there was little chance of recovery. Coit praised the lieutenant's actions in the battle. "He behaved splendidly throughout the day," Coit wrote, and he said that Goddard conducted himself as a brave and skillful officer.

When Goddard was wounded, Coit sent him to the rear immediately in the care of three men. Coit saw him later at the hospital: Goddard was conscious but "feeling rather discouraged about himself." Goddard said that he did not expect to live, but he was ready to go. At four in the morning, when he was put in an ambulance for the landing so he could be taken to Fortress Monroe, he was "feeling brighter." But three days later, on Wednesday, May 11, Coit wrote in a letter, "Hear nothing from Alf. Goddard but fear everything."[23] Alf Goddard had died on Monday, May 9, two days before the date of this letter.[24]

The action on May 7, the second battle of Port Walthall Junction as it was called, was another missed opportunity by the Army of the James. The Federals suffered 345 casualties compared with the Confederates' 184, and the Confederates were able to buy time in order to bring up reinforcements.

On the evening of May 7, Major General George Pickett, commanding the Confederate defenses at Petersburg and fearful of an attack on that city, ordered

Brigadier General Bushrod Johnson, in command of their forces at Port Walthall Junction, to abandon that position and move south to positions behind Swift Creek. General Johnson immediately ordered the troops to be marched out that night. The next day, Sunday May 8, was quiet as the Confederates rushed to strengthen Petersburg, while the Federals continued to strengthen Bermuda Hundred. On the following day, May 9, however, the Union army began moving again as General Butler ordered the Union troops to once again advance on Port Walthall Junction and destroy the railroad.[25]

Battle of Swift Creek

On Monday, May 9, Brooks' First Division of the Eighteenth Corps marched out early and reached Port Walthall Junction about 9 a.m. The two brigades of the First Division were deployed into line of battle on the battlefield of May 7, where many of the Federal casualties still lay unburied. These were the First Brigade under Brigadier General Gilman Marston and the Second Brigade under Brigadier General Hiram Burnham. Together they would lead the advance of the Eighteenth Corps.[26] The Federal troops reached the Richmond & Petersburg Railroad without opposition, and upon orders from General Brooks (commanding the First Division), General Burnham moved his brigade (which included the Eighth) down the railroad in the direction of Petersburg.

Meanwhile, the bulk of the Eighteenth Corps advanced down the Richmond Turnpike, with General Heckman's First Brigade (of the Second Division) in the lead. Heckman's brigade encountered Confederate pickets as they neared Swift Creek, which crossed the Turnpike, but they continued to advance, pushing the pickets back. The Confederate forces were located on the far side of Swift Creek (the south side), and an advanced detachment consisting of portions of General Hagood's South Carolina brigade was positioned on the north side of the creek.

As Heckman came into view of the Confederates, he deployed his brigade into lines of battle, straddling the turnpike. Due to some confusion with orders, the Confederate units north of the Creek, led by the 11th South Carolina, attacked the Federals. After a stiff fight and some deadly volley fire from Heckman's lead regiments, the 25th Massachusetts and 27th Massachusetts, the Confederate forces withdrew across the bridge over Swift Creek.[27]

As the main force of the Eighteenth Corps engaged the Confederates at the turnpike, Burnham's brigade, advancing down the railroad to the east, also encountered Confederates north of Swift Creek. Burnham immediately ordered his troops into line of battle on the left of the railroad (the east side). He deployed skirmishers and attacked the Confederates, driving them back across the creek. Then Burnham advanced his line further, nearly up to the Shippen house. He sent the 10th New Hampshire forward in support of Colonel Henry Hunt's Battery, which had taken position between that house and the railroad, and was shelling the enemy's bridges over the creek.

When Confederate sharpshooters posed a problem, Burnham found a solution.

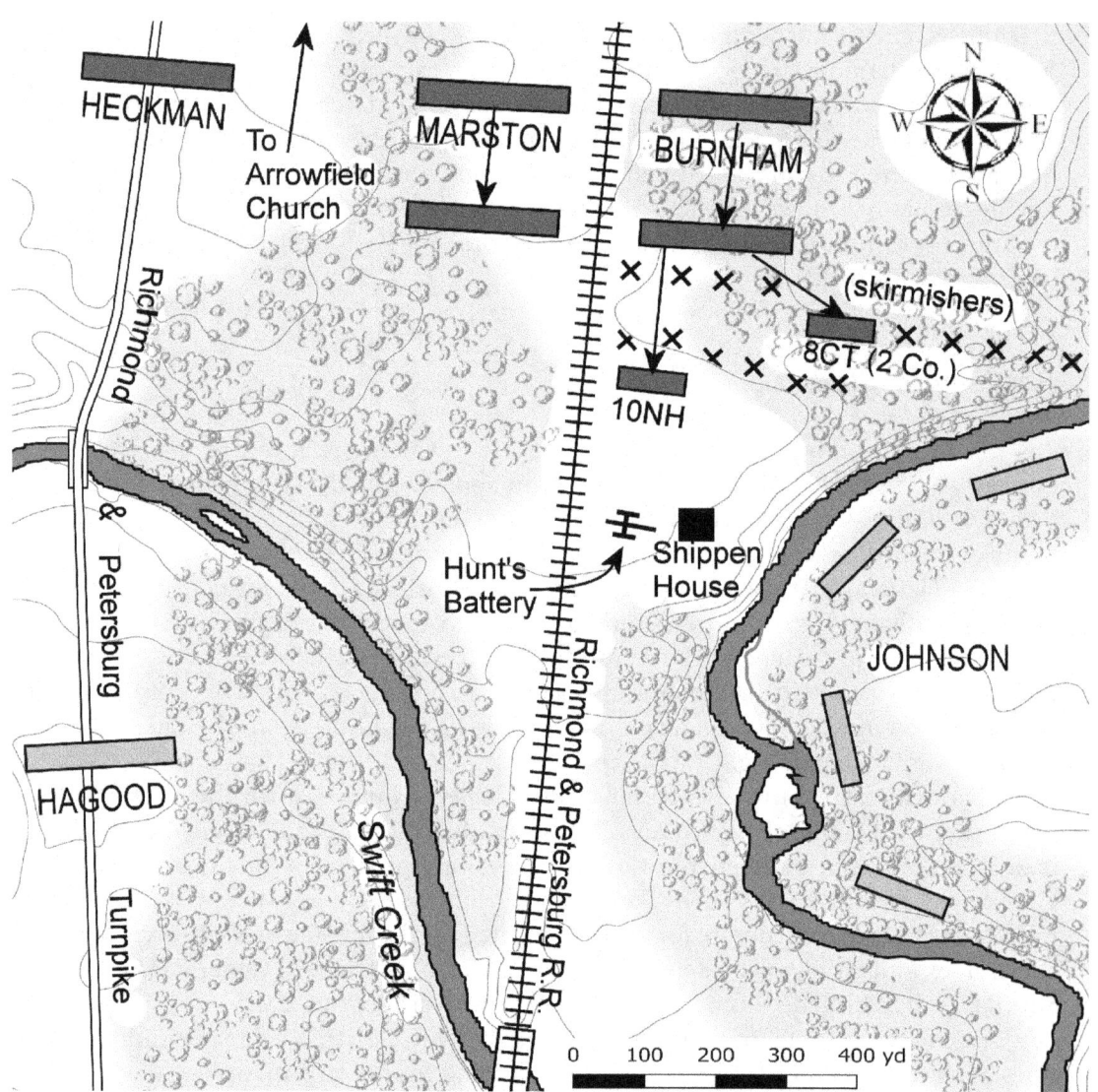

Map 17. Battle of Swift Creek, Virginia, May 9, 1864.

In his report, he wrote, "Being considerably annoyed by the enemy's sharpshooters on the opposite side of the creek to the left of the Shippen house, I strengthened my skirmish line with the two flank companies of the Eighth Connecticut Volunteers, armed with Sharps rifles, and ordered them to drive the enemy out or silence their fire, which they soon did." That night Burnham modified his line by order of General Brooks, now placing the Eighth on the west side of the railroad to fill the gap between their brigade and that of General Marston.[28]

The two flank companies of the Eighth were Company G, commanded by Captain Roger Ford, and Company K, commanded by Captain John McCall. Ford wrote in his diary that they were ordered to hold a position on the creek, which they held until nightfall, when they were ordered to rejoin the regiment, arriving back at 8 p.m. The next day, Tuesday, May 10, Ford indicated that they worked on destroying the railroad, while "The Rebels are throwing Shell at us but doing very little harm." At 3 p.m., they received orders to fall back, as the 8th Connecticut was serving as rear guard, but "the Rebels" were taken by Surprise and did not follow us very closely.[29]

Wednesday, May 11, was a day of rest for the Army of the James. While the Eighteenth Corps had fought the battle of Swift Creek on May 9, the Tenth Corps had also been engaged, fighting a Confederate division that had come down from Drewry's Bluff, in the battle of Chester Station on May 10. No movements were planned for May 11, and the Federals stayed behind their entrenchments. The Confederates, however, took advantage of this lull that Butler was allowing them. Desperate to fortify Richmond against the threat of the Army of the James, the Confederates simply marched 11,000 of their troops up the Richmond Turnpike from Petersburg, passing the entire front of the Army of the James, and filled positions in the entrenchments of Drewry's Bluff and Richmond.[30]

At 9:30 p.m. on the night of May 11, Butler issued his orders for the next day. His plan was not so much a general advance on Richmond but rather more of a demonstration against the Confederate forces they encountered. General Smith was ordered to take all the troops from his Eighteenth Corps that he could spare and "demonstrate against the enemy up the turnpike ... pressing the enemy into their intrenchments with the endeavor to turn them on the left, if not too hotly opposed.... It is intended to develop [by this movement] the entire strength of the enemy in the direction of Richmond, and, if possible, either to force them within their intrenchments or turn them, as the case may be." One division from the Tenth Corps was to be lent to General Smith; the remainder of the Tenth Corps was to be held in reserve and to defend against any movements by the Confederates from Petersburg.[31]

Battle of Drewry's Bluff

Burnham's Second Brigade, including the 8th Connecticut, moved out from camp at 7 a.m. on Thursday, May 12. On reaching the Richmond turnpike, they turned north in the direction of Drewry's Bluff. Near Dr. Cheatham's house, they encountered Confederates and deployed into line of battle. The Second Brigade formed on the left of the turnpike. Brigadier General Godfrey Weitzel's Second Division was on its right, and Colonel Horace T. Sanders' Third Brigade was on its left. Skirmishers were sent out to engage the Confederates. Ordered to advance, they pushed the enemy back, with the line of battle continuing to move up in support. The advance continued until the Confederates were driven behind Proctor's Creek.

On the next day, Friday, May 13, the skirmishing resumed, and the Confederates were steadily forced back. By afternoon, the skirmishers had passed the Half-Way House on the turnpike, and reached the outer line of the Confederate entrenchments. That evening, believing that the Confederates had evacuated their works, skirmishers conducted a reconnaissance to determine if the Confederates were gone. Instead, they found that a considerable force was still there. However,

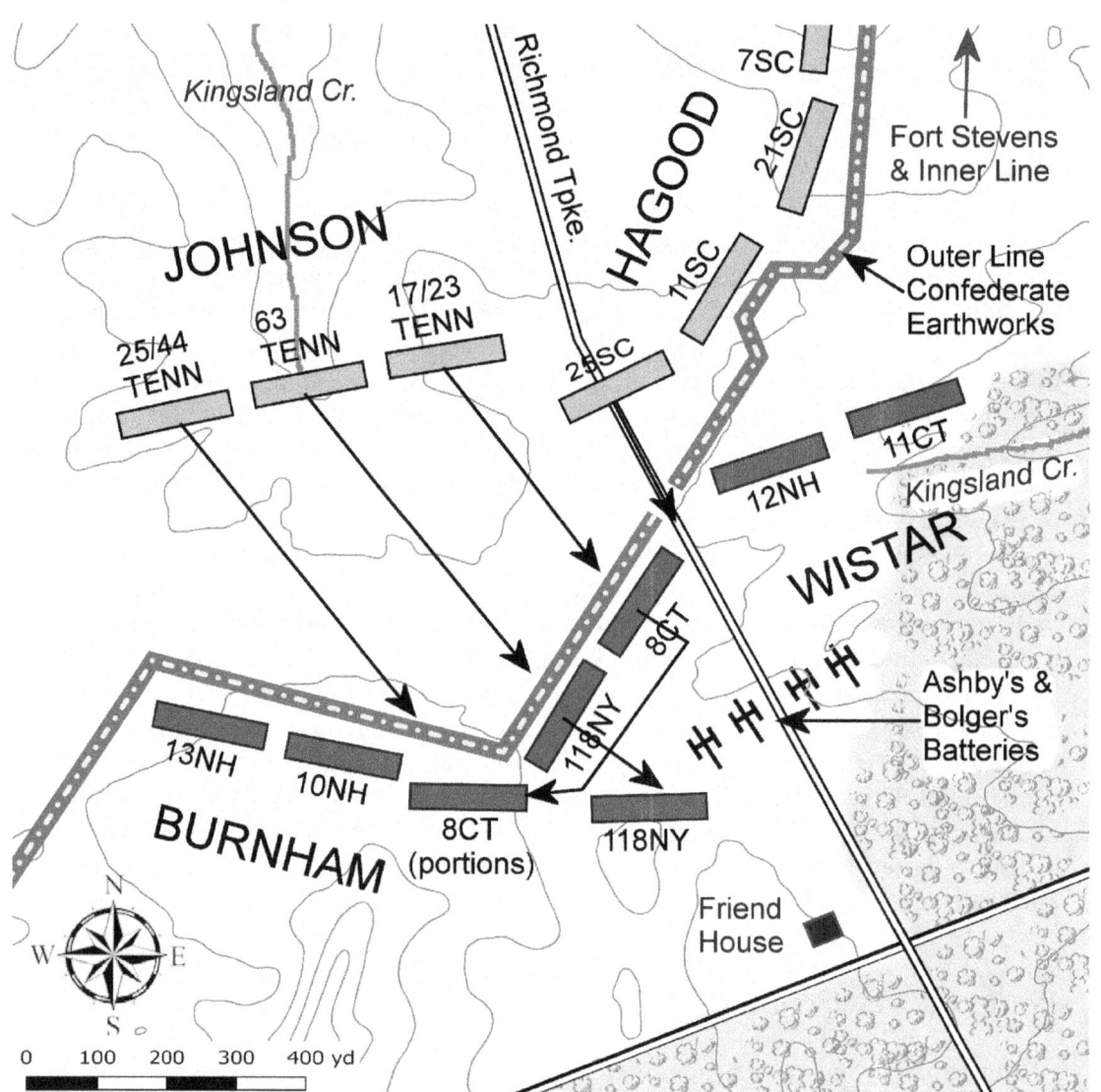

Map 18. Battle of Drewry's Bluff, Virginia, May 16, 1864.

on the morning of Saturday, May 14, when Burnham's brigade advanced and occupied the entrenchments, they discovered that the trenches had been evacuated later that night. The Confederate troops had retired to a stronger set of earthworks on the right side of the turnpike, from which they fired artillery against the Federals as they moved into the Confederate's now-abandoned entrenchments. General Burnham deployed his brigade in line of battle under the cover of the breastworks, with his right resting on the turnpike.[32]

In his report, Lieutenant Colonel Martin B. Smith, having assumed command of the Eighth in place of the wounded Colonel Ward, wrote that the 8th Connecticut was constantly in the front, from May 12 to May 16, much of the time acting in conjunction with the 118th New York Volunteers as a reserve for the skirmishers.[33]

Chapter 7. Deep Creek to Drewry's Bluff

Sergeant Seth Plumb, in a letter home, added some detail:

> The line of battle was formed after reaching the Richmond and Petersburg pike, our brigade well in the advance as usual. This line of battle moved slowly in skirmishing with the enemy till it reached the outer works around Fort Darling which it occupied Saturday morning. This line of battle marched under heavy fire much of the way, and all along through where our regiment marched you can see where the men lay flat on their faces often for hours at a time and with their fingers they scraped the mud up into a kind of work to protect them. The men were without even rubber blankets and it showered every few hours through the whole 48 hours. Saturday morning our troops reached the outer works and soon silenced the guns in the next line of works a little way ahead, but did not advance on them.[34]

Captain Roger Ford wrote that from the captured works they could see a "very large Fort in sight about 800 yards in front of us supposed to be Fort Darling" and that the works they captured were about six or eight miles in length.[35] The fort that they actually saw was Fort Stevens. Fort Darling was the fort at the easternmost part of the line, at Drewry's Bluff, overlooking the James River. It appears, however, that the name Fort Darling was commonly used to describe the entire line of defensive works in this area.

The next day, Sunday, May 15, was quiet, but Monday, May 16, more than made up for it. The Confederates had planned a major assault against the Federal right for early on the May 16, hoping to fold the Federal right back onto the center.[36] The Federal right was held by General Weitzel's Second Division of the Eighteenth Corps. Its left rested on the Richmond Turnpike. The Federal center consisted of General Brooks' First Division. On the right of the division was Burnham's Second Brigade, and its rightmost regiment was the 8th Connecticut, with its right resting on the Richmond Turnpike. Because of an angle in the captured Confederate breastworks now occupied by the Federals, where the line of entrenchments turned and ran to the north, the 8th Connecticut and the regiment to its left, the 118th New York, faced more to the left oblique than straight at the Confederate positions, with the right of the Eighth being somewhat "in the air."[37]

At 4:45 a.m. on Monday, May 16, the Confederate division of Major General Robert Ransom, consisting of four brigades, attacked Weitzel's positions on the Federal right. Weather became an important factor in that morning's battle because the area was covered by a dense fog, with visibility down to just a few feet. In addition, the Federals has strung telegraph wire across their front, tied shin high to tree stumps and stakes, to slow any advances made against them. Initially, the Confederate's attack had success, but confusion from the fog and the wire caused heavy losses, and Federal resistance stalled the advance.[38]

Meanwhile, a division commanded by Confederate Major General Robert Hoke was to attack the Federal center and left to prevent the Federals from reinforcing their right. At about 6:30 a.m., two of Hoke's brigades, those of Johnson and Hagood, moved forward against Brooks' Division. Hagood's rightmost regiment, the 25th South Carolina, engaged the 8th Connecticut and the 118th New York, while the remainder of his regiments remained behind the line of breastworks running to the northeast.[39]

Since the 8th Connecticut was the rightmost regiment in the Federal center, and since it was positioned along breastworks that accentuated their exposed right, the Eighth immediately felt the brunt of Hoke's attack. They were attacked from three sides. Captain Henry C. Hall described the frantic situation that morning:

> I never saw such fighting as I saw that day. Our men stood on one side of a breastwork and the rebs the other firing, bayoneting, and clubbing each other face to face. Once I was ordered to move my company to cover the left of our regt when the rebs were flanking us and when I got them there the rebs stood in line twenty deep not fifteen feet in front of us. We commenced firing and the rebs advanced upon us, in five minutes they were on three sides of us and coming round on the fourth when we fell back, upon the 118th N.Y. and the rebs after us charging up to the points of our bayonets like madmen. The 118th began to falter and I jumped up on the breastwork in front of them to cheer them on when a huge Tennesean charged on me. I drew my pistol and told him to drop his gun, he obeyed and came over the breastwork my prisoner instead of capturing me. That place soon got too hot and we retired slowly to a position occupied by the 10th N.H. where we again formed our line and contested the ground for a while.[40]

Lieutenant Colonel Martin B. Smith, commanding the Eighth, stated in his official report that when the Confederates charged the Federal troops to their right, and drove them, it exposed the right flank of the Eighth. Seeing this, Lieutenant Colonel Smith said that he ordered three companies to protect this flank, but they could not, and they fell back. His report said that the Eighth held their position for some time, until flanked on both right and left, at which point they fell back and took a position between the 10th New Hampshire and the 118th New York. When the 118th New York fell back, the 8th Connecticut took its position next to the 10th New Hampshire and remained there until noon, when ordered to fall back.[41]

Charles Coit wrote in a letter home that the position of the 8th Connecticut in the breastworks was such that they were "flanked before the fighting had commenced except that one or two Co's held a small fort at the right of our line, this they held until the Rebs were on the breastworks with them. Then Lieutenant Colonel Smith, who was commanding us ordered us to fall back." However, Coit wrote, the companies became separated in the fog, and the regiment broke up, with some men becoming lost. A portion of the men of the Eighth, though, were able to rally on the colors, and the unit reengaged.[42]

Brigadier General Burnham's report on the battle was not kind to Lieutenant Colonel Smith or sympathetic to the situation in which the Eighth's troops had found themselves in. He wrote: "The attack [on the Brigade] now became more furious, when Lieut. Col. M.B. Smith, commanding the Eighth Connecticut Volunteers, on the extreme right of my brigade, next to the pike, after making but feeble resistance, abandoned the line of fortifications in a very discreditable manner, and ordered his regiment to fall back, which it did in considerable confusion."[43]

Brigadier General Brooks, commanding the First Division, echoed Burnham's report, although perhaps with a little less rancor: "I regret to have to report that the commanding officer of the Eighth Connecticut, occupying the extreme right, withdrew that regiment from a position that was susceptible of being turned, but before it was sufficiently endangered. It might have caused trouble to the rest of the line."[44]

In their comprehensive book *The Military and Civil History Connecticut During the War of 1861–1865,* Croffut and Morris quoted Chaplain Moses Smith, who said the fallback by the Eighth was justifiable:

> The Eighth Connecticut occupied the right of the left center, and were soon attacked. Our lieutenant-colonel, Martin B. Smith, then in command, had remarked the day previous, to the general commanding our division, that the right and left center were not united: ... but no protection was given to that place or to our right. On Monday morning, as the right line was being pressed, and while the fog was so dense that a man could not be seen at a distance of ten paces, the enemy in mass came pouring in at our right.
>
> The only alternative seemed to be, fall back, or be captured. But for an hour our men battled them: sometimes mixed with the enemy, sometimes driving them; but constantly exposed to the enfilading fire, and the enemy gaining. At length, to prevent capture, our lieutenant-colonel gave the order to fall back. For this order, he was at first blamed, and the heroic old Eighth reported as having "skedaddled." That some men straggled in the fog is true; but be it remembered that the regiment was already so flanked, that the right was compelled to pass within the breastworks, and go down the rebel side, and then over those works, to rejoin the regiment.[45]

One other viewpoint—from the regiment next in line, the 118th New York Volunteers—may be helpful. In its regimental history, the author, John Lovell Cunningham, formerly a major in that regiment, wrote that the situation had been hopeless:

> [T]he line was giving way on our right. Heckman's Brigade seemed to have fallen back, and we were beginning to receive an enfilading and rear fire. The 8th Connecticut on our immediate right was being doubled back, company by company. Still no orders from Brigade or Division headquarters.... [T]he enemy was surrounding us, and now so near as to be reached with our bayonets, with hand-to-hand encounters. This was destruction, and company commanders directed each man to act for himself in getting to the rear.... [N]o use to rally. There are too many of the enemy on front and flank—too many brave fellows lying in yonder ditch—to make further defense reasonable.[46]

All indications from first person accounts are that the right of the brigade (and the division), that being the 8th Connecticut and the 118th New York, was overwhelmed by the Confederate attack. The terrain played an important role here—the breastworks held by these units were at an angle, leaving the right rear of the line unprotected. In addition, there was no physical connection with the division to their right—the breastworks did not continue to the adjacent regiments but rather turned and ran back toward Fort Stevens. The turnpike, splitting the divisions, served more as a barrier than as a unifying link. And even the Confederate attacks were separate and apart from each other, accentuating the other differences. Add to this the weather—an impenetrable fog that isolated men and units. Finally, there is no evidence that command ever attempted to rectify the situation or send aid that might have stemmed the tide at this crucial first assault by the Confederates, if in fact they could have, given the fog. This was truly the Eighth's own "Bloody Angle."

Consider, however, this comment by Captain Charles Coit, who took command of the 8th Connecticut whenever Lieutenant Colonel Smith was unavailable: "From all reports I don't think Col. Smith behaved very well the last day, I wish Col. Ward had been with us."[47]

Burnham's Second Brigade fought that morning, aided by the telegraph wire strung out in front, until 10 a.m., when General Brooks ordered the brigade withdrawn to the edge of the woods behind them. Soon thereafter they were pulled back to the Half-Way House, with skirmishers left to hold Friend's house in the rear of their original position. The Second Brigade (except for the 10th New Hampshire which was left to support a battery), then formed as the extreme left of the Eighteenth Corps in a line of battle on the right of the turnpike. At 3 p.m. they advanced, but finding no resistance from the Confederates, marched back to camp.[48]

Captain Charles Coit of the 8th Connecticut was in charge of the skirmishers left at the Friend house by General Burnham, and Coit had been in command of the brigade picket line the night before. After fighting and falling back with the skirmishers, he dismissed the men and sent them back to their companies. Later, after rallying strays and other men found in the woods, he was ordered by General Brooks to hold a line with these men, which he did for two hours. General Burnham then ordered Coit to deploy the men as skirmishers and cover the retreat of the troops. Coit complied, taking a position around "a large brick house," the Friend house. He was ordered to hold that line as long as possible, and he did just that until about 6 p.m., when they were attacked by a Confederate line of battle. They fired a volley and fell back, just as they were met by an officer sent to recall them. They arrived back at camp just after the Eighth did.[49]

Lieutenant Colonel Smith's report listed the casualties from May 12 to May 16 as seven killed, thirty wounded, and twenty-eight missing.[50] The one commissioned officer killed was Captain John McCall of Company K, whose company, along with Captain Ford's Company G, had earlier been sent out at Swift Creek by General Burnham to clear the area of sharpshooters. McCall was a Norwich man and a good friend of Captain Coit.[51]

There was one other casualty worthy of note, a death that had a great impact on Sergeant Seth Plumb, one of the narrators in this book. As may be recalled, since the Deep Creek days, Plumb was the sergeant in charge of the Eighth's Pioneer Corps. A few days before the early morning attack in the fog, the Pioneer Corps of the Eighth was consolidated with the Pioneer units in the other regiments of the brigade, under an officer who was made their leader. In the battle of May 16, the Pioneers were assigned to the breastworks of the 13th New Hampshire and fought there during the engagement. When the units fell back, Plumb went to find the Eighth, and learned that his best friend from Litchfield, First Sergeant Edward Wadhams—a man with whom he had enlisted—had been killed.

Seth Plumb left the Pioneers Corps that day. He was promoted to First Sergeant of Company E in Ed Wadham's place. He later wrote to his family at home:

> [M]y dearest earthly friend ... was killed last Monday in a battle near Fort Darling. Edward Wadhams is no more on earth, how hard it is for me to give him up Heaven only knows. He was more to me than all the rest of my friends in the army beside a hundred times.... When we fell back I went to find the 8th, and then learnt that Ed was left dead at the breast works. The ball went just inside of the left shoulder and passed into the region of the heart probably as he died instantly. I felt very bad that I could not see him after he was dead, but such is war.[52]

After their return to camp, the Eighth went back to the drudgery of strengthening their defenses. First, they were ordered to move their camp, but before they could become established, the entire regiment was sent out to "slash" the woods in front of the rifle pits that were being constructed. (Slashing consists of cutting down all the trees in an area, at a height of three to four feet above ground, so that the tops of the trees fall towards the enemy, forming a barrier difficult to overcome.) Captain Coit, in charge of the Eighth, reported that the men were kept working all night; they were not relieved until 7 p.m. the following evening, having spent "over thirty hours continuous chopping after so many hard work fighting."[53]

For the next week or so, the Eighth's time was spent between work details and falling in under arms to defend against expected attacks or movements of the enemy. On Saturday, May 29, the Eighth marched out at 5 p.m., arrived at Bermuda Hundred Landing about 8:30 p.m., and went into camp. At 4 a.m. the following morning, the men boarded the transport barge *John Haswell*, which was towed into the stream and anchored. At 7:30 a.m., the boat weighed anchor, and the Eighth started for Fortress Monroe.[54]

CHAPTER 8

Cold Harbor, Petersburg, Fort Harrison

While the Army of the James bolstered its defenses at Bermuda Hundred, south of Richmond, Lieutenant General Ulysses S. Grant and the Army of the Potomac were slugging it out with Major General Robert E. Lee north of Richmond. After hard fighting at Spotsylvania, Grant moved south on May 20 to challenge Lee at Hanover Junction, near the North Anna River. After fighting there, Grant moved south again, crossing the Pamunkey River on May 28 at Hanover Town, heading for Cold Harbor, a crossroads where five roads met.[1] As Grant wrote in his memoirs: "Cold Harbor was important to us because while there we both covered the roads back to White House (where our supplies came from), and the roads south-east over which we would have to pass to get to the James River below the Richmond defences."[2]

To strengthen his forces for the attack, Grant obtained the transfer of the Eighteenth Corps from Major General Benjamin F. Butler's Army of the James to the Army of the Potomac. The Eighteenth Corps, 16,000 strong, was led by Major General William F. "Baldy" Smith. As Grant recalled:

> On the 26th I informed the government at Washington of the position of the two armies; of the reinforcements the enemy had received; of the move I proposed to make; and directed that our base of supplies should be shifted to White House, on the Pamunkey.... Orders had previously been sent through Halleck, for Butler to send Smith's [Eighteenth] corps to White House. This order was repeated on the 25th, with directions that they should be landed on the north side of the Pamunkey, and marched until they joined the Army of the Potomac.[3]

Lee, aware of this reinforcement, arranged for a transfer of his own. He moved Major General Robert Hoke's division north—7,000 men at Bermuda Hundred—to join Lee's Army of Northern Virginia.

General "Baldy" Smith assembled an impromptu flotilla to transport the Eighteenth Corps, including the 8th Connecticut, from the Bermuda Hundred landing to either West Point or White House on the Pamunkey River. While they were within Union lines on Bermuda Hundred, the Eighth received orders to get ready to move.

Cold Harbor

Captain Charles Coit, now commanding the regiment, described the Eighth's preparation for their move to Cold Harbor. On Friday, May 27, they were pulled from the earthworks near the Howlett Line back towards Bermuda Hundred. They finally got some deserved rest from the front, sleeping all night for the first time in a while. The next day, they were all put in line. After dark, in the rain, they were marched back still further towards Bermuda Hundred. As the regiment's commander, Coit got to ride Colonel Ward's horse, and as he told his family, he would much rather ride than walk.[4]

In a letter home, Sergeant Seth Plumb reported on the move from Bermuda Hundred and the march from White House. The regiment marched to the Bermuda Hundred landing on Saturday, May 28, he said, then boarded transports Sunday morning with the rest of the Eighteenth Corps.[5] At first, the men of the Eighth were glad to get away from the stalemate on their bottled-up peninsula, but they were soon in a rage over the accommodations on their leaky barge.[6]

They proceeded to White House, Virginia, on the Pamunkey River. They arrived on Monday night, May 30, then Tuesday afternoon started their forced march towards Richmond. The weather was sultry, the heat was extreme. Exhaustion and heat stroke caused many stragglers.[7]

On Tuesday, May 31, cavalry from both sides battled over the crossroads at Cold Harbor, and the final disposition that day left it in Federal hands. Major General Horatio G. Wright's Sixth Corps began to come up to Cold Harbor the next day around 10 a.m.[8]

On Wednesday afternoon, June 1, the Eighth was on the march, following the Sixth Corps near the Chickahominy, ten miles northeast of Richmond. Word came that the 2nd Connecticut Heavy Artillery was close by. They soon met stragglers from the unit, who confirmed the news.[9]

Captain Charles Coit, who commanded the Eighth that day, wrote in his official report that they had been misdirected. They resumed their march at 6 a.m. towards New Castle, only to learn later that their objective was Cold Harbor. They arrived at that destination late in the afternoon. The Eighth was halted near the enemy lines, where they rested about an hour, then formed in line of battle.[10]

In his memoirs, Grant explained his plan for making use of "Baldy" Smith's Eighteenth Corps at Cold Harbor: "Smith, who was coming up from White House, was also directed to march directly to Cold Harbor, and was expected early on the morning of the 1st of June; but by some blunder the order which reached Smith directed him to Newcastle instead of Cold Harbor. Through this blunder Smith did not reach his destination until three o'clock in the afternoon, and then with tired and worn-out men from their long and dusty march."[11]

The Eighteenth Corps, with the Eighth, slowly made their way to their designated position in line between Wright's Sixth Corps and Major General Gouverneur K. Warren's Fifth Corps. "Baldy" Smith was ordered to connect with General Wright on his left and Warren on his right. General Smith soon discovered, once on the ground, that he could not possibly do both. "My scant force would not have filled the space between the 5th and 6th Corps, and, making that connection, I should have had no lines with which to make an attack.... As I could not obey both requirements of the order, I determined to aid in the attack, and began formation of my lines immediately."[12]

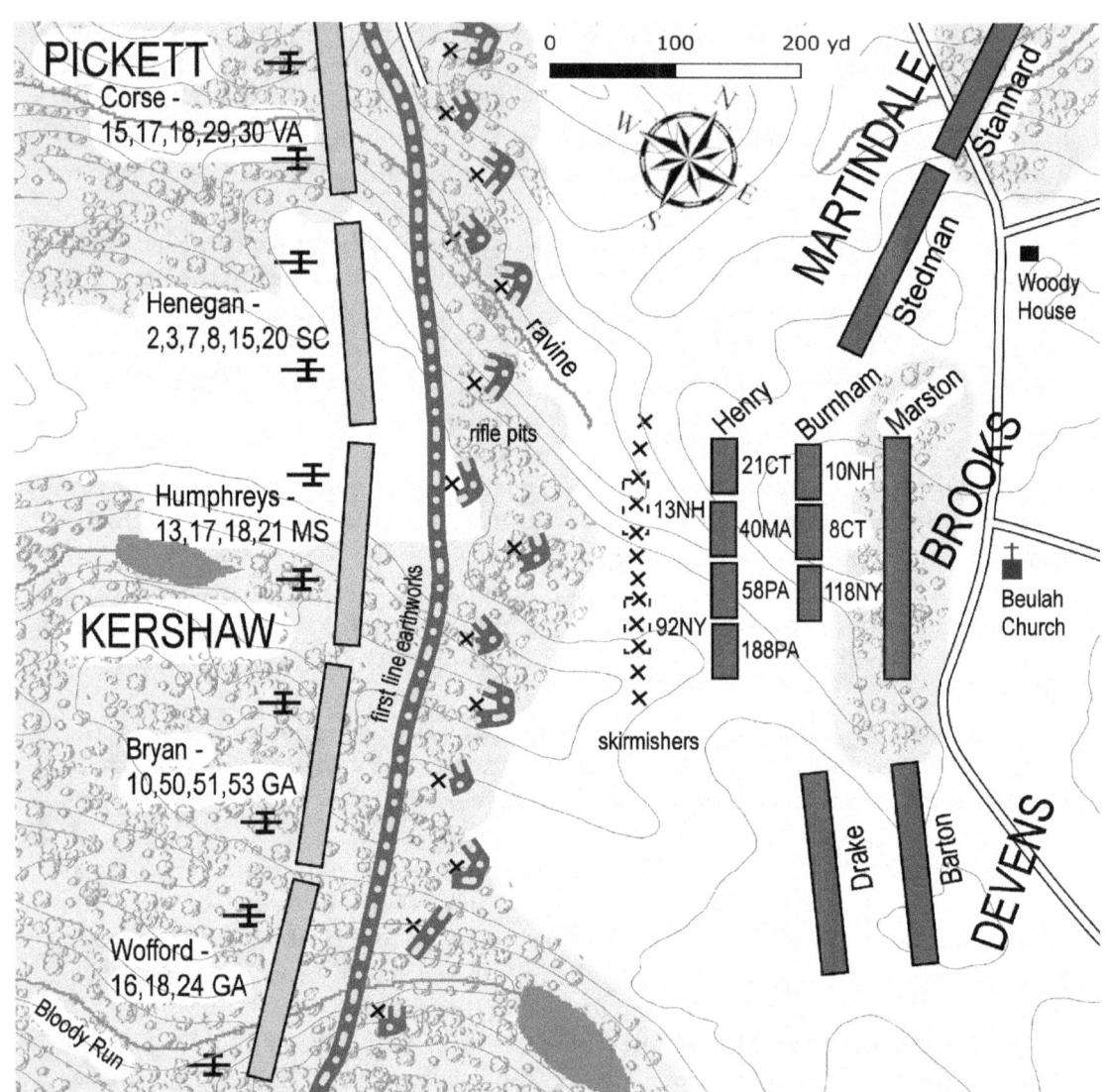

Map 19. Battle of Cold Harbor, Virginia, June 1, 1864, 6:00 p.m.

Smith's lines were now deployed. Brigadier General Charles Devens, Jr.'s, Third Division got into position on Wright's right about 4 o'clock. Brigadier General William T.H. Brooks' First Division was positioned about 5 o'clock, extending the line to Beulah Church, and "anchoring the right end of the Union line on Mr. Allison's road in front of the Woody house."[13]

General Brooks described what his command did in his official report. Upon arrival at Cold Harbor, his division was formed to the right of Devens' division, along the Bethesda Church road. Brooks formed his division in three parallel lines for the fighting ahead.

The first line was composed of Colonel Guy V. Henry's Third Brigade—the 21st Connecticut, 40th Massachusetts, 58th Pennsylvania, and the 188th Pennsylvania.

The 92nd New York, with the 13th New Hampshire from Brigadier General Hiram Burnham's Second Brigade, were thrown out as skirmishers.

The second line of Brooks' division was composed of the other regiments in Burnham's brigade—the 118th New York, the 8th Connecticut, and the 10th New Hampshire. The Eighth was between the 10th New Hampshire to their right, and the 118th New York to their left.[14]

The third line was Brigadier General Gilman Marston's First Brigade, posted in reserve, in line of battalions, each in column of divisions.[15]

Opposite Brooks' division, including Burnham's brigade, the Confederates were well entrenched and well prepared. These works were not transient or freshly dug. They were a substantial part of the permanent outer ring of the Richmond defenses. Arrayed in the trenches and works in front of the Eighth were Brigadier General Joseph B. Kershaw's division, of Richard H. Anderson's First Corps, Army of Northern Virginia.[16]

Burnham's first line advanced though woods 200 or 300 yards wide and emerged into an open space about 100 yards wide. The second line, including the Eighth, moved forward, in support of the advanced line, and halted about 100 yards behind it. The first line attacked and was met by the enemy skirmisher's fire from the protection of their rifle pits, along the edge of a pine grove, and from the enemy's main line, about 200 yards distant. General Burnham, in his official report, later wrote that this charge was successful. "The pits were charged and the enemy driven to his main line. This was done without much loss, except in the 13th New Hampshire."[17]

The second line, made up of the rest of Burnham's brigade, including the Eighth, then moved forward with Henry's brigade on its left, through the woods, and out into the clearing. General Brooks called a momentary halt, but then he ordered Burnham's brigade forward to support those who had gained a foothold on the main works to their left. Burnham withdrew the 13th New Hampshire and the 10th New Hampshire to the rear. He ordered the 118th New York and the 8th Connecticut to continue forward until they filled the space between the 58th Pennsylvania and those on their left. There, they halted and threw out pickets. These two regiments were ordered to intrench during the night.[18]

As Burnham advanced the 118th New York and the 8th Connecticut, they faced Brigadier General Benjamin G. Humphrey's Mississippi brigade, which consisted of the 13th, 17th, 18th, and 21st Mississippi Regiments. As the remainder of Burnham's brigade moved forward right, with the 13th New Hampshire in front and 10th New Hampshire behind, they were engaged by Colonel John W. Henagan's South Carolina brigade, which consisted of the 2nd, 3rd, 7th, 8th, 15th, and 20th South Carolina Regiments. There was also some friendly fire coming into the 13th New Hampshire from the left as Colonel Henry's brigade refused its right flank.[19]

About 7 p.m., when the remainder of their brigade was moved to the right, the 8th Connecticut advanced across the clearing and into the woods beyond. There they constructed breastworks, and sent out scouts, who determined that the pickets of the brigades to the right and the left did not connect, so pickets were sent out to cover their front. Coit reported the loss in the Eighth as two killed and four wounded.[20]

General Ulysses Grant described the success of their first moves of June 1. "By six o'clock in the afternoon Wright and Smith were ready to make an assault. In front of both the ground was clear for several hundred yards and then became wooded. Both charged across this open space and into the wood, capturing and holding the first line of rifle-pits of the enemy, and also capturing seven or eight hundred prisoners."[21]

Stalemate

Then the battle became a stalemate. The advanced line, with the 8th Connecticut and the 118th New York, was dug in and pinned down directly in front of the enemy works. Reliefs tried to rotate in after dark. General Smith's Eighteenth Corps was successful breaking through and holding the enemy rifle pits and first trenches. They were stretched out, however, and dangerously low on ammunition. The Eighteenth Corps had been ordered to move without trains, and were short of everything needed to continue the attack. Their hospital borrowed supplies from General Wright's hospital, and the infantry acquired ammunition it needed in the same manner. General "Baldy" Smith and his corps were in no condition to renew the attack on June 2. General Smith made Major General George G. Meade, commanding the Army of the Potomac, aware of it during the evening of June 1. The planned morning attack was thus postponed to late afternoon, and then again, until the next day.[22]

General Grant praised the Eighteenth Corps in his summary of the first day's results.

> Smith's corps also gained the outer rifle-pits in its front. The ground over which this corps (18th) had to move was the most exposed of any over which charges were made. An open plain intervened between the contending forces at this point, which was exposed both to a direct and a cross fire. Smith, however, finding a ravine running towards his front, sufficiently deep to protect men in it from cross fire, and somewhat from a direct fire, put Martindale's division in it, and with Brooks supporting him on the left and Devens on the right[see note], succeeded in gaining the outer probably picket rifle-pits. Warren and Burnside also advanced and gained ground which brought the whole army on one line.[23]

At daylight, June 2, General Burnham moved the 8th Connecticut and the 118th New York to the right in order to connect with the 10th New Hampshire, and in so doing, relieved a portion of Colonel Henry's Third Brigade. General Burnham's brigade remained in this position, strengthened the rifle pits, and sustained desultory fire.[24]

In his official report, Captain Coit reported that on June 2, before daylight, the Eighth was ordered to relieve the 40th Massachusetts on the front line. The Eighth moved to the front to fill the spot vacated on the left of the 10th New Hampshire. There, under heavy fire, they completed work on breastworks within 200 yards of the enemy's works. Coit reported their loss that day as one killed and six wounded.[25]

First Sergeant Albion Brooks dashed off a letter home announcing the movements, the changes, and the possibilities. "You see that we have changed base. I cannot write but just a word. We can hear Grant's cannon and probably will be near in a few hours. Give my love to all. We are expected to move every moment. My health is very good and I hope for the best."[26]

It was the first sergeant's last letter home. On June 2, Albion Brooks was struck by a bullet in the left abdomen, and it came out above his right hip. Chaplain Moses Smith informed his family, writing that "about one quarter before 9 o'clock last evening (June 3rd, '64) he quietly breathed his last. He was perfectly conscious to the end.... He said that God's will was right and he could trust all to Him."[27]

A Massive Attack

Now the battle intensified. Grant ordered Meade to execute another massive attack all along the line on the morning of Friday, June 3. General "Baldy" Smith moved three brigades to the front for the attack—Gilman Marston's, George J. Stannard's, and Griffin A. Stedman's brigades. He moved Burnham's brigade, with the Eighth, back to the third line, holding them in reserve. They did not participate in the assault on that fateful morning.[28]

General Burnham later reported that the attack began at 5 a.m. on June 3. The 10th New Hampshire, under Lieutenant Colonel John Coughlin, was deployed as skirmishers in advance of the attacking column. They captured some of the enemy's first line of rifle pits, and remained in the front, holding their gains gallantly, but with great suffering. The remaining three regiments, including the Eighth, were held in reserve until about noon.

General Brooks then ordered Burnham's forces to the left, where they took position on the right of the Sixth Corps. The troops were massed in column by division to storm the enemy's main works. The 21st Connecticut, under Lieutenant Colonel Thomas Burpee, was added to the column. But then, the order to attack was countermanded. Burnham moved his troops to a more sheltered position farther right, where they remained until dark.[29]

Subsequently, on the night of June 3, Brooks ordered Burnham to relieve elements of Henry's brigade from the front.[30] Captain Coit's official report describes how the Eighth advanced to the front again to relieve the 25th Massachusetts from Brigadier General George J. Stannard's First Brigade of Brigadier General John H. Martindale's Second Division. During the night the Connecticut men completed the breastworks that the Massachusetts troops had started.[31]

The men of the Eighth hugged the ground, pinned in place, yards apart for that night and the next day. Sergeant Seth Plumb described how they were lying in about twelve parallel lines, ten rods apart, each protected by a breastwork. The Eighth was within speaking distance of the Confederate line. In spite of the heavy losses, Plumb said the troops had confidence in General Grant, and "Baldy" Smith was still popular with the men.[32] Coit reported the losses of the Eighth on June 3 as one killed and twelve wounded.[33]

Amid the carnage and suffering, there was a moment of synchronicity. Private William H. Plumb of the 2nd Connecticut Heavy Artillery, and his brother, Sergeant

Seth Plumb of the 8th Connecticut, were able to meet on the field of battle. The Eighteenth Corps had encountered the Sixth Corps on the march to Cold Harbor, so each brother knew the other was nearby. They were able to meet on that infamous June 3. Seth Plumb wrote home of their brotherly encounter.

> The first news that I will give you is this, that while so many of our dear Litchfield boys have been killed and are dieing, Will and I have been permitted to meet, and have spent a good part of yesterday and to day together. Now for particulars. A week ago last Saturday we marched to the landing at Bermuda Hundred, and embarked with the 18th Corps Sunday morning for the White House on the Pamunkey. We arrived there Monday night, and on Tuesday after noon set out for Richmond Wednesday after noon we came upon the road where the 6th Corps of the Army of the Potomac had just pafsed over and in a few minutes some one said the 2nd Conn is just ahead. this seemed to good to be true, but soon we saw some of their straglers and found that it was ever so. We halted soon as we were in the presence of the enemy, and Elvin Oaks of Co. A came to enquire for me, and I learnt from him that Will was along, and the boys of the 2nd all right. In about an hour from that we were drawn up in line of battle and went into the fight. the 6th Corps being on the left of the 18th (the 2nd is in the 2nd Brigade 1 Division 6th Corps) This was the last we heard of the 2nd till yesterday morning as we were kept at the front, as usual. Then I could stand it no longer and ran away from my regiment, and found the 2nd and Will not more than half a mile from us. Imagine our feelings as we embraced each other. I took Will back with me to the 8th as we were on the front line and I could not stay away. Last night we were relieved from the front and are now within 150 rods of the camp of the 2nd and of course we are together to day.[34]

Brother William Plumb also wrote of their visit. "I was with Seth most all day yesterday, he is well and strong and full of hope, we thought many times yesterday of the sad, sad news that had gone home to many families in Litchfield, while we were permitted to meet in health, to rejoice over our own good luck, and mourn for those that were very near and dear to us."[35] It would be the last time the Plumb brothers saw each other on this earth.

On Saturday, June 4, at 3 a.m., Burnham reported the 13th New Hampshire and the 118th New York relieved a portion of Colonel Henry's brigade on the front line of the rifle pits. The 8th Connecticut was moved to the right and even further to the front, where they relieved from the front line the 2nd New Hampshire of Brigadier General Griffin A. Stedman, Jr.'s, Second Brigade from Martindale's Second Division. Burnham's three regiments held that front line, strengthening the pits and skirmishing with the enemy until the evening of June 4, when they were relieved by Marston's brigade. "On the evening of the 4th my command was relieved by General Marston. From that time to the present, I have alternated with the other brigades of the division in holding the front line every third day," General Burnham later wrote.[36]

Captain Coit, in his official report, said that on Saturday, June 4, between 3 and 4 a.m., under orders from General Martindale, the 8th Connecticut advanced to the extreme front and relieved the 2nd New Hampshire, where they began and finished a line of breastworks, connecting on the left with works built by the 13th New Hampshire. Around midnight they were relieved by the 139th New York and withdrawn to the rear lines. Losses for the Eighth on June 4 were one killed and six wounded.[37]

In a letter home, Coit mentioned they had been engaged constantly for four days with losses every day. He said they had been fighting behind breastworks, which limited casualties to about thirty killed and wounded. About midnight on Saturday, June 4, they were relieved from the front lines and rested in the rear lines.[38]

Coit also reported that the Eighth remained in their last position on Sunday, June 5, with one man wounded, until the evening of June 6, when they moved to the front again to relieve the 92nd New York. There, the Eighth remained for twenty-four hours, supporting the 10th New Hampshire, with one man wounded. The Eighth was relieved on June 7, by the 139th New York, withdrawing to the rear lines until the evening of June 9. They suffered one killed and one wounded.[39]

Coit wrote home that the Eighth was about to move to the front for the next twenty-four hours, but whether in the front or the rear, the danger was much the same. He said that if the men would just stay down, they would remain safe, yet it was virtually impossible to stay down like that for hours and days. Even a flinch to adjust some discomfort was enough to draw deadly fire. So, there they laid in trenches and traverses, in a dozen parallel lines, the first just a few rods apart from their foes.[40]

Captain Coit's official report stated the full recapitulation of the Eighth's losses for the Cold Harbor actions were thirty-seven casualties: six killed, thirty-one wounded.[41]

Around this same time, reports came that some soldiers of the Eighth were among the Union prisoners the Confederate forces had captured over the past several months, notably from the actions on Bermuda Hundred. Most of the captured enlisted men were sent to the infamous Andersonville, Georgia, prison, where many Union soldiers died. Croffut and Morris wrote that "about the 1st of June, a large number of prisoners came in [to Andersonville] from Butler's army, including twenty-four of the Eighth Connecticut, fifty-two of the Seventh, a hundred and thirty of the Eleventh, and fifteen of the Twenty-first."[42]

Private Andrew Byrne, of Company B, recorded a chronology of some of the Eighth's casualties at Cold Harbor:

> Jun. 1 Wed.—marched again at 5 o'clock in the morning met the rebel in the afternoon skirmishing and driving into his rifle pits and after a hard fight took his first lines
>
> Jun. 2 Thu.—fighting and driving him by charges out of successive lines of rifle pits all day and night. Andrew Gordon, Bill Darby, and McCann wounded, Bill Long killed, in the front all day and night
>
> Jun. 3 Fri.—fighting all day at Coal Harbour gaining steadily on some points of the line, but holding ours on the whole. Walter Smithson wounded.[43]

For thirteen days, from May 31 until the night of June 12, the 8th Connecticut, with the rest of the Eighteenth Corps, and the Army of the Potomac, laid in front of the Cold Harbor lines in the earthworks and rifle pits, rotating to the front every third day, and to the rear for two days. The battle of Cold Harbor was over.

Advance on Petersburg

Grant now executed another movement advancing south by the left flank. His plan to secretly cross the Army of the Potomac to the south of the James River was risky. His strategy included taking Petersburg, cutting the railroads to the south and west of the city, while keeping Lee locked in place with the Union forces north of the James.

Personality clashes in the Union command affected the fate of the Eighth. General Butler was a political appointment, and General Smith was a West Point professional. It was widely known that they did not have good opinions of each other. The antagonism spilled over after Cold Harbor.

Butler was not supportive of Grant's plans or the costly battle at Cold Harbor. Butler still had his eye on Petersburg. Before they had begun the siege at Cold Harbor, Butler had proposed an attack on Petersburg, and he now convinced Grant to return General Smith and the Eighteenth Corps to him for the purpose of taking Petersburg by surprise. General Smith (like Butler) had openly criticized General Meade, and indirectly, Grant, for the actions at Cold Harbor, making for further drama.

Grant agreed to Butler's plan, so General Smith was ordered back to the Army of the James. "On the 12th, Smith was ordered to move at night to White House, not to stop until he reached there, and to take boats at once for City Point, leaving his trains and artillery to move by land," Grant wrote later in his *Personal Memoirs*.[44] Now Grant began his coordinated advance on Petersburg. He ordered Major General Winfield S. Hancock's Second Corps to march toward Petersburg. General Smith's Eighteenth Corps boarded the transports at White House and arrived at Point of Rocks on Bermuda Hundred on June 14, in advance of the rest of the army.

In a letter home on June 18, Captain Coit told his family how the Eighth moved from the Cold Harbor front, back to Bermuda Hundred, and then into the action in front of Petersburg. He said transports took them to Point of Rocks about noon on June 14, where they marched back from the river about a mile and a half to their old camp. Coit said every man was exhausted and needed rest. But an orderly arrived from headquarters that night with orders Coit read by the light of a match. He was to rouse the regiment, eat breakfast, and be ready to march by 2 a.m.[45] Coit's official report about the attack on Petersburg said that at 2 a.m. on June 15, the Eighth, 200 men strong, on the right of the brigade, moved across the Appomattox River on pontoons and out the road towards Petersburg. They marched south along that route until midmorning.[46]

Butler ordered General "Baldy" Smith and the Eighteenth Corps to attack the substantial earthwork defenses northeast of Petersburg named the Dimmock Line. General Smith was deliberate in his approach after the Cold Harbor experience. Smith's reconnaissance of the Confederate works found they were well defended by artillery. Unsure of rumors that Lee was on his way with reinforcements, General Smith delayed the attack, and as a result, lost much of the element of surprise. As one critic later said of Smith, "He lost his nerve, perhaps because of the formidable character of the Confederate works, or perhaps because of a recurring bout with malaria, but his hesitation may have lost him the opportunity to shorten the war by nearly a year."[47]

While General Smith was busy assessing the situation, his forces arrayed for the battle were greeted with skirmishing by the enemy. The Eighth's line engaged and advanced on their outer pickets and rifle pits.

Broadway Landing, Virginia, pontoon bridge across the Appomattox (Library of Congress, Prints and Photographs Division, Civil War Photographs, LC-B811-2625). The 8th Connecticut Volunteers crossed this bridge moving back and forth from their camp at Point of Rocks to the Petersburg front in June 1864.

General Smith's Third Division of black troops, under Brigadier General Edward W. Hinks, pushed in, carried the first line of works, and captured a gun and several hundred men. General Hinks, on the left of the line, took four redoubts, but the main salient on the line, across a broad valley, and on the right of Burnham's brigade, was defended by redoubts, and covered by rifle pits.

Captain Coit's official report described how Hinks's division captured the first line. Then the left wing of the Eighth regiment was deployed as skirmishers to the left of the road under Captain William J. Roberts of Company I. The Eighth advanced, contacted the enemy, then deployed the right wing as skirmishers. The color guard was sent to the rear.[48]

The Eighth's line advanced and drove the enemy about a quarter mile until they encountered the strong Confederate fortifications. The skirmishers were supported with a line of battle by the 13th New Hampshire and a detachment of the 118th New York.[49] Using trees and bushes as cover, the men advanced as close to the works as the cover allowed. Deliberate fire kept the enemy in check and silenced the guns for a time. Around noon, the enemy charged the center of the brigade line, but were repulsed with considerable loss. Around 6 p.m., the Eighth's two companies with Sharps rifles, Company G and Company K, at the center of the line, had expended their sixty rounds, and were unable to procure more ammunition of that caliber. They were relieved by two companies of the 118th New York, who were placed in the center of the Eighth's line.

By this time, General Smith had Brigadier General August V. Kautz's cavalry division deployed and the artillery support was in position. The entire Eighteenth Corps of infantry was in line arrayed along the north and east facing portions of the enemy defenses. "Baldy" Smith finally ordered the full general attack by brigade heavy skirmish lines at 7 p.m.[50]

Those orders came to General Burnham, and the Second Brigade skirmish line was sent forward. The 13th New Hampshire was on the left, eight companies of the Eighth and two of the 118th New York were on the right. With a cover from sixteen cannon, the brigade skirmish line charged the rifle pits and forts and quickly took the works in their front, to the surprise of all, capturing five guns and 250 prisoners.[51]

Captain Charles Coit described the attack. The Eighth advanced through dense jungle, which offered protection from enemy fire, and kept their losses slight. Coit reported twelve casualties in the charge, and eight earlier in the day. His troops captured cannons and prisoners. The enemy resistance was slim, which allowed the success of the skirmish line attack. As Coit said later, "The Rebs were greatly disgusted that they had been whipped by a skirmish line."

During the attack, Coit wrote, the soldiers were informed that General Smith stood only a few yards in the rear of their line, and when they gained the works, he jumped up and down and shouted "Victory! Victory!" while waving his hat. He mounted his horse, and he and General Brooks were inside the works immediately. Coit added, "Where do you suppose our Brigadier was? Just where he always is at such times—not in the front."[52]

General Smith and General Brooks ordered the advance to continue. Immediately, the line was pushed forward a few hundred rods, about two-thirds of a mile, to the rear of the fort. They immediately advanced to a hill in the rear of the works, within two miles of Petersburg, and directly in front of the enemy's inner line of defenses along Harrison Creek. But darkness was now falling, and General Smith decided not to continue the advance. At the end of his letter, Coit wrote, "We are now posted around a house owned by a family by name of Friend, on a knoll in plain sight of Petersburg."[53]

There they built breastworks, provided support, and remained in place until 6:30 p.m. on June 17, when the Eighth was relieved by the 3rd Vermont from the Sixth Corps. The Eighth then marched back that night, and re-crossed the Appomattox River to Point of Rocks.

Coit reported the casualties of the Eighth as two killed and seventeen wounded.

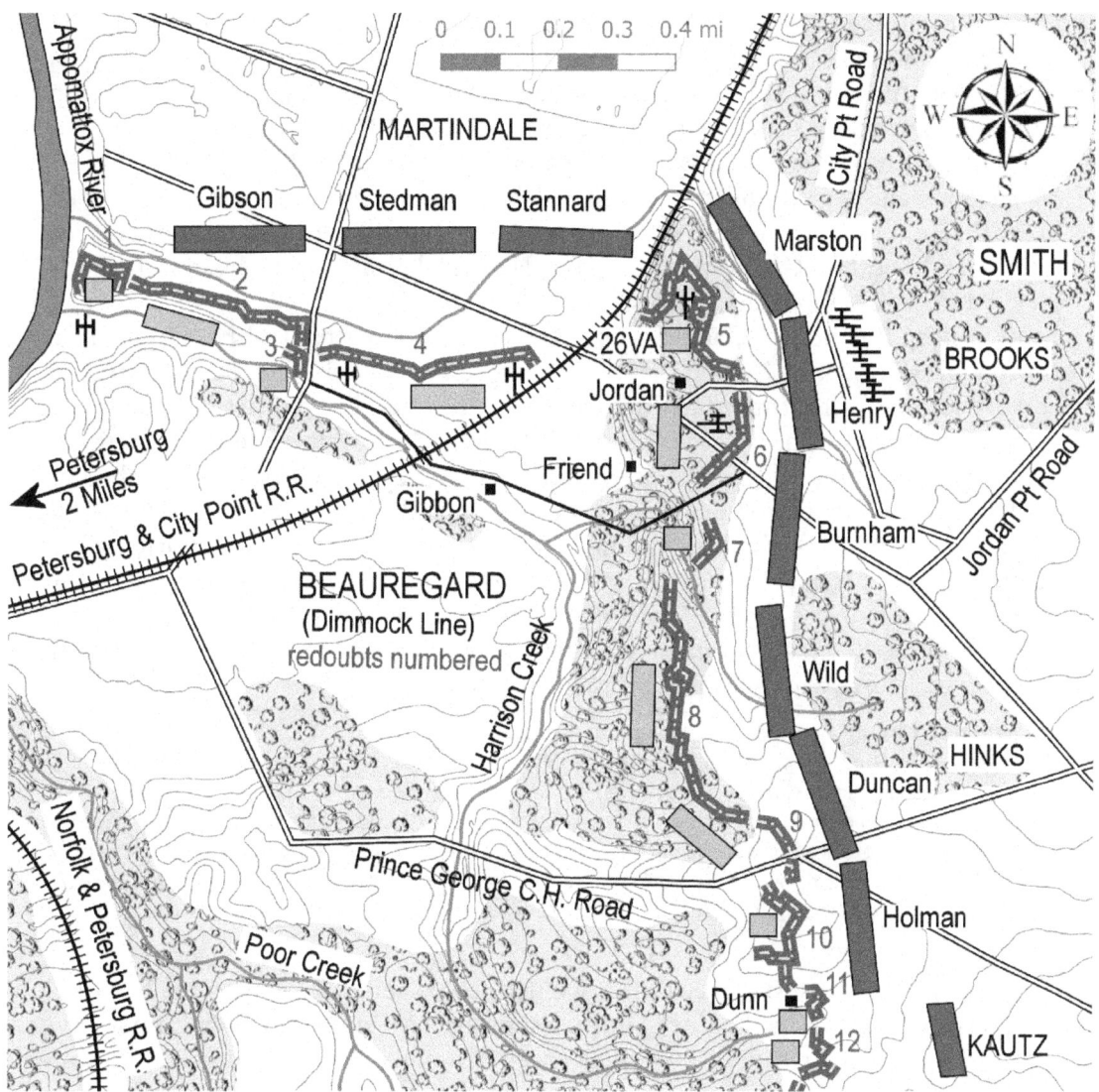

Map 20. Second Battle of Petersburg, Virginia, June 15, 1864, 7:00 p.m.

He finished his report with this simple statement: "The behavior of the whole command, officers and men, was in the highest degree commendable."[54]

General William Brooks' First Division, and General John Martindale's Second Division, had captured a mile of works around the salient of Redoubt 5, but the Confederates continued to hold their fortifications further to the left, to the right, and to the rear of the point of attack.[55] "Baldy" Smith's three divisions had driven General Henry A. Wise's Virginia brigade back to Harrison's Creek, but did not advance further that night. The Confederates held, dug in, and resisted for another nine and a half months.[56] Grant later wrote, "I believed then, and still believe, that Petersburg could have been easily captured at that time."[57]

Captain Coit said General Burnham had praised him for the Eighth's contributions to the June 15 attack. "And here let me copy from Genl Burnham's report of action at Petersburg June 15. I would also commend Capt. Chas. M. Coit Commdg 8th Connt Vols. for his good behavior on that occasion and the prompt manner in which he supported Col. Stevens' 13th N.H."[58]

Chaplain Moses Smith wrote of the losses suffered by the regiment: "Of the dead, Sergeant Fitz G. Hollister was as worthy a man as ever graced the ranks of the Eighth. He was difficult, but intelligent; retiring, but influential, and faithful even unto death, both to God and his country. He is embalmed in the hearts of all who really knew him. Dead, he yet lives."[59]

During the month, Chaplain Smith watched the regiment shrink in terms of both officers and men. He said that there had been no superior officers for duty. Colonel Ward had not returned to duty from wounds at Walthall Junction, Lieutenant Colonel Martin B. Smith was on the sick list and in the hospital, there was no major, and Captain Henry M. Hoyt, the senior captain, was detailed to brigade staff. Thus, the regimental command devolved upon Captain Charles Coit much of this time, and he proved to be a faithful and honorable leader. The regiment reported about 200 men and only ten officers during this period. Since leaving Yorktown on May 31, the regiment had lost about 50 percent of their fighting strength.[60]

On June 18, Captain Coit wrote home that his troops, with a break from the front, had returned to their old Bermuda Hundred camp.

> I am really living again. Am in my wall tent (mine as commander of Regt.) with my baggage at hand, have on clean underclothes + have just partaken of a good supper—ham hashed with potatoes, pickles, fresh bread, dried applesauce, + coffee with milk + white sugar—pretty good bill of fare. Yesterday p.m. we—the 18th Corps or at least a portion of it—were relieved from our position in front of Petersburg by the 6th Corps + we marched back to our old Camp. This Camp we occupied a day + a night before we sailed for White House + again a night when we returned from W.H. before this advance on Petersburg + now we return again.[61]

On June 19, just one week after Cold Harbor, general orders were issued by Major General William "Baldy" Smith assigning the Eighteenth Corps, First Division command to Brigadier General George J. Stannard, replacing General William T.H. Brooks.[62]

The Siege of Petersburg

The 8th Connecticut now rotated back to the front to join the siege around Petersburg.

On Tuesday, June 21, at 2.30 a.m., the regiment was roused and left Point of Rocks at 4 a.m. for Petersburg. They arrived at the rear lines there about 9 a.m. They were supposed to relieve the Sixth Corps in the front line, but the Confederate guns made the move impossible during daylight. So, the Eighth laid in a field for the day roasting under the hot sun. Captain Coit thought that the time could have been better spent back in their camp where they could sort through baggage and paperwork. About 8 p.m., the Eighth moved to the front, where they were assigned a position in the second line of entrenchments.

Chapter 8. Cold Harbor, Petersburg, Fort Harrison

> We strengthened this line during the night + dug covered ways +c. Our line (8th Reg) ran through the yard connected with a fine brick house + the pit that I had dug for my head qts was magnificently shaded by the fine trees, mulberry +c—then the Regt that I relieved had left a tete a tete, (i.e., a sofa aint it) a mahogany table + chair which they had confiscated + these I moved into my pit + perhaps I did not have luxurious quarters for the forty eight hours that I habituated there.[63]

Coit said there was no certainty to his tenure in command of the regiment. "No one knows when Col. Ward or Col. Smith will return—may at any time. Do you know that as long as I command the Regt I receive just ten dollars ($10) per month less pay than when commanding a Co.?"[64]

The siege work and trench life were taking a toll on the men of the Eighth, as Chaplain Moses Smith wrote on July 20.

> A month of siege-work; lying in the trenches; eyeing the rebels; digging by moonlight; broiling in the sun; shooting through a knot-hole; shot at if a head is lifted; artillery compliments passing and repassing; our lives endangered by shells from both sides; officers falling; comrades dying; everybody wearied by the monotony, and exhausted by heat and watching.....
>
> Here we have remained constantly under the enemy's fire. Occasionally, for one or two days, the regiment has been withdrawn from the pits beyond bullet-range, but not from artillery-shots. Rebel sharpshooters and rebel mortars have been busy on us, both while in the front and when relieved. In return, our men have played the sharpshooter, and burrowed underground.[65]

The chaplain described the mounting losses of the Eighth, both officers and men. The siege had brought suffering and death to the regiment.

> Twenty casualties have occurred in our regiment during these thirty days. Most of the wounds have been severe, and five of the men are dead. Among our losses we sorrowfully record three honored captains,—Roger M. Ford, commanding Company G, wounded in the right leg; Elam T. Goodrich, commanding Company H, wounded in the hip; and Henry C. Hall, commanding Company F, instantly killed by a rifle-ball. It is said "Death loves a shining mark."... So, among the non-commissioned dead. No man in Company B can fill the vacancy caused by the death of Sergeant Joseph Glover. Youthful, tender-hearted, honoring religion, faithful to every duty, true to his calling, and loved by all, he fell in a moment, and we mourn his loss.[66]

It was now July. Sergeant Seth Plumb composed a good description of the situation the Eighth was now experiencing. He told of the duty at the front two days, then in the rear two days. Since the rotations happened in the night, and the watching was constant, the soldiers got little sleep at the front.

> The orders there were for not a man to sleep in the night but for every man to have his eyes and ears open, the rebel picket line being but a few rods in front of us. All day yesterday from day light till after the stars began to show for more than 16 hours I lay in a little pit all alone without once stepping out of it, exposed to the burning sun, but I do not feel the effects of it much to day, though I did think one time that the sun would dissolve this Plum. For the sake of my friend as well as my own I obliged orders and kept covered as much as possible for a man to show his head was only to make a target for many rebel sharp shooters.[67]

Seth Plumb said that since so many officers had been lost, some companies were commanded by sergeants. The tactical situation was difficult. The Eighth, now part of Stannard's division, was on the right of the line, close to the banks of the

Appomattox River. Across the river, Confederate batteries were at right angles to their line to hit them in the flank and rear. On Thursday, June 30, those batteries opened from every direction, until the smoke hid the sun. The men stuck to their shelters and hardly anyone was hurt.

Sergeant Plumb told of a Confederate charge a week earlier in front of the line that the Eighth held. The rifle pits they were in the day before were the ones that the Confederates took, but those pits proved fatal to the Confederates in the end. Plumb also said a thirty-pound gun that played on the city every fifteen minutes had set a fire Thursday night that caused a commotion heard from the city. He said the mortars were especially deadly, since they dropped shells straight down, right into their trenches.[68]

In his next letter home, Plumb described the unrelenting nature of the battle.

> War rages almost uninterruptedly, as it has from the 15th of June, when we first took the fortifications. The bringing of artillery and the popping of musketry has become to us like the ticking of the clock to you, and it would seem hardly natural to be where we could not hear it. At times the firing will break out along the line as if an attack was being made, and all stand ready with their pieces in their hands and bayonets fixed ready to receive them. We are on duty at this front 4 days at a time now, then we go to the rear for 2 days.[69]

In a letter July 3, Captain Coit told his family that Colonel Ward had returned, and that the Eighth was taking still more casualties among the officers and soldiers in the ranks.

> Saw Col. Ward this a.m.—he has arrived but is not strong + probably will not go out with us tonight. Capt. Goodrich was wounded quite severely last Friday. We were both lying side by side at the time and as he raised up to arrange his coat under his head as a pillow a bullet struck him in the small of the back just escaping the bone. If it had penetrated an inch farther it would have been mortal. It will be sore but not dangerous. I have lost the best man in my Co. Sergt. Joseph Glover in addition to other excellences he was a real Christian. I don't know how he can be spared in the Co.[70]

Coit said that commanding the regiment was challenging, but he was reluctant to pass the baton back to Colonel Ward.

> I gave one man in Co. I the choice of "doing his duty under fire or being shot the next time he failed—this was while at Coal Harbor–+ since he has proved a first-rate soldier in every respect." At the same time, I gave all the Regt to understand the same and we have had no shirks since to my knowledge. I suppose I date from Head Qts. today for the last time for the present at least for Col. Ward intends to join us to night + take command. I must own I am rather sorry. After commanding a Regt for nearly two months + two such months it will seem rather tame to return to my Co. Col. Ward is not strong yet by any means + I hope he may wish me to assist him tho' I don't expect it we are so short for Company Officers—part of the time have had but six for ten Co's.[71]

Captain Coit described how he was thankful for the help and support the relief societies were providing for the men of the Eighth, especially for the fresh vegetables they were now receiving. He said that both the U.S. Sanitary Commission and the Christian Commission were doing great work, but vast supplies didn't go very far in the huge army. Coit said the men even received pickles, and the officers were able to buy and feast on new potatoes from the commissary. Coit said that the Sanitary

Commission had sent onions, but the officers didn't get any because the stores were always issued to the men first. On this campaign, Coit said, the men lived better than the officers.[72]

Life in the trenches at the front was miserable. When the regiment was sent to the front on the night of July 19, Coit said they waded in mud for a couple miles to reach the front lines, where they found the trenches flooded with water, and the bottoms a mass of mud. There was little chance of sleep that night. Coit said he passed the night on a board six inches wide and four feet long that he placed across the trench, with his rubber poncho over him. The poncho kept him dry from the rain, but perspiration soaked him through from the inside. It rained through the middle of the next day, but then turned delightful.[73]

Changes in High Command

From June through July, the fate of the Eighth was roiled in army command politics. Grant did not like Butler, Butler did not like Smith, and Smith did not like Butler. The three of them wrote plenty about hard feelings and counter arguments. As the war fighting waned, the infighting waxed.

Based on the limited success of "Baldy" Smith's advances on Petersburg back on June 15, Grant relieved him from command of the Eighteenth Corps on June 19. General Smith had been close with Grant in the 1863 Western Theater, and Smith expected Butler had encouraged Grant to remove him. Butler had complained to Grant of General Smith's insubordination to orders to push the attack on Petersburg on June 15 and 16.[74]

In Washington, Lincoln issued Order No. 225 to remove the Eighteenth Corps from the Army of the James, and naming General Smith to command. Butler responded to the news:

> The order No. 225 was sent to me directly from Washington, and paragraph I. reads as follows:—
>
> "The troops of the Department of North Carolina and Virginia serving with the Army of the Potomac in the field under Major-General Smith will constitute the Eighteenth Army Corps, and Maj.-Gen. William F. Smith is assigned by the President to the command of the Corps. Maj.-Gen. B.F. Butler will command the remainder of the troops in the Department, having his headquarters at Fortress Monroe."
>
> Upon receiving the order, I called upon General Grant with it, showed it to him, and asked him if this was his act and his desire,—and if so, would he kindly tell me what act or fault of mine had caused such action on his part. He replied: "But I don't want this."[75]

Grant actually did not want this change. He wanted the Eighteenth Corps to stay where it was. So, he rescinded the order, then relieved General Smith. Smith replied: "The only reason given me by General Grant at our first interview was that I had severely criticized General Meade [after Cold Harbor], and had instigated an attack upon General Hancock in the 'New York Tribune.' This was highly absurd."[76]

As a result of all this intrigue, the Eighteenth Corps was returned to General Butler's Army of the James, and Major General Edward O.C. Ord was placed in command of the corps.

When Captain Coit heard about the dismissal of "Baldy" Smith as Eighteenth Corps commander, he told his family that the men of the Eighth had full confidence in Smith. Coit related this anecdote.

> I have said considerable about our Genl Smith in this letter but I have one thing more to add. Late yesterday I rec'd an order to have 2 officers + about 100 men report for fatigue duty to a Major Tyler of the Genl's staff. They so reported but the Major thought it was then too late to do the work + dismissed them to report this morning. This morning they reported + were set at work repairing a road. After working two or three hours Genl Smith passed that way + immediately dismissed them as he expressly stated because it was Sunday. The 8th never cheered but one Genl but if we remain much longer under Baldy I think he will hear from us.[77]

In another letter, Coit again praised General Smith, and said he was not impressed with General Ord, the Eighteenth Corps command replacement.

> Genl Smith was really beloved by all his troops + all had perfect confidence in his abilities and were ready to go where ever he ordered. Why he of all men should have been relieved no one can imagine except that he was not on good terms with Burnside + Hancock so we hear.....
> Genl Ord I met at his Hd. Qts. the day he assumed command of the Corps. I spoke only a word with him, I was Div Off of Day + answered for our Division, but I heard him talk considerably—was not particularly pleased, he does not look at the person he is conversing with, his appearance is soldierly but not particularly great.[78]

Soldiers often tell a simpler story of their experiences, and they did that during the continuing siege around Petersburg. One soldier of the Eighth wrote:

> We are in the pits two, and sometimes four days at a time, through night and day, rain and sun, mud and water. When a shell comes bowling along, down we all go with a jerk. There is nothing lost, I notice, by being polite. We have to lie low, of course; and when we are relieved, and get behind our breastworks, it is not much better; for, if a head or hand is lifted in sight, fifty bullets are sent after it. The enemy's guns have a good range upon our camps, and sometimes open upon us about midnight, supposing us sound asleep after our fatigue in the trenches, and keep us awake all night, and many times drive us to our gopher-holes. Thus, we stand the storm; our works growing stronger day by day, and our faith strengthening with our works.[79]

Sergeant Plumb said their duty in the trenches was getting more dangerous. He said their division was positioned on the line from the Appomattox River to a little beyond the City Point railroad.

> Our lines are in plain sight of the city and less than a mile from it. The boys regulate their watches by the city clock. Our lines are first a picket line. About 8 rods in rear of that a line of breast works with a traverse every rod or two to protect us from the enfilading fire from over the river. In rear of this about 20 rods is the 2d line of breast works, with many guns and mortars mounted in forts along its whole length, back of this on the hills there are other works but they are no infantry in them. The picket line is not occupied now in the day time which is a great relief.
> Our position this time is on the front line. It is not safe for a man to show his head above the works and watch is kept though between sand bags on top of the works. At dusk however all musketry firing ceases in front of our Division and the pickets from both sides go out in plain sight of each other.[80]

Plumb described picket duty one night when the moon made it nearly as light as day. Pickets from the opposing sides were posted about the same time. Both sides marched towards each other, so it was breathlessly exciting, but no shots were fired, and everything was quiet, to the satisfaction of those lives so near each other. The night before, the Confederates hurled a few mortar rounds at them. The Union reply was to fire all the guns and mortars on the Union line for nearly two hours. The city was thrashed, and the enemy driven into their holes for their audacity. He said the Confederates seemed to be looking for news about their recent advance on Washington, D.C. "The last time that we were out the rebels were very anxious to get some of our newspapers to find out about their troops in Maryland but we would not exchange, so they concluded that they had taken Washington and Baltimore certainly."[81]

Sergeant Plumb said he read in the newspaper that he had received a commission as a second lieutenant by Governor William Buckingham. "I was quite surprised to see this morning in a Norwich paper of the 21st that I was commissioned 2 Lieutenant on the 15th of this month. I heard nothing of this before but suppose that my commission will arrive soon. I don't know what company I shall be assigned to, but probably to Co. H or G as they have no 2nd Lieutenant. Direct letters to me as Sergt till I get my commission."[82]

The Crater

General Grant realized that the chance to carry Petersburg by surprise had slipped away by the beginning of July. Since the middle of June, the Union forces had completed a long series of works, strong enough to be held easily, from the Appomattox River to points south of the city. The Confederates had also hardened their defenses so that direct assault was not practical. Their line now ran from the Appomattox, and stretched away to the southwest of the city. Burnside's Ninth Corps occupied prime ground, within 150 yards of the enemy line. In their front was a fort at a re-entering angle to the works. Burnside convinced Grant he could dig a mine under the fort, and load it with a large amount of powder. On July 30, the Federal forces would explode the powder in mine, rush in with an assault, and gain a foothold in the resulting breech in the line.[83]

The Ninth Corps lay directly in front of the mine, ready for the assault. General Ord's Eighteenth Corps was ready to directly follow as the reserve. His men laid on the ground all night, ready to spring into the gap after Burnside's men.[84]

When the mine exploded, chaos reigned, but the assault was fatally flawed. The history of this event has long been told, and blame enough has been made. Colonel Griffin A. Stedman of the Third Division spoke for all the Eighteenth Corps when he wrote, "Then we asked, why we were not sent in? Why is the 18th Corps kept back? We can carry the position, let us go! But it was not permitted."[85]

Captain Coit witnessed the whole affair from the Eighth's support position, poised to join the ensuing advance. He described how the Eighteenth Corps moved to the right to occupy the trenches of the Ninth Corps as they massed for the charge. From that position, the Eighth could see the whole affair: the explosion, the charge, and the retreat. He described the explosion as very grand, beyond anything he had ever seen.

The Ninth Corps troops charged in, carried the fort with little loss, and extended along the rifle pits to the right and left. Coit said he could see the colors of many Union regiments both to the right and left of the fort. After a few hours, a heavy force of black troops was sent forward to reinforce the success. Though the Confederates had advanced on Union lines, they had been repulsed. From their position, the Eighth added their fire on the opposing lines to prevent their flanking fire on the Union thrusts. But there was a panic and retreat among the black soldiers, Coit said; the black soldiers suddenly began a full run for the rear, like a flock of sheep, without cause or reason, and most of the men had thrown away their guns.

The lines to the right and left of the fort were abandoned, and immediately occupied again by the Confederates. The remaining troops there were left alone and exposed to flank fire in addition to that in front from three pits. These troops held the fort alone for three or four hours. No attempt made to reinforce them, and they were forced to surrender. Coit wrote:

> Leaving them there for so long time unsupported is to me most unaccountable. Oh, how we felt to see the only troops who had fought well march over the embankment + surrender. Everything has been gained + now everything has been lost + we leave most ignominiously whipped besides. The charging party to which our troops actually surrendered was much smaller than themselves but they were suffering heavily from the fire on the flanks and they could not retreat. Our loss from 4800 to 4900.[86]

Captain Coit said that the new base camp of the Eighth was very close to the breastworks of the Petersburg standoff. The troops switched their camps between the Bermuda Hundred side and the Petersburg side of the Appomattox River on a regular basis.

> I think I have not written particularly of our new Camp—we are much nearer the front than before but in a much more secure place. We are Camped in quite a deep ravine + therefor entirely sheltered from any chance shot flying this way. My tent Hd. Qts. is pitched in the side of the hill + we have a shade of boughs built over it but best of all within six feet of the door we have a hard tack box set in the bank, the bottom is covered with pebbles, bushes entirely shade it and it is always over flowing with the clearest, coolest + best water I have seen in Virginia.[87]

On August 18, Coit reported a camp emergency and natural disaster that befell the men of the Eighth in front of Petersburg. "We have had a great freshlet here sweeping through the ravine where a large portion of our Corps were encamped carrying away Camps + everything, my Co. lost knapsacks + almost everything fortunately my tent was on the side hill + escaped. Quite a number of lives were lost none from the 8th but two were so badly injured as to oblige sending them to Hospital."[88]

Bermuda Hundred Again

Near the end of August, Coit announced the Eighth was moving from the Petersburg front trenches back to the Bermuda Hundred lines.

Chapter 8. Cold Harbor, Petersburg, Fort Harrison

> Another Sabbath + we are all hard at work fixing up our new Camp at this place. Yesterday our Brigade, the last of our Corps, was relieved by the 10th Corps + we marched here + now occupy ground lately held by that Corps. Oh what a relief it is to get away from the constant firing that we had become so accustomed to at Petersburg. It seems that until today I had supposed that I had ceased to notice it truly like Sunday excepting the constant pounding of the men as they build bunks +c. We occupy on old camp ground on a fine dry flat of land + find nice arbors built under which we pitch our tents. Arbors are built the whole length of the Company streets + every tent in camp will have a good shade over it.[89]

Coit reported that Chaplain Moses Smith was now sick, but his commander had displayed a miraculous recovery. "Our Chaplain has gone to Hospt. sick. He had lost his appetite + had made several attempts to get leave to visit his wife who has been at Norfolk during the summer. Col. Ward has had a Brigade offered him + suddenly recovers his health. He assumes command of 3d Brigade of this Div next Monday. Has done no duty with Regt."[90]

On August 31, the Eighth was organized with the Eighteenth Corps under General Edward O.C. Ord. Their First Division commander was General Joseph B. Carr, and their Second Brigade commander was Colonel Edger M. Cullen. The Eighth was, at the time, commanded by Captain Charles Coit.[91] But Coit soon learned that he would be relieved of command by an officer from division headquarters. "Capt. Hoyt is relieved from duty at Div. Hd. Qts. + will return to the Regt + of course take command, tomorrow, he being my senior. Col. Ward told me this a.m. that he was very sorry. Lt. Foss act. adjt. is quite unwell today + it's the worst day in the month for him to be off duty."[92]

Coit pointed out that a new Federal policy would lengthen the period of service for an officer in the Union army. Perhaps this change suggested that the army needed more officers or that there were new financial stresses that kept the national government from recruiting new officers or incentivizing officers to stay. At any rate, the War Department issued orders that said no officer in a three-year regiment would be entitled to his discharge until he had served, in his present rank, a full three years. Coit thought it rather severe, unjust, and dishonorable on the part of the government. This policy penalized those who had sought or had received promotions, he said. And even though the Army of the Potomac might not pay officers for six or eight months, an officer who asked for credit from the Commissary Department to eat would be charged back one or two rations per day at the rate of 30 cents each. Coit said that was twice the rate if the officer paid for the food with cash. Since the officers could only draw food that the Commissary had on hand after feeding the rank and file, the officers did not eat as well as the men—and had to pay for the privilege![93]

Sergeant Plumb described their regimental camp and their situation now on the Bermuda Hundred line in a letter home on September 4.

> The 18th Corps is now strengthened along the line of Bermuda Hundred fortifications and our brigade is on the extreme right of this line within half a mile of the James river and within sight of some of the buildings of Richmond.....
> The rebels here in our front are very friendly to our pickets, and there is no firing. the men visit each other and change papers, make trades, in spite of orders. There are two splendid springs between the lines within a few rods of each other, the rebels use one and we the other,

and there is where they meet. They tell our men to vote for McClellan and the war will be over. I think if we would vote for Jeff Davis it would be too.

We are encamped on good ground a little way from the breast works, and only keep men on the picket line. It is very much easier here than it was in front of Petersburg, and we drill every day. There is a very fine view of the river towards Richmond from here.[94]

On September 16, five soldiers from the Eighth were captured at "Cox's Mill."[95] It is south of the Appomattox River, in Prince George County, near Garysville, Virginia, between Sycamore Church on the Old Stage road, and Cocke's Mill on Powell's Creek, and about twelve miles east of Petersburg. Their capture may have been related to Wade Hampton's "Beefsteak Raid," when Confederates captured Union beef grazing near Coggin's Point on Edward Ruffin's plantation.[96] "Hampton's force captured more than 2,468 cattle, along with 11 wagons, and 304 prisoners, leading them back to the Confederate lines at 9 a.m. on September 17."[97]

On September 18 and 19, 1864, five soldiers of the Eighth were reported captured in the vicinity of Fort Powhatan, on the James River.[98] "A detail of twenty-five men from the Eighth was sent to establish a line of telegraph from City Point to Fort Powhatan; when sixteen [five] were captured by Wade Hampton in a raid within our lines after beef."[99]

Fort Harrison and Chaffin's Bluff

General Ulysses Grant described the Union strategy for the overall operations now to be conducted north of the James. "On the 28th of September, to retain Lee in his position, I sent Ord with the 18th corps, and Birney with the 10th corps, to make an advance on Richmond, to threaten it. Ord moved with the left wing up to Chaffin's Bluff; Birney with the 10th corps took a road farther north; while Kautz with the cavalry took the Darby road, still farther to the north."[100]

Indeed, on Chaffin's Bluff, on the north bank of the James River, just to the east of Richmond, stood a formidable line of works engineered as part of the defensive perimeter of the city. The main earthwork in the line was called Fort Harrison. "Named after Lieutenant William Harrison, a Confederate engineer, it was the largest in the series of fortifications that extended from New Market Road to the James River that also included Forts Brady, Hoke, Johnson, Gregg, and Gilmer. These earthworks were designed to protect the strategically important Chaffin's Bluff on the James."[101]

The 8th Connecticut Volunteers were now part of the Second Brigade of the First Division of the Eighteenth Corps in the Army of the James. The Second Brigade was now commanded by Brigadier General Hiram Burnham, the First Division commanded by Brigadier General George J. Stannard, and the Eighteenth Corps commanded by Major General Edward O.C. Ord. The Army of the James was still commanded by Major General Benjamin F. Butler.[102]

> On the afternoon of the 28th, Butler faced his army to the right, and moved in the evening towards the James. At nine in the evening, the 18th Corps had arrived at Aiken's Landing, and the 10th had crossed the Appomattox, and was hurrying forward. At two in the morning, the

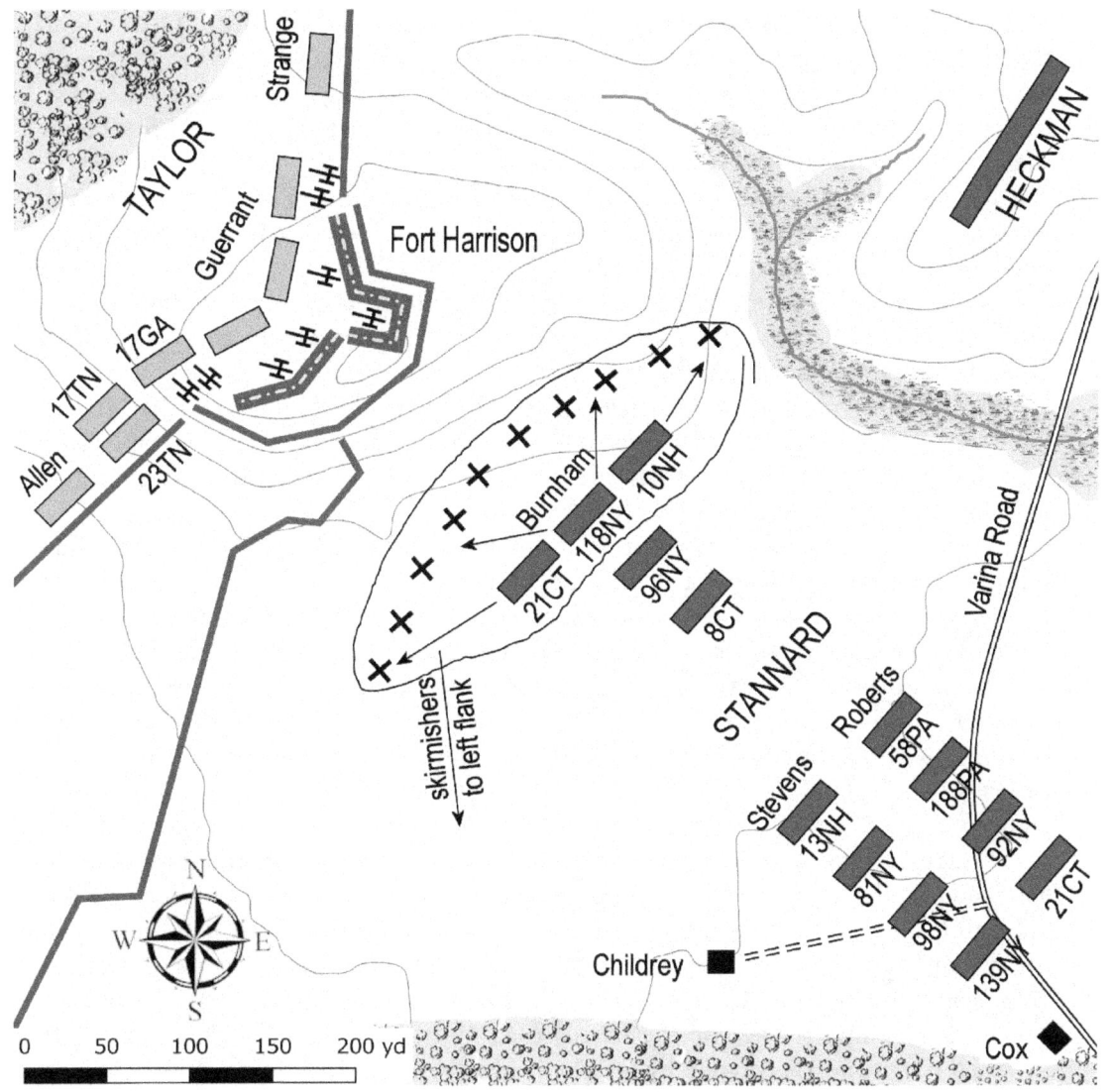

Map 21. Battle of Fort Harrison, Virginia, September 29, 1864, 6:00 a.m.

18th Corps began moving over the pontoon-bridge; and by four they were all over, massed in column by division, and moving up the Varina Road, on familiar ground.[103]

General George Stannard's First Division was selected by General Edward Ord to lead the Eighteenth Corps assault on Fort Harrison. General Stannard's official report recorded that Ord ordered Stannard to move from camp on Bermuda Hundred to Aiken's Landing on the James River at 9 p.m. on September 28. He received written orders to cross the river on pontoons at 3 a.m. on September 29, which was done, and completed by 4 a.m. Stannard headed his division out the Varina road, in the direction of the enemy works on Chaffin's Bluff, with Burnham's Second Brigade in the lead, followed by the First Brigade under Colonel Aaron F. Stevens, and the Third Brigade under Colonel Samuel H. Roberts.[104]

Confederate pickets around Chaffin's Bluff reported the crossing of Ord's Eighteenth Corps at Aiken's Landing before dawn. Major Richard C. Taylor, in charge locally, notified General Ewell, who notified Generals Bragg and Lee, who directed reinforcements from Petersburg to march to their support. They would not reach the fort in time. Major Taylor ordered Lieutenant John Guerrant and his Goochland Artillery to man the guns of the fort. Captain Cornelius Allen and the Lunenburg Artillery were at Battery X to the right of the fort. He ordered Major James Strange and the 1st Virginia Reserves to the left of the fort.[105]

Major James Moore of the 17th Georgia commanded five companies defending in the fort itself. Captain John H. Martin hurried his three companies of the 17th Georgia back to the fort from the New Market line.[106]

Regiments from General Henry L. Benning's brigade were also rushed to the fort. As the Federals advanced, the garrison in the fort may have been as few as two hundred men. Major Taylor's total effective force in the immediate vicinity of the fort was around 800 men.[107]

Stannard reported that, prior to marching, the 10th New Hampshire commanded by Colonel Michael T. Donohue, and the 118th New York commanded by Lieutenant Colonel George F. Nichols, exchanged their muskets for Spencer repeating rifles. Once on the north banks, they were deployed as skirmishers and flankers.[108]

Burnham's brigade was led by a skirmish line commanded by the senior officer, Colonel Michael T. Donohue, of the 10th New Hampshire. Donohue's line led the column up the Varina road from the landing, and through the woods about three miles, with the 118th New York on the left, and the 10th New Hampshire on the right.[109]

The rest of Stannard's division was put in column by division and moved along the road parallel to the river. A few moments after dawn, the skirmishers leading the column found the enemy pickets and proceeded to drive them through the woods for two or three miles. As they advanced, they swept away the enemy pickets of the 17th Tennessee and 23rd Tennessee, pushing them back towards their main works.[110]

As the column pushed up the Varina road, they halted at the edge of the woods between the properties owned by families named Cox and Childrey. There they all beheld the open ground before the fort on the crest of the ridge. General Burnham alerted Stannard and Ord to the situation. Burnham reported a strong line of earthworks mounting heavy guns. The command staff went forward to reconnoiter. Burnham convinced Ord that the Second Brigade should attack at once, without delay. Before they emerged from the woods onto open ground, General Stannard directed Burnham at once to carry the works by assault.[111]

The Eighth then provided two companies for the division skirmish line. It is likely that it was Company G and Company K, since they carried Sharp's rifles, and were regularly designated for skirmish companies. Seven companies from 21st Connecticut of the Third Brigade, under Lieutenant Colonel James F. Brown, were also added to the skirmish line for the assault.[112]

The skirmishers were followed by the 96th New York in line of battle, then the eight remaining companies of the 8th Connecticut, in column of divisions.[113]

The Second Brigade column was followed by Colonel Stevens's First Brigade in

Chapter 8. Cold Harbor, Petersburg, Fort Harrison

column of divisions to the left of the road, and by Colonel Roberts's Third Brigade in column of divisions, to the right of the road.[114]

General Ord ordered Brigadier General Charles A. Heckman's Second Division to support with a coordinated attack on the fort to the right of Stannard's division. Heckman, however, marched too far to the north before turning west, got tangled in swamp, and could not attack Harrison. Stannard's First Division could wait no longer for the support, and stepped off about 6 a.m. to carry Fort Harrison alone.[115]

Along the crest of the hill was a large square fort mounting about eight guns, surrounded by a ditch ten feet deep. To the left and right stretched rifle pits and redoubts with one or two guns each, enfilading the approach in every direction.[116]

Stannard then ordered Colonel Aaron F. Stevens with his First Brigade in column on the left, and Colonel Samuel H. Roberts with his Third Brigade in column on the right, to immediately push forward behind Burnham's Second Brigade assault column.[117]

> The column here left the road, and, inclining to the left, moved directly across a heavy plowed field toward the principal work. The distance was about 1,400 yards, and while traversing this space my command, with the exception of my skirmishers, not having as yet discharged a musket, was exposed to a plunging fire of artillery and musketry, galling in the extreme and caused them to become somewhat broken.[118]

The column moved directly into the face of the storm. The skirmish line was no longer sweeping enemy skirmishers or pickets. Donohue wheeled them off to the left to cover the south flank of the column.[119] This unmasked the assault column's steady advance towards the fort. The Second Brigade advanced, with bayonets fixed, and arms at right shoulder shift, with the 96th New York in the lead.[120] The Eighth was right behind them, in a storming column of divisions.

> This was a gallant charge across nearly a mile of open field to Chaffin's Bluff. The new recruits vied with the veterans. Now the muzzles of the rebel guns frowned from Fort Harrison directly in the front; now little puffs of smoke revealed an alert foe, and the batteries showered destruction upon the advancing column; now the Eighth deployed in line of battle, and closely followed by the rest of the division, dashed away over the field. It was a fearful distance to traverse such a field under such a fire. Without a moment's delay, the brigade moved to the position assigned it, and advanced through a dense slashing, and under a heavy artillery-fire, to the assault. The enemy's gunboats, in the meantime, dropped down the James, and threw a heavy cross-fire into the assaulting columns.[121]

As the column closed on the fort, the hail of iron thrown against them became more furious. The column obliqued to the right and gained the shelter of a swale a hundred yards in front of the fort walls, but under the reach of the guns. There, exhausted, they stopped, caught their breath, then reformed their lines.

Generals Ord, Stannard, and Burnham watched the assault column from the edge of the woods. Stannard said: "The column, however, pushed gallantly forward until it reached the base of the hill upon which the battery was situated, when it came to a halt, from sheer exhaustion."[122]

It seemed the advance was moving too slow. The opportunity might be lost to the Confederate reinforcements bearing down on them. Stannard sent orders to Colonels Stevens and Roberts with the column to hurry it up.

[Col.] Roberts was, nevertheless, an effective combat leader who could both halt and resume the attack in the immediate presence of the foe. Even before receiving his superior's orders, he made his own decision that the brief respite had gone on long enough…. "Now men," he continued, "just two minutes to take that fort! Just minutes, men!"

Regimental and brigade formations had long since been lost, and it was now a vast blue wave of hopelessly intermingled units that surged up the hill towards the fort.

Once in the fosse, the Federals boosted, clawed, clambered, and with ladders of bayoneted rifles rammed into the wall—climbed their way up the scarp and rampart for the decisive struggle.[123]

Stannard reported on the urgency for the final push of the assault:

> The enemy were now moving up from their left considerable re-enforcements, and, fearing that the assault would fail by reason of the delay, I sent Captain Kent, acting assistant adjutant-general of the division, to move the column at once to the assault. It was owing to his efforts, and, he reports, to the assistance of Colonel Donohoe, that, a few moments later, the head of the column gallantly mounted the parapet of Battery Harrison, drove the enemy from his guns, and planted the "Stars and Stripes" on one of its massive traverses.[124]

Fort Harrison had been successfully captured. General Stannard reported the success of the assault, the capture of the fort, and the loss of General Hiram Burnham. "Our captures included 16 pieces of artillery of various calibers and about 50 prisoners, including a lieutenant-colonel in command of the works…. The column had scarcely entered the works when the brave Brigadier-General Burnham was mortally wounded by a musket-ball in the bowels. He survived but a few moments."[125]

Captain Charles Coit added particular items regarding the Eighth's role in the assault on Fort Harrison. They were proud the flags of the Eighth had once again been planted on Confederate works.

> Lt. Col. Smith was wounded at the head of the Regt early in the charge + Foss called to me to take command + then down he fell. Neither are dangerously wounded.
>
> The colors of the 8th + 96th N Yk mounted the work at the same time, they were the first. I think I captured the first prisoners in the fort. After getting inside we formed the Regt + pressed forward from one barrack to another driving the Rebels and the 8th had the front for some time.
>
> In advance of all other Regts, Genls Ord + Burnham were both wounded inside the fort. Capt. Hoyt came up that night + took command.[126]

Once the fort and prisoners had been secured, the troops began make improvements to protect the fort from counterattack from the west. Stannard's First Division was moved to the south side of the fort, and put in line facing towards the James River in the direction of the Confederate pontoon bridge that would bring Confederate reinforcements from the south side. There, in line and under arms, they spent the night, the Eighth included.

The next day, Friday, September 30, brought the expected Confederate counterattack. General Stannard reported the defense and the repulse. He recorded that the enemy had been heavily reinforced during the night, and were positioned to make an assault to retake the fort. The enemy gunboats continued shelling from their nine-inch guns in support. About midday, Stannard said he received word of enemy preparations for an assault on his right. He moved the First Brigade from the left to the extreme right to bolster any weakness there. Stannard credited the Third Division for working through the night to strengthen the works on the left and center of the fort, but the right was still open. Stannard reported that his command, from when they entered the works, had spent their time improving the works with an eye towards enclosing the defense, but it had not yet been completed.

About 12:30 p.m., the enemy threw three lines upon the right, while opening with two batteries of field guns on the center and left, in support. Stannard held back until the Confederates could be seen emerging from the brush, when his men opened with a most effective fire.

> The enemy's furious onset had been in the meantime repulsed with musketry alone, driving him to cover, and leaving an immense number of dead and wounded in front of my right. He, however, quickly reformed, and with his accustomed yell tried the same position a second time. Finding that my ammunition was getting low, I had a few moments before sent a staff officer with an order to bring up a wagon from my ordnance train....
>
> Captain Brydon gallantly held his mules, three of which were shot while he was thus occupied, while Lieutenants Burbank and Cook, of my staff, distributed the ammunition to the command. I mention this circumstance thus particularly because it was owing to the promptness with which my order was obeyed and the gallant manner in which it was executed that my command was enabled to repulse the enemy's second and his successive assaults.
>
> During the progress of this second attempt to carry our position, I received a musket-ball in the right arm, which shattered the bone above the elbow and necessitated my removal from the field and amputation on my arrival at the hospital.[127]

Captain Charles Coit recollected his memory of the Confederate counterattack that day. "The Rebs made two heavy charges on our immediate front the next day + we mowed them down terribly. The ground was covered with their killed + wounded + we took many prisoners. The weather raining most of the time. Am well as possible but have hardly had any sleep since leaving Camp."[128]

The fighting for Fort Harrison and Chaffin's Bluff was now over. General Grant summarized the resulting gains and losses:

> Stannard's division of the 18th corps with General Burnham's brigade leading, tried an assault against Fort Harrison and captured it with sixteen guns and a good many prisoners. Burnham was killed in the assault. Colonel Stevens who succeeded him was badly wounded; and his successor also fell in the same way.... In the afternoon a further attempt was made to advance, but it failed. Ord fell badly wounded, and had to be relieved; the command devolved upon General Heckman, and later General Weitzel was assigned to the command of the 18th corps.... Lee ... attempted to retake the works which we had captured by concentrating ten brigades against them. All their efforts failed, their attacks being all repulsed with very heavy loss. In one of these assaults upon us, General Stannard, a gallant officer who was defending Fort Harrison, lost an arm.[129]

The losses in the Eighth during the attack were equally severe.

> The casualties of the Eighth were eight killed and sixty-five wounded. Among the killed were Lieut. James B. Kilbourne, Lieut. Charles N. Irwin, ... William H Durfee, Gilbert G. Reynolds, William H. Peterson, William A. Smith, and other brave men.[130]
>
> Lieut.-Col. Martin B. Smith, leading the regiment, was wounded severely in the leg. Among the wounded were also Capt. Samuel S. Foss, John A. Rathbun, Amos L. Keables, and Thomas S. Weed.

Chaplain Moses Smith wrote that there was

one other name I must mention among our honored dead. Our rolls record him only as an enlisted man, with rank of sergeant; for although having been commissioned, he had never been mustered as lieutenant. But fairer character never graced a soldier's uniform, and he lives embalmed in the affections of home and in the hearts of his comrades. He led in the closing prayer of that last meeting an hour before the march; and his last words as the column moved for the charge were respecting "that good meeting." Even the casket in which such a jewel has been carried is prized; and, as we write here in camp, weeping friends are preparing in the burying-ground of Litchfield, Conn., the grave of our dear comrade, Seth F. Plumb.[131]

Captain William S. Hubbell, of the 21st Connecticut, and medal of honor recipient at Fort Harrison, remarked on the opportunity lost, and the politics of the consequences.

Had we known the full extent of our victory, we might have easily entered Richmond on the 29th of September, as the road was open before us. Nevertheless, we seized the most advanced approach to the Rebel capital and the point from which its captors issued forth on the day when Richmond fell.[132]

General Butler remarked in wrath, 'that if we had not stopped to cackle like an old hen over her eggs, we should have taken Richmond on that day.' But our leaders were all killed or disabled, and Butler himself, who ought to have marshalled us for the onset, was busily engaged with crowing on a safe perch several miles from the sight of carnage and the smell of gunpowder.[133]

General Stannard summarized the full significance of their success. This was written in his official report filed while recuperating from the loss of his arm at home in Vermont.

The record will scarcely show an instance where so small a body of men carried so strong a position as the works on Chaffin's farm, and after a loss of one man in five, held their position without assistance against all attempts to dislodge them by an enemy vastly superior in numbers and nearly all composed of fresh troops. The whole number of pieces of artillery captured by my command in the works on Chaffin's farm, including Battery Harrison (now called Fort Burnham, in honor of the gallant and lamented general), was 22.[134]

Fort Harrison was renamed by the Union army to Fort Burnham after its capture, to honor that general's leadership and heroic death. The fort was held against all Confederate attempts to re-capture it, but the foothold gained north of the James was not successfully expanded during the remainder of the war.[135]

The lack of more brigade and regimental reports on this action was due to heavy losses among those commanding officers. There was no official report filed by anyone from the Eighth, but their story was told in the other heroic reports by those alongside them.

Commendations

On October 11, 1864, Major General Benjamin F. Butler, commanding the Army of the James, announced commendations for member soldiers for exemplary service during the season's campaign. Special recognition was noted for three members of the Eighth.

William S. Simmons and Jacob Bishop, color-sergeants of the Eighth Connecticut Volunteers, are commended for planting their colors on the parapet of the fort among the earliest.

Sergeants Bishop and Simmons are promoted to second lieutenants in the U.S. Colored Troops, with the approval of the President.

Corpl. Nathan E. Hickock, Eighth Connecticut Volunteers, has honorable mention for his gallantry in capturing a rebel battle-flag, and is recommended to the Secretary of War for a medal. His colonel will see that he has his warrant as a sergeant.[136]

Corporal Nathan E. Hickok, Company A, was awarded the Medal of Honor, with the citation for capturing a flag at Fort Harrison. It was possibly the garrison flag from the parapet of the Grand Traverse.[137]

In an interesting scenario, once again the Eighth was embroiled in competition honoring their colors. Captain Coit mentioned it in one of his letters. General Butler specifically called attention to the issue in the official record. "Sergt. Lester Archer, of the Ninety-sixth New York, has honorable mention for his gallantry in placing the colors of his regiment on Battery Harrison. There is a generous rivalry between the color bearers of the Eighth Connecticut and the Ninety-sixth New York as to which were the first in planting their colors—so nearly equal were they that it is difficult to say which were in advance. May that rivalry always continue."[138]

Chaplain Moses Smith also reported on the commendations that the regiment received. "For meritorious deeds on the morning of September 29, Fort Harrison is to be inscribed upon our banner."[139] He repeated specifics exclamations from the field. "Justly did our Division Commander, Gen. Stannard, remark as he was carried wounded from the field, 'I have had the honor to lead the best Division in the whole army.' But we are proud to record the fact, that being assigned the post of honor at the head of the storming column, the heroic old Eighth, to a man, did its duty, and who could ask for more?"[140]

Discharges Term Expired

Between September 20 and October 13, 111 soldiers of the Eighth were discharged from army service, their three years enlistment term having expired.[141]

In the case of the 8th Connecticut veteran volunteers, the discharges reduced their regimental strength significantly just before the operations against Fort Harrison. It must have left a strange taste in the mouths of those who, up until that time, had been brothers-in-arms with those that had just gone home. It must have also been anxious times for those who had re-enlisted to once again be called to battle, knowing those who did not re-enlist were safely on their journey home.

> The regiment at this time [Oct. 7, 1864] lost the services of Surgeon Melancthon Storrs of Hartford, who resigned and returned home, after three years of devotion to the good of the soldiers.... So manifest was his excellence, that, when he was sent for a special purpose to Washington, Dr. McMellan, a surgeon of the regular army, in charge of the mammoth hospital near Fort Monroe, in indorsing his orders, added the statement that Dr. Storrs was "the most efficient surgeon ever on duty at this hospital."[142]

The command structure and officer's corps of the Eighth was becoming somewhat eroded. Many were contemplating military advancement opportunities that stretched the brotherhood thin. Captain Coit, on October 17, 1864, describes the loss of several of the Eighth's officers as time marched on. As he wrote, "I am now willing someone else should try their hand on the two or three officers + 100 men who still remain to uphold an unstained reputation which I know I have faithfully labored + largely contributed to build up…. Including Capt. Hoyt, six of our officers have been mustered out within a week. Dr. Storrs, Quartermaster Dougherty, Lieuts Breed, Stevens, + Lane."[143]

Chaplain Moses Smith wrote home, too, to report the changes in personnel. He listed those who were discharged when their terms expired: Captain Hoyt, Lieutenants Ambrose Dougherty, John Lane, Emerson Stevens, and Thomas Weed. He said that Colonel Ward commanded the Brigade, and that Captain Coit, recently commissioned Major, was acting Assistant Adjutant General in the brigade staff. Chaplin Smith said that Captain Elam Goodrich, now commanding the regiment, had the affection of the men and deservedly received commendations from superior officers.[144]

Fair Oaks

After the Battle of Fort Harrison, the Eighteenth Corps remained holding the lines hard won north of the James River. The center was now on Fort Burnham, and extended south to the James, and north along the outer Richmond defenses past the New Market, Darbytown, Charles City, and Williamsburg roads. Picket duty, and manning the trenches in front of Richmond with resolute readiness were the perpetual orders of the day.

The Eighth was organized as part of the Eighteenth Corps under Brevet Major General Godfrey Weitzel, but not attached to a division or brigade. Colonel John Ward was commander of record, but Captain Goodrich was physically commanding the Eighth, while Ward was absent sick.[145]

At about this time, the 8th Connecticut was assigned as Eighteenth Corps Provost Guard. They served at the Corps Headquarters located near Fort Burnham, on the property of the Cox house.[146] The Eighth was camped in an adjacent field close by.

Because the presidential election was approaching, the White House needed an offensive action to show the voters new progress in the prosecution of the war. Grant planned an attack on Petersburg by the Second Corps. To lock Confederate troops in place north of the James, Grant directed Butler to send Terry's Tenth Corps forward on the Darbytown road, and Weitzel's Eighteenth Corps forward on the Williamsburg road, near Fair Oaks, but they were not to attack or engage any entrenched positions.[147]

Butler's orders for the coordinated actions on the Darbytown road and at Fair Oaks were issued to move on October 27. Terry was to demonstrate along the Alexander Line, while Weitzel probed north and attempted to find and turn the Confederate left flank.[148]

Confederate General James Longstreet had been ordered back to command of the First Corps north of the James, replacing General Richard H. Anderson, on

Chapter 8. Cold Harbor, Petersburg, Fort Harrison

October 17.[149] As Terry and his Federal troops did not press the attack on the Darbytown road, Longstreet correctly surmised the real target was to the north of White Oak Swamp, near Fair Oaks Station.[150]

As Weitzel advanced along the Williamsburg road, Longstreet deployed the Home Guard, and then the Hampton Legion and the 24th Virginia Cavalry were engaged to delay the advance. Longstreet ordered General Charles W. Field's division to double-quick to the north and bolster their support. Fields sent four brigades—Texas, South Carolina, Georgia, and Alabama—and they crippled the attack.[151] "Capt. Charles M. Coit of the Eighth, serving on the staff of the commander [Bvt. Major General Godfrey Weitzel, Eighteenth Corps], received a severe wound, which it was feared would be mortal but, after a doubtful struggle between life and death, he rallied, and recovered. He was an accomplished and fearless officer, and had often led the regiment in battle."[152]

Chaplain Moses Smith wrote to the family of the wounds that Coit received.

> He was wounded yesterday p.m. and has to-day started on board a Hospital steamer with others for Chesapeake Hospital, Hampton, Va. The wound was severe. It was apparently a shrapnel shot, the ball broke the collar bone and entered the cavity of the chest. Of course, his first thoughts were respecting his dear loved Mother and he desired me to write you immediately. We hope for the best. We know that he is in the hands of a kind Father where we believe he loves and who knows all the feelings.[153]

Coit survived and convalesced in the U.S. Army Hospital at Fortress Monroe for several months. He later returned to the regiment at the beginning of May 1865.[154]

The Eighth had two soldiers captured at Fair Oaks that day—Private Patrick Warner, of Company I, and Sergeant Nathan Hickok, of Company A. They may have been on Special Duty with the command, or otherwise ordered out during this engagement. Hickok had won the Medal of Honor for capturing a flag at Fort Harrison. After Hickok's capture, there is no further record of him in either army. It could be that he died that day of wounds, and was buried unknown in an unmarked grave.[155]

Chaplain Smith described the circumstances for the Eighth, back at Corps Headquarters, during the action. "The Eighth being on guard did not participate. Our men could scarcely contain themselves as they listened to the thunder of artillery on both right and left, and knew that earnest work was progressing, and they were not taking an active part."[156]

The rest of the Eighth suffered no casualties at Fair Oaks since they were serving as the Provost Guard for the Eighteenth Corps at the time, and thus they were held in reserve.[157] It is probable that, with the constantly diminishing numbers in the Eighth, they were considered too small to operate as a regiment, and thus given alternate duties. The Eighth continued in this capacity for the remainder of the campaign and into winter quarters.

Chapter 9

Richmond, Lynchburg, and Home

November 1864 brought Thanksgiving to the Army and the 8th Connecticut. The holiday was observed on the fourth Thursday of the month, which President Lincoln had declared a national holiday only a year before. While the Eighth was wanting for the fixings of a good old New England Thanksgiving feast, they were sent fresh recruits in the form of draftees and substitutes to bolster their ranks. Chaplain Moses Smith said he was hopeful about the regiment's new manpower now.

"On Nov. 29th, 95 out of 100 sent, actually arrived," the chaplain wrote. "They seem to promise well. We now have an aggregate of nearly 300 in the old Eighth. So, you see, we are not dead yet. Nor do we propose to yield while rebellion and slavery, the primal cause of rebellion, resist our national authority."[1]

Just days before Thanksgiving, however, the Eighth had an unwelcome duty to perform. On November 21, the regiment was called to execute five deserters from Company G of the 1st Connecticut Heavy Artillery. As Moses Smith wrote later in the *Connecticut War Record*, "It was a hard place for the Chaplain, for Capt. Morgan, who commanded the squads, and for our men who did the summary deed. But they faithfully performed the requirement, and with the sharp sound, 'fire,' each prisoner fell insensible. I can but feel that the influence will prove imminently salutary."[2]

Reorganization and Promotions

In December of 1864, the Eighteenth Corps was dissolved as part of a change that signified yet another attempt to find the right combination of military leaders to carry out Lieutenant General U.S. Grant's strategy to end the war.

GENERAL ORDERS, NO. 297.

WAR DEPARTMENT, December 3, 1864.

Adjutant General's Office. Washington,

By direction of the President of the United States, the following changes will be made in the organization of the "Army of the James"

  1. The 10th and 18th Army Corps will be discontinued.

  2. The white infantry troops of the 10th and 18th Army Corps, now with the Army of the James, will be consolidated under the direction of the Major General commanding the Department of Virginia and North Carolina [Butler], and will constitute a new Corps, to be called the 24th Corps.

  3. The colored troops of the Department of Virginia and North Carolina will be organized into a new Corps, to be called the 25th Corps.

4. The present Corps Staff and the artillery of the 18th Corps will be transferred to the 24th, and the present Corps Staff and artillery of the 10th to the 25th Corps.

5. Major General E.O.C. Ord is assigned to the command of the 24th Corps, and Major General G. Weitzel to the command of the 25th Corps.

By order of the Secretary of War:

E. D. TOWNSEND, Assistant Adjutant General.

Crofutt and Morris later explained what these changes meant to the Eighth. "The white troops of the 10th Corps were consolidated with those of the 18th, in a new corps known as the 24th; and the Eighth Connecticut was detailed to guard headquarters."[3]

The biggest change in the new orders was, of course, that President Lincoln relieved Major General Benjamin F. Butler from command of the Department of Virginia and North Carolina, and the Army of the James, at the request of General U.S. Grant. Once Lincoln had issued General Order No. 1, Grant informed Butler of the change, and replaced Butler with General Edward O.C. Ord on January 8, 1865.[4]

Grant wrote to Secretary of War Edwin M. Stanton in early 1865 asking free rein to relieve Butler from military service. Since Stanton was traveling outside Washington, D.C., at the time "Grant appealed directly to Lincoln for permission to terminate Butler, noting 'there is a lack of confidence felt in [Butler's] military ability' In General Order Number 1, Lincoln relieved Butler from command of the Department of North Carolina and Virginia and ordered him to report to Lowell, Massachusetts."[5]

Grant recorded this fact quite simply in his memoirs. "At my request, Major-General B.F. Butler was relieved, and Major-General E.O.C. Ord assigned to the Department of Virginia and North Carolina."[6]

"When Ord assumed command of the Army of the James from Butler on January 1, 1865, John Gibbon took command of the XXIV Corps and led it ably," one historian wrote.[7] Major General John Gibbon then issued General Orders No. 18 on January 31, which relieved the 8th Connecticut of duty as the Twenty-Fourth Corps Headquarters Guard, and returned them to their brigade.[8]

Lieutenant Colonel Martin B. Smith, who had commanded the Eighth till he was wounded at Fort Harrison was discharged from the service on January 13, 1865. He had never completely recovered from his wounds to resume his duties.[9] But on his trip home from the front after his discharge, the retired officer was part of a very unlikely event in which he snatched victory from defeat.

> On the 4th of February, Lieut.-Col. Whitaker achieved a brilliant exploit. The famous rebel raider, Harry Gilmor, had charged through Maryland, destroyed the Baltimore and Washington Railroad, captured a major-general and many officers on the train and escaped across the Potomac. Among the passengers on the train that was stopped and burned by Gilmor was Lieut-Col. M.B. Smith of the Eighth. He slipped his watch and pocket-book into his boot-leg; and, when a soldier demanded his boots, he saved them by appealing to an officer. Col. Smith was made prisoner; but, while the raiders were busy with plunder, he sauntered off to a neighboring house, concealed himself, and escaped that night to our lines. Col. Whitaker was designated by Sheridan's chief of staff to lead three hundred picked men, and capture the bold raider. He straightway chased and captured Gilmor, and delivered him over to the Federal authorities.[10]

In a report on December 20, Chaplain Smith described the current strength of the regiment—300 men present, and about 250 men ready for duty. He hoped for more recruits to take the place of those who left the service on account of disability.

> Since I last wrote, Lieut. Col. Smith, Lieut. Foss, Act. Adj. Capt. Roberts, Co. I, and Lieut. Vorra, Co. K, all having received severe wounds during the past year, have been honorably discharged. Lieut. Pelham, Co. G, has been dismissed from service. Dr. Bigelow has been mustered full Surgeon. George W. Farnham, lately Drum Major, is now 1st Lieut., Co. C, and Adjutant William M. Pratt has accepted the Majority. Col. Ward commands the Brigade.
>
> Our roster of line officers is much reduced, but one valuable addition is at hand. Roger M. Ford, who has served from the onset of the war, first as a three-month man, then as an officer with two promotions in this regiment, but was wounded in June last before Petersburg, and very much to his disappointment, was discharged on account of disability, has recently re-enlisted as a private and returned to the regiment. You may well believe that he has been most cordially welcomed by all, and that a commission for his former position, Capt., Co. G, is forthcoming.[11]

Four Connecticut regiments—the 8th, the 11th, the 21st, and the 29th—still held the lines north of the James. Adjutant William B. Pratt was promoted to major on February 22, 1865, after the position was declined by Captain Charles M. Coit.[12] Pratt was subsequently promoted to lieutenant colonel on May 12, 1865.[13] When Captain Coit was again commissioned to be a major, he again declined, as he had done the previous year.[14] Coit had been breveted a lieutenant colonel on March 13, 1865, while recovering from wounds suffered at Fair Oaks.[15]

Colonel John E. Ward, who had commanded the Eighth since March 1863, was discharged from the service on March 14, 1865. Having been wounded at Port Walthall Junction the previous May, he at times had commanded the division, but he had only occasionally resumed his duties with the regiment.[16]

On to Richmond

Now the final campaign began. The official records documented the Union Army order of battle for the Appomattox Campaign from March 29 to April 3, 1865. The 8th Connecticut's commander was Major William M. Pratt, and the unit was part of the Second Brigade that included six other regiments—the 5th Maryland, the 10th New Hampshire, the 12th New Hampshire, the 96th New York, the 118th New York, and the 9th Vermont. The Second Brigade was commanded by Colonel Michael T. Donohue.

The Second Brigade and its seven regiments were part of the Third Division, with Brigadier General Charles Devens commanding, and the division was part of the Twenty-fourth Corps, with Major General John Gibbon commanding. The corps was part of the Army of the James, with Major General O.C. Ord commanding. Ord reported to Lieutenant General U.S. Grant, who was the commander of all Union forces.[17]

Chaplain Moses Smith wrote a summary of the Eighth's role in the fall of Richmond. In the final chain of events, he said, the First and Second Divisions of the Twenty-fourth Corps moved around to the left to cooperate with General Sheridan to roll up on Lee's right. The Third Division, including the 8th Connecticut, held their position on the extreme right of the entire line. Chaplain Smith said the activities of the Third Division were meant to cause confusion among the Rebels. The Federals held reviews, conducted marches, struck and pitched tents, left the front, and returned again.

Because of this deception, the Confederates failed to realize that two-thirds of the Corps had moved to the left, and pushed the attack at Five Forks.[18] That set off a chain reaction which resulted in the collapse of the defense of the Confederate capital the next day.

As Chaplain H.S. DeForest of the 11th Connecticut wrote, "Many heroes have fought for this day, and died without the sight. The heroes of this battle are those who broke the rebel lines yesterday, and forced Lee to send a telegram to Jeff. Davis, which cut short his devotions, and called him out of church to begin his flight. But by the fortunes of war we are permitted to see and feel the long-expected day. It is a day never to be forgotten by us till days shall be no more."[19]

When that fateful morning brought the fall of Richmond, the Eighth, from their position nearby, beheld the explosions, fires, and alarms in the city.

> We do not lay any claim to the honor of first entering the late Rebel capital.... Furthermore, we are happy to say that our regiment has not, at any time, been located in the city. Our men have been on duty there from the first, and continue to be, but we have been allowed to keep our camp at a respectable distance from the filth and vermin, vile liquor, and vile women of that nest of treason.... About two weeks we enjoyed Fulton Hill on the S.E. of Richmond, and since have occupied the suburbs of Manchester, on the opposite side of the James.[20]

The 1st Connecticut Battery, the 8th Connecticut, and the 21st Connecticut were among the first to move forward into the Confederate capital.[21] General Lee finally surrendered on April 9, 1865, at Appomattox, about 80 miles from Richmond. The Civil War was virtually over.

On April 27, Major General John Gibbon, commanding the Twenty-Fourth Corps issued General Order No. 51 from Richmond inviting representative soldiers to be honored in Washington, D.C., where they would witness the presentation of colors surrendered by Lee's Army to the government of the United States. From the Eighth, Private Henry Steele, of Company B, was named in the orders.[22]

Chaplain Smith said the men now felt like they were engaged in the toughest campaign of their service. It was terribly hard to do nothing. "Besides, homesickness charges down upon our front, flank, and rear. If you hear that the Veteran Eighth has capitulated [to homesickness], you must not be greatly surprised. We can sustain the attack a little longer, but shall soon need a reinforcement of orders headed, Homeward, Ho!"[23]

Charles M. Coit, now a Brevet Lieutenant Colonel, was also responsible for public relations. In May, 1865, Headquarters advised him some dignitaries from home were visiting and wished to see him. He went to Richmond to meet and dine with them. The next morning, he was awakened early and told General Owens wished him to join in escorting the party on a tour of the fortifications. Coit wrote,

> At the Arlington House Mr. Birnie with 15 or 16 others + Rev Mifses Buckingham + Parson, Mifses Ripley + Atwater + al—took possession of the four horse Hd. Qts. establishment +

two ambulances that Genl Devens had supplied + off we started for Fort Harrison—or as it is now called—Ft. Burnham—Major Elder + myself [on] horseback. At Ft. Burnham met Genl + Mrs. Curtis. Mrs. C. inquired after Mo + Sis—Ate our luncheon in the rebel fort Endwell + then home again.

Did not I tell them how the old 8th put the first colors on Ft. Harrison + how I commanded then. Didnt I waive my hat + swing my arms, + describe to them how the shot + shell ploughed thro' our massed column +c +c +c. Well you know that's my style. The whole face of the country there has been so changed by the cutting down of forests on both sides that I could hardly recognize it as the familiar ground that we occupied last October.[24]

Lynchburg

Lynchburg had long been identified as a strategic location since railroads from the west and south converged there from the Shenandoah Valley and ran east to Richmond. Grant knew this was an important place to control.

After the fall of Richmond, and the surrender at Appomattox, the 8th Connecticut and 11th Connecticut were sent to Lynchburg, where they remained several months, doing quasi-military and quasi-police duty.[25]

On May 27, 1865, Brevet Lieutenant Colonel Charles Coit decided that it was time to resign and head home. He wrote to his family, "Have just returned from Division Hd. Qts.—rode over as a Captain + back as a Civilian. I am truly out of the service. I feel real 'gay' as Dr. Dan used to say. I shall start for the North probably the first of next week."[26]

The Army once again reorganized to administer post-war provost and police duties. In that move, the Eighth was designated a member of the new Second Independent Brigade, which consisted of seven regiments. In his official report, General A.H. Terry wrote:

> The Third Division of the Twenty-fourth Army Corps is dissolved and the troops hitherto composing it will hereafter constitute the First and Second Independent Brigades of that corps. ... The Second Independent Brigade will consist of the following-named regiments: Eleventh Connecticut Volunteers, Eighty-first New York Volunteers, Eighth Connecticut Volunteers, Fifty-eighth Pennsylvania Volunteers, One hundred and eighty-eighth Pennsylvania Volunteers, Ninety-eighth New York Volunteers, and Ninth Vermont Volunteers.[27]

In May 1865, Chaplain Moses Smith wrote the troops were not happy that they had not been released from duty. "The boys are very indignant at detention in service. One can hardly wonder, but we hope that, for their own honor and that of the State, they will endure that which is much harder than actual campaigning—the monotony, restraint, and temptations of camp life in days of peace."[28]

Muster Out

And now it was time for the regiment to begin its final days of service, as Stephen R. Smith wrote in 1889.

> The regiment was mustered out on the 12th of December, 1865, after four years and two months of service—having served a longer term than other Connecticut regiments except the

Chapter 9. Richmond, Lynchburg, and Home

First Artillery and the Thirteenth Infantry. Its tattered colors in the Capitol at Hartford speak more eloquently of its service than pen can do, and the brave men who helped to make and maintain its honorable record will not have suffered and died in vain if the blessings of constitutional liberty are duly appreciated by those in whose behalf, they laid down their lives.[29]

In their 1868 book, Croffut and Morris described the homecoming of the troops.

They came home in December, had a reception in Hartford befitting their long and arduous service, and were mustered out. Rowland Swift addressed the Eighth, and Ezra Hall addressed the Eleventh, in terms of grateful welcome; and the companies and soldiers departed to find more personal greetings in glad hearts and homes. The regiments had generally marched, camped, and fought side by side, and shared a. twin-chronicle of heroic deeds, and a long list of gallant dead.[30]

Casualties of the Eighth Regiment

Killed in action	72
Died of wounds	40
Died of disease	132
Discharged prior to muster-out of regiment	610
Missing at date of muster-out of regiment	11

Conclusion: After the War

Regimental Association

After they mustered out in December of 1865, the veterans of the 8th Connecticut continued their friendships and decided to form a regimental association. They held their first public rank and file reunion in Meriden in 1870.[1] They met annually in convention well into the twentieth century, ending around 1930. We know about the organization's meetings by the silk annual meeting ribbons available as militaria, artifacts, and antiques, and by newspaper reports about their meetings. We have not found official minutes or public records of their activities, though they may be obscurely archived somewhere.

Sometimes the group held joint meetings with other regiments, particularly those of Harland's brigade, as the numbers of veterans attending diminished over time. The day they preferred for their annual reunions was September 17, the anniversary of the memorable Battle of Antietam.

The usual proceedings of the association did what such groups usually do—they adopted resolutions, they elected officers, they reviewed their membership rolls, and they honored those who had "answered the final roll call." One item they seemed to discuss often was where to hold their next reunion. The events always culminated in a grand collation, with tables spread with bounty for the veterans to enjoy.

The social time after the official meetings was a highlight for the old boys—the handshakes and story swapping, all punctuated with hearty laughter. The veterans would sometimes share souvenirs to illustrate their stories. On September 17, 1896, *The Meriden Daily Journal* reported that at their twenty-seventh reunion in Meriden, "Comrade [Joseph H.] Jewett showed pieces of the Eighth's state and national colors that were shot off at the trenches in front of Petersburg and Richmond, which he secured."[2]

Three sites were favorites for the annual event. Meriden was one of the most visited cities, since it was home to the largest number of members of any town. Norwich was also a favorite, since that city was home to many of the original officers of the Eighth. Hartford was also repeatedly visited over the years, because of its central location and its status as the state capital.

The association elected officers each year, and prominent members served as president. Among them were Edward Harland, Henry Hoyt, James Russell, William Hagadon, J. Henry Garrigus, William McCarty, Isaac Williams, Ashbel Bartram, John Lane, Frederick Gallup, Jay Nettleton, John Rathbun, Melancthon Storrs,

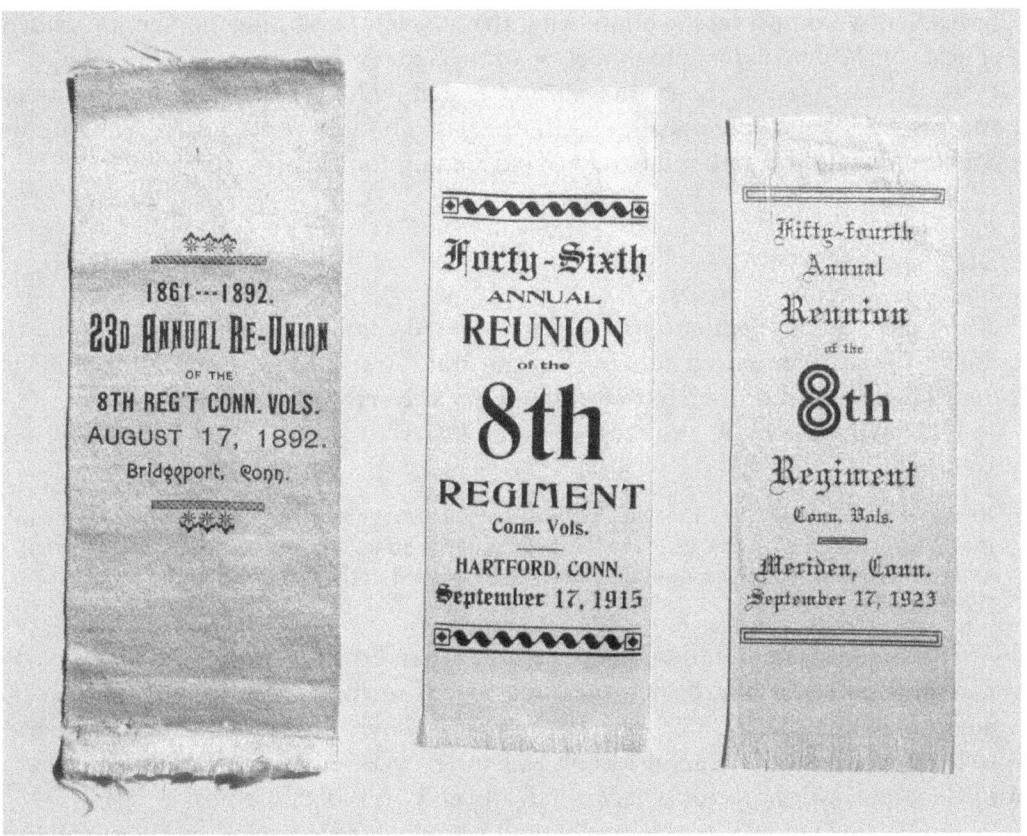

Eighth Connecticut reunion ribbons (photograph by the authors).

Andrew Gordon, Albert Thomas, Edward Pelton, Horace Garrigus, Frederick Jackson, and Charles Upham.

But as the twentieth century came, the reunions began to grow smaller. On September 19, 1911, the *Norwich Bulletin* reported, "When the fifty members of the Eighth regiment, Connecticut volunteers, held their annual reunion in Meriden, Saturday, and re-elected Edward Harland of Norwich president for life, it was stated that of the 1,027 men who marched out of Connecticut in '61 only 156 are now living."

On September 16, 1914, *The Meriden Daily Journal* posted a notice of the forty-fifth reunion of the Eighth Regiment, which included this appeal. "This is the anniversary of the battle of Antietam, where our dear old regiment lost 194 of our comrades, and we are losing them now, not by shot and shell, but by the call of the Great Commander. What is left of us, let us gather together on that day, and clasp hands once more."

Harlow Chapin was secretary and treasurer for some time, but when he died in 1895, no official records were recovered. Timothy E. Hawley started over to build a roster to sustain the association.[3] But when Hawley died, the records of the association again were not recovered. In 1929, the group issued urgent pleas to gather contacts for the living veterans, estimated at just twenty-one old soldiers.[4]

That year, 1929, marked the last documented reunion of the Eighth Regiment

Connecticut Volunteers association. After that, the few remaining members attended as guests of the final association meeting of the Sixteenth Connecticut in 1931.

In the early years, the events were attended by hundreds, then dozens, then handfuls, and finally, precious few. Still, the passion for reuniting each year and for reaffirming their brotherhood had been paramount for almost sixty years.

Battle Flag Day

As the new Connecticut State Capitol neared completion, the state decided to transfer the many honored colors from the State Arsenal to the new Hall of Flags constructed to display them in the west wing of the new building.

On March 11, 1879, the Connecticut Legislature approved the following resolution:

> Resolved by this Assembly, That the comptroller, adjutant general, and quartermaster general shall be a board to have charge of the battle flags of the State, now stored in the State Arsenal, and they are directed to cause suitable cases to be erected in the Capitol, and the flags placed therein.[5]

The adjutant general then was none other than Edward Harland, the first colonel of the Eighth. The board appointed to oversee the transfer set the date for the ceremony as September 17, 1879—the anniversary of the battle of Antietam. Harland and the board invited General Joseph R. Hawley to be chief marshal for the event, and General Hawley graciously accepted, and ably served at that post.[6]

On Battle Flag Day, each Connecticut regiment, represented by the surviving veterans, was invited to bear their colors in procession from the State Arsenal to the Hall of Flags.

When the flags at the arsenal were examined, curators described the condition of the Eighth's battle flags as follows: "Eighth—One national flag, hopeless; two state flags and one national in poor condition, but can be carried as fixed. (One state flag was presented by the 'Sons of Connecticut in New York.')."[7]

When Battle Flag Day dawned on September 17, 1879, the veterans gathered in great strength. More than 10,000 Connecticut veteran soldiers participated, and more than 100,000 citizens attended.

The *Hartford Courant* described the event in a report worthy of note for all time. "To-day the old flags of the war, which have been stored in unnoticed honor in the State Arsenal, will be carried by the reverent hands of those who fought under them and saved them, to their final resting place in the Capitol of the State, there to hang in everlasting testimony of the sacrifice a free people are willing to make for liberty."[8]

The Eighth reported that 250 of their men were present.[9] The men selected their officers for the day—Captain Henry M. Hoyt and Adjutant Henry R. Jones. Several former field officers attended: Edward Harland, Thomas D. Sheffield, and Dr. Melancthon Storrs. The color bearers were Thomas W. Bishop, Thomas J. Hubbard, Heber S. Ives, and Orlow Root.[10]

All the regimental flags were paraded from their storage at the State Arsenal

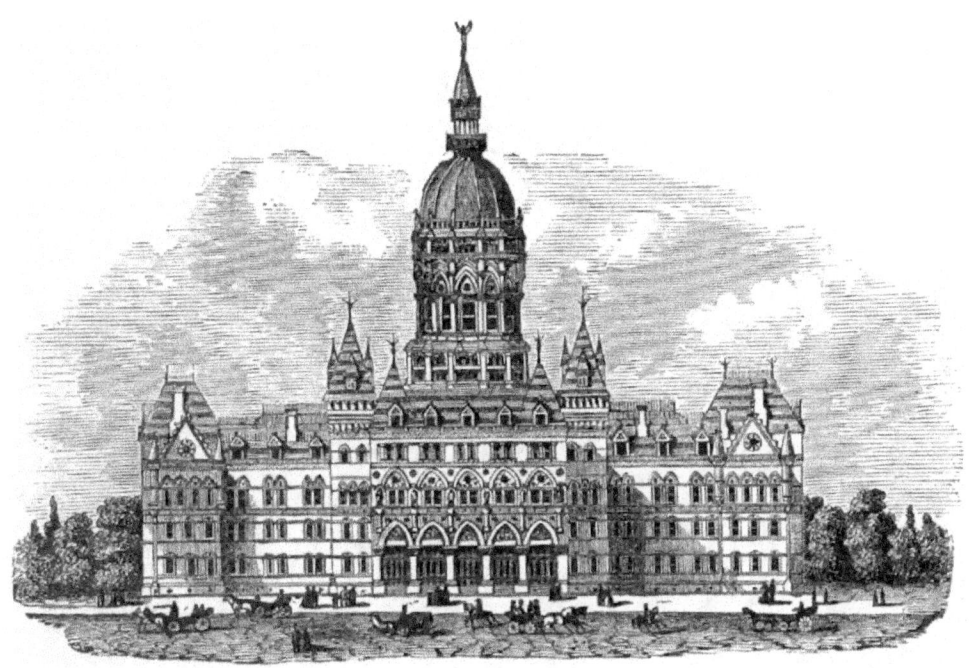

State Capitol (in Joseph R. Hawley, *History of Battle Flag Day: September 17, 1879*).

through the streets of Hartford to the Connecticut State Capitol, where they were presented to the state. Governor Charles B. Andrews accepted the flags on behalf of the citizens of Connecticut. In his speech, he said: "Lovingly then, and tenderly, let us lay them away in the motherly arms of the State whose trophies they now become, that they may teach these lessons of patriotism and of duty to all future generations."[11]

A book commemorating the celebrations that day records each of the stories of the regimental color bearers. The story of the Eighth's color bearers reads thusly:

> Wm. H. Cone of Company C was the first color-bearer, but after his promotion [March 1, 1862], Henry E. Strickland was entrusted with the flag. The honor was not misplaced, as Strickland at the battle of Newberne was the first man to plant his colors on the entrenchments. At the battle of Antietam, he was mortally wounded, but as he fell the flag was seized by Lt. Col. Appelman, subsequently Secretary of State of Connecticut, and held in the face of the enemy until Sergeant [then Private] Walker of Company D took Strickland's place in the ranks.
>
> After the Eighth reenlisted, Sergeant Thomas J. Hubbard of Torrington was appointed color-sergeant, and carried the national color until the battle of Walthall, Va., May 1, 1864, where his elbow was shattered by a minnie ball. Although the arm was completely crushed, Hubbard still clung to his color for a considerable distance, advancing with the line of battle. Finally, he was relieved by Sergeant Orlow J. Root, at present of Pine Meadow, who carried the flag through the remainder of the engagement. He also came home with it, depositing it at the State Arsenal when the regiment was mustered out of service.[12]

The old color bearers then proceeded to carry their banners inside the building, and enshrined them in glass cases. There, in the Hall of Flags, they still rest, and there they can be viewed and cherished today.

Placing the Flags in the Capitol (in Joseph R. Hawley, *History of Battle Flag Day: September 17, 1879*).

Antietam Monument

In September 1891, Colonel J.C. Broatch of the 14th Connecticut, led the planning for a regimental excursion to the Antietam battlefield. He conceived of erecting a monument there to the regiment. The following February, at the Grand Army of the Republic Encampment in Willimantic, Broatch offered a resolution to propose to the Connecticut General Assembly, then in session, to make appropriations available for the erection of monuments to all Connecticut troops on the battlefields where they fought. The resolution was adopted at the encampment, and a committee presented it to the legislature. On June 14, 1893, the Connecticut Legislature approved appropriations for any monument proposed to be erected by a Connecticut regimental or battery association. Each association would submit its proposal to the state quartermaster general, who would approve an expense to the state not to exceed $1,000.[13]

The 8th, 11th, 14th, and 16th Connecticut regiments all appointed committees to develop proposals. The regimental committee for the Eighth was made up by John S. Lane, Henry R. Jones, Isaac Williams, Harlow Chapin, and Frederick Gallup. Under Colonel J.C. Broatch and General J.B. Clapp, the four committees decided to work together. Each regiment selected and procured land to build their monuments on the Antietam battlefield. Lieutenant John S. Lane of Milford purchased the ground upon which the monument of the Eighth was to be placed and presented it to the regiment. The Eighth and the Eleventh awarded contracts to create the monuments to Stephen Maslen of Hartford. The committees decided their regiments would conduct a joint excursion to dedicate their monuments departing on October 8, 1894.[14]

The veterans of the Eighth joined that Antietam excursion to the Sharpsburg, Maryland, battlefield on a trip to dedicate all four Connecticut monuments erected there. The excursion started from Jersey City, New Jersey, at 1 p.m. on October 8. The veterans and their families took the Baltimore and Ohio Railroad through Allentown, Reading, Harrisburg, and Gettysburg, Pennsylvania, and then through Pen Mar and Hagerstown, Maryland, to Sharpsburg. Later, they would go to Harpers Ferry, West Virginia, and Washington, D.C. The group would return through Baltimore and Philadelphia.

The number of tickets was limited to 400, or 100 per regiment. Tickets cost $8.50, and accommodations at Gettysburg, Sharpsburg, and Washington, D.C., cost $1.50 to $2 per night.[15]

When they arrived at Sharpsburg, the veterans of the 8th, 11th, 14th, and 16th Connecticut regiments solemnly dedicated the stone monuments to their comrades who had fallen at Antietam. Each monument was placed at the location of the farthest advance in their trials of that battle.

The 8th Connecticut dedicated its monument on October 11, 1894, at the 2 p.m. ceremony in which Lieutenant John S. Lane of Meriden presided. The Sharpsburg Band played, and a chorus of several Connecticut veterans sang. It was a double quartet that had organized on the train. Singers from the Eighth were S. Jay Nettleton, Frederick Gallup, and Charles Jackson.[16] Corporal A.E. Bartram read the prayer, and Captain H.R. Jones gave the address. Then he read this eternal charge.[17] "O comrades! Who, weary with the march and the onset, have heard the tattoo call, drawn the curtain of your tents and fallen asleep—to you, we who remain, in the name of our grateful commonwealth, dedicate this perpetual memorial. Be it ours to tend it, and ours to accept the legacy which you have left us—devotion until death, to a Union saved and reunited."[18]

The history of the Eighth Regiment Connecticut Volunteer Infantry does not end here. With the words above, the soldiers of the Eighth have charged us, today, with keeping their legacy alive. This book is our good faith step in that direction.

Antietam dedication ribbon (courtesy Tad Sattler Private Collection).

* * *

Monument Details

The Eighth's monument is quite remarkable in its own right. It is along the Harpers Ferry Road in Sharpsburg, but a little out of the way. If you are heading north, there is a sign posted on the east side of the road, at the walking path to the monument. The best descriptions of the work and where to find are from the Stone Sentinels project.

> The monument is a granite pillar with alternating rough hewn and finished segments. A relief of a haversack, bayonet and belt is at the bottom of the front of the monument. A relief of a crossed anchor and cannon on a shield, the symbol of the Union 9th Corps, is at the top of the front of the monument. The monument was dedicated on October 11, 1894.
>
> Front [west side]:
> 8th Conn.
> Vol. Infantry
> 2d Brig.
> 3d Div.
> 9th Corps.
> Back [east side]:
> 8th Conn. V.I.
> No. Engaged—400
> Killed and Wounded—194

Eighth Connecticut monument (courtesy National Park Service).

The monument to the 8th Connecticut Infantry is southeast of Sharpsburg (39°27"08.6"N, 77°44'37.3"W). It can be reached by a paved walking path that starts from the east side of Harpers Ferry Road about 0.5 mile south of Main Street (Maryland Route 34) in Sharpsburg. The path heads east and then north about 380 yards toward the 9th New York Monument. The 8th Connecticut monument is 30 yards east of the path and just south of the 9th New York Monument.[19]

War Department Marker

The U.S. War Department erected several iron plaques across the battlefield at Sharpsburg. There are 238 markers erected between 1890 and 1906.[20] There is one on

Branch Avenue, looking over the area around the 16th Connecticut monument, then known as "Connecticut Park,"[21] describing the actions by the Eighth and the rest of Harland's brigade.

> On the morning of the 17th, Harland's Brigade moved from its position southeast of Burnside Bridge. The 11th Connecticut, deployed as skirmishers, preceded Crook's Brigade in its assault on the bridge and was repulsed with great loss. During the forenoon the remaining Regiments of the Brigade moved down the left bank of the Antietam, crossed at Snavely's Ford and, moving up the right bank of the stream, formed line on the left of the Division, Ewing's Ohio Brigade in support. At about 3 p.m., the Brigade advanced in the direction of Sharpsburg. The 8th Connecticut passed to the west of this point and the 16th Connecticut and 4th Rhode Island were in the 40 acre cornfield east, when they were attacked in flank by the right of A.P. Hill's Division and compelled to retire to the cover of the high ground near the bridge.[22]

Appendix A: Record of Service

Eighth Connecticut Volunteers

Summary

The Eighth Regiment Connecticut Volunteer Infantry was in existence from muster in starting September 21, 1861, until muster out on December 12, 1865. This service spanned four years, two months, and 21 days, or a total of 1544 days.

The following statistics were derived from the official State of Connecticut adjutant-generals records.[1]

1593	Total Men Who Served	288	Deserted
1014	Mustered Before Leaving State	5	Deserters Executed
74	Killed in Battle	444	Promotions
388	Wounded in Battle	71	Reductions
54	Wounded, then Died	34	Resignations
81	Captured	313	Re-Enlisted Veterans
1	Missing in Action	111	Discharged Term Expired
119	Died of Sickness	108	Transferred (USN 32, VRC 42)
356	Discharged Disability	288	Mustered Out
113	Discharged in Service	91	From Beginning, Mustered Out
9	Discharged Dishonorable	46	No Further Record (lost track)
358	Drafted or Substitute	5	Discharged, Later Re-Enlisted

Dyers Compendium

8th REGIMENT CONNECTICUT VOLUNTEER INFANTRY.[2]

ORGANIZATION:

Organized at Hartford September 21, 1861.
Left State for Annapolis, Md., October 17.
Attached to Parke's Third Brigade, Burnside's Expeditionary Corps, to April 1862.
1st Brigade, 3rd Division, Dept. of North Carolina, to July 1862.
2nd Brigade, 3rd Division, 9th Army Corps, Army of the Potomac, to April 1863.

2nd Brigade, 2nd Division, 7th Army Corps, Department of Virginia, to July 1863.
2nd Brigade, Getty's Division, U.S. Forces, Dept. Va. and N.C., to January 1864.
Sub-District Albemarle, N.C., Dept. of Va. and N.C., to April 1864.
2nd Brigade, 1st Division, 18th Army Corps, Dept. of Va. and N.C., to August 1864.
Provost Guard, 18th Army Corps to December 1864.
Provost Guard, 24th Army Corps, Dept. of Virginia to February 1865.
2nd Brigade, 3rd Division, 24th Army Corps, to July 1865.
2nd Provisional Brigade, 24th Army Corps, to August 1865.
Dept. of Virginia to December 1865.

SERVICE:

Duty at Annapolis, Md., till January 6, 1862.
Burnside's expedition to Hatteras Inlet and Roanoke Island, N.C., January 7–February 8, 1862.
Battle of Roanoke Island February 8.
At Roanoke Island till March 11.
Moved to New Berne, N. C., March 11–13.
Battle of New Berne March 14.
Operations against Fort Macon March 23–April 26.
Skirmish Fort Macon April 12.
Capture of Fort Macon April 26.
Duty at New Berne till July.
Moved to Morehead City July 2, thence to Newport News, Va., July 3–5 and duty there till August 1.
Moved to Fredericksburg, Va., August 1–5 and duty there till August 31.
Moved to Brooks' Station, thence to Washington, D.C., August 31–September 3.
Maryland Campaign September–October.
Frederick, Md., September 12.
Turner's Gap, South Mountain, September 14.
Battle of Antietam September 16–17.
Duty in Pleasant Valley till October 27.
Movement to Falmouth, Va., October 27–November 19.
Battle of Fredericksburg, Va., December 12–15.
Burnside's 2nd Campaign, "Mud March," January 20–24, 1863.
Moved to Newport News February 6–9.
thence to Suffolk March 13.
Siege of Suffolk April 12–May 4.
Fort Huger, April 19.
Edenton Road April 24.
Nansemond River May 3.
Siege of Suffolk raised May 4.
Dix's Peninsula Campaign June 24–July 7. "Blackberry Raid"
Expedition from White House to South Anna River July 1–7.
Moved to Portsmouth, Va., and duty there till March 1864.
Expedition to South Mills October 12–14, 1863.

Outpost duty at Deep Creek March 13 to April 18, 1864.
Moved to Yorktown April 18–21.
Butler's operations on south side of the James and against Petersburg and Richmond May 4–28.
Occupation of City Point and Bermuda Hundred May 5.
Port Walthall Junction, Chester Station, May 7.
Swift Creek, or Arrowfield Church, May 9–10.
Operations against Fort Darling May 12–16.
Battle of Drewry's Bluff May 14–16.
On Bermuda Hundred front May 17–27.
Moved to White House Landing, thence to Cold Harbor, May 27–June 1.
Battles about Cold Harbor June 1–12.
Assaults on Petersburg June 15–18.
Siege of Petersburg and Richmond June 16, 1864, to April 2, 1865.
Mine explosion Petersburg, July 30, 1864 (Reserve).
On Bermuda Hundred front August 25–September 27.
Fort Harrison, New Market Heights, September 28–29.
Chaffin's Farm, September 29–30.
Duty in trenches before Richmond till April 1865.
Battle of Fair Oaks October 27–28, 1864.
Occupation of Richmond April 3 and duty there and at Lynchburg, Va., till December.
Mustered out December 1865.

LOSSES:

Regiment lost during service:
8 Officers and 112 Enlisted men killed and mortally wounded and
3 Officers and 141 Enlisted men by disease.
Total 264.

Official Records[3]

The returns of the army report the organization as it existed at any particular point in time over the course of the war. Relevant entries covering the Eighth are listed below.

Official Records, Series I, Volume IX, Serial 9, p. 382
    January 31, 1862,
    Department of North Carolina Maj. Gen. Ambrose E. Burnside
    Coast Division Maj. Gen. Ambrose E. Burnside
    Third Brigade Brig. Gen. John G. Parke
    8th Connecticut Col. Edward Harland
    Brigaded with: 9 NY, 53 NY, 4 RI, 5 RI

Official Records, Series I, Volume IX, Serial 9, p. 382
    April 30, 1862,

Department of North Carolina Maj. Gen. Ambrose E. Burnside
Coast Division Maj. Gen. Ambrose E. Burnside
Third Brigade Brig. Gen. John G. Parke
8th Connecticut Col. Edward Harland
Brigaded with: 9 NJ, 4 RI, 5 RI, 1st US Battery C

Official Records, Series I, Volume LI, Serial 107, p. 727
July 25, 1862
Ninth Corps Maj. Gen. Ambrose E. Burnside (7/22/62)
Third Division Brig. Gen John G. Parke
Second Brigade
8th Conn Col. Edward Harland
Brigaded with: 11 CV, 4 RI

Official Records, Series I, Volume XIX, Serial 27, p. 178
September 1862
Army of the Potomac Maj. Gen. George B. McClellan
Ninth Corps Maj. Gen. Ambrose E. Burnside, Maj. Gen. Jesse Reno, Brig. Gen. Jacob D. Cox
First Division Brig. Gen. Orlando B. Wilcox
Third Division Brig. Gen. Isaac P. Rodman
Second Brigade Col. Edward Harland
8th Connecticut Lt. Col. Hiram Appelman, Maj. John E. Ward
Brigaded with: 11 CT, 16 CT 4 RI

Official Records, Series I, Volume XXI, Serial 31, p. 53
December 31, 1862
Army of the Potomac Maj. Gen. Ambrose E. Burnside
Ninth Corps Brig. Gen. Orlando B. Wilcox
Third Division Brig. Gen. George W. Getty
Second Brigade Col. Edward Harland
8th Connecticut Maj. John E. Ward, Capt. Henry M. Hoyt
Brigaded with: 11 CT, 15 CT, 16 CT, 21 CT, 4 RI

Official Records, Series I, Volume XXV, Serial 40, p. 619
January 31, 1863
Army of the Potomac Maj. Gen. Joseph Hooker
Ninth Corps Maj. Gen. John Sedgewick
Third Division Brig. Gen. George W. Getty
Second Brigade Col. Edward Harland
8th Connecticut Lt. Col. John E. Ward
Brigaded with: 11 CT, 15 CT, 16 CT

Official Records, Series I, Volume XVIII, Serial 26, p. 575
March 31, 1863
Dept of Virginia Maj. Gen. John A. Dix
Seventh Corps Maj. Gen. John A. Dix

Getty's Division Brig. Gen. George W. Getty
Second Brigade Brig. Gen. Edward Harland
8th Connecticut Col. John E. Ward
Brigaded with: 11 CT, 15 CT, 16 CT

Official Records, Series I, Volume XVIII, Serial 26, p. 576
April 30, 1863
Dept of Virginia Maj. Gen. John A. Dix
Seventh Corps Maj. Gen. John A. Dix
Getty's Division Brig. Gen. George W. Getty
Second Brigade Brig. Gen. Edward Harland
8th Connecticut Col. John E. Ward
Brigaded with: 11 CT, 15 CT, 16 CT

Official Records, Series I, Volume XVIII, Serial 26, p. 678
May 31, 1863
Dept of Virginia Maj. Gen. John A. Dix
Seventh Corps Maj. Gen. John A. Dix
Getty's Division Brig. Gen. George W. Getty
Second Brigade Brig. Gen. Edward Harland
8th Connecticut Col. John E. Ward
Brigaded with: 11 CT, 15 CT, 16 CT

Official Record+8+s, Series I, Volume XXVII, Serial 45, p. 619
June 30, 1863
Dept of Virginia Maj. Gen. John A. Dix
Seventh Corps Maj. Gen. John A. Dix
Second Division Brig. Gen. George W. Getty
Second Brigade Brig. Gen. Edward Harland
8th Connecticut Col. John E. Ward
Brigaded with: 11 CT, 15 CT, 16 CT

Official Records, Series I, Volume XXIX, Serial 49, p. 619
August 31, 1863
Dept of Virginia and North Carolina Maj. Gen. John G. Foster
Portsmouth—Getty's Division—Brig. Gen. George W. Getty
Second Brigade Brig. Gen. Edward Harland
8th Connecticut Col. John E. Ward
Brigaded with: 11 CT, 15 CT, 16 CT

Official Records, Series I, Volume XXIX, Serial 49, p. 619
December 31, 1863
Dept of Virginia and North Carolina
Army of the James Maj. Gen. Benjamin F. Butler
Eighteenth Corps
Portsmouth—Getty's Division—Brig. Gen. George W. Getty
Second (Harland's) Brigade Col. Francis Beach

8th Connecticut Capt. Henry M. Hoyt
Brigaded with: 15 CT, 16 CT

Official Records, Series I, Volume XXXIII, Serial 60, p. 482
January 31, 1864
Dept of Virginia and North Carolina
Army of the James Maj. Gen. Benjamin F. Butler
Eighteenth Corps William F. Smith
Portland—Heckman's Division—Brig. Gen. Charles A. Heckman
Third Brigade Col William H.P. Steere
8th Connecticut (detachment) Lt. Col. John Coughlin
Brigaded with: 23 MA, 10 NH, 13 NH, 9 NJ, 4 RI

Also

Subdistrict of the Albemarle Brig. Gen. Henry W. Wessels
Harland's Brigade Col. Francis Beach
8th Connecticut Col. John E. Ward
Brigaded with: 15 CT, 16 CT

Official Records, Series I, Volume XXXIII, Serial 60, p. 427
April 30, 1864
Dept of Virginia and North Carolina
Army of the James Maj. Gen. Benjamin F. Butler
Eighteenth Corps Maj. Gen. William F. Smith
First Division William T.H. Brooks
Second Brigade Hiram Burnham
8th Connecticut Col. John E. Ward
Brigaded with: 10 NH, 13 NH, 118 NY

Official Records, Series I, Volume XXXVI, Serial 69, p. 427
May 31, 1864
Dept of Virginia and North Carolina
Army of the James Maj. Gen. Benjamin F. Butler
Eighteenth Corps Maj. Gen. William F. Smith
First Division Brig. Gen. William T.H. Brooks
Second Brigade Brig. Gen. Hiram Burnham
8th Connecticut Capt. Charles M. Coit
Brigaded with: 10 NH, 13 NH, 118 NY

Official Records, Series I, Volume XL, Serial 81, p. 552
June 31, 1864
Dept of Virginia and North Carolina
Army of the James Maj. Gen. Benjamin F. Butler
Eighteenth Corps Maj. Gen. William F. Smith
First Division Brig. Gen. George J. Stannard
Second Brigade Brig. Gen. Hiram Burnham
8th Connecticut Capt. Charles M. Coit
Brigaded with: 10 NH, 13 NH, 118 NY

Official Records, Series I, Volume XL, Serial 82, p. 1124
   July 31, 1864
   Dept of Virginia and North Carolina
   Army of the James Maj. Gen. Benjamin F. Butler
   Eighteenth Corps Maj. Gen. Edward O.C. Ord
   First Division Brig. Gen. Hiram Burnham
   Second Brigade Col. Edgar M. Cullen
   8th Connecticut Capt. Charles M. Coit
   Brigaded with: 10 NH, 96 NY, 118 NY

Official Records, Series I, Volume XLII, Serial 88, p. 621
   August 31, 1864
   Dept of Virginia and North Carolina
   Army of the James Maj. Gen. Benjamin F. Butler
   Eighteenth Corps Maj. Gen. Edward O.C. Ord
   First Division Brig. Gen. Joseph B. Carr
   Second Brigade Col. Edgar M. Cullen
   8th Connecticut Capt. Charles M. Coit
   Brigaded with: 5 MD, 10 NH, 12 NH, 96 NY, 118 NY

Official Records, Series I, Volume XLII, Serial 89, p. 1124
   October 31, 1864
   Dept of Virginia and North Carolina
   Army of the James Maj. Gen. Benjamin F. Butler
   Eighteenth Corps Bvt. Maj. Gen. Godfrey Weitzel
   Unattached 8th Connecticut Col. John E. Ward

Official Records, Series I, Volume XLII, Serial 89, P. 1124
   December 31, 1864
   Dept of Virginia and North Carolina
   Army of the James Maj. Gen. Benjamin F. Butler
   Twenty-fourth Corps Maj. Gen. Edward O.C. Ord
   Headquarters Guard 8th Conn Col. John E. Ward

Official Records, Series I, Volume XLVI, Serial 96, p. 334
   January 31, 1865
   Department of Virginia
   Army of the James Maj. Gen. Edward O.C. Ord
   Twenty-fourth Corps Maj. Gen. John Gibbon
   Headquarters Guard 8th Conn Col. John E. Ward

Official Records, Series I, Volume XLII, Serial 96, p. 749
   February 28, 1865
   Department of Virginia Maj. Gen. Edward O.C. Ord
   Twenty-fourth Corps Maj. Gen. John Gibbon
   Third Division Brig. Gen. Charles Devens
   Second Brigade John E. Ward

8th Conn Maj. William M. Pratt
Brigaded with: 5 MD, 10 NH, 12 NH, 96 NY, 118 NY, 9 VT

Official Records, Series I, Volume XLVI, Serial 95, p. 334
March 30, 1865
Union Forces Lt. Gen. Ulysses S. Grant
Twenty-fourth Corps Maj. Gen. John Gibbon
Third Division Brig. Gen. Charles Devens
Second Brigade Col. Michael T. Donohue
8th Conn Maj. William M. Pratt
Brigaded with: 5 MD, 10 NH, 12 NH, 96 NY, 118 NY, 9 VT

Official Records, Series I, Volume XLVI, Serial 97, p. 1036
April 30, 1865
Twenty-fourth Corps, Maj. Gen. John Gibbon
Third Division Brig. Gen. Charles Devens
Second Brigade Col. Michael T. Donohue
8th Conn Maj. William M. Pratt
Brigaded with: 5 MD, 10 NH, 12 NH, 96 NY, 118 NY, 9 VT

Appendix B: Biographies of Narrators and Notables

Hiram Appelman

Hiram Appelman was born in Groton, Connecticut, on June 23, 1825. His father, John F. Appelman, was a ship captain who came to Groton from Wolgart, Prussia in 1806.[1] His mother was named Matilda.[2] When Hiram was old enough, he went to work in the dry goods business in Groton. In 1849, Hiram cast his lot with the rest of the gold rushers, and went to California. He went first to San Francisco, and then to Sacramento. He was a successful businessman there until he returned to Connecticut in 1856. Once back, he shortly set out for Kansas. He stayed there two years, and returned once again to Groton in 1858. He began school to study to become an attorney.[3]

When the war started, Hiram put his studies aside, and enlisted for ninety-days service with

Hiram Appelman (courtesy Mystic River Historical Society, Inc., Mystic, Connecticut).

the 2nd Connecticut Volunteer Infantry on April 22, 1861. He was mustered as Private in Rifle Company C on May 7, 1861. He served with the Second at the first battle of Bull Run, and was mustered out with the rest of the regiment on August 7, 1861.[4]

Hiram Appelman enlisted in the 8th Connecticut Volunteers on September 11, 1861. He was mustered as Captain of Company G on September 21, 1861. He was promoted to Major on December 23, 1861, and was again promoted to Lieutenant Colonel on March 28, 1862. Appelman was wounded slightly at the battle of Fort Macon in April 1862. However, he was severely wounded while leading the regiment at the battle of Antietam on September 17, 1862. That wound forced him to resign on December 23, 1862.[5] He had a bullet lodged in his leg for the rest of his life.[6]

Appelman returned to studying law, and was admitted to the bar in Connecticut in February of 1863.[7] He applied for U.S. Pension on March 19, 1863.[8] Hiram married Delia Augusta Haynes Appelman on December 28, 1866.[9] They had a daughter, Amelia Cook Appelman, on September 10, 1867,[10] and a son, Hiram H. Appelman, on October 18, 1869.[11]

Hiram was active in Republican politics in the state. He served as Secretary of State from 1869 to 1870 and again from 1871 to 1873. He was obliged to resign his position due to continuing complications from his Antietam wound.[12]

Hiram Appelman died of consumption at Fort Griswold, Groton, on September 4, 1873,[13] at the age of 48. He is buried in Elm Grove Cemetery in Mystic, Connecticut.[14]

* * *

Albion Dennis Brooks

Albion Dennis Brooks was born on May 9, 1843, in Carthage, Maine.[15] His mother was Abigail Eustis Brooks, the second wife of his father, George E. Brooks, a school teacher. Abigail was the sister of George's first wife, Anna Eustis Brooks.[16] Albion had two half-sisters, Pamela and Emily E., and two half-brothers, George H. and William E. Brooks. His father died in 1845 when Albion was about two years old. His mother remarried Abijah Landers, and they moved to Kingfield, Maine. When his mother died in 1857, his half-sister Emily took him in. She taught school first in Carthage, Maine, then Jay, Maine, then East Haverhill, Massachusetts. It was there she met and married Samuel Clayton Kingman of South Reading, Massachusetts. Clayton obtained work with the Wheeler and Wilson Manufacturing Company, a maker of sewing machines, located in Connecticut. The three moved first to Watertown, Connecticut, then to Bridgeport, Connecticut. Albion also worked in the factory and went to school in both towns. Albion went back to South Reading in 1857 to work with Clayton's father in the U.S. Post Office there. After two years, Albion returned to work in Clayton's shop in Bridgeport once again.[17]

When the war began, Clayton enlisted, but was rejected by the surgeons for

Albion Dennis Brooks (courtesy Special Collections Library, Pennsylvania State University).

being too small. Albion begged to go in his place.[18] The 8th Connecticut Volunteers were first stationed in Annapolis, Maryland, and Albion made his way there and enlisted in the Eighth on November 26, 1861. He was mustered as Private in Company A that same day. He was later promoted Corporal on March 28, 1862, and to Sergeant on September 17, 1862, being the day of the battle of Antietam. He was again promoted to First Sergeant on September 25, 1862. Albion served faithfully with the Eighth, and re-enlisted on December 24, 1863.[19]

Albion was mortally wounded in the forward rifle pits at the battle of Cold Harbor, Virginia, on June 2, 1864.[20] He died the next day, June 3.[21] It was Albion's express wish, that should he die, his body was to be sent North, and buried beside his mother.[22] There he rests today, in the Riverside Cemetery in Kingfield, Maine.[23]

"Out of the Ranks"
by Emily Brooks Kingman on hearing of the death of her brother[24]

Out of the ranks Our Father has called him,
Away from the tumult of war and the strife;
To mansions eternal Angels have borne him;
From death he has passed into glorious life.

Never again through the wearisome marches
Will falter his step though his heart may be strong.
Never again in the lonely night watches
Will he sigh for the right, while beholding the wrong?

Never may drum-beat "the battle call" sounding,
Awake him from dreaming of friends and of home,
For above the roar of cannon resounding
He heard the sweet message, "Beloved one come."

Oh friend! Do you know, do you feel the deep meaning?
Of words that a Savior's love only could send?

On his last failing sight their glory was beaming,
"Lo I am with you, even unto the end."

Bridgeport, Conn, June 11, 1864
In Memory of Albion D. Brooks, Co. A,
8th Conn. Vols., killed at Cold Harbor, Va.,
June 2, 1864

* * *

Oliver Cromwell Case

Oliver Cromwell Case was born on December 22, 1839, in Simsbury, Connecticut. His parents were Job Case and Abigail Griswold Phelps Case. Oliver had two older brothers, Ariel Job and Alonzo Grove Case. He later had a younger sister, Abbie Jane Case Phelps.[25]

On September 16, 1861, three-year recruiting was occurring and Oliver enlisted in the 8th Connecticut Volunteers. He was mustered as Private in Company B on September 25, 1861. Subsequently, he was transferred to Company A on October 1, 1861.[26]

He served during the early battles of the Eighth, but was killed in action at the battle of Antietam, on September 17, 1862.[27]

He was buried in the Antietam National Cemetery at Sharpsburg, Maryland.[28] He was later sent home and buried in the Hop Meadow Cemetery in Simsbury, Connecticut.[29]

Oliver C. Case grave, Simsbury, Connecticut (photograph by the authors).

* * *

Charles Morgan Coit

Charles Morgan Coit was born on March 29, 1838, in Norwich, Connecticut. His mother was Sarah Perkins Grosvenor Coit, the third wife of his father, Charles Coit. He had a sister, Ellen G. Coit, and a younger brother, George D. Coit. His father served the U.S. Army in the War of 1812 and had risen to Colonel at the time of his death in 1855.

Charles M. Coit became secretary and treasurer of the Chelsea Savings Bank in Norwich.[30] Charles also helped his mother, sister, and brother manage the family's several rental properties.

Charles enlisted in the 8th Connecticut Volunteers on September 13, 1861. He was mustered First Lieutenant and Adjutant on the regimental staff. He was promoted to Captain of Company B on March 27, 1862. He served in that capacity for much of the Eighth's hard service. In addition, he also served as the commander of the Eighth when the senior officers were unable to serve due to wounds or illness. Charles Coit was wounded late in the war at the battle of Fair Oaks, Virginia, October 27, 1864. After a long hospitalization, he recovered and returned to service with the Eighth. He was offered promotion to Major twice, a position that he declined. He was breveted Lieutenant Colonel on March 13, 1865. Charles subsequently resigned, and was discharged on May 27, 1865.[31]

Charles Morgan Coit (in D. Hamilton Hurd, *History of New London County, Connecticut*).

Charles returned to life in Norwich, Connecticut. He married Mary B. Hillard on June 18, 1872, at Norwich, and had two sons, Charles and Augustus. Charles M. Coit died by drowning on July 3, 1878, while sailing a yacht in New London, Connecticut, harbor. He had attempted to save the life of his son Charles, who had fallen overboard.[32] His son survived, but Charles did not.

Charles M. Coit is buried in Yantic Cemetery, in Norwich, Connecticut.[33]

* * *

Roger Morgan Ford

Roger Morgan Ford was born on December 22, 1834, in New Marlborough, Massachusetts, where his father was from.[34] His parents were Roger W. Ford and Emily Ford. He was the third of six children listed on the 1850 U.S. Census, when the family was recorded as residing in North Haven, Connecticut.[35] Roger M. Ford was documented enlisting in the U.S. Army in 1855 at 21 years old.[36]

Roger married Phoebe A. Mason Ford in 1858, and took up residence in New Jersey, where they had a son, William H., in 1859. Roger went to Meriden, Connecticut, in 1859 to work in the silver-plating trade there. It appears Phoebe and the children remained in New Jersey during that time.[37]

At the start of the war, Roger enlisted from Meriden, Connecticut, in the 1st Connecticut Volunteer Infantry on April 18, 1861. He was mustered as Private in Company F on April 22, 1861. He served his three-month term, and was mustered out with the regiment on July 31, 1861.[38]

Roger again enlisted on September 18, 1861, when he joined the 8th Connecticut Volunteers. He was mustered as Second Lieutenant in Company K on September 23, 1861. He was promoted to First Lieutenant on March 18, 1862, and was again promoted to Captain of Company G on February 7, 1863. He was wounded in front of Petersburg, Virginia, on June 25, 1864, and was discharged on September 2, 1864. Roger always was a fair and honest man. After he recuperated as a citizen at home, he once again enlisted in the Eighth at New Haven on January 5, 1865. He was mustered as Private in Company E on that day. He was soon promoted to First Sergeant of Company E on February 6, 1865, then promoted to Captain of Company G for the second time on March 1, 1865. Roger was mustered out at the end of the regiment's service on December 12, 1865.[39]

Roger Morgan Ford (courtesy Matthew E. Reardon Private Collection).

After the war, Roger became a policeman for the city of Meriden. He probably brought the family to Meriden in 1869, since the 1870 U.S. Census lists their daughter, Nettie N. Ford born in New Jersey in 1868, but their third child, Ida M. Ford, born in Connecticut in 1870.[40] In 1889, at age 55, Roger and Phoebe had another daughter, Kazel Ford. He lived in Meriden for the rest of his life.[41]

Roger M. Ford died on March 25, 1902, and is buried at Walnut Grove Cemetery, Meriden, Connecticut.[42] Roger Ford's war diary was found in a warehouse in Meriden in 2015 and was donated to the New England Civil War Museum in Rockville, Connecticut.

* * *

Lucius W. Fox

Lucius W. Fox was born on January 21, 1842, in Litchfield, Connecticut. His father was Marcus Fox, a shoemaker and farmer, and his mother was Marcia Minerva Hubbell Fox. Lucius was the oldest of six children. He had two brothers, Sheldon and Henry Fox, and three sisters, Julia, Emma, and Marcia. The family bought a farm and moved to Washington, Connecticut.[43]

Lucius enlisted in the 8th Connecticut Volunteers on September 27, 1861, and was mustered as Private in Company I that day. Lucius served courageously throughout his enlistment. In December 1863, he chose not to re-enlist in the regiment for another three years. The following fall, Lucius Fox was discharged, term expired, on September 26, 1864.[44]

Lucius W. Fox (courtesy Matthew E. Reardon Private Collection).

Upon his return from the war, Lucius married his fiancée, Elma G. Shriver, in 1864.[45] They had a son, Louis G. Fox, born in 1866. In about 1869, Lucius took his wife and son to Nebraska to homestead there. Their daughter, Ida May Fox, was born in 1870 while in Nebraska. They all returned to Connecticut after only 18 months.[46]

The 1880 U.S. Census found Lucius farming in Harwinton, Connecticut, living with his wife, Elma G., and their children, 14-year-old Louis and 10-year-old Ida.[47] The 1900 U.S. Census again listed Lucius and family as farming in Harwinton.[48] After being married about 40 years, his wife Elma died.[49] After two years, Lucius, at the age of 68, remarried to Sarah A.T. Fox and moved to Torrington, Connecticut.[50] The 1920 U.S. Census then places Lucius living at 133 Brown Street, West Haven, Connecticut,[51] with only his second wife, Sarah Fox.[52]

Lucius Fox died on January 14, 1926, a week short of his 84th birthday. He is buried in Pine Grove Cemetery in Ansonia, Connecticut.[53]

* * *

Henry C. Hall

Henry C. Hall was born in 1840 in Newtown, Connecticut. Henry married Emily J. Hall and they had three children. Their first child, Albert H. Hall, born in 1858, died in infancy. Arthur B. Hall is the other name found.[54]

Henry enlisted in the 8th Connecticut Volunteers on September 14, 1861. He was mustered as Sergeant in Company I on September 21, 1861. He was promoted to First Sergeant on March 15, 1862. He was commissioned and promoted Second Lieutenant on April 29, 1862, and then promoted to First Lieutenant on May 6, 1862. He served as Acting Adjutant of the regiment during that fall and winter. He was promoted again to

Henry C. Hall. Tad Sattler, photographer (courtesy of the Andrew M. Morgan Collection, Connecticut State Library).

Captain of Company F on February 7, 1863. Henry was wounded at the battle of Drewry's Bluff on May 17, 1864.[55]

Henry Hall died from a sharpshooter's bullet in the trenches in front of Petersburg, Virginia, on July 11, 1864.[56] He was buried with military and Masonic honors at Wooster Cemetery, Danbury, Connecticut, on July 24, 1864.[57]

* * *

Edward Harland

Edward Harland was born on June 24, 1832, in Norwich, Connecticut. His parents were Henry Harland and Fanny Harland. They had four children, Hally, Edward, Harriet, and Hannah Harland.[58]

"He was descended from an English watchmaker who immigrated to the colonies just a few years before the Americans declared their independence."[59]

Edward Harland graduated with a law degree from Yale University in 1853. He was admitted to the bar two years later, and became a prominent citizen of Norwich.[60]

"Upon graduation from Yale, he studied for the Connecticut bar in the law offices of John Turner Wait, father of the future Lieutenant Marvin Wait of the 8th Connecticut and, in 1855, Harland was elected as secretary of the Connecticut State Democratic Convention. By 1860, Ned Harland's political involvement had transitioned to the new Republican party as he served as one of the floor managers for the Lincoln-Hamlin Ball."[61]

At the start of the war, Edward Harland raised a company for the 3rd Connecticut Volunteer Infantry. He was elected, commissioned, and mustered as Captain of Rifle Co. C. He served the three-month term of the regiment and was mustered out with them on August 12, 1861.

"As the 8th Connecticut

Edward Harland (in WA. Croffut and J.M. Morris, *The Military and Civil History of Connecticut During the War of 1861–1865*).

Volunteer Infantry gathered at Camp Buckingham in Hartford in late September of 1861, Connecticut Governor, William A. Buckingham, selected Edward 'Ned' Harland of Norwich to serve as the regimental commander."[62]

> On September 3, 1861, the Hartford Daily Courant announced his appointment as the Lieutenant Colonel of the 6th Connecticut Infantry Regiment serving under Colonel John Chatfield, previously the commander of the 3rd Connecticut Volunteer Infantry.
>
> Harland's assignment as the second in command of the 6th Connecticut was extremely short. Within two days of his appointment, the Hartford Daily Courant would again announce a new position for the Norwich lawyer as Colonel of the newly forming 8th Connecticut Volunteer Infantry Regiment.[1] In testament to Edward Harland's status and character, he was presented with an expensive sword by the New-London County bar upon his commissioning as the Colonel of the 8th Connecticut.[2] One month later, Harland received another useful gift, this time from his alma mater. In early October of 1861, Ned Harland was "presented with an elegant field glass by members of the Yale Class of 1853, who were associated with him in the 'Owl Club' at the school.[4]"[63]

He was commissioned and mustered as Colonel of the 8th Connecticut Volunteers on October 5, 1861. He was discharged from the Eighth and promoted to Brigadier General of Volunteers on November 29, 1862. He resigned from the U.S. Army on June 22, 1865.[64]

> Thirty-three-year-old Edward Harland returned to Norwich after the war where he enjoyed great success in a number of endeavors. After first returning to his law practice, Harland next served a number of terms in both houses of the Connecticut legislature, and sat for a time as a probate judge. Continuing a distinguished career as a public servant, Harland also served on the state board of pardons and as the Adjutant General of the Connecticut state militia. In 1890 the aging bachelor was named president of the Chelsea Savings Bank.[65]

Edward Harland, indeed, served two terms in the State House of Representatives, and one in the State Senate, and was a Judge of Probate from 1862 to 1876.[66]

General Edward Harland was elected in 1875 as the first commander, establishing the Department of Connecticut of the Grand Army of the Republic.[67]

Harland was the State Adjutant General on Battle Flag Day in 1879, and made major contributions to that patriotic event.[68]

He was also very active over the years in the Eighth Connecticut Volunteers Veteran Association of surviving veteran members. The regiment presented a large, framed portrait of General Harland to the Sedgewick Post, G.A.R. No.1 of Norwich. Edward Harland was a member and past commander of that post.[69] At the Eighth's annual reunion meeting in 1911, Edward Harland was elected as the Association's President for Life.[70]

Harland also helped to establish the W.W. Backus Hospital in Norwich.[71]

"Harland suffered from chronic emphysema during the final ten years of his life; indeed, this affliction was listed as the cause of his death, which came on March 9, 1915, in Norwich, Connecticut. He was eighty-two years of age."[72]

Edward Harland never married. He is buried in Yantic Cemetery, in Norwich, Connecticut.[73]

* * *

Henry Morris Hoyt

Henry Morris Hoyt was born on October 12, 1834. His father was Philo W. Hoyt, 23 years old, and his mother was Clarissa L. Stevens Hoyt, 20 years old.[74]

The 1860 U.S. Census found Henry living in Bridgeport, Connecticut, in the residence of Catherine Wood, likely as a boarder. His occupation was listed as a printer.[75]

Henry M. Hoyt. Tad Sattler, photographer (courtesy Andrew M. Morgan Collection, Connecticut State Library).

When the war started, Henry enlisted, from Bridgeport, in the 1st Connecticut Volunteer Infantry on April 20, 1861. He was commissioned and mustered as First Lieutenant in Company H on April 23, 1861. He served and was mustered out at the end of their ninety-day term on July 31, 1861.[76] He subsequently enlisted, from Bridgeport, in the 8th Connecticut Volunteer Infantry on September 21, 1861, and was commissioned and mustered First Lieutenant in Company A on September 25, 1861. He was soon promoted to Captain of Company A on December 25, 1861. He was discharged, his term expired, on October 15, 1864.[77]

After the war, "Major" Henry M. Hoyt became publisher of the Bridgeport newspaper, *Morning News*, and sustained it as a reliable media standard on that city's scene.[78]

Hoyt was also active with the regiment's veteran association. He served as an officer, and attended annual reunions. He was also involved in the Battle Flag Day ceremonies on September 17, 1879, at the Connecticut state capitol building dedication.

Henry Hoyt died, at age 50, on April 2, 1885. He was buried in section 19 of Mountain Grove Cemetery, in Bridgeport, Connecticut.[79]

* * *

Nathan E. Hickok

Nathan E. Hickok was probably born in 1839, in Danbury, Connecticut.[80]

Nathan E. Hickok of Danbury, enlisted in the 8th Connecticut Volunteers on October 1, 1861. He was mustered as Private in Company A on October 2, 1861. He served throughout the campaigns of the Eighth, and re-enlisted on December 24, 1863. He was promoted to Corporal on February 22, 1864. Nathan Hickok captured an enemy flag during the storming of Fort Harrison on September 29, 1864. He was promoted Sergeant on October 1, 1864, in recognition of his bravery. Nathan Hickok was captured by the enemy at the battle of Fair Oaks, Virginia, on October 29, 1864. There is no further record of his whereabouts or demise.[81] Nathan could have been wounded, captured, and died without identification by the enemy. He was recorded as 5 feet 3 inches tall, with blue eyes, and dark hair on his enlistment form. His first enlistment listed him as a laborer, and his re-enlistment listed him as a paper maker.[82]

Nathan E. Hickok was, perhaps posthumously, awarded the Medal of Honor on April 6, 1865. The citation reads:

> The President of the United States of America, in the name of Congress, takes pleasure in presenting the Medal of Honor to Corporal Nathan E. Hickok, United States Army, for extraordinary heroism on 29 September 1864, while serving with Company A, 8th Connecticut Infantry, in action at Chaffin's Farm, Virginia, for capture of flag.[83]

Nathan E. Hickok, while being a hero, also became an unknown. He is memorialized in his home town. In the Wooster Cemetery in Danbury, Connecticut, there stands a monument honoring local men in unknown graves who were "Soldiers Who Did Not Return."[84] There is a small plaque on the back side of the base, reading "Nathan Hickok, Awarded Cong. Medal of Honor, April 6, 1865."[85] In recent times, April 2004, a small stone monument was also placed in a more visible location near the larger monument.[86] It also has a plaque that reads "In Memory of Corporal Nathen E. Hickok, Medal of Honor, Civil War—April 6, 1865."[87]

Nathan E. Hickok, Army Medal of Honor, 1864 (Army Heritage Museum Collection, Carlisle, PA).

* * *

Fitz Greene Hollister

Fitz Greene Hollister was born on April 17, 1837, in Washington, Connecticut.[88] His father was Preston S. Hollister, a farmer, and his mother was Phoebe H. Hollister. He was the oldest of three sons, including Clarence and Arthur Hollister.[89] Fitz grew up and worked on the family farm.

Fitz enlisted in the 8th Connecticut Volunteers on September 21, 1861, and was mustered as Private in Company I that same day. He was promoted to Corporal on October 11, 1863. Fitz re-enlisted on December 24, 1863. He was promoted again to Sergeant on February 12, 1864. Fitz was killed in action near Petersburg, Virginia, on June 15, 1864.[90] He was shot in the chest while skirmishing during the advance.[91]

Fitz Greene Hollister (courtesy Gunn Memorial Library and Museum, Washington, CT).

Fitz Hollister is buried in the Old Judea Cemetery Washington, Connecticut.[92]

* * *

William Lyman Huntington

William Lyman Huntington was born on August 23, 1833, in Lebanon, Connecticut. His father was Simeon, and his mother Achsah Clark Huntington.[93] He had three siblings, Sarah, Ira Clark, and Clarissa Williams Huntington.[94] William grew up, and married 27-year-old Eunice C. Perry Huntington on May 18, 1859, in Worchester, Massachusetts.[95]

William enlisted in the 8th Connecticut Volunteers from Lebanon on September, 3, 1861. He was mustered as Private in Company D on September 21, 1861. He was promoted to Sergeant on February 10, 1862. William was wounded in the battle of Antietam, September 17, 1862. He recuperated, and served throughout the following years. He was promoted to First Sergeant on January 9, 1863. He re-enlisted on December 24, 1863. William was wounded again at the battle of Port Walthall Junction on May 7, 1864. Subsequently, he was transferred to the 37th Company, 2d Battalion, Veterans Reserve Corps. During that service, he clerked at the Quartermaster General's Office in Washington, D.C. He was discharged as Private from 36th Company on September 5, 1866.[96]

After the war, in February 1867, William announced he was leaving Lebanon to travel by boat for California with his friend, Daniel Hutchinson.[97] He wrote from the Lance Ranch in Loreto, Baja California, Mexico. He was working as a ranch hand, and in a mine located there.[98] He contracted typhoid fever, and was invited to move to Marysville, California, north of Sacramento, to manage an estate there for the Hutchinson family.[99] He wrote home about experiencing a major earthquake there.[100] William worked in Marysville until around May 1869, when he wrote from Mammoth, California, where he had taken work in a saw mill.[101] He mentioned that he had been ill with ague a few times since leaving Marysville, but had fought it back. William finally returned to Connecticut from California in the middle of November 1869.[102]

William Lyman Huntington (courtesy Houghton Library, Harvard University, Boston, MA).

William and his family appear in the 1880 U.S. Census. They were residing and farming in Lebanon, Connecticut. William and Eunice listed a son, Ira Clark Huntington, born in 1862. His mother-in-law, Mary Perry, was also living with them.[103]

William Huntington died on March 13, 1905. He is buried in Center Cemetery, Lebanon, Connecticut.[104]

* * *

William Henry Johnson

William Henry Johnson was born on March 4, 1833, in Alexandria, Virginia, to his free black parents. With nothing more than a Sunday school education, he left home in 1845 at twelve years of age, and went to Philadelphia, Pennsylvania, where he learned the hairdressing trade. He moved to Albany, New York, in 1851. There he met abolitionist Stephen Myers, and got actively involved in the Underground

Railroad. Albany was a major stop along the route to freedom in Canada. William returned to Philadelphia in 1855, and continued with the Underground Railroad as an abolitionist and activist.[105]

William married Sarah Ann Davis Stewart in 1852. Sarah was the daughter of John G. Stewart, editor of *The North Star and Freeman's Advocate*, an Albany newspaper published by Stephen Myers.[106] Together, over the years, William and Sarah had six children. William H. was born in 1859, Sarah in 1861, Stewart in 1866, Emma in 1869,[107] Anna in 1875,[108] and Grant U. in 1878.[109]

William Henry Johnson was part of the Banneker Literary Institute in Philadelphia, where he publicly wrote and spoke against slavery. In 1859, he was compelled to leave Philadelphia to escape prison due to his assistance to fugitive slaves having drawn too much attention. He moved to Norwich, Connecticut, and was living there when the war started.[110]

William was not allowed to enlist, due to his color, so he joined the 2nd Connecticut Volunteers as an "independent man." He served and fought with them at the first battle of Bull Run. William wrote to the Boston newspaper *Pine & Palm*, "We lost everything—life, ammunition, and honor. We were driven like so many sheep into Washington, disgraced and humiliated."[111] He also wrote for Frederick Douglass's Rochester paper, *The North Star*.[112]

After the Second mustered out, he returned to Norwich, and soon joined the 8th Connecticut Volunteers, again as an "independent man." William served and fought with the Eighth at the battles of Roanoke and Newbern. He published letters from the front describing his experiences with the Eighth in the *Pine & Palm*.[113] In one letter from Newbern, he described himself ready for the fight. "This may be the last line from me; for now, I go into the field armed with a revolver and a sure rifle; and shall take my post to defend the colors of my regiment."[114] After Newbern, his health began to fail, and rheumatism forced him to leave the Eighth in June 1862. He returned once again to Albany. There, he took up

William Henry Johnson (in William H. Johnson, *Autobiography of Dr. William Henry Johnson*).

work as a recruiting agent, raising black troops for the Fourteenth Congressional District.[115]

William Henry Johnson was a "Free-Soiler" who trained with anti-slavery notables like Garret Smith, Frederick Douglass, John C. Freemont, the Rev. Henry Garnet, and many others. William was also active in politics. He attended his first Republican National Convention before the war in 1856. William was appointed a delegate to the Republican National Convention in 1864.[116]

The 1870 U.S. Census found William and Sarah living in Albany with their first four children, William, Sarah, Stewart, and Emma. William's occupation was listed as a barber.[117]

Starting in 1892, William published and edited his own paper, *The Calcium Light*, at Albany. He was present at the national convention in 1872 when U.S. Grant was nominated, and again in 1900 when William McKinley was nominated and re-elected.

William Henry Johnson wrote the constitution of the New York Equal Rights Committee, and was elected its chairman from 1866 to 1873. He was elected in 1887 to the Republican State Committee as a member at large. In 1888 he attended the Chicago national convention that nominated Benjamin Harrison for President.[118]

In 1891, William drafted legislation which was passed, prohibiting discrimination against black people by the insurance industry. In 1900, a bill sponsored by William was passed that repealed all New York laws which prohibited the free and equal accommodation of black children in public schools. That law was signed by Governor Theodore Roosevelt, who presented the signing pen to William to commemorate his efforts.[119]

William Henry Johnson became a Master Mason in the Jepthah Lodge No. 13, Albany, in 1862. He held several offices of increasing importance, culminating as Grand Master in 1882. He craved knowledge beyond the Blue Lodge, and achieved the thirty-third degree in the Scottish Rite on March 19, 1883.[120]

The 1900 U.S. Census found the Johnsons living in Albany with daughters Sarah, Emma, and Anna.[121] The 1910 U.S. Census found William, age 77, and Sarah, age 74, boarding at the John W. Caldwell residence in Albany. William listed his occupation as elevator man at the hospital.[122]

Wife Sarah Johnson died on April 10, 1918.[123] William Henry Johnson died on October 3, 1918. He was 85 years old. He is buried, with the rest of his family, in Albany Rural Cemetery, in Menands, New York.[124]

* * *

Wolcott Pascal Marsh

Wolcott Pascal March was born in Brooklyn, New York, on March 15, 1839. The 1850 U.S. Census lists his father as Edward Marsh, and mother as Matilda Marsh. The Marsh family was living and farming in New Hartford, Connecticut. They had three children, Wolcott P., Edward W., and Myron G. Marsh.[125]

Wolcott moved to Hartford, Connecticut, and worked as a merchant, engaged in selling knives.¹²⁶ When the war started, Wolcott Marsh enlisted in the 1st Connecticut Volunteers from Hartford, on April 18, 1861. He was mustered as Private in Rifle Company A on April 22, 1861. Wolcott Marsh was married to Anna Cecilia Thompson Marsh on May 8, 1861, in Hartford, Connecticut.¹²⁷ Wolcott and the regiment were mustered out of service on July 31, 1861.¹²⁸

Wolcott Marsh returned home, then enlisted again on October 2, 1861, this time in the 8th Connecticut Volunteers. He was mustered as Second Lieutenant in Company A on October 2, 1861. He was promoted First Lieutenant on December 24, 1861. He was again promoted, as Captain of Company F on March 28, 1862. Marsh suffered severely, probably from malaria contracted during the North Carolina campaign of early 1862. He resigned with a medical discharge after the battle of Fredericksburg, on December 22, 1862.¹²⁹

After he returned home, in the spring of 1863, Wolcott bought a farm in the East Weatogue section of Simsbury, Connecticut, where he may have raised tobacco. He also worked in a store in Hartford in the winter. Wolcott and Anna sold that farm in 1865, and bought another farm in Bloomfield, Connecticut. The Marsh family moved once again in 1866, this time to Canton Street in Hartford, Connecticut. Sometime in 1867 or 1868, Wolcott moved his family to Springfield, Massachusetts. There, Wolcott started a new business selling shoes.¹³⁰

Wolcott and Anna were listed in the 1870 U.S. Census as having a son Wolcott Howard in 1863, a daughter Annie in 1865, and a daughter Mary Munson in 1866. It recorded them living in Springfield, Massachusetts, and Wolcott's occupation as a merchant.¹³¹ They had a son, Frank J. in 1868, but he died in 1870 prior to the census.¹³²

Wolcott Pascal Marsh (courtesy Sandra Marsh Mercer and Jerry Mercer Family Collection).

The family again

moved, perhaps to the Dakota Territory, thence to Elmira, New York, but returned to Springfield, Massachusetts. Wolcott still suffered from the malaria contracted during the war, and his doctor advised him to move to a milder climate. In 1890, Wolcott sold his shoe business, and took the family by train to California. They chose Ontario, California, where he bought a ten-acre orange grove, and built a new house.[133]

Wolcott Marsh died of complications from his chronic illness on August 3, 1894.[134] Wolcott is buried in Bellevue Memorial Park, in the Upland section of Ontario, California.[135] The Army Pension Office declared Wolcott an Invalid on February 2, 1893, and declared Anna his Widow on October 6, 1894.[136] After Wolcott's death, his son Howard operated the orange grove and took care of Anna. She had a stroke around 1902. She was paralyzed, but lived on until December 1912.[137]

* * *

Samuel Jay Nettleton

Samuel Jay Nettleton was born on December 24, 1832, in Washington, Connecticut. His father was Samuel Nettleton, and his mother was Sarah Canfield Nettleton.[138] The 1860 U.S. Census showed Sarah widowed, living in Washington, Connecticut, with five children, Sarah Abigail born 1821, Celia Jane born 1827, Susan Amelia born 1830, Samuel Jay born 1832, and Henry Selden born about 1838.[139]

Jay enlisted in the 8th Connecticut Volunteers on September 14, 1861. He was mustered as Corporal in Company I on September 21, 1861, under the name of Jay T. Nettleton of Washington, Connecticut. He was promoted to Sergeant on March 15, 1862, and again to First

Samuel Jay Nettleton (courtesy Gunn Memorial Library and Museum, Washington, CT).

Sergeant on November 8, 1863. Jay was discharged for term expired on September 20, 1864.[140]

After the war, Jay promptly married Martha Ann Stevens in Fishkill, New York, and lived together in Washington.[141] Jay is recorded in the 1880 U.S. Census as living in Litchfield, Connecticut, where he was farming for an occupation. His wife was Martha Nettleton. Together, they had nine children: Sarah C., Amelia S., Mary W., Anna A., Fitz G., Ceclia S., Lucy M., William M., and an unnamed infant.[142]

His second marriage was to his first wife's younger sister, Sarah Irene Stevens.[143]

In the 1910 U.S. Census lists Jay living in Washington with his second wife, Sarah I. Nettleton, and daughter Lucy M.[144]

Samuel Jay Nettleton died on August 17, 1912. He is buried in Washington Cemetery on the Green, Washington, Connecticut.[145] The Army Pension Office recorded Jay as Invalid on June 3, 1890, and declared Sarah I. Nettleton as Widow on October 17, 1916.[146]

* * *

Seth Frederick Plumb

Seth Frederick Plumb was born on August 27, 1836, in Litchfield, Connecticut. The 1850 U.S. Census showed his father Frederick W. Plumb, and his mother Huldah S. Plumb. They had five children. John L. born in 1832, Seth F. born in 1836, Lemira E. born in 1840, William H. born in 1842, and Charles E. born in 1846.[147]

Prior to the war, Seth farmed land he owned, and sold cordwood from his wood lots off of Brush Hill Road. In the winter, he taught in a one room schoolhouse on Harris Plains at the foot of Brush Hill.[148]

The 1860 U.S. Census listed Seth living with his brother John, his wife Lucy, and their two-year-old son, Frederick. They all lived on John's farm on Knox Road, close by to Brush Hill.[149]

Seth Plumb enlisted, at 25

Seth Frederick Plumb (courtesy private family collection).

years old, in the 8th Connecticut Volunteers on September 6, 1861. He was mustered Sergeant in Company E on September 25, 1861. He was promoted First Sergeant on May 16, 1864. He was commissioned Second Lieutenant on July 17, 1864, but was never mustered. He was killed in action at the battle of Fort Harrison on September 29, 1864.[150]

Seth Plumb is buried in West Cemetery, in Litchfield, Connecticut.[151] The Litchfield post of the Grand Army of the Republic was named in his honor, the Seth F. Plumb GAR Post No. 80.[152]

* * *

Joseph E. Shadek

Joseph E. Shadek, also known as Joseph Shedek, enlisted in the Eighth on September 20, 1861. He was mustered in as a Private in Company A, and later, on November 25, 1862, was promoted to Corporal.[153]

The earliest record we found for Shadek was from a city and business directory showing that he lived in New York City during the period from 1856 to 1858, with his occupation listed as painter. Similar records for the periods from 1869 through to 1875 also show him living there, again listing him as a painter. In 1864 (also with a New York City address), he was naturalized as a U.S. citizen, his prior nationality being given as Italian.[154]

Shadek's connection to Connecticut and the Eighth may have come from the fact that he knew Wolcott P. Marsh, who was from Hartford, and who was mustered in as a 2nd Lieutenant in Company A. It is Marsh's letters home to his wife that give us some insight into the artist. Marsh frequently mentioned the paintings Shadek made, and wrote of their accuracy in depicting the chosen scene correctly. Marsh sent some of these pictures home, occasionally complaining that Shadek needed "good colors" and paints. In a letter dated April 3, 1862, Marsh asked his wife to obtain and send him a sketch book, in which he could get Shadek to sketch all the places the regiment has been.[155] Perhaps this book is Shadek's sketchbook that now resides in the Bridgeport Public Library in Bridgeport, CT.

In another letter, this dated May 11, 1862, Marsh asked his wife if she was aware that Shadek's family was "burned out" when a store in Hartford named Rockwell's burned. He mentioned that the Shadeks lost everything including a valuable library and all of Joseph Shadek's paintings, models, paints and tools.[156]

Rockwell's Store was located at the corner of Morgan Street and Front Street in Hartford. It burned on April 21, 1862, in the midst of a flood from the nearby Connecticut River.[157] Front Street was an area where many Italian immigrants resided. It may be that this was where Shadek's family lived.

On December 13, 1862, Joseph Shadek was discharged from service due to disability, presumably illness.[158] Coincidently, Wolcott Marsh resigned from the Eighth on December 22, also for medical reasons.[159]

One last bit of information sheds some additional light on Shadek's life. A U.S. Veteran's Administration Pension Payment Certificate reflects that Joseph E.

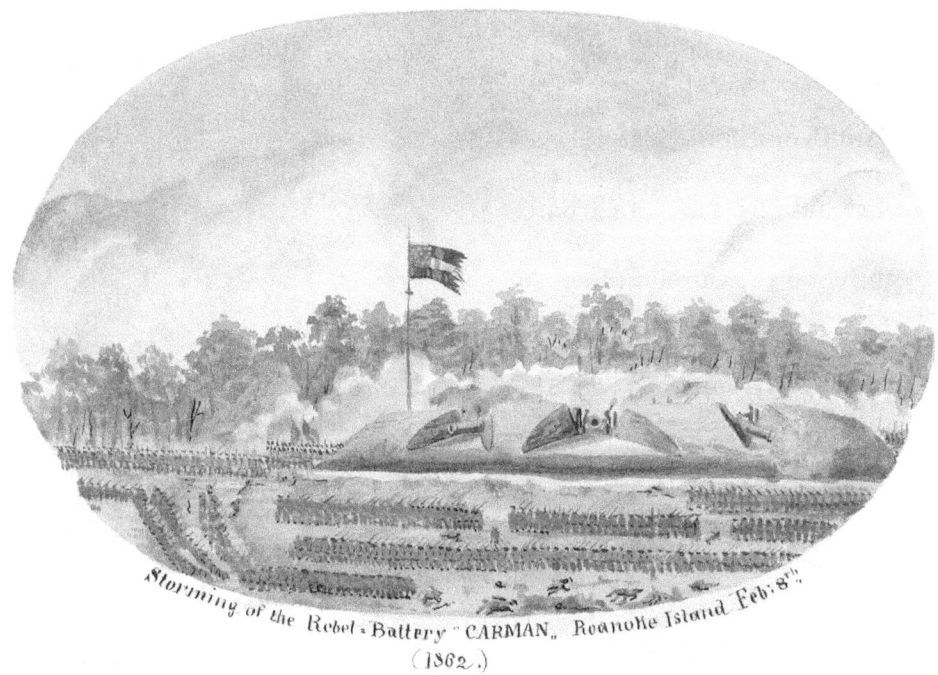

Storming the Rebel Battery "Carman" Roanoke Island, North Carolina, February 8, 1862 (Joseph E. Shadek Civil War Sketchbook. Courtesy Bridgeport History Center, Bridgeport Public Library).

Shadek, a veteran of Company A of the Eighth Conn. V. I., died on December 2, 1920, leaving a widow by the name of Mary T. Shadek.[160]

* * *

Martin B. Smith

Martin B. Smith was born on July 12, 1827, in New York.

The 1850 U.S. Census found him living in Plymouth, Connecticut, with his wife Polly C. Frost Smith, their sons, three-year-old Robert M. and one-year-old Edward W. Smith. They also lived with Polly's father, mother, and brother.[161] The 1860 U.S. Census found Martin living in Waterbury, with the addition of a third son, Frances, born in 1851.[162]

Martin B. Smith of Waterbury, enlisted in the 8th Connecticut Volunteers on September 6, 1861. He was mustered as Captain of Company E on September 25, 1861. He was promoted to Lieutenant Colonel on May 1, 1863. Martin Smith was wounded in the attack on Fort Harrison on September 29, 1864. He continued in service, frequently reporting sick, until he was discharged on January 13, 1865.[163]

After the war, Martin returned home, but then moved his family to Collins, Ohio, where he worked as U.S. Postmaster.[164] His wife Polly died there on January 15, 1879.[165]

Martin B. Smith. Tad Sattler, photographer (courtesy Andrew M. Morgan Collection, Connecticut State Library).

Martin B. Smith died, at the age of 72, on October 27, 1899. Martin died of Bright's Disease,[166] a chronic nephritis, characterized by swelling, high blood pressure, and heart disease.[167] He is buried in the East Townsend Cemetery, Townsend Township, Huron County, Ohio.[168]

* * *

John Edward Ward

John Edward Ward of Norwich was born in 1839 and enlisted in the 3rd Connecticut Volunteers on April 25, 1861. He was mustered Sergeant in Rifle Company D on May 11, 1861. He was promoted to First Lieutenant on May 20, 1861, but not mustered. He fought at the first battle of Bull Run. He was mustered out at the close of the ninety days service of the regiment, on August 12, 1861.[169]

John E. Ward enlisted in the 8th Connecticut Volunteers on August 27, 1861. He was mustered as Captain of Company D on September 21, 1861. He was promoted to Major on March 28, 1862, and promoted again to Lieutenant Colonel on December 23, 1862. John Ward was promoted to Colonel of the regiment on March 9, 1863. Ward was wounded at the battle of Port Walthall Junction on May 7, 1864. He was discharged on March 14, 1865.[170]

The 1870 U.S. Census found

John Edward Ward (courtesy Scott Hann Private Collection).

him living in Norwich, Connecticut, boarding with the Woodmansee family. His occupation was listed as a life insurance agent.[171] John applied for a U.S. Pension on December 1, 1883.[172]

John E. Ward died November 7, 1886, at the age of 49 years old, in Sault Sainte Marie, Michigan. He is buried in Cypress Cemetery, in Old Saybrook, Connecticut.[173]

* * *

Marvin Wait

Marvin Wait was born January 23, 1843, in Norwich, Connecticut. His father was John Turner Wait, a prominent lawyer of that city, and his mother was Elizabeth Rudd Wait.[174] The 1860 U.S. Census listed the family residing in Norwich, with John and Elizabeth having son Marvin, and two daughters, Ann E. and Mary E. Wait. They also listed two female domestics and a male laborer living with them.[175]

Marvin Wait of Norwich enlisted in the 8th Connecticut Volunteers on October 3, 1861. He was mustered as Private in Company D on October 5, 1861. He was promoted to Second Lieutenant of Company A on December 24, 1861. Marvin was promoted again to First Lieutenant on March 28, 1862, but not mustered. Marvin Wait was killed in action at the battle of Antietam on September 27, 1862.[176] The sorrow over a young and promising lad was lamented in the summary of the regiment's history by J.H. Vaill:

> Its death-roll included Lieutenant Marvin Wait of Norwich, son of Connecticut's honored citizen, John T. Wait. Enlisting as a private soldier when but eighteen, the story of his heroic fortitude amid the carnage of battle will be preserved

Marvin Wait (in D. Hamilton Hurd, *History of New London County, Connecticut*).

upon Connecticut's historic page along with that of Nathan Hale, the youthful martyr spy. Though severely wounded in his right arm Lieutenant Wait refused to go to the rear, and seizing his sword with his left hand, encouraged his men to press on, until he fell riddled by bullets.[177]

Marvin Wait is buried in Yantic Cemetery in Norwich, Connecticut. The inscription on his grave stone reads:

"In Memory of Lieutenant Marvin Wait"
Co. A 8th Regt Conn. Vol.
Born at Norwich Jan 21, 1843
Killed while gallantly leading his men in the bloody conflict at
Antietam, Maryland, Sept 17, 1862
He died with his young fame about him for a shroud.[178]

Appendix C: Flags of the Eighth

Connecticut has a long history of serving our country, and rising to the call of our nation, our state, and our flags. Connecticut Civil War battle flags were carried, followed, and defended over their years of service, and were witness to several hard-fought battles. The final return of the flags to the state symbolized success. The colors of the Eighth Regiment Connecticut Volunteer Infantry, with those of every state regiment, now reside at the Connecticut State Capitol in the Hall of Flags.

Eighth Connecticut Volunteer Infantry flags (in Steven W. Hill, *Connecticut Battle Flags: The Civil War*).

Appendix C

Flag Descriptions

In 1989, the Capitol Battle Flag Sub-commission was established with Monsignor Joseph Devine as Chairman. We owe much of the documentation and preservation to the dedicated subcommittee members, led by Geraldine Caughman. The following are modern day descriptions from their State Capitol Visual Survey conducted in 1990.[1]

The first National color (accession 1990-000-081) was made of red, white, and blue silk. It measured six feet on the hoist (height or vertical dimension), and (probably) six feet, six inches on the fly (width or horizontal dimension.) The canton measured 39 inches on the hoist, and 37 inches on the fly. The canton is painted with a national shield device with an eagle with spread wings upon the shield, holding arrows in its claws. There were (probably) 34 gold stars painted in a random pattern surrounding the eagle and shield design. On the middle stripe, the last short red one, painted in gold, capital block letters, "EIGHTH REGT. C.V."

The battle honors on the first national color are painted in black on white stripes, and black on red stripes, on the obverse as follows: "Antieta[m], Suffol[k], Roanoke Island, South Mountain, Sep.., Newbe[rn], Fredericksburg, Dec. [13], Fort Macon, and Hill's Point, April 19."[2]

Eighth Connecticut Volunteers first national flag (Office of Legislative Management, Connecticut General Assembly).

The staff was made of pine, stained dark walnut, and measured a height of 10 feet, including a nine-and-a-half-inch brass finial of an open spade design. The staff was cut in two and joined using a brass sleeve. The staff bears a state arsenal tag that reads "8th National." The flag is mounted to the staff with a closed sleeve mount. The finial is brass, nine and a half inches long, an open spade design, and in good condition.[3]

There are subtle differences between this flag and other similar flags in the Capitol collection. For example, this is the only painted eagle on a national flag that is grasping arrows in his claws. The maker of this flag is unknown.[4]

The first State color (accession 1990-000-080) was made of blue silk. It measured 70 inches on the hoist, and (probably) six feet, four inches on the fly. The silk is surrounded by a three-inch gold fringe on three sides, omitting the sleeve. The flag is painted with a central device. The design is of a Connecticut State seal next to and in front of a national shield. There is an eagle sitting on the seal, with both wings outspread, head to the right. There is a gold scroll under the seal and shield that reads in black paint, "Qui Transulit Sust." on the obverse, and "Eighth Regiment Conn. Vols." on the reverse.

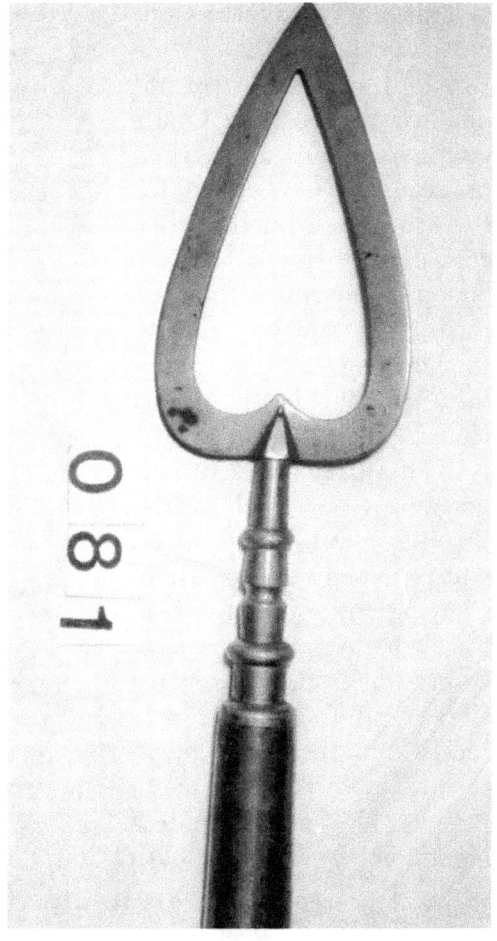

Eighth Connecticut Volunteers finial (Office of Legislative Management, Connecticut General Assembly).

The battle honors on the first state color are painted in gold on the obverse as follows: "Roanoke Island, Feb. 7th, 1862," "Fort Macon, Apl. 26th, 1862," "Antietam, Sep. 17, 1862," "Suffolk, Apl. 11th, 1863," "Newbern, March 14, 1862," "South Mountain. Sep. 14, 1862," "Fredericksburg, Dec. 14, 1862," "Hill's Point, Apl. 19, 1863."

The staff was made of cherry in one piece, with a dark stain. There is no ferrule on the bottom of the staff. There is a silver plate two and a half inches by four inches on the staff, reading "Presented to the 8th Regt. C.V. by the Sons of Connecticut residing in New York, October, 1861." The staff is 115 inches tall, including a brass finial of the open spade design. The flag is attached to the staff by a sleeve mount. The finial is also of brass, an open spade design, with the tip shot away.[5]

"The maker of the regimental color of the 8th CVI is also unknown. It does not appear to be the work of F.F. Rice, of Hartford, Connecticut." Rice was the painter of several other early war Connecticut flags.[6]

"During the summer of 1863, Connecticut Quartermaster William Aiken ordered two new colors for the 8th. Based on the worn condition of the battle honors on the fly end of their old flags, they did not receive the new flags until long after the April 19th Battle of Fort Huger."[7]

This first stand of colors were flown with honor, through many hard battles, and returned to the State of Connecticut in the middle of June 1863. A second stand of colors was issued to replace the originals. They were received by the regiment, in the field at Portsmouth, about June 20, 1863, according to a letter home by Captain Charles Coit.

Eighth Connecticut first state flag (Office of Legislative Management, Connecticut General Assembly).

> The second set of colors also received hard usage: therefore, Mrs. Katherine Richey, the conservator, was able to salvage only a small part of the flags. From the shape of the scroll, we know that the blue regimental color would have resembled the second regimental color issued to the 5th CVI with scenes from Bartlett's book, American Scenery, painted on the front side and pictures of the Charter Oak and Judge's Cave painted on the reverse side.[8]

The second National flag (accession 1990-000-082) now measures 66 inches on the hoist, 29 inches on the fly, with canton hoist of 35 inches and fly of 29 inches. There is much of the original flag now missing. There is a two-inch twisted fringe of gold top and bottom, but not on the shortened fly. There are 10 gold painted two-inch stars randomly place on canton.

The staff is one piece of pine, 113½ inches long, and stained dark. It appears to be handmade, and may not be the original staff for this flag. The flag is sleeve mounted to the staff. There is no ferrule. The finial is brass nine and a half inches long, with an unusual threaded base. It is of the open spade design.

Due to the 1939 conservation, it is impossible to determine the original design of this flag. It could not be determined if the original canton was of a Connecticut or Quartermaster design. The stripes measure five inches wide, but Quartermaster flags normally measured five and a half inches.[9]

The second State flag (accession 1990-000-083) currently measures 41 inches on the hoist and 34½ inches on the fly. It is of painted blue silk, with a four-inch gold

 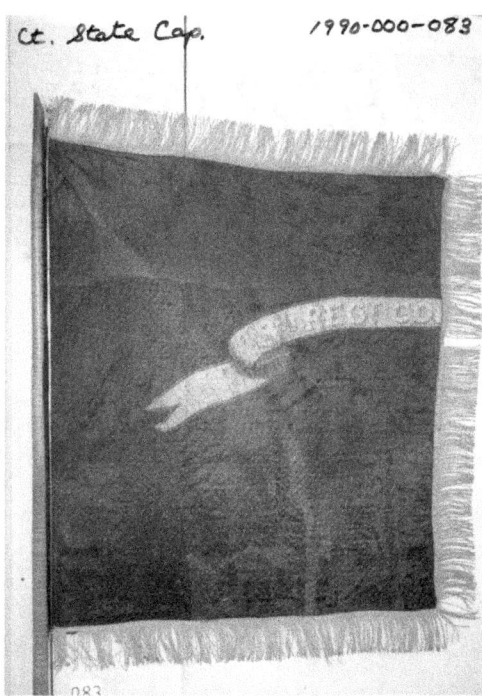

Left: Eighth Connecticut Volunteers second national flag (Office of Legislative Management, Connecticut General Assembly). *Right:* Eighth Connecticut Volunteers second state flag (Office of Legislative Management, Connecticut General Assembly).

fringe. There is only a portion of the scroll on the original flag left. It bears the identification "8th Regt. Co." However, based on comparison to other flags in the collection, this flag would have been similar to that of the 28th C.V.I.

The staff is of tiger maple, measuring 102 inches. It is broken off at the top. There is about 19 inches missing from the bottom. The staff is two pieces, with a brass sleeve and stop collar. There is no ferrule. The flag mount is of the eye and rod type. There is no finial extant. There is an arsenal tag reading "8th C.V. Infantry State."[10]

The second State flag was provided by Connecticut, and presumed to be similar to those issued to many other regiments during that time. The following is from the 5th Conn. description in Caughman's book, *"Qui Transtulit Sustinet"*:

> …has four painted scenes as part of its central device. On the obverse of this flag, are two pictures that were copied from "American Scenery" illustrated by William Bartlett. One is titled, "Bridge at Norwich," and the other is titled, "View from Mount Holyoke." The 5th, 6th, 8th, 14th, 21st, 23rd, 24th, 25th, 26th, and 28th are the Connecticut regiments that carried flags with scenes painted on them. These flags were painted by the Tiffany & Co. of New York, at a cost of $125 each. … Only three flags, the 5th, 23rd, and 28th, have pictures of the Charter Oak and Judge's Cave on one side [reverse]. (It is possible that the flags of the 6th, 8th, and 14th were also painted with the Charter Oak and Judge's Cave, but there is not enough of the flags extant to be sure.)[11]

Twenty-Sixth Connecticut Volunteers state flag (Office of Legislative Management, Connecticut General Assembly).

Interpretations

The state survey and Caughman's book refer to the accession 1990-000-081 national and 1990-000-080 state flags as the first issued stand of colors, and the accession 1990-000-082 national and 1990-000-083 state flags as the second issued set. There are some points that support that conclusion. These would include the observation that the banner scroll on 084 matches almost exactly the same scrolls found on the 26th and 28th Connecticut regiment state flags, thus placing that style flag around September 1862, not 1861. The battle honors painted in black on the 081 flag do look as if they may have been incrementally placed on the flag in the field. A letter from Captain Charles Coit describes the situation near Fredericksburg on November 11, 1862.

> Yesterday there was a grand review of the command of Gen. Sumner by that general composed of the 2nd and 9th Corps. As the old general rode past our colors he suddenly wheeled his horse around and riding up close to them stopped and sat gazing at them some moments then road on. Whether he was reading the names of the different battles in which we have been on them inscribed or counting the bullet holes I do not know. But it was a proud moment for the noble old 8th, and every heart swelled with pride and satisfaction.
>
> As the General and Staff approached the regit. (8th) our Division General Getty was heard to say to General Sumner thus, "This General is the 8th Conn." and as the General was looking at the colors one of his staff a Lieut. Col. read the names of battles on our flag out loud. "Roanoke Is., Newbern, Pt. Macon, South Mountain, Antietam" (The two last are not on flag but he repeated them over as though they were.) "Well no wonder they are a small regit."[12]

Interestingly, these primary sources refer only to "the flag" implying that only one was used. That may support the possibility that the 081 national was indeed the first, and accumulated battle honors while the 080 state flag saw little use. The artistic quality of the battle honors uniformly painted in gold on the 083 state flag suggest the honors were not done incrementally in the field over time. One explanation could be that when 081/080 were returned to the state in 1863, the battle honors were then replicated from 081 to 080 for the traveling patriotic displays that were common at that point in the war.

Yet, there are points that support the alternate conclusion, with 082/083 being the first issued set, and 081/080 constituting the second issue in 1863. The overall condition of the 081/080 flags is considerably better than the other flag set. The 082/083 set is nearly destroyed, and could suggest that they are older, saw more severe service, and had to be retired. Caughman's book notes a letter from Private Allen Dauchy, on May 28, 1863, that he describes their flag before it was returned to Connecticut: "it is cut up and torn with shot and shel so it is not much beter than a lot of Red, White, and blue Ribons."[13] This might suggest that the 083 state flag was indeed a new issue in 1863 because the battle honors appear up to date for that time and professionally done in gold lettering.

But whichever set was old and which were new, the soldiers loved all their colors the same. Charles Coit summarizes it all from Portsmouth, Virginia, on June 21, 1863: "By the way we have within a day or two recd a splendid new set of colors from the State + sent our old ones back to Hartford. If you go to H. be sure to see

The Hall of Flags in the Connecticut State Capitol (the George F. Landegger Collection of Connecticut Photographs in the Carol M. Highsmith's America, Library of Congress, Prints and Photographs Division).

them—you can't know how much we love them—may our new ones be kept as free from all suspicions of dishonor as those."[14]

So, while there are so many colorful details known about each of the flags, it seems difficult or impossible to definitively determine precisely which stand of colors truly came first. But it is an interesting pursuit to try to find more puzzle pieces that might complete the picture, and solve the mystery. We encourage all readers to decide for themselves.

And so there they rest. The battle flags of the Eighth, along with every military organization from Connecticut, past to present, are enshrined at the Connecticut State Capitol, in the Hall of Flags. We owe a debt of gratitude to everyone who carried, guarded, or served under those waving banners. They all have earned their place in the history of our state and our nation.

* * *

Appendix D:
Arms and Equipment of the Eighth

The Eighth was formed in September of 1861, which was a time of transition for Connecticut regiments when it came to the uniform, arms, and equipment they were issued. Unlike the earlier militia regiments, which wore state uniforms, the volunteer infantry regiments formed in 1861 received a combination of the state and federal uniforms. Like most Civil War regiments, the early days of the Civil War reflected a variation in Connecticut uniforms and equipment.

Uniforms

As to the basic uniform itself, the state and federal uniforms were similar. They consisted of dress uniforms of single-breasted dark blue frock coats with dark blue trousers, and for fatigue purposes, dark blue sack coats. In December 1861, Federal regulations were revised to authorize light blue trousers,[1] and the Eighth began receiving these in early 1862. Officers' uniforms, which they were required to purchase themselves, followed general guidelines but also reflected the variations of tailor-made uniforms and personal preferences.

In a letter dated November 12, 1861, Private John Merriam described their uniform: "Our color is blue a dark blue (darker than the regular army) coat pants and all. We have a tall Kossuth hat."[2]

In a letter from North Carolina dated April 23, 1862, Sergeant Seth Plumb wrote that they drew new clothes that week, consisting of a coat, trousers, and blouse (i.e., sack coat). He went on to say that he and some other men from Litchfield were sending their old clothes home. He wrote: "[T]he pants I drew just after the battle, the coat and blouse drew at Hartford. Our clothes are lighter than those we had in the winter, the color of our coats and blouse is blue black and our pants are sky blue, those pants I send home are much lighter color than those I have now. We wore our under clothes and woolen shirts yet and probably will all summer if we are in camp. We drew no shirts except under shirts, so those shirts I got from home have been just the thing."[3]

For headgear, Federal regulations required both officers and enlisted men to wear for dress the Model 1858 Dress Hat, which were black felt hats more commonly known as Hardee hats.[4] For fatigue purposes, forage caps were called for. There is evidence that the soldiers of the Eighth were issued or obtained Hardee hats. Private John Merriam's letter referenced above mentions a "tall Kossuth hat." The term Kossuth hat refers to a slouch hat named for Lajos Kossuth, Governor-President of the Kingdom of Hungary during the revolution of 1848–1849, and is another term for the Model 1858 hat.[5] Charles Coit mentions waiting for his "regulation hat" in a letter dated October 3, 1861, and then in a letter dated November 8, 1862, writes, "Our regulation hats that we ordered while in Newbern have been chasing us around ever since + have come to hand this afternoon. If we had not engaged them I don't think many of us would pay $3 for one. They are very easy, warm, shed rain, durable + quite showy but I shall stick to my old Cap for marches, +c."[6]

In a photograph of Captain James Moore of Company D, he poses with a Hardee hat,[7] as does then Corporal Jay Nettleton in an early photograph (see Appendix B). Finally, a painting by Joseph Shadek titled "Eve Amusements Decbr 24th 1861. Camp Annapolis" showing men of Company A of the Eighth celebrating Christmas Eve, depicted these men wearing slouch hats which appear to be Hardee hats.[8]

There were two state variations in the uniform of the Eighth that stood out prominently. One was the overcoat or "greatcoat" as they are also known. Along with some of the other early Connecticut volunteer infantry regiments, the Eighth was issued gray satinet overcoats,[9] and their use is often mentioned in the letters and writings of members of the Eighth. At the battle of Newbern, for instance, it is reported that in one encounter Confederate troops declined to fire on the Eighth, it is believed in part because they were wearing these gray overcoats at the time.[10]

Another notable state variation in the uniform of the Eighth is the wearing of state buttons instead of the federal eagle buttons. The use of state buttons on infantry uniforms was very common during the Civil War, and Connecticut was no exception. The fact that the major button manufacturers in the United States were located in Waterbury, Connecticut, helped as well. Coat and cuff buttons were made for both

Left: Enlisted men's coat button (photograph by the authors). *Right:* Officer's coat button (photograph by the authors).

officers and enlisted men. Officer buttons were three-piece staff buttons with the State coat of arms depicted, while enlisted men's buttons were two-piece buttons with the Great Seal of the State. These buttons were used extensively by Connecticut troops during the Civil War.[11]

Ordnance

In the category of longarms used by the regiment, there was also a mix of the makes, models, and types of weapons issued and used. In a Summary Statement of Ordnance and Ordnance Stores on Hand for the quarter ending December 31, 1862, on file in the records of the Office of the Chief of Ordnance, the 8th Connecticut was listed as having reported the following armament:

> 171 U.S. Rifles, sword bayonet, model 1840, 1845, Calibre .58
> 92 Sharp's Breech-loading Rifles, triangular bayonet, Calibre .52
> 17 Springfield Rifled Muskets, model 1855, 1861, N.A. and contract, Calibre .58
> 4 Enfield Rifled Muskets, Calibre .58 and .577[12]

What exactly were these weapons? Let's examine some of these categories.

Springfield Rifled Muskets, model 1855, 1861, N.A. and contract, Calibre .58

Eli Whitney, Jr., son of the famous inventor, took over his father's Whitney Armory in New Haven, Connecticut, in 1842 and continued producing arms there. Between 1842 and 1865 Whitney produced fourteen different models of military longarms. But of these, only four were U.S. models fully conforming to the requirements of the War Department. The others were termed by Whitney as "good and serviceable" weapons and were non-regulation arms.[13] A proverbial Connecticut Yankee, Whitney often incorporated into his products surplus or condemned parts purchased at government auctions, and sold the guns to less discriminating state militias.[14]

In September of 1861, Whitney sold to the State of Connecticut an estimated 350 longarms identified as "minie muskets with Maynard primers." These were Whitney Model 1855 rifle muskets produced by the Whitney Armory and patterned after the U.S. M1855. The Maynard primers used in these rifles were from a lot of condemned locks purchased by Whitney from the Springfield Armory earlier that year. The locks were dated 1858 but otherwise unmarked. When the muskets were completed, the locks were marked "E.WHITNEY" over "N.HAVEN." These muskets were immediately issued by the State of Connecticut to its troops. There are two cited examples of these weapons which exist today and both have regimental markings on them. One is marked "8 CV/A18" and the other is marked "11 CV." It may be that the 17 Springfields listed on the Summary Statement were comprised of or at least contained some of these longarms.[15]

U.S. Rifles, sword bayonet, model 1840, 1845, Calibre .58

At the regimental level, in a Quarterly Return of Ordnance and Ordnance Stores for the fourth Quarter of 1862, First Lieutenant Andrew M. Morgan of Company F reported that his company was issued five Springfields and 10 "Whitney rifled muskets calibre .58."[16] No other rifles were mentioned. In the Summary Statement referenced above, which listed the returns by company, Company F was reported as having five "Springfield Rifled Muskets, model 1855, 1861, N.A. and contract, Calibre .58" and 10 "U.S. Rifles, sword bayonet, model 1840, 1845, Calibre .58." It is logical to conclude that both forms were referring to the same ten longarms.

It is possible that the term "U.S. Rifles, sword bayonet, model 1840, 1845, Calibre .58" was intended to describe the US Model 1841 rifle, also known as the "Mississippi" rifle.

The M1841 was the standard issue musket of the United States from its adoption until it was replaced by the Model 1855 Springfield. Its nickname originated during the Mexican War when Colonel Jefferson Davis of the Mississippi Rifles insisted on the M1841 for his regiment. The Mississippi was a two-banded rifled musket, the first standard U.S. rifle to use the percussion lock system. It was originally .54 caliber, but was altered in 1855 to .58 caliber, in order to use the .58 caliber Minié ball. Many of the older Mississippi rifles were also changed to .58 caliber after 1855. In addition, the M1841 was modified to accept the sword bayonet and to add a new long range rear sight.[17]

From 1842 to 1855, Whitney received orders from the U.S. War Department for 27,600 M1841 rifles, which were delivered. The last 1,100 of these (produced in 1855) had the modifications for the Minié ball and for the extended range.[18]

Were the 171 rifles listed in the Summary Statement M1841 Mississippis? Company F's return simply referred to them as "Whitney rifled muskets calibre .58." One argument against the proposition that they were M1841 rifles is that Company F's return reported 15 "Bayonet scabbards," with no number given for "Bayonet scabbards for sword bayonets." The M1841 was modified to utilize the sword bayonet.

The designation "U.S. Rifles, sword bayonet, model 1840, 1845, Calibre .58" in the Summary Statement is not helpful in describing the particular weapons the Eighth had. In addition, the authors are aware of only a very few longarms that bear markings identifying them as belonging to the 8th Connecticut, and these examples are the Whitney Model 1855 rifle muskets.

The Summary Statement referred to above also reports the armament of the 11th Connecticut for the fourth quarter of 1862. That regiment reported 201 of the "Springfield Rifled Muskets, model 1855, 1861, N.A. and contract, Calibre .58," 72 Sharps Breech-loading Rifles, but none of the U.S. Rifles, model 1840, 1845, reported under the Eighth. These differences may shed some light on the weapons issue. In that regard, consider the following statement made by Captain Charles Coit of Company B of the Eighth, in a letter dated July 18, 1862, "I wish the 8th had as good arms as the 11th [Connecticut]. They have the Springfield + we the Whitney rifle.—the latter aint worth two cents + the worst of it is that the men all know + feel it."[19] Some months earlier, while adjutant of the Eighth, Coit had written that there was talk of condemning their arms. He added, "I don't know but they (the muskets) may be good enough but they certainly are not well finished. [T]he ramrods are continually breaking + many of the locks were out of order when we received them, so the Capts say."[20]

Perhaps the 171 rifles listed under the U.S. Rifles category in the Summary Statement for the Eighth are in fact part of the lot of 350 Whitney Model 1855 rifled muskets that the State of Connecticut purchased in September of 1861. The terminology used to describe the category could have been chosen for a variety of reasons, including mistake. And the 17 weapons listed for the Eighth under the Springfield Rifled Muskets category, could actually be just that—genuine Springfields that made their way into the ranks of the Eighth. Jay Nettleton of Company I wrote in a letter dated October 22, 1861, "We got our arms last Tuesday. They are a Rifle similar to Enfield or Minnie [Springfield?] & use the Enfield cartridges."[21] The only rifles reported for Nettleton's Company I in the Summary Statement were the U.S. Rifles model 1840, 1845.[22]

The Whitney M1855 employed several features appearing on Whitney's Enfield series including a 40" long barrel identical to that on Whitney's long Enfield rifle musket, bored to .58 caliber. The front sight was constructed such that it doubled as the lug of the socket bayonet, presumably of the Enfield pattern.[23]

Another possibility is that the "Springfields" were part of Whitney's June 27, 1861, contract with the State of Connecticut to produce 6,000 Model 1861 Springfield pattern rifle muskets, but these also suffered from quality control issues.[24] Perhaps in time more information or more identified specimens will come to light to help resolve these issues.

Sharp's Breech-loading Rifles, triangular bayonet, Calibre .52

Another notable arm carried by the Eighth was the .52 caliber Sharp's Breech-loading rifle. The Summary Statement referenced above reflects that the Eighth had 92 Sharps on hand at the end of 1862. The Company breakdown of that number is Co. G—40, Co. K—45, Co. B—4, Co. C—2, and Co. D—1.[25] The reason for the high numbers for Companies G and K is because these were the flank companies, and for that reason, were given the weapons with greater firepower through increased speed in reloading. These flank companies also served as the primary skirmishers for the regiment, so the increased firepower was important in that function as well.

The source of the Sharps rifles that the Eighth used is well established. The Sharps Rifle Manufacturing Company had first arranged to sell a number of long (36" barrel) NM1859 Sharps rifles with saber attachment to the Egyptian Government, and then offered them to the Ordnance Department, but ultimately, they were sold to the State of Connecticut on April 20, 1861. Sharps delivered 740 rifles to Connecticut on May 7. Five hundred and seventy-six of these rifles were issued to the 2nd Connecticut Volunteer Infantry, a three month regiment which fought at First Bull Run. After the Second's term expired and its men were mustered out, the rifles were issued to the 8th Connecticut and the 11th Connecticut.[26]

Cook's Tent of Company A, 8th Regiment Connecticut Volunteers, Roanoke Island (Joseph E. Shadek Civil War Sketchbook. Courtesy Bridgeport History Center, Bridgeport Public Library).

Equipment

The Eighth appears to have been supplied with standard infantry equipment. However, early in the War, Charles Coit does comment in several of his letters home about deficiencies in what the Eighth was issued. At one point in late 1861, he describes the Eighth as the being "well drilled, best disciplined + worst equipped Regt in the Division."[27]

For tents, early in the War the Eighth used Sibley tents, wall tents and "common tents," that is, wedge tents.[28] One type of common or wedge tent is called a double bell wedge tent, which has a bell at either end with the entrance on the long side. The Eighth used this style of wedge tent as is shown in Joseph Shadek's painting of Christmas Eve 1861 cited above, and also in his painting entitled "Coock's tent of Co A 8th Rgt. C.V. Roanoke Isl."[29]

On May 8, 1862, the Eighth received new Sibley tents while in North Carolina. The Sibleys were round with a twelve foot diameter and a center pole also of twelve feet. They could accommodate up to twenty men.[30] Charles Coit wrote that "only one tent is allowed to the three officers of a Co. but we are permitted to keep one of our old wall tents, so the Capts. take the new Sibley's + give their Lieuts the old wall tents."[31] In addition, the Sibleys were floored.[32]

Arms and Equipment of the Eighth

In September 1862 the Eighth was issued shelter tents[33] which became the standard for the enlisted men of the regiment for the remainder of the War. Officers, of course, had better quarters, living in larger tents or assigned housing, when available, although they too used shelter tents when necessary.

Overall, the Eighth appears to have been well supplied. An Account Book for Company F, which lists the items each soldier was issued and its cost, show soldiers receiving pants, drawers, shirts, socks, shoes, a cap, a blouse (sack coat), a dress coat, an overcoat, as well as a blanket, canteen and haversack.[34]

* * *

Appendix E: The Modern Eighth Connecticut Volunteers

Header from Seth Plumb October 26, 1863, letter (courtesy private family collection).

The Eighth Regiment Connecticut Volunteer Infantry, Company A, Incorporated

A Civil War Living History Organization

Living history spans many activities, but commonly denotes the pursuit of like-minded people physically portraying our predecessors and reenacting their making of history. It is an immersive process, involving contributing factors of the minds, the methods, and the materials of their world.

Minds address the who, the individuals, backgrounds, families, occupations, experiences, beliefs, and motivations. Methods encompass the how to operate the Union army, including the Army Regulations rules and procedures, the Infantry Tactics formations and drills, the Military Customs roles and responsibilities, and the Articles of War governing laws. Materials cover the what, the physical things used, the clothes and uniforms, weapons and ammunition, camp equipment, shelters, rations, medical services, and pay.

These facets are combined in coordinated activities, capturing the essence of life experienced in those times. Living history is generally presented as interactive interpretations for the public, although there are equally enlightening closed to the public experiences. The common goals of living history organizations are to emulate, educate, and commemorate the legacy of those heroes and patriots that we portray.

Our organization's mission is embodied in the following statement. "The Eighth Regiment Connecticut Volunteers, Company A, Inc. is a non-profit volunteer organization formed to portray an infantry company of the 8th Regiment Connecticut Volunteer Infantry during the Civil War, and in so doing educate and promote our Civil War heritage."[1]

The organization has members with many years of experience in Civil War reenacting. Many of the charter members are still active today. The unit is affiliated with the United States Volunteers[2] at the national level, and the New England Brigade[3] at the regional level. The unit is organized under a set of by-laws, guiding the operation of the unit, and is governed by an annually elected Executive Board. We are insured, incorporated, and are a federal 501(c)(3) not-for-profit organization.

The purpose of our unit is to educate both members and public alike, and in so doing promote our Civil war heritage. We are an organization with a deep interest in the Civil War. We strive to accurately portray the regiment, its times, and the soldiers who comprised the Eighth. We conduct on-going research and continuously work to improve our portrayals and impressions.

We are involved in a wide spectrum of activities and events, including living histories and first-person impressions, school programs, scripted battle scenarios, tactical maneuvers, drills, parades, memorial and commemorative events, research and discussion groups, historic preservation activities, and National Park Service invitational events.

The unit is active year-round, but especially during the "campaign" season from April to October. We travel to many historic locations. We have fought on and near original battlefields, at original garrison forts, and many National Park Battlefield Monuments. We also participate in a good share of community events in and around Connecticut.

Our organization has a standing History Committee for the research and development of the history of the regiment. Many members and friends have dedicated years of effort to amass, transcribe, and review the primary source materials that made the writing of this book possible.

Footer from Seth Plumb October 26, 1863, letter (courtesy of private family collection).

* * *

Appendix F: Map Notes

Preparation

Historical accounts need visual augmentation to be best understood. These maps have been prepared with regard to documented descriptions, military reports, contemporary cartography, and related modern works. The battle maps depict the military dispositions and deployments prior to the specific action or operation the Eighth Connecticut Volunteers were engaged in. In the case of subsequent positions, arrows denote these movements accordingly. Please also refer to the symbols legend for the several annotations utilized.

These maps were created to render as faithful a picture of the story of the Eighth Connecticut Volunteers as accurately as possible. While no map can be perfect, we consulted many resources for these maps, and in the known cases, our assumptions are noted. In addition, all specific resources referenced in preparation of these maps are cited in this section. There are so many sources are available today. Reviewing these specific references can prove to be thoroughly entertaining, and also educational.

* * *

Map References and Notes

Map 1. Burnside Expedition, North Carolina, January–June 1862.
   Virginia GIS data

Map 2. Battle of Roanoke Island, North Carolina, February 8, 1862.
   North Carolina GIS data
   Foster, John G. *Sketch of Roanoke Island, N.C. February 8.* Washington, D.C.: Government Printing Office, 1862. Map. https://www.loc.gov/item/99447477/.

Map 3. The Battle of New Bern, North Carolina, March 14, 1862.
   North Carolina GIS data
   Sneden, Robert Knox. *Plan of the Battle of Newberne, North Carolina: fought March 14th. [1862]* Map. https://www.loc.gov/item/gvhs01.vhs00079/.
   Sauers, Richard A. *A Succession of Honorable Victories: The Burnside Expedition in North Carolina.* Dayton, OH: Morningside House, 1996, 263.

Trotter, William R. *Ironclads and Columbiads: The Civil War in North Carolina, The Coast.* Winston-Salem, NC: John F. Blair Publisher, 1989, 112–113.

Map 4. The Siege of Fort Macon, North Carolina, April 1862.
Colton, G. Woolworth. *The war in North Carolina. Map of the entrance to Beaufort harbor, N.C. showing the position of Fort Macon, etc.* [S.l., 1861] Map. https://www.loc.gov/item/99447458/.

Map 5. Route of March to Sharpsburg, Maryland, September 1862.
Virginia and Maryland GIS data
United States Topographical Bureau, Jubal Anderson Early, Alfred Landon Rives, William Ludwell Sheppard, and United States Army. Corps of Topographical Engineers. *Part of map of portions of the milit'y dept's of Washington, Pennsylvania, Annapolis, and north eastern Virginia.* 1864. Map. https://www.loc.gov/item/2002627442/.

Map 6. Positions of the Eighth, Battle of Antietam, Maryland, September 17, 1862.
Maryland GIS data
United States War Department. *Atlas of the battlefield of Antietam, prepared under the direction of the Antietam Battlefield Board, lieut. col. Geo. W. Davis, U.S.A., president, gen. E.A. Carman, U.S.V., gen. H Heth, C.S.A. Surveyed by lieut. col. E.B. Cope, engineer, H.W. Mattern, assistant engineer, of the Gettysburg National Park. Drawn by Charles H. Ouran. Position of troops by gen. E.A. Carman. Published by authority of the Secretary of War, under the direction of the Chief of Engineers, U.S. Army, 1908.* Washington, D.C.: Government Printing Office, 1908. Map. https://www.loc.gov/item/2008621532/.

Map 7. Final Attack of the Eighth, Antietam, Maryland, September 17, 1862.
Maryland GIS data
United States War Department. *Atlas of the battlefield of Antietam, prepared under the direction of the Antietam Battlefield Board, lieut. col. Geo. W. Davis, U.S.A., president, gen. E.A. Carman, U.S.V., gen. H Heth, C.S.A. Surveyed by lieut. col. E.B. Cope, engineer, H.W. Mattern, assistant engineer, of the Gettysburg National Park. Drawn by Charles H. Ourand. Position of troops by gen. E.A. Carman. Published by authority of the Secretary of War, under the direction of the Chief of Engineers, U.S. Army, 1908.* Washington, D.C.: Government Printing Office, 1908. Map. https://www.loc.gov/item/2008621532/

Map 8. Route of March to Fredericksburg, Virginia, November 1862.
Maryland and Virginia GIS data
Guernsey, Alfred H., and Henry Mills Alden. *Harper's Pictorial History of the Civil War, Vol.2.* Chicago: Puritan Press Co., 1894, 246

Map 9. Vicinity of Fredericksburg & Falmouth, Virginia, December 1862.
Virginia GIS data
U.S. Geological Survey. *Topographic map of Fredericksburg and vicinity, Virginia, showing battlefields.* [S.l, 1931] Map. https://www.loc.gov/item/99439199/.
U.S. National Archives. *Sketch showing position of pontoon bridges and guns covering them, at Fredericksburg, Va., December 11–15, 1862.* RG 77, Fortification File, Drawer 150, Sheet 29. Map. https://unwritten-record.blogs.archives.gov/2018/12/12/mapping-the-battle-of-fredericksburg/.
Map of Fredericksburg, Va., and vicinity. [1862] Map. https://www.loc.gov/item/2005625032/.

Map 10. Positions of the Eighth, Battle of Fredericksburg, Virginia, December 13, 1862.
Virginia GIS data
O'Reilly, Francis A. *The Fredericksburg Campaign, Winter on the Rappahannock* (Baton Rouge: Louisiana State University Press, 2003), 416.
U.S. Geological Survey. *Topographic map of Fredericksburg and vicinity, Virginia, showing battlefields.* [S.l, 1931] Map. https://www.loc.gov/item/99439199/
Map of Fredericksburg, Va., and vicinity. [1862] Map. https://www.loc.gov/item/2005625032/.

Appendix F

Map 11. Vicinity of Hampton Roads, Virginia, Spring 1863.
Virginia GIS data
Worret, Ch., Thomas Jefferson Cram, Ethan Allen Hitchcock, and United States Army. Department of Virginia. *Copy of a map military reconnaissance Dep't Va.: Hampton Roads and Norfolk regions, Va.* [1862] Map. https://www.loc.gov/item/2003630497/.

Map 12. Vicinity of Fort Huger & Suffolk, Virginia, April 1863.
North Carolina GIS data
Soederquist, Oscar. *Military map of Suffolk & vicinity for Majr. Genl. J.A. Dix.* [?, 1863] Map. https://www.loc.gov/item/99439125/.
United States. War Department. Map of Nansemond River and Vicinity, map, 1899; Washington, D.C. (https://texashistory.unt.edu/ark:/67531/metapth284644/; accessed May 24, 2021), University of North Texas Libraries, The Portal to Texas History, https://texashistory.unt.edu; crediting UNT Libraries Government Documents Department.

Map 13. Route of March on "The Blackberry Raid," July 1863.
North Carolina and Virginia GIS data
Sommers, S.L., and Albert H Campbell. *Map of Prince George Co., Va. 1864.* Map. https://www.loc.gov/item/2002627462/
Confederate States of America. Army. Dept. of Northern Virginia. Chief Engineer's Office and Edward Porter Alexander. *Map of the counties of Charles City, Goochland, Hanover, Henrico, King William, New Kent, and part of the counties of Caroline and Louisa, Virginia.* [S.l.: Chief Engineer's Office, D.N.V., 1864] Map. https://www.loc.gov/item/gvhs01.vhs00354/

Map 14. Vicinity of Richmond & Petersburg, Virginia, May 1864.
Virginia GIS data
Guernsey, Alfred H.; Alden, Henry Mills, *Harper's Pictorial History of the Civil War, Vol.1*, Chicago, IL: Puritan Press Co., 1894, p.388

Map 15. Second Battle of Port Walthall Junction, May 7, 1864, p.m.
Order of Burnham's Brigade, except 8CV, is assumed, not documented.
Virginia GIS data
Gilmer, Jeremy Francis, and Henry L Penfield. *Map of the country between Richmond and Petersburg.* New York: H.L. Penfield, Lith, 1864. Map. https://www.loc.gov/item/lva0000003/.
Forman, Robert J. et al. *Bermuda Hundred Campaign Tour Guide.* Chesterfield, VA: The Chesterfield Historical Society, 2010, 14.

Map 16. Second Battle of Port Walthall Junction, May 7, 1864, p.m.
Virginia GIS data
Gilmer, Jeremy Francis, and Henry L Penfield. Map of the country between Richmond and Petersburg. New York: H.L. Penfield, Lith, 1864. Map. https://www.loc.gov/item/lva0000003/.
Forman, Robert J. et al. *Bermuda Hundred Campaign Tour Guide.* Chesterfield, VA: The Chesterfield Historical Society, 2010, 15.
Robertson, William G. *Back Door to Richmond: The Bermuda Hundred Campaign April–June 1864.* Baton Rouge: Louisiana State University Press, 1987, 87.

Map 17. Battle of Swift Creek, Virginia, May 9, 1864.
Virginia GIS data
Gilmer, Jeremy Francis, and Henry L Penfield. Map of the country between Richmond and Petersburg. New York: H.L. Penfield, Lith, 1864. Map. https://www.loc.gov/item/lva0000003/.
United States Army. Corps, 10th. Engineer Office. Sketch no. 4 of roads between H.-Q. 10th Army Corps and Swift Creek on the south: with enemy's 2nd line of intrenchements sic around Drury's Bluff on the north. [1864] Map. https://www.loc.gov/item/99446516/.
Robertson, William G. *Back Door to Richmond: The Bermuda Hundred Campaign April–June 1864.* Baton Rouge: Louisiana State University Press, 1987, 114.

Map Notes

Map 18. Battle of Drewry's Bluff, Virginia, May 16, 1864.
Virginia GIS data
Gilmer, Jeremy Francis, and Henry L. Penfield. *Map of the country between Richmond and Petersburg.* New York: H.L. Penfield, Lith, 1864. Map. https://www.loc.gov/item/lva0000003/.
Robertson, William G. *Back Door to Richmond: The Bermuda Hundred Campaign April–June 1864.* Baton Rouge: Louisiana State University Press, 1987, 183.

Map 19. Battle of Cold Harbor, Virginia, June 1, 1864, 6:00 p.m.
Virginia GIS data.
Rhea, Gordon C., *Cold Harbor—Grant and Lee May 26–June 3, 1864*, Baton Rouge: Louisiana State University Press, 2002, 239

Map 20. Second Battle of Petersburg, Virginia, June 15, 1864, 7:00 p.m.
Order of Martindale's Division is assumed, not documented.
Hinks's Division, aka Hincks prior to and after war.
Virginia GIS data
Sommers, S.L., and Albert H. Campbell. *Map of Prince George Co., Va.* 1864. Map. https://www.loc.gov/item/2002627462/.
The struggle of Petersburg. The lines of rebel intrenchments carried by our troops. June 15–17. [S.l, 1864] Map. https://www.loc.gov/item/99448482/.

Map 21. Battle of Fort Harrison, Virginia, September 29, 1864, 6:00 a.m.
Virginia GIS data
Battle of Chaffin's Farm, Sept. 29th: topography of 1894: roads, houses, trees, etc., from Campbell and Chambliss maps: positions and routes assumed from descriptions in official records. [?, 1894] Map. https://www.loc.gov/item/lva0000125

GIS Data

Elevation

https://edcftp.cr.usgs.gov/Contours/final_by_state/
https://edcftp.cr.usgs.gov/Contours/preliminary_by_state/

U.S. Geological Survey, National Geospatial Program, Reston, VA: U.S. Geological Survey, September 9, 2019
USGS NED 1/3 arc-second Contours for Richmond E, Virginia 20190909 1 × 1 degree FileGDB 10.1
USGS NED 1/3 arc-second Contours for Richmond W, Virginia 20190909 1 × 1 degree FileGDB 10.1
USGS NED 1/3 arc-second Contours for Norfolk E, Virginia 20190909 1 × 1 degree FileGDB 10.1
USGS NED 1/3 arc-second Contours for Norfolk W, Virginia 20190909 1 × 1 degree FileGDB 10.1
USGS NED 1/3 arc-second Contours for Roanoke E, Virginia 20190909 1 × 1 degree FileGDB 10.1
USGS NED 1/3 arc-second Contours for Roanoke W, Virginia 20190909 1 × 1 degree FileGDB 10.1
USGS NED 1/3 arc-second Contours for Manteo W, North Carolina 20190829 1 × 1 degree FileGDB 10.1

USGS NED 1/3 arc-second Contours for Rocky Mount E, North Carolina 20190829 1 × 1 degree FileGDB 10.1

USGS NED 1/3 arc-second Contours for Rocky Mount W, North Carolina 20190829 1 × 1 degree FileGDB 10.1

USGS NED 1/3 arc-second Contours for Washington E, Maryland 20191212 1 × 1 degree FileGDB 10.1

USGS NED 1/3 arc-second Contours for Washington W, Maryland 20191212 1 × 1 degree FileGDB 10.1

Hydrology

U.S. Geological Survey, National Geospatial Program, *NHD 20200616 for Maryland State or Territory Shapefile Model Version 2.2.1*, Reston, VA, 2020

U.S. Geological Survey, National Geospatial Program, *NHD 20200616 for North Carolina State or Territory Shapefile Model Version 2.2.1*, Reston, VA, 2020

U.S. Geological Survey, National Geospatial Program, *NHD 20200615 for Virginia State or Territory Shapefile Model Version 2.2.1*, Reston, VA, 2020

Transportation

U.S. Geological Survey, National Geospatial Technical Operations Center, *USGS National Transportation Dataset (NTD) for Virginia 20210316 State or Territory Shapefile*, Reston, VA, 2021

U.S. Geological Survey, National Geospatial Technical Operations Center, *USGS National Transportation Dataset (NTD) for Maryland 20210329 State or Territory Shapefile*, Reston, VA, 2021

U.S. Geological Survey, National Geospatial Technical Operations Center, *USGS National Transportation Dataset (NTD) for North Carolina 20210329 State or Territory FileGDB 10.1*, Reston, VA, 2021

* * *

Chapter Notes

Introduction

1. Frederick P. Todd, *American Military Equipage, Volume 3* (Westbrook, CT: The Company of Military Historians, 1978), 605, 675–676.
2. Seth Plumb to Sister, beyond Sharpsburg, MD, September 23, 1862, Private Collection.

Chapter 1

1. Stephen R. Smith, et al., eds., *Record of Service of Connecticut Men in the Army and Navy of the United States During the War of the Rebellion* (Hartford, CT: Case, Lockwood, and Brainard Co., 1889), 1, 18, 34.
2. W.A. Croffut and John M. Morris, *The Military and Civil History Connecticut During the War Of 1861–65* (New York: Ledyard Bill, 1868), 101.
3. Croffut and Morris, *Connecticut During the War*, 100.
4. Smith, et al., *Connecticut Men*, 220.
5. Croffut and Morris, *Connecticut During the War*, 120.
6. Croffut and Morris, *Connecticut During the War*, 123.
7. Croffut and Morris, *Connecticut During the War*, 126.
8. "Recruiting for the Army," *Narragansett Weekly*, August 29, 1861.
9. Croffut and Morris, *Connecticut During the War*, 123.
10. Smith, et al., *Connecticut Men*, 34.
11. Croffut and Morris, *Connecticut During the War*, 121.
12. Smith, et al., *Connecticut Men*, 220.
13. F. Perry Close, *The History of Hartford Streets* (Hartford, CT: Connecticut Historical Society, 1969), 19.
14. Hilliard B. Ferris to Brother, Hartford, CT, September 20,1861, Connecticut State Library, Hartford, CT.
15. Ferris to Brother, Hartford, CT, September 25, 1861.
16. Ferris to Brother, Hartford, CT, October 3, 1861.
17. Charles M. Coit to Mother, Hartford, CT, October 3, 1861, The Gilder Lehrman Collection, The Gilder Lehrman Institute of American History, New York, NY.
18. Coit to Gen. Casey, Hartford, CT, October 11, 1861.
19. Seth F. Plumb to Friends, Hartford, CT, October 17, 1861, Helga J. Ingraham Memorial Library, Litchfield Historical Society, Litchfield, CT. Note that Mystic is not a town, but rather a village, a part of the towns of Groton and Stonington.
20. Coit to unknown, Hartford, CT, October 14, 1861.
21. Samuel Jay Nettleton to Friends at Home, Jamaica, Long Island, NY, October 22, 1861 in *Life Through Letters: Samuel Jay's Story*, David DeMeo and Reece Holman, eds. (Washington, CT: Gunn Memorial Museum, 2012), n.p.
22. Ferris to Brother, Jamaica, Long Island, NY, October 20, 1861. Americans called their weapons "minnis" or "minies" because they fired a minié ball, designed by Claude-Étienne Minié. The projectile was a conical shaped bullet, but people called it a ball because, until this time, ammunition had always been ball-shaped.
23. Croffut and Morris, *Connecticut During the War*, 124.
24. U.S. War Department, *The War of the Rebellion: A Compilation of the Official Records of the Union and Confederate Armies* (Washington, D.C.: U.S. Government Printing Office, 1880), Series III, Volume I, Serial 122, 578.
25. Oliver C. Case to Sister, Jamaica, Long Island, NY, October 20, 1861, Simsbury Historical Society, Simsbury, CT.
26. Nettleton to Friends, Jamaica, Long Island, NY, October 22, 1861, n.p.
27. Case to Sister, Jamaica, Long Island, NY, October 28, 1861.
28. Case to Sister, Jamaica, Long Island, NY, October 31, 1861.
29. Henry C. Hall to Brother Alex, Jamaica, Long Island, NY, October 31, 1861, Henry C. Hall papers, 1861–1864, David M. Rubenstein Rare Book and Manuscript Library, Duke University, Durham, NC.
30. Smith, et al., *Connecticut Men*, 327.
31. Nettleton to Friends at Home, Jamaica, Long Island, NY, October 22 ,1861, n.p. We believe

that the term "Reg." as used here is meant to refer to regimental drill.

32. Coit to unknown, Jamaica, Long Island, NY, October 27, 1861. We could not find a definition for the phrase "up to the handle" but we believe that in this context it means "completely" or "fully" and was an allusion to a sword or knife penetrating its target all the way to its hilt.

33. Croffut and Morris, *Connecticut During the War*, 124.

34. Coit to unknown, Jamaica, Long Island, NY, October 24, 1861.

35. Hall to Brother Alex, Annapolis, MD, November 6, 1861.

36. Nettleton to Friends, Annapolis, MD, November 6, 1861, n.p.

37. Coit to Mother, Jamaica, Long Island, NY, November 1, 1861.

38. Hall to Brother Alex, Jamaica, Long Island, NY, October 31, 1861.

39. Case to Sister, Perryville, MD, November 3, 1861. Perryville is located on the northeast bank of the Susquehanna River where it meets Chesapeake Bay. Havre de Grace is on the opposite bank of the river.

40. Smith, et al., *Connecticut Men*, 4, 330.

41. Wolcott P. Marsh to Wife, Perryville, MD, November 5, 1861 in *Letters to a Civil War Bride*, Sandra Marsh Mercer and Jerry Mercer, eds. (Westminster, MD: Heritage Books, 2006), 105, 109–111.

42. Richard A. Sauers, "A Succession of Honorable Victories" *The Burnside Expedition in North Carolina* (Dayton: Morningside House, 1996), 49–50.

43. Nettleton to Friends at Home, Annapolis, MD, November 6, 1861, n.p.

44. Marsh to Wife, Annapolis, MD, November 5, 1861, 112.

45. Coit to Mother, Sister and Brother, Annapolis, MD, November 6, 1861.

46. Plumb to Friends, Annapolis, MD, November 13, 1861, Litchfield Historical Society.

47. Coit to Mother, Annapolis, MD, November 13, 1861. The identity of White is unknown.

48. Hall to Brother Alex, Annapolis, MD, November 24, 1861.

49. Plumb to Brother Charley, Annapolis, MD, November 23, 1861, Litchfield Historical Society.

50. Marsh to Wife, Annapolis, MD, November 17, 1861, 133.

51. Case to Sister, Annapolis, MD, November 11, 1861.

52. Case to Sister, Annapolis, MD, November 28, 1861.

53. Marsh to Wife, Annapolis, MD, November 29, 1861, 153.

54. Coit to unknown, Annapolis, MD, November 24, 1861. John E. Ward, of Norwich, had earlier served in the same rifle company as Col. Harland, and later rose to the rank of colonel of the 8th Connecticut.

55. Nettleton to Friends at Home, Annapolis, MD, December 9, 1861, n.p.

56. Coit to Mother, Annapolis, MD, November 13, 1861.

57. Coit to Mother, Annapolis, MD, November 13, 1861.

58. Coit to unknown, Annapolis, MD, January 1, 1862.

59. Croffut and Morris, *Connecticut During the War*, 127.

60. Plumb to Friends, Annapolis, MD, November 13, 1861, Litchfield Historical Society.

61. Nettleton to Friends at Home, Annapolis, MD, December 18, 1861, n.p.

62. Case to Sister, Annapolis, MD, December 21, 1861.

63. Nettleton to Friends at Home, Annapolis, MD, December 9, 1861, n.p.

64. Plumb, letter to Friends, November 13, 1861, Litchfield Historical Society.

65. Marsh to Wife, Annapolis, MD, December 9, 1861, 166.

66. Case to Sister, Annapolis, MD, December 16, 1861.

67. John L. Merriam to Friend, Annapolis, MD, December 7, 1861, Lincoln Memorial Shrine, A.K. Smiley Library, Redlands, CA.

68. Nettleton to Friends, Annapolis, MD, December 18, 1861, n.p.

69. Plumb to Friends, Annapolis, MD, December 19, 1861, Litchfield Historical Society.

70. Case to Sister, Annapolis, MD, December 21, 1861.

71. Plumb to Friends, Annapolis, MD, January 5, 1862, Litchfield Historical Society.

72. Plumb to Friends, Annapolis, MD, December 19, 1861, Litchfield Historical Society.

73. Case to Sister, Annapolis, MD, December 21, 1861.

74. Croffut and Morris, *Connecticut During the War*, 130.

75. Nettleton to Friends at Home, Annapolis, MD, December 18, 1861, n.p.

76. Case to Sister, Annapolis, MD, December 21, 1861.

77. Plumb to Friends, Annapolis, MD, December 29, 1861, Litchfield Historical Society.

78. Case to Sister, Annapolis, MD, December 30, 1861.

79. Case to Sister, Annapolis, MD, January 3, 1861.

80. Case to Sister, Annapolis, MD, December 30, 1861, and Annapolis, MD, January 7, 1861.

81. Coit to Mother Sister and Brother, Annapolis, MD, December 29, 1861.

82. Coit to unknown, Annapolis, MD, December 26, 1861.

Chapter 2

1. George B. McClellan, *McClellan's Own Story* (New York: Charles L. Webster & Company, 1887), 203–204.

2. John G. Barrett, *The Civil War in North*

Carolina (Chapel Hill: University of North Carolina Press, 1963), 66–67.

3. William R. Trotter, *Ironclads and Columbiads: The Civil War in North Carolina, The Coast* (Winston-Salem, NC: John F. Blair, Publisher, 1989), 68.

4. Ambrose E. Burnside, *The Burnside Expedition* (Providence, RI: N. Bangs Williams & Company, 1882), 9.

5. Trotter, *Ironclads and Columbiads*, 69–70.

6. Richard A. Sauers, *"A Succession of Honorable Victories": The Burnside Expedition in North Carolina* (Dayton, OH: Morningside House, 1996), 66.

7. Burnside, *The Burnside Expedition*, 9.

8. McClellan, *McClellan's Own Story*, 206.

9. Samuel Jay Nettleton to Friend Lewis, January 5, 1862, in *Life Through Letters: Samuel Jay's Story*, David DeMeo and Reece Holman, eds. (Washington, CT: Gunn Memorial Museum, 2012), n.p.

10. Charles M. Coit to unknown, onboard *Brookman*, January 6, 1862, The Gilder Lehrman Collection, The Gilder Lehrman Institute of American History, New York, NY.

11. W.A. Croffut and John M. Morris, *The Military and Civil History Connecticut During the War of 1861–65* (New York: Ledyard Bill, 1868), 162.

12. Henry C. Hall, ed., *America's Successful Men of Affairs* (New York: The New York Tribune Association, 1895), 112–113. Sauer identifies the ship as the "H.D. Brookman" as does Coit, who also uses "H.J." in one of his letters. Croffut and Morris gives the bark's name as "J.P." It is likely that the bark was acquired from the shipping firm of H.D. & John U. Brookman of New York City which owned a large number of vessels and was in business during this time. It was made up of the brothers Henry D. Brookman and John Ulmore Brookman. This could explain the H.D. prefix or possibly the H.J. We will hereafter refer to the bark as the *Brookman*, unless specifically quoting a source.

13. Wolcott P. Marsh to Wife, onboard *Chasseur*, January 23, 1862, in *Letters to a Civil War Bride*, Sandra Marsh Mercer and Jerry Mercer, eds. (Westminster, MD: Heritage Books, 2006), 188.

14. Coit to unknown, onboard *Brookman*, January 6, 1862.

15. Croffut and Morris, *Connecticut During the War*, 163.

16. Coit to unknown, Annapolis, MD, January 8, 1862, and Coit to All, January 11, 1862.

17. Burnside, *The Burnside Expedition*, 12.

18. Coit to All, Annapolis, MD, January 11, 1862.

19. Coit to All, Annapolis, MD, January 11, 1862.

20. Burnside, *The Burnside Expedition*, 13–15.

21. Seth F. Plumb to Friends, Hatteras Inlet, NC, January 17, 1862, Litchfield Historical Society, Litchfield, CT.

22. Marsh to Wife, Hatteras Inlet, NC, January 13, 1861, 175–177.

23. Marsh to Wife, Hatteras Inlet, NC, January 13,1861, 175.

24. Trotter, *Ironclads and Columbiads*, 71.

25. Marsh to Wife, Hatteras Inlet, NC, January 13, 1861, 176, 179.

26. Burnside, *The Burnside Expedition*, 18.

27. Plumb to Friends, Hatteras Inlet, NC, January 17, 1862, Litchfield Historical Society.

28. Coit to unknown, onboard *Brookman*, January 18 and January 23, 1862.

29. Marsh to Wife, onboard *Chasseur*, January 17, 1861,181–183.

30. Marsh to Wife, onboard *Chasseur*, January 23, 1861, 188–189.

31. Coit to unknown, onboard *Brookman*, January 23, 1862.

32. Coit to unknown, onboard *Brookman*, January 23, 1862, and Hatteras Inlet, NC, January 28, 1862.

33. Sauers, *Honorable Victories*, 121.

34. Burnside, *The Burnside Expedition*, 21.

35. Sauers, *Honorable Victories*, 137.

36. Marsh to Wife, Hatteras Inlet, NC, January 29, 1861, 200–202.

37. Coit to Mother Sister and Brother, onboard *Sentinel*, January 31, 1862.

38. Coit to unknown, onboard *Sentinel*, February 1, 1862.

39. Coit to unknown, onboard *Sentinel*, February 1, 1862.

40. Coit to Mother Sister and Brother, onboard *Sentinel*, February 3, 1862.

41. Burnside, *The Burnside Expedition*, 22.

42. Marsh to Wife, onboard *Chasseur*, February 5, 1862, 217. Sauers states that on January 17, Burnside, realizing that he had more troops than he needed for Roanoke, ordered the 6th New Hampshire and the 11th Connecticut to disembark and join the garrison at Hatteras Inlet as a reserve. To compensate General Parke for the loss of the 11th Connecticut, he ordered the 9th New York to join Parke's command. See Sauer, *Honorable Victories*, 130.

43. Coit to unknown, onboard *Sentinel*, February 5, 1862.

44. Trotter, *Ironclads and Columbiads*, 75–77.

45. Barrett, *The Civil War in North Carolina*, 74–75.

46. Sauers, *Honorable Victories*, 165–167. The official reports indicate a variety of times that the Federal ships opened fire (see Sauer, *Honorable Victories*, 168).

47. Nettleton to Friends at Home, Roanoke Island, VA, February 9, 1862, n.p.

48. Barrett, *The Civil War in North Carolina*, 77.

49. Burnside, *The Burnside Expedition*, 23.

50. Marsh to Wife, onboard *Chasseur*, February 7, 1862, 218.

51. Nettleton to Friends at Home, Roanoke Island, VA, February 9, 1862, n.p.

52. Nettleton to Brother Charles, Roanoke Island, VA, February 25, 1862, n.p.

53. Nettleton to Brother Charles, Roanoke Island, VA, February 25, 1862, n.p.

54. Burnside, *The Burnside Expedition*, 19.

55. Nettleton to Brother Charles, Roanoke Island, VA, February 25, 1862, n.p.
56. Marsh to Wife, onboard *Chasseur*, February 7, 1862, 219.
57. Sauers, *Honorable Victories*, 47–48. Note that Sauers lists the *Chasseur* as having two 12-pounder Wiards and the *Zouave* as having one 30-pounder Parrott and two 12-pounder Wiards (page 480). However, both Nettleton's and Marsh's accounts appear to indicate that the *Chasseur* was armed with two 30-pounder Parrotts and one 6-pounder Wiard.
58. Sauers, *Honorable Victories*, 143–145.
59. U.S. War Department, *The War of the Rebellion: A Compilation of the Official Records of the Union and Confederate Armies* (Washington, D.C.: U.S. Government Printing Office, 1880), Series I, Volume IX, Serial 9, 105. No. 21 Report of Brig. Gen. John G. Parke, February 8, 1862.
60. U.S. War Department, *Official Records*, Series I, Volume IX, Serial 9, 74. No.1, Report of Brig. Gen. Ambrose E. Burnside, U.S. Army.
61. Marsh to Wife, onboard *Chasseur*, February 7, 1862, 219, and Wolcott Marsh to Wife, on Roanoke Island, February 10, 1862, 220.
62. Nettleton to Brother Charles, Roanoke Island, VA, February 25, 1862, n.p.
63. Marsh to Wife, Roanoke Island, NC, February 16, 1862, in *Letters*, 225. "Spiking a gun" was a method of temporarily disabling a cannon by hammering a barbed steel spike into the touch hole; it could be removed, but it was difficult. Soldiers could also drive a bayonet into the touch-hole and break it off, leaving the blade's tip embedded.
64. Nettleton to brother Charles, Roanoke Island, VA, February 25, 1862, n.p.
65. Coit to Mother Sister and Brother, onboard *Sentinel*, February 10, 1862.
66. U.S. War Department, *Official Records*, Series I, Volume IX, Serial 9, 108. No. 22, Report of Col. Isaac P. Rodman, 4th Rhode Island Infantry, February 10, 1862. Rush Hawkins, the colonel of the 9th New York, always maintained that it was the charge of his regiment that broke the Confederate line, but this has been disputed by many, including General Foster. See Barrett, *The Civil War in North Carolina*, 81–82. In fact, by the time the New York regiment reached the fort, the Confederates were already pulling back, having been flanked by Reno's division (led by the 21st Massachusetts) on the Rebel right flank and by Foster's division (led by the 23rd Massachusetts) on their left flank. See Trotter, *Ironclads and Columbiads*, 84–86.
67. U.S. War Department, *Official Records*, Series I, Volume IX, Serial 9, 74. No. 1, Report of Brig. Gen. Ambrose E. Burnside, February 8, 1862.
68. Nettleton to Brother Charles, Roanoke Island, VA, February 25, 1862, n.p.
69. Marsh to Wife, Roanoke Island, NC, February 10, 1862, 222.
70. Coit to Mother Sister and Brother, onboard *Sentinel*, February 10, 1862.
71. Barrett, *The Civil War in North Carolina*, 83–87.
72. Barrett, *The Civil War in North Carolina*, 90–91.
73. Mark Mayo Boatner III, *The Civil War Dictionary* (New York: David McKay Company, Inc., 1959) 619–620.
74. Sauers, *Honorable Victories*, 200–203.
75. Sauers, *Honorable Victories*, 226–227.
76. Marsh to Wife, Roanoke Island, NC, February 16, 1862, 226.
77. Coit to Old home & the dearest ones there, Roanoke Island, VA, February 20, 1862.
78. Nettleton to Brother Charles, Roanoke Island, VA, February 25, 1862, n.p.
79. Marsh to Wife, Roanoke Island, NC, February 19, 1862, 233–234.
80. Coit to All, Roanoke Island, VA, March 4, 1862, and Oliver C. Case to Sister, Roanoke Island, VA, March 4 and March 11, 1862, Simsbury Historical Society, Simsbury, CT.
81. The common spelling of the city name during the war was "Newbern." The authors determined to use the current common spelling of "New Bern" in the text to enable name recognition and further studies. It will be noticed in notes on letters written, the soldiers used "Newbern" in their addresses.
82. Sauers, *Honorable Victories*, 233–235.
83. Marsh to Wife, onboard *Chasseur*, March 11, 1862, 255.
84. Marsh to Wife, onboard *Chasseur*, March 11, 1862, 255–257.
85. Marsh to Wife, onboard *Chasseur*, March 12, 1862, 257–258.
86. Oliver C. Case to Sister, Newbern, NC, March 15,1862, Simsbury Historical Society, Simsbury, CT.
87. U.S. War Department, *Official Records*, Series I, Volume IX, Serial 9, 74. No. 1, Report of Brig. Gen. Ambrose E. Burnside, March 14, 1862.
88. U.S. War Department, *Official Records*, Series I, Volume IX, Serial 9, 97. No. 15, Report of Brig. Gen. John G. Parke, March 14, 1862.
89. U.S. War Department, *Official Records*, Series I, Volume IX, Serial 9, 74. No. 1, Report of Brig. Gen. Ambrose E. Burnside, March 14, 1862.
90. Coit to All, Newbern, NC, March 15, 1862.
91. Case to Sister, Newbern, NC, March 15, 1862.
92. Marsh to Wife, Newbern, NC, March 18, 1862, 261.
93. Case to Sister, Newbern, NC, March 15, 1862.
94. U.S. War Department, *Official Records*, Series I, Volume IX, Serial 9, 97. No. 15, Report of Brig. Gen. John G. Parke, March 14, 1862.
95. U.S. War Department, *Official Records*, Series I, Volume IX, Serial 9, 74. No. 1, Report of Brig. Gen. Ambrose E. Burnside, March 14, 1862.
96. U.S. War Department, *Official Records*, Series I, Volume IX, Serial, 97. No. 15, Report of Brig. Gen. John G. Parke, March 14, 1862.

97. U.S. War Department, *Official Records*, Series I, Volume IX, Serial 9, 236. No. 16, Report of Col. Edward Harland, March 14, 1862.

98. Case to Sister, Newbern, NC, March 15, 1862. Private Philo A. Matson of Company A is listed in the *Record of Service of Connecticut Men* book as having been wounded and deserted on March 14, 1862. In a letter of April 6, 1862, Lieutenant Wolcott Marsh wrote, "Philo Matson was a long lean lank round shouldered fellow. We did not know he had gone home till two or three days ago. There was no more need of his going home on account of his wound than of me. As it was but slight." See *Letters to a Civil War Bride*, 285.

99. Coit to All, Newbern, NC, March 15, 1862, and Coit to Mother, Sister and Brother, Newbern, NC, March 17, 1862.

100. U.S. War Department, *Official Records*, Series I, Volume IX, Serial 9, 97. No. 15, Report of Brig. Gen. John G. Parke, March 14, 1862.

101. U.S. War Department, *Official Records*, Series I, Volume IX, Serial 9, 223. No. 11, Report of Lieut. Col. William S. Clark, March 14, 1862.

102. Croffut and Morris, *Connecticut During the War*, 173.

103. Case to Sister, Newbern, NC, March 15, 1862. The "gray coats" that Case refers to are the gray greatcoats that were the original Connecticut state issue. Marsh wrote that "we charged into the battery the rebels thought our regr. were friends on account of our overcoats & did not discover their mistake for several minutes" (Marsh to Unknown, March 18, 1862, 264).

104. Joseph R. Hawley, *History of Battle Flag Day: September 17, 1879* (Hartford, CT: Lockwood & Merritt, 1880), 118

105. Coit to All, Newbern, NC, March 15, 1862.

106. Case to Sister, Newbern, NC, March 15, 1862.

107. Coit to Mother, Sister, and Brother, Carolina City, NC, April 4, 1862.

108. U.S. War Department, *Official Records*, Series I, Volume IX, Serial 9, 97. No. 15, Report of Brig. Gen. John G. Parke, March 14, 1862.

109. U.S. War Department, *Official Records*, Series I, Volume IX, Serial 9, 103. No. 19, Report of Major John Wright, March 14, 1862.

110. U.S. War Department, *Official Records*, Series I, Volume IX, Serial 9, 236. No. 16, Report of Col. Edward Harland, March 14, 1862.

111. Marsh to Wife, Newbern, NC, March 18, 1862, 262–263.

112. Case to Sister, Newbern, NC, March 15, 1862.

113. Marsh to Wife, Newbern, NC, March 18, 1862, 261.

114. Sauers, *Honorable Victories*, 300.

115. Marsh to Wife, Newbern, NC, March 18, 1862, 262, 290.

116. Case to Sister, Newbern, NC, March 15, 1862.

117. Sauers, *Honorable Victories*, 303.

118. Marsh to Wife, Newbern, NC, March 18, 1862, 263.

Chapter 3

1. Paul Branch, Jr., *The Siege of Fort Macon* (Morehead City, N.C.: Herald Printing Co, 1982), 1–5, 18–21.

2. Branch, *Siege of Fort Macon*, 22–23.

3. Samuel Jay Nettleton to Sister Abbie, Carolina City, NC, March 28, 1862, in *Life Through Letters: Samuel Jay's Story*, David DeMeo and Reece Holman, eds. (Washington, CT: Gunn Memorial Museum, 2012), n.p.

4. Charles M. Coit to unknown, onboard *Sentinel*, March 20, 1862, The Gilder Lehrman Collection, The Gilder Lehrman Institute of American History, New York, NY, and Charles Coit to All, Carolina City, NC, March 27, 1862.

5. Coit to All, Carolina City, NC, March 27, 1862.

6. Coit to All, Carolina City, NC, March 27, 1862.

7. Nettleton to Sister Abbie, Carolina City, NC, March 28, 1862, n.p.

8. Nettleton to Sister Abbie, Carolina City, NC, March 28, 1862, n.p. The night of March 21 was spent at Newport. Before the Federal advance, Colonel White had sent a raiding party to destroy the railroad bridge over the Newport River, which it did, but it failed to destroy the Beaufort Road bridge. From Carolina City, Parke sent a surrender demand to Colonel White, who declined. See Richard A. Sauers, *"A Succession of Honorable Victories": The Burnside Expedition in North Carolina* (Dayton, OH: Morningside House, 1996), 310–314.

9. Wolcott P. Marsh to Wife, Carolina City, NC, March 31, 1862 in *Letters to a Civil War Bride: Captain Wolcott P. Marsh*, Sandra Marsh Mercer and Jerry Mercer, eds. (Westminster, MD: Heritage Books, 2006), 271.

10. Nettleton to Sister Abbie, Carolina City, NC, March 28, 1862, in *Life Through Letters*, n.p.

11. Coit to All, Carolina City, NC, March 27, 1862.

12. Branch, *Siege of Fort Macon*, 26.

13. Marsh to Wife, Carolina City, NC, March 31, 1862, 272–273, 276. It was not uncommon at this time for Union officers to hire the services of former slaves as cooks and servants.

14. Branch, *Siege of Fort Macon*, 27.

15. Marsh to Wife, Carolina City, NC, April 1, 1862, 276–277.

16. Sauers, *Honorable Victories*, 315.

17. Branch, *Siege of Fort Macon*, 32.

18. Sauers, *Honorable Victories*, 317.

19. Marsh to Wife, Bogue Banks, NC, April 3, 1862, 278–280.

20. Coit, letter to Mother, Sister, and Brother, Carolina City, NC, April 4, 1862. Coit's letter refers to Company B being at Beaufort; this is believed to be an error and it is in fact Company E. Coit had just been promoted to captain of Company B. Marsh also confirms that it was Company E stationed at Beaufort (*Letters to a Civil War Bride*, 277, 299), as does Sergeant Seth Plumb of Company

E (Plumb, Letter to Friends, On the Banks of the Neuse, May 6, 1862, Litchfield Historical Society, Litchfield, CT).

21. Coit to unknown, Morehead City, NC, April 16, 1862.

22. Sauers, *Honorable Victories*, 316.

23. Marsh to Wife, Bogue Island, NC, April 6, 1862, 284. Coit reported that Johnson had been sick ten days with fever. John Merriam, Coit's orderly sergeant in Co. F, was a relation and went home with the body. Coit to Mother, Sister, and Brother, Carolina City, NC, April 4, 1862.

24. Coit to All, Morehead City, NC, April 21, 1862.

25. W.A. Croffut and John M. Morris, eds., *The Military and Civil History Connecticut During the War of 1861-65* (New York: Ledyard Bill, 1868), 177–178.

26. Mark Mayo Boatner III, *The Civil War Dictionary* (New York: David McKay Company, Inc., 1959), 720.

27. Coit to All, Morehead City, NC, April 21, 1862.

28. Sauers, *Honorable Victories*, 318.

29. Branch, *Siege of Fort Macon*, 41–43.

30. Croffut and Morris, *Connecticut During the War*, 179.

31. Marsh to Wife, Bogue Island, NC, April 14, 1862, 291–293. The reference to Company L is in error—there was no Company L. It would have to have been either Company B, C or F. Companies D and K were in Morehead City and Company E was in Beaufort.

32. Marsh to Wife, Bogue Island, NC, April 14, 1862, 292–293.

33. Croffut and Morris, *Connecticut During the War*, 179.

34. Steven R. Smith, et al., *Record of Service of Connecticut Men in the Army and Navy of the United States During the War of the Rebellion* (Hartford, CT: Case, Lockwood, and Brainard Co., 1889), 342.

35. Croffut and Morris, *Connecticut During the War*, 179.

36. Coit to All, Morehead City, NC, April 21, 1862. The three batteries were as follows: Lieutenant Flagler's four, 10-inch mortars were about 1,680 yards from the fort. Captain Morris's battery of three, 30-pound Parrott Rifles were about 200 yards in front of Flagler and slightly to the right; Lieutenant Prouty's battery of four, 8-inch mortars was 200 yards in front of Morris and to the right near the beach on the ocean side, about 1,280 yards from the fort. Branch, *Siege of Fort Macon*, 45.

37. Croffut and Morris, *Connecticut During the War*, 180. Alexander was in Company G and was later discharged for disability in August of 1862. *Record of Service of Connecticut Men*, 348.

38. Marsh to Wife, Bogue Island, NC, April 23, 1862, 305–306.

39. Coit to All, Morehead City, NC, April 21, 1862.

40. Croffut and Morris, *Connecticut During the War*, 180.

41. Oliver C. Case to Sister, Bogue Island, NC, April 28, 1862. Simsbury Historical Society, Simsbury, CT.

42. Branch, Siege of Fort Macon, 54–58.

43. Marsh to Wife, Bogue Island, NC, April 27, 1862, 308–309.

44. Marsh to Wife, Bogue Island, NC, April 27, 1862, 309.

45. Marsh to Wife, Bogue Island, NC, April 27, 1862, 310–311.

46. Marsh to Wife, Bogue Island, NC, April 28, 1862, 311–312. Marsh and Company A were with Captain Morris' battery of three 30-pounder Parrott Rifles about 1,480 yards from the fort. The first shot was fired by Captain Morris himself about 5:40 a.m. The eight shells that Marsh said followed were from Flagler's battery of four 10-inch mortars to the left rear and Prouty's battery of four 8-inch mortars to the right front. See Branch, *Siege of Fort Macon*, 45, 60. The four gunboats Marsh mentions were the *Daylight*, the *State of Georgia*, the *Chippewa*, and the *Gemsbok* under the command of Commander Samuel Lockwood. Sauers, *Honorable Victories*, 333.

47. Branch, *Siege of Fort Macon*, 84–85.

48. Branch, *Siege of Fort Macon*, 85–88.

49. Croffut and Morris, *Connecticut During the War*, 180–181.

50. Marsh to Wife, Bogue Island, NC, April 28, 1862, 312.

51. Coit to unknown, near Newbern, NC, May 8, 1862.

52. Marsh to Wife, near Newbern, NC, May 4, 1862, 319–320.

53. Seth F. Plumb to Friends, Banks of the Neuse, May 6, 1862, Litchfield Historical Society. Oliver Case of Company A noted that they had taken "the young wheelbarrow," "a small, stern wheel steamer taken from secesh," from Carolina City to Morehead City (letter to Sister, 8 May 1862).

54. Plumb to Friends, Banks of the Neuse, June 7, 1862, Litchfield Historical Society.

55. Croffut and Morris, *Connecticut During the War*, 255.

56. Case to Sister, Newbern, NC, May 8, 1862.

57. Coit to unknown, near Newbern, NC, May 8, 1862. He later wrote that the men are just as well off—all tents are floored (Coit to unknown, near New Berne, NC, May 20, 1862).

58. Plumb to Friends, Banks of the Neuse, May 13, 1862, Litchfield Historical Society.

59. Case to Sister, Newbern, NC, May 8, 1862.

60. Coit to All, South of Newbern, NC, May 5, 1862.

61. Marsh to Wife, near Newbern, NC, May 29, 1862, 331–333.

62. Coit to unknown, near Newburn, NC, June 2, 1862.

63. Case to Sister, Newbern, NC, June 3, 1862.

64. Croffut and Morris, *Connecticut During the*

War, 255. They state that the Eighth was particularly hit by "bilious fever."

65. Plumb to Friends, Banks of the Neuse, May 26, 1862, Litchfield Historical Society.

66. Coit to unknown, Camp of 8th, June 1, 1862.

67. Coit to All, Newbern, NC, June 28, 1862.

68. William Marvel, *Burnside* (Chapel Hill: University of North Carolina Press, 1991), 98.

69. Marsh to Wife, Morehead City, NC, July 2, 1862, 397.

70. Coit to unknown, Morehead City, NC, July 5, 1862.

71. Coit to unknown, onboard *Guide*, July 7, 1862. Wolcott Marsh wrote that the *Guide* was a black, side-wheel steamer formerly called the *Admiral*. He had spent the nights in Morehead City at the Macon House, a three-story hotel built in 1860. See *Letters to a Civil War Bride*, 401.

72. Ronald H. Bailey and the Editors of Time-Life Books, *Forward to Richmond* (Alexandria, VA: Time-Life Books, 1983), 89–91.

73. Marsh to Wife, onboard *Guide*, July 7, 1862, 404–405.

74. Coit to unknown, on ship at Ft. Monroe, VA, July 9 1862.

75. Coit to All, Newport News, VA, July 14, 1862.

76. Plumb to Friends, Norfolk, VA, July 9, 1862, Litchfield Historical Society.

77. Marsh to Wife, onboard *Donelson*, July 12, 1862, 405.

78. Coit to Brother, Newport News, VA, July 18, 1862.

79. Coit to All, Newport News, VA, July 30, 1862.

80. Smith et. al., *Connecticut Men*, 339, and Croffut and Morris, *Connecticut During the War*, 256.

81. Marvel, *Burnside*, 98–100.

82. Case to Sister, near Fredericksburg, VA, August 7, 1862.

83. Case to Sister, near Fredericksburg, VA, August 7, 1862.

84. Case to Sister, near Fredericksburg, VA, August 7, 1862; Coit to All, opposite Fredericksburg, VA, August 9, 1862; and Jay Nettleton to Friends and Sister, Fredericksburg, VA, August, 8, 1862, n.p.

85. Nettleton to Friends and Sister, Fredericksburg, VA, August, 8, 1862, n.p.

86. Marsh to Wife, Fredericksburg, VA, August 10, 1862, 433.

87. Coit to All, opposite Fredericksburg, VA, August 9, 1862.

88. Nettleton to Friends at Home, Fredericksburg, VA, August, 18, 1862, n.p.

89. Plumb to Friends, August 10, 1862, Litchfield Historical Society.

90. Marvel, *Burnside*, 103–104.

91. Coit to All, Fredericksburg, VA, August 13, 1862.

92. Coit to All, Fredericksburg, VA, August 26, 1862.

93. Nettleton to Brother, Fredericksburg, VA, August, 29, 1862, n.p.

94. Marsh to Wife, Falmouth, August 30, 1862, 446–447.

95. Coit to All, Fredericksburg, VA, August 28, 1862.

96. Plumb to Sister, Aquia Creek, VA, September 2, 1862, Litchfield Historical Society.

97. Coit to All, Aquia Creek, VA, September 3, 1862.

98. Marsh to Wife, Washington, D.C., September 6, 1862, 449. Croffut and Morris report that they camped south of the White House, near the Washington Monument. See Croffut and Morris, *Connecticut During the War*, 259. In 1862 the Potomac River was near to and just west of the Washington Monument.

99. Coit to unknown, Washington, DC, September 6, 1862.

100. Croffut and Morris, *Connecticut During the War*, 259.

101. Marsh to Wife, Washington, D.C., September 6, 1862, 449. The grounds that Marsh refers to where the three Connecticut regiments camped in 1861 is located two miles north of the Capitol, on the lands of a wealthy banker named Corcoran, who called his place Glenwood (Croffut and Morris, *Connecticut During the War*, 83). Coit reported their camp as "off from 7th Street somewhat" (Coit to unknown, Washington, D.C., September 6, 1862).

102. Marvel, *Burnside*, 110–112.

103. Ezra A. Carman, *The Maryland Campaign of September 1862, Vol 2:-Antietam*, Thomas Clemens, ed. (El Dorado Hills: Savas Beatie LLC, 2012), 537.

Chapter 4

1. Ronald H. Bailey and the Editors of Time-Life Books, *The Bloodiest Day* (Alexandria, VA: Time-Life Books, 1984), 8.

2. George B. McClellan, *McClellan's Own Story* (New York: Charles L. Webster & Company, 1887), 549.

3. William Marvel, *Burnside* (Chapel Hill: University of North Carolina Press, 1991), 112–113. Note that Leesborough is now known as Wheaton, Maryland.

4. Wolcott P. Marsh to Wife, near Shepherdstown, WV, September 21, 1862, in *Letters to a Civil War Bride: Captain Wolcott P. Marsh*, Sandra Marsh Mercer and Jerry Mercer, eds. (Westminster, MD: Heritage Books, 2006), 457.

5. Roger M. Ford, diary, September, 8, 1862, New England Civil War Museum, Rockville, CT.

6. Charles M. Coit to unknown, Washington, D.C., September 6, 1862, The Gilder Lehrman Collection, The Gilder Lehrman Institute of American History, New York, NY.

7. Samuel Jay Nettleton to Brother & Home Friends, near Sharpsburg, MD, September, 24,

1862, in *Life Through Letters: Samuel Jay's Story*, David DeMeo and Reece Holman, eds. (Washington, CT: Gunn Memorial Museum, 2012), n.p.

8. Marsh to Wife, near Shepherdstown, WV, September 21, 1862, 457–458. Note that Ariel Case was married to the sister of Wolcott Marsh's wife, Anna.

9. Ford diary, September, 9, 1862, and Jay Nettleton to Brother & Friends, near Sharpsburg, MD, September 24, 1862, n.p.

10. Marsh to Wife, near Shepherdstown, WV, September 21, 1862, 458. And see Jay Nettleton to Brother & Home Friends, near Sharpsburg, MD, September, 24, 1862, regarding departure time.

11. Marsh to Wife, near Shepherdstown, WV, September 21, 1862, 458, and Nettleton to Brother & Friends, near Sharpsburg, MD, September 24, 1862, n.p. Note that the National Road was one of the first Federal projects and ran from Cumberland, Maryland west to Ohio, opening the way west. An eastern extension ran to Baltimore and was known as the National Pike or Baltimore National Pike ("National Road," Wikipedia, accessed May 1, 2021, https://en.wikipedia.org/wiki/National_Road).

12. Ford diary, September, 12,1862.

13. Nettleton to Brother & Friends, near Sharpsburg, MD, September 24, 1862, n.p., and Marsh to Wife, near Shepherdstown, WV, September 21, 1862, 459.

14. Marvel, *Burnside*, 114–115.

15. Nettleton to Brother & Friends, near Sharpsburg, MD, September 24, 1862, n.p. We believe the reference to "Reno's Division" meant his former Second Division. He was given command of the Ninth Corps on September 3.

16. Marsh to Wife, near Shepherdstown, WV, September 21, 1862, 459.

17. Marsh to Wife, near Shepherdstown, WV, September 21, 1862, 460.

18. Ford diary, September 13, 1862.

19. Marvel, *Burnside*, 115.

20. Janet B. Hewett, *Supplement to the Official Records of the Union and Confederate Armies* (Wilmington, NC: Broadfoot Pub. Co., c. 1994–2001), 796. Record of Events—v.3. Connecticut troops (Union, 1st–8th Regiments)—v. 4. (serial no. 16) Connecticut troops (Union, 9th–28th Regiments), Vol. 3.

21. Nettleton to Brother & Friends, near Sharpsburg, MD, September 24, 1862, n.p., and Ford diary, September 13, 1862.

22. Marsh to Wife, near Shepherdstown, WV, September 21, 1862, 460.

23. Marsh to Wife, near Shepherdstown, WV, September 21, 1862, 460–461.

24. Marvel, *Burnside*, 117–122.

25. Marsh to Wife, near Sharpsburg, MD, September 23, 1862, 461.

26. Marsh to Wife, near Shepherdstown, WV, September 21, 1862, 461–462.

27. Nettleton to Brother & Friends, near Sharpsburg, MD, September 24, 1862, n.p.

28. Marsh to Wife, near Sharpsburg, MD, September 23, 1862, 462.

29. Nettleton to Brother & Friends, near Sharpsburg, MD, September 24, 1862, n.p.

30. Marsh to Wife, near Sharpsburg, MD, September 24, 1862, 467.

31. Marsh to Wife, near Sharpsburg, MD, September 24, 1862, 467, and Ford diary, September 16, 1862. Note that Harland's report of the battle stated that "strong pickets" were placed 300 yards in front of the line (O.R., Series I, Volume 19, No. 151, Report of Edward Harland, September 3–20, 1862).

32. Stephen R. Smith, et al., *Record of Service of Connecticut Men in the Army and Navy of the United States During the War of the Rebellion* (Hartford, CT: Case, Lockwood, and Brainard Co., 1889), 617.

33. Ezra A. Carmen, *The Maryland Campaign of September 1862, Volume 2: Antietam*, ed. Thomas G. Clemens (El Dorado Hills, CA: Savas Beatie, 2012) 2:401–402. See also U.S. War Department, *Official Records*, Series I, Volume 19, No. 151, Report of Col. Edward Harland, 8th Connecticut Infantry, September 22, 1862. Carmen puts the 16th Connecticut to the left of the Eighth whereas Wolcott Marsh reports them to the right (see Marsh, 468).

34. U.S. War Department, *The War of the Rebellion: A Compilation of the Official Records of the Union and Confederate Armies* (Washington, D.C.: U.S. Government Printing Office, 1880), Series I, Volume 19, Serial 27, 452. No. 151, Report of Edward Harland, September 3–20, 1862.

35. Marsh to Wife, near Sharpsburg, MD, September 24, 1862, 468.

36. U.S. War Department, *Official Records*, Series I, Volume 19, serial 27, 452. No. 151, Report of Edward Harland, September 3–20, 1862. See Carmen, *The Maryland Campaign*, 397, 401. Carmen's maps place the brigade in their first new position at 7:30 a.m., in the ravine at 8 a.m., and then on the ridge at 10:30 a.m. The 11th Connecticut is shown as remaining on the Rohrbach Lane until it moves towards Burnside Bridge.

37. Marsh to Wife, near Sharpsburg, MD, September 24, 1862, 469.

38. Marvel, *Burnside*, 128, 137.

39. Carmen, *The Maryland Campaign*, 2:426–428.

40. Carmen, *The Maryland Campaign*, 2:427–428, and U.S. War Department, *Official Records*, Series I, Volume 19, Serial 27, 452. No. 151, Report of Edward Harland, September 3–20, 1862. Carmen puts the distance from Snavely's Ford to the Burnside Bridge, in a direct line, at 1,275 yards.

41. Carmen, *The Maryland Campaign*, 2:428–429, and U.S. War Department, *Official Records*, Series I, Volume 19, Serial 27, 455. No. 153, Report of Lieut. Col. Joseph B. Curtis, September 3–20, 1862.

42. Marsh to Wife, near Sharpsburg, MD, September 24, 1862, 470.

43. Carmen, *The Maryland Campaign*, 2:429, and U.S. War Department, *Official Records*, Series I, Volume 19, Serial 27, 452. No. 151, Report of Edward Harland, September 3–20, 1862.

44. Marsh to Wife, near Sharpsburg, MD, September 24, 1862, 470.

45. Carmen, *The Maryland Campaign*, 2:435, 2:448–449.

46. Marsh to Wife, near Sharpsburg, MD, September 24, 1862, 470.

47. Carmen, *The Maryland Campaign*, 2:405, 426, 440–441.

48. Carmen, The Maryland Campaign, 2:447–449.

49. Henry C. Hall to Sister, Mouth of Antietam Creek, October 5, 1862, Duke University Library, Durham, NC.

50. Carmen, *The Maryland Campaign*, 2:440–441, 2:449–450, 2:457, 2:466, and U.S. War Department, *Official Records*, Series I, Volume 19, Serial 27, 452. No. 151, Report of Edward Harland, September 3–20, 1862. Carmen added the identity of the two North Carolina regiments.

51. Nettleton to Brother & Friends, near Sharpsburg, MD, September 24, 1862, n.p.

52. Carmen, *The Maryland Campaign*, 2:458. McIntosh's battery consisted of a 10-pound Parrott rifle, a three-inch Ordnance rifle, a 12-pound Napoleon and a 12-pound howitzer. Curt Johnson and Richard C. Anderson, Jr., *Artillery Hell* (College Station: Texas A&M University Press, 1995), 94. The howitzer and all the battery's caissons were left at Blackford's house. The Pee Dee artillery unit was named after a region in South Carolina, and the region got its name from Pee Dee tribe of Native Americans who lived there.

53. Hall to Sister, Mouth of Antietam Creek, October 5, 1862.

54. Ford diary, September 17, 1862.

55. Upham as quoted in Carmen, *The Maryland Campaign*, 2:459; Clemens comments that Carmen didn't give a source for the quote. Clemens also states that neither Harland in his report, nor Ward in his report, mentions Company K being detached, but Carmen was unequivocal about it happening. It is confirmed in W.A. Croffut and John M. Morris, *The Military and Civil History Connecticut During the War of 1861–65* (New York: Ledyard Bill, 1868), 272.

56. Hall to Sister, Mouth of Antietam Creek, October 5, 1862.

57. Nettleton to Brother & Friends, near Sharpsburg, MD, September 24, 1862, n.p.

58. Carmen, *The Maryland Campaign*, 2:449–462, 2:470–471.

59. It is not clear which Confederate troops were on the Eighth's right flank, although there are several references in primary sources to the fact that they were being fired on from three sides, as in the quotes above. Marsh's mention of fire from a "high hill" on the right could perhaps be a reference to Cemetery Hill.

60. Coit to All, near Sharpsburg, MD, September 19, 1862.

61. Marsh to Wife, near Sharpsburg, MD, September 24, 1862, 470–471.

62. Ford diary, September 17, 1862.

63. Hall to Sister, Mouth of Antietam Creek, October 5, 1862.

64. Carmen, *The Maryland Campaign*, 2:462.

65. Carmen, The Maryland Campaign, 2:462

66. Marsh to Wife, near Sharpsburg, MD, September 24, 1862, 471–472.

67. Nettleton to Brother & Friends, near Sharpsburg, MD, September 24, 1862, n.p.

68. Croffut and Morris, *The Military and Civil History Connecticut During the War of 1861–65*, 272–273.

69. Coit to All, near Sharpsburg, MD, September 19, 1862.

70. Coit to unknown, near Sharpsburg, MD, September 19 [18], 1862.

71. Seth F. Plumb to Friends, beyond Sharpsburg, MD, September 20, 1862, Private Collection. George refers to George Booth. Both Booth and Ferris were in the color guard.

72. *Memorial of Marvin Wait* (New Haven: Thomas J. Stafford, Printer, 1863), 3, 10–11.

73. Marsh to Wife, near Sharpsburg, MD, September 26, 1862, in *Letters to a Civil War Bride*, 475–476. Note that "In Place, Rest" is a command where the soldiers no longer need be at attention and can relax their stance, although they must remain in formation.

74. Plumb to Friends, beyond Sharpsburg, MD, September 20, 1862, Private Collection.

75. Plumb to Sister, beyond Sharpsburg, MD, September 23, 1862, Private Collection.

76. Smith et al., *Connecticut Men*, 338.

77. Marsh to Wife, near Sharpsburg, MD, September 26, 1862, 476–477. In an earlier letter, Marsh had related that Oliver Case was buried in a separate grave by his brothers, Ariel and Alonzo. Ariel was Marsh's brother-in-law, being married to the sister of Anna Marsh (Marsh, 463).

78. Nettleton to Brother, Sisters & Mother, Antietam, MD, September 30, 1862, n.p.

79. Coit to All, near Sharpsburg, MD, September 19, 1862.

Chapter 5

1. Seth F. Plumb to brother Will, Antietam Iron Works, October, 3, 1862, Private Collection.

2. Charles M. Coit to All, Pleasant Valley, MD, October, 10, 1862, The Gilder Lehrman Collection, The Gilder Lehrman Institute of American History, New York, NY.

3. Samuel Jay Nettleton to Brother & Sister, Pleasant Valley, MD, October, 8, 1862 in *Life Through Letters: Samuel Jay's Story*, David DeMeo and Reece Holman, eds. (Washington, CT: Gunn Memorial Museum, 2012), n.p.

4. Coit to Lieut. Eaton, Pleasant Valley, MD, October, 10, 1862.

5. Coit to All, Washington, D.C., October, 22, 1862.
6. Coit to All, Washington, D.C., October, 22, 1862.
7. Coit to Mother, Sister, and Brother, Pleasant Valley, MD, October 16, 1862; Coit to All, Washington D.C., October 22, 1862; and Coit to All, Pleasant Valley, MD, October 25, 1862.
8. William Marvel, *Burnside* (Chapel Hill: University of North Carolina Press, 1991), 155–157.
9. Coit to All, Wheatland, VA, October 31, 1862.
10. Nettleton to Friends, Carter's Run, VA, November 9, 1862.
11. Roger M. Ford diary, November 2, 1862, New England Civil War Museum, Rockville, CT.
12. Ford diary, November 3, 1862.
13. Nettleton to Friends at home, Carter's Run, VA, November 9, 1862, and Ford diary, November 3, 5, 6, 7, 1862. Coit reported that the troops the brigade was sent to support were those of cavalry General Pleasanton.
14. Coit to All, Warrenton Junction, VA, November 17, 1862.
15. George B. McClellan, *McClellan's Own Story* (New York: Charles L. Webster & Company, 1887), 648, 650.
16. Coit to All, Warrenton Junction, VA, November 17, 1862.
17. Ford diary, November 10–19, 1862.
18. Coit to All, near Fredericksburg, VA, November 20, 1862
19. Coit to All, near Fredericksburg, VA, November 20, 1862, and Coit to All, near Fredericksburg, VA, November 21, 1862.
20. Wolcott P. Marsh to Wife, near Fredericksburg, VA, November 27, 1862, in *Letters to a Civil War Bride: Captain Wolcott P. Marsh,* Sandra Marsh Mercer and Jerry Mercer, eds. (Westminster, MD: Heritage Books, 2006), 495.
21. Coit to Old Folks at Home, opposite Fredericksburg, VA, November 23, 1862.
22. National Park Service, brochure, *Chatham: The Lacy House,* accessed May 4, 2021, https://www.nps.gov/frsp/learn/historyculture/chatham.htm.
23. Henry C. Hall to brother Alex, Falmouth, VA, December 8, 1862, Duke University Library, Durham, NC.
24. Coit to Old folks at home, Opposite Fredericksburg, VA, November 23, 1862, and Hall to brother Alex, Falmouth, VA, December 8, 1862.
25. Hall to brother Alex, Falmouth, VA, December 8, 1862.
26. Coit to Old Folks at Home, opposite Fredericksburg, VA, November 23, 1862.
27. Plumb to brother Charley, opposite Fredericksburg, VA, December 3, 1862, Private Collection.
28. Marsh to Wife, Lacy House, VA, November 30, 1862, 498.
29. Hall to brother Alex, Falmouth, VA, December 8, 1862.
30. Marsh to Wife, Lacy House, VA, November 30, 1862, 498.
31. Hall to brother Alex, Falmouth, VA, December 8, 1862.
32. U.S. War Department, *The War of the Rebellion: A Compilation of the Official Records of the Union and Confederate Armies* (Washington, D.C.: U.S. Government Printing Office, 1880), Series I, Volume 21, Serial 31, 199. No.31, Report of Maj. Thomas S. Trumbull, December 19, 1862.
Note that the 4½-inch rifled gun ("4.5 inch siege rifle") fired shells weighing about 30 pounds. These were different from the 4.2-inch Parrott rifle. See "Siege artillery in the American Civil War," *Wikipedia,* accessed May 12, 2021, https://en.wikipedia.org/wiki/Siege_artillery_in_the_American_Civil_War.
Note, too, that the First Connecticut Artillery appears to have also been known as the First Connecticut Heavy Artillery and as the First Regiment C.V. Heavy Artillery. See Stephen R. Smith, et al., eds., *Record of Service of Connecticut Men in the Army and Navy of the United States During the War of the Rebellion* (Hartford, CT: Case, Lockwood, and Brainard Co., 1889), 1,18,34.
For a photograph of Battery M on Stafford Heights overlooking Fredericksburg, see *Rebels Resurgent: Fredericksburg to Chancellorsville,* 164–165. The photograph appears to confirm that Battery M fielded three guns. Note, however, that this picture was taken on the heights south of the Lacy House, below Fredericksburg, at the site they had moved to after the Lacy House.
Wolcott Marsh confirmed that the 1st Connecticut "struck their tents and moved off since dark" on December 10. Marsh to Wife, Lacy House, VA, December 10, 1862, 511.
33. Coit to All, Lacy House, VA, December 19, 1862.
34. Nettleton to Celia and Guy, Fredericksburg, VA, November 23, 1862.
35. Wesley Brainerd, "The Pontoniers at Fredericksburg," in *Battles and Leaders of the Civil War,* Clarence C. Buel and Robert U. Johnson, eds. (New York: Century Co., 1884–1888), 3:121.
36. U.S. War Department, *Official Records,* Series I, Volume 21, Serial 31, 175. No. 20, Report of Maj. Ira Spaulding, December 12, 1862.
37. Ed Malles, ed., *Bridge Building in Wartime, Colonel Wesley Brainerd's Memoir of the 50th New York Volunteer Engineers* (Knoxville: University of Tennessee Press, 1997), 107–108.
38. Malles, *Bridge Building,* 110-112.
39. Malles, *Bridge Building,* 112- 114.
40. Plumb to Friends, near Fredericksburg, VA, December 16, 1862, Private Collection. Capt. Hoyt's report and Lt. Ford's diary both indicate that it was General Getty who came to the Eighth's camp.
41. Plumb to Friends, near Fredericksburg, VA, December 16, 1862, Private Collection. Plumb put the distance from the Lacy House to the upper pontoon bridge at about 30 rods (495 feet).
42. Smith et al., *Record of Service of Connecticut Men,* 338, 352.

43. *The* [New Haven, CT] *Daily Palladium*, December 20, 1862, 2.
44. Coit to All, Fredericksburg, VA, December 14, 1862.
45. Ford diary, December 11, 1862.
46. Marsh to Wife, Falmouth, VA, December 21, 1862, 514–516, 519.
47. U.S. War Department, *Official Records*, Series I, Volume 21, Serial 31, 349. No. 138, Report of Capt. Henry M. Hoyt, December 17, 1862.
48. U.S. War Department, *Official Records*, Series I, Volume 21, Serial 31, 331. No.128, Report of Brig. Gen. George W. Getty, December 28, 1862., and U.S. War Department, *Official Records*, Series I, Volume 21, Serial 31, 310. No. 110, Report of Brig. Gen. Orlando B. Willcox, January 7, 1863.
49. U.S. War Department, *Official Records*, Series I, Volume 21, Serial 31, 169. No.17, Report of Brig. Gen. Daniel P. Woodbury, December 12, 1862.
50. U.S. War Department, *Official Records*, Series I, Volume 21, Serial 31, 175. No. 20, Report of Maj. Ira Spaulding, December 12, 1862.
51. *Elmira* [NY] *Weekly Advertiser And Chemung County Republican*, December 27, 1862, 2.
52. *The Penn-Yan* [NY] *Democrat*, January 2, 1863, 1.
53. Malles, *Bridge Building*, 116.
54. U.S. War Department, *Official Records*, Series I, Volume 21, Serial 31, 169. No. 17, Report of Brig. Gen. Daniel P. Woodbury, December 12, 1862.
55. U.S. War Department, *Official Records*, Series I, Volume 21, Serial 31, 310. No. 110, Report of Brig. Gen. Orlando B. Willcox, January 7, 1863.
56. Ford diary, December 12, 1862; and Plumb to Friends, near Fredericksburg, VA, December 16, 1862, Private Collection.
57. U.S. War Department, *Official Records*, Series I, Volume 21, Serial 31, 33. No.128, Report of Brig. Gen. George W. Getty, December 28, 1862.
58. Plumb to Friends, near Fredericksburg, VA, December 16, 1862, Private Collection.
59. U.S. War Department, *Official Records*, No.128, Report of Brig. Gen. George W. Getty, December 28, 1862. Also see U.S. War Department, *Official Records*, Serial 31, Page 201, Chapter XXXIII, No. 32, Report of Captain Otto Diederichs, Battery A, First Battalion New York Light Artillery, December 19, 1862.
60. Plumb to Friends, near Fredericksburg, VA, December 16, 1862, Private Collection.
61. U.S. War Department, *Official Records*, Series I, Volume 21, Serial 31, 310. No. 110, Report of Brig. Gen. Orlando B. Willcox, January 7, 1863.
62. U.S. War Department, *Official Records*, Series I, Volume 21, Serial 31, 331. No.128, Report of Brig. Gen. George W. Getty, December 28, 1862, and U.S. War Department, *Official Records*, Series I, Volume 21, Serial 31, 310. No. 110, Report of Brig. Gen. Orlando B. Willcox, January 7, 1863.
63. U.S. War Department, *Official Records*, Series I, Volume 21, Serial 31, 347. No. 137, Report of Col. Edward Harland, December 17, 1862.
64. Plumb to Friends, near Fredericksburg, VA, December 16, 1862, Private Collection.
65. Plumb to Friends, near Fredericksburg, VA, December 16, 1862, Private Collection; W.A. Croffut and John M. Morris, *The Military and Civil History Connecticut During the War of 1861–65* (New York: Ledyard Bill, 1868), 294.
66. "Judge Montgomery Slaughter, Sr.," *Find a Grave*, accessed June 8, 2021, https://www.findagrave.com/memorial/5225343/montgomery-slaughter. Find a Grave located the grave in the Fredericksburg Cemetery, Fredericksburg, Fredericksburg City, VA.
67. Marvel, *Burnside*, 196.
68. Plumb to Friends, near Fredericksburg, VA, December 16, 1862, Private Collection.
69. U.S. War Department, *Official Records*, Series I, Volume 21, Serial 31, 331. No.128, Report of Brig. Gen. George W. Getty, December 28, 1862; U.S. War Department, *Official Records*, Series I, Volume 21, Serial 31, 310. No.110, Report of Brig. Gen. Orlando B. Willcox, January 7, 1863; and U.S. War Department, *Official Records*, Series I, Volume 21, Serial 31, 347. No.137, Report of Col. Edward Harland, December 17, 1862.
70. National Park Service, brochure, *Chatham: The Lacy House*, accessed May 16, 2021, https://www.nps.gov/frsp/learn/historyculture/chatham.htm.
71. Coit to All, Lacy House, VA, December 19, 1862.
72. Coit to All, Lacy House, VA, December 19, 1862.
73. Plumb to Friends, near Fredericksburg, VA, December 16, 1862, Private Collection.
74. Plumb to Father, near Fredericksburg, VA, December 30, 1862, Private Collection.
75. Plumb to Friends, near Fredericksburg, VA, January 23, 1863, Private Collection; William K. Goolrick and Editors of Time-Life Books, *Rebels Resurgent: Fredericksburg to Chancellorsville* (Alexandria, VA: Time-Life Books, 1985), 93–98.
76. Ford diary, January 21–23, 1863.
77. Goolrick, *Rebels Resurgent*, 93–98.
78. Ford diary, February 6–8, 1863, and Coit to All, off Fort Monroe, VA, February 8, 1863. We believe that the ship referred to was the *John Brooks* was built in 1859, and apart from government use in the Civil War, spent her career along the New England coast. "Category: John Brooks (ship, 1859)," *Wikimedia Commons*, accessed June 6, 2021, https://commons.wikimedia.org/wiki/Category:John_Brooks_(ship,_1859).
79. Plumb to Sister, Newport News, VA, February 15, 1863, Litchfield Historical Society, Litchfield, CT. Coit identified the monitor as the *Nehant* in a letter: Coit to All, Newport News, VA, February 10, 1863. The body of water known as Hampton Roads is one of the world's largest natural harbors (more accurately a roadstead or "roads"). The U.S. Navy built more than sixty Monitor-type vessels during the Civil War.
80. Coit to All, Newport News, VA, February 9, 1863.

81. Plumb to Miss LE Plumb, Newport News, VA, February 9, 1863, Private Collection.
82. Nettleton to brother Henry, Newport News, VA, February 13,1863.
83. Nettleton to brother Henry, Newport news, VA, February 13, 1863.
84. Coit to All, Newport News, VA, March 9, 1863.
85. Nettleton to brother Henry, Newport News, VA, March 7, 1863.
86. "History of Baseball," *Wikipedia*, accessed June 16, 2021, https://en.wikipedia.org/wiki/History_of_baseball.
87. Plumb to Miss LE Plumb, Newport News, VA, February 9, 1863, Private Collection.
88. Plumb to Friends, Newport News, VA, March 3, 1863, Private Collection.
89. Plumb to Brother and Cousin, Newport News, VA, March 11, 1863, Private Collection.
90. Coit to All, Newport News, VA, February 10, 1863.
91. Coit to All, Newport News, VA, March 4, 1863.
92. This quote is from part of a letter, presumably to All, written by Charles Coit from Gaskins Mills, VA, with no date given. However, the Eighth spent one week there beginning November 7, 1862.

Chapter 6

1. Steven A. Cormier, *The Siege of Suffolk: The Forgotten Campaign April 11–May 4, 1863* (Lynchburg, VA: H.E. Howard, Inc., 1989), 15.
2. William Huntington to sister Ellen, Suffolk, VA, March 19, 1863, Houghton Library, Harvard University, Boston, MA.
3. Huntington to sister Ellen, Suffolk, VA, March 19, 1863.
4. Seth F. Plumb to sister Lemira, Suffolk, VA, March 18, 1863, Private Collection.
5. John M. Morris, *The Connecticut War Record* (New Haven), August 1863, 11.
6. W.A. Croffut and John M. Morris, *The Military and Civil History Connecticut During the War of 1861–65* (New York: Ledyard Bill, 1868), 331.
7. Croffut and Morris, *Connecticut During the War*, 475.
8. "Siege of Suffolk," *Wikipedia*, accessed April 12, 2021, https://en.wikipedia.org/wiki/Siege_of_Suffolk.
9. U.S. War Department, *The War of the Rebellion: A Compilation of the Official Records of the Union and Confederate Armies* (Washington, D.C.: U.S. Government Printing Office, 1880), Series I, Volume 18, Serial 26, 575. Abstract of Returns of Maj. Gen. John A. Dix, March 31, 1863.
10. Albion Brooks to Family, July 15, 1863, Special Collections Library, Pennsylvania State University, University Park, PA.
11. Plumb to sister Lemira, Suffolk, VA, April 21, 1863, Private Collection.
12. Opinion of the Judges of the Supreme Court, 30 Conn. 591, 1862 WL 941 (Conn.)
13. Terrance Adams, *History of Absentee Voting in The State Constitution*, September 7, 2012. https://www.cga.ct.gov/2012/rpt/2012-R-0379.htm.
14. Charles Coit to Family, Suffolk, VA, April 10, 1863, The Gilder Lehrman Collection, The Gilder Lehrman Institute of American History, New York, NY.
15. Jay Nettleton to Family, Suffolk, VA, April 10, 1863, in *Life Through Letters: Samuel Jay's Story*, David DeMeo and Reece Holman, eds. (Washington, CT: Gunn Memorial Museum, 2012), n.p.
16. Morris, *Connecticut War Record*, 11.
17. Morris, *Connecticut War Record*, 11.
18. Coit to Family, Suffolk, VA, April 17, 1863.
19. Stephen R. Smith, et al., eds., *Record of Service of Connecticut Men in the Army and Navy of the United States During the War of the Rebellion* (Hartford: Case, Lockwood, and Brainard Co., 1889), 330.
20. Croffut and Morris, *Connecticut During the War*, 478.
21. Cormier. *The Siege of Suffolk*, 23.
22. Cormier, *The Siege of Suffolk*, 128.
23. John S. Salmon, *The Official Virginia Civil War Battlefield Guide* (Mechanicsburg: Stackpole Books, 2001), 170.
24. Cormier, *The Siege of Suffolk*, 142.
25. Cormier, *The Siege of Suffolk*, 148.
26. Plumb to sister Lemira, Suffolk, VA, April 21, 1863, Private Collection.
27. Plumb to sister Lemira, Suffolk, VA, April 21, 1863, Private Collection.
28. Plumb to sister Lemira, Suffolk, VA, April 21, 1863, Private Collection.
29. Morris, *Connecticut War Record*, 11–12.
30. Cormier, *The Siege of Suffolk*, 150.
31. U.S. War Dept., *Official Records*, Series 1, Volume 18, Serial 26, 304. Report No. 15, Report of Brig. Gen. Geo. W. Getty, May 12, 1863
32. Huntington to sister Ellen, Suffolk, VA, April 30, 1863.
33. Cormier, *The Siege of Suffolk*, 153.
34. Coit to Family, Suffolk, VA, April 23, 1863.
35. Smith et al., *Connecticut Men*, 327–358.
36. Cormier, *The Siege of Suffolk*, 150
37. Huntington to sister Ellen, Suffolk, VA, April 21, 1863.
38. Plumb to sister Lemira, Suffolk, VA, April 28, 1863, Private Collection.
39. Huntington to sister Ellen, Suffolk, VA, May 14, 1863.
40. U.S. War Dept., *Official Records*, Series 1, Volume 18, Serial 26, 314. No. 21, Report of Col. J. Edward Ward, May 6, 1863.
41. Croffut and Morris, *Connecticut During the War*, 334.
42. Coit to All, Suffolk, VA, April 23, 1863.
43. Coit to All, Suffolk, VA, April 23, 1863.
44. Smith et al., *Connecticut Men*, 329.
45. Coit to All, Suffolk, VA, May 2, 1863.
46. Coit to All, Suffolk, VA, May 3, 1863.
47. Plumb to sister Lemira, Suffolk, VA, May 5, 1863, Private Collection.

48. Croffut and Morris, *Connecticut During the War*, 335.
49. Morris, *Connecticut War Record*, 12.
50. Morris, *Connecticut War Record*, 12.
51. Plumb to sister Lemira, Suffolk, VA, May 6, 1863, Private Collection.
52. Coit to All, Suffolk, VA, May 10, 1863.
53. Coit to All, Suffolk, VA, May 16, 1863.
54. Coit to All, Suffolk, VA, May 21, 1863.
55. Plumb to sister Lemira, Suffolk, VA, May 24, 1863, Private Collection.
56. Coit to All, Suffolk, VA, May 26, 186.3
57. Plumb to sister Lemira, Suffolk, VA, May 24, 1863, Private Collection.
58. Allen Dauchy to cousin MaryLib, Suffolk, VA, May 28, 1863, Lewis Leigh Collection, U.S. Army Heritage and Education Center, Carlisle, PA; Geraldine S. Caughman, *Qui Transtulit Sustinet: Connecticut Battle Flag Collection, Volume I* (Wethersfield, CT: Caughman Associates, 2006), 59. This source includes the verbatim text of the letter.
59. Plumb to sister Lemira, Suffolk, VA, May 31, 1863, Private Collection.
60. Plumb to sister Lemira, Suffolk, VA, May 31, 1863, Private Collection.
61. Plumb to sister Lemira, Suffolk, VA, June 7, 1863, Private Collection.
62. Coit to All, Portsmouth, VA, June 17, 1863.
63. Nettleton to Family, Portsmouth, VA, June 20, 1863.
64. Croffut and Morris, *Connecticut During the War*, 336.
65. Seth Plumb to sister Lemira, Portsmouth, VA, June 21, 1863, Helga J. Ingraham Memorial Library, Litchfield Historical Society, Litchfield, CT.
66. Coit to All, Portsmouth, VA, June 21, 1863.
67. Croffut and Morris, *Connecticut During the War*, 337.
68. Coit to All, Portsmouth, VA, June 22, 1863.
69. "White House, Virginia," *Wikipedia*, accessed August 30, 2021, https://en.wikipedia.org/wiki/White_House,_Virginia.
70. "White House (plantation)," *Wikipedia*, accessed August 30, 2021, https://en.wikipedia.org/wiki/White_House_(plantation).
71. Croffut and Morris, *Connecticut During the War*, 338.
72. Plumb to sister Lemira, Yorktown, VA, July 11, 1863, Private Collection.
73. Nettleton to Family, Portsmouth, VA, July 15, 1863.
74. Plumb to sister Lemira, Portsmouth, VA, July 15, 1863, Litchfield Historical Society.
75. Coit to All, White House, VA, July 7, 1863.
76. Coit to All, Yorktown, VA, July 11, 1863.
77. Plumb to sister Lemira, Portsmouth, VA, July 15, 1863, Litchfield Historical Society.
78. Plumb to sister Lemira, Portsmouth, VA, July 19, 1863, Private Collection.
79. Croffut and Morris, *Connecticut During the War*, 339.
80. Nettleton to Family, Portsmouth, VA, July 15, 1863.
81. Plumb to sister Lemira, Portsmouth, VA, July 27, 1863, Private Collection.
82. Croffut and Morris, *Connecticut During the War*, 340.
83. Huntington to sister Ellen, Portsmouth, VA, July 17, 1863.
84. Plumb to sister Lemira, Portsmouth, VA, July 19, 1863, Private Collection.
85. Croffut and Morris, *Connecticut During the War*, 476.
86. U.S. War Dept., *Official Records*, Series 1, Volume 27, Serial 45, 827. General Orders No. 262, August 1, 1863.
87. U.S. War Dept., *Official Records*, Series I, Volume 29, Serial 49, 619. Abstract of Returns, Maj. Gen. Benjamin F. Butler, December 31, 1863.
88. Plumb to sister Lemira, Portsmouth, VA, August 2, 1863, Private Collection.
89. Plumb to sister Lemira, Portsmouth, VA, August 9, 1863, Litchfield Historical Society.
90. Plumb to sister Lemira, Portsmouth, VA, September 4, 1863, Private Collection.
91. Huntington to sister Ellen, Portsmouth, VA, July 23, 1863.
92. Plumb to sister Lemira, Portsmouth, VA, August 9, 1863, Litchfield Historical Society.
93. Plumb to sister Lemira, South Mills, NC, August 22, 1863, Private Collection.
94. Huntington to sister Ellen, South Mills, NC, August 26, 1863.
95. Huntington to sister Ellen, South Mills, NC, August 28, 1863.
96. Brooks to Family, South Mills, NC, August 23, 1863.
97. Ford diary, September 5–9, 1863. New England Civil War Museum, Rockville, CT.
98. Brooks to Family, Portsmouth, VA, September 12, 1863.
99. Morris, *Connecticut War Record*, 60.
100. Plumb to sister Lemira, Portsmouth, VA, September 17, 1863, Private Collection.
101. Plumb to sister Lemira, Portsmouth, VA, September 17, 1863, Private Collection.
102. Morris, *Connecticut War Record*, 86.
103. Croffut and Morris, *Connecticut During the War*, 478.
104. Plumb to sister Lemira, Portsmouth, VA, October 19, 1863, Private Collection.
105. Brooks to Family, Portsmouth, VA, October 9, 1863.
106. "2Lt. Alanson L. Sanborn," *Find a Grave*, accessed June 21, 2021, www.findagrave.com/memorial/134931282/alanson-l.-sanborn. This site contains a copy of the *New York Times* newspaper article from July 14, 1863, detailing the story.
107. Plumb to sister Lemira, Portsmouth, VA, October 26, 1863, Private Collection.
108. Huntington to sister Ellen, Portsmouth, VA, November 9, 1863.
109. Henry C. Hall diary, November 9, 1863,

David M. Rubenstein Rare Book & Manuscript Library, Duke University, Durham, NC.
110. G.W. Farnum, *Connecticut War Record*, 121.
111. Ford diary, November 26, 1863.
112. Plumb to sister Lemira, Portsmouth, VA, November 21, 1863, Private Collection.
113. Farnum, *Connecticut War Record*, 107.
114. Nettleton to Family, Portsmouth, VA, December 2, 1863.
115. John Merriam to Etta Morton, Portsmouth, VA, November 27, 1863, Lincoln Memorial Shrine, A.K. Smiley Public Library, Redlands, CA.
116. Croffut and Morris, *Connecticut During the War*, 461.
117. Ford diary, December 17, 1863.
118. Nettleton to Family, Portsmouth, VA, December 2, 1863.
119. Plumb to sister Lemira, Portsmouth, VA, December 16, 1863, Private Collection.
120. Huntington to sister Ellen, Portsmouth, VA, Dec. 13, 1863.
121. Smith, et. al., *Connecticut Men*, 327–328. The Eighth's regimental summary history by J.H. Vaill.
122. Huntington to sister Ellen, Portsmouth, VA, Dec. 13, 1863.
123. Croffut and Morris, *Connecticut During the War*, 520.
124. Croffut and Morris, *Connecticut During the War*, 521–522. Many of the state's newspapers published the text of the speech. See, e.g., "Reception of the Eighth and Eleventh Regiments. A Grand Ovation!" *The Hartford Daily Courant* (Hartford, CT), Jan. 16, 1864.
125. Ford diary, January 10–April 1, 1864.
126. Croffut and Morris, *Connecticut During the War*, 536.

Chapter 7

1. W.A. Croffut and John M. Morris, *The Military and Civil History Connecticut During the War of 1861–1865*. (New York: Ledyard Bill, 1868), 536
2. Samuel Jay Nettleton to Friends, Deep Creek, VA, March 28, 1864, in *Life Through Letters: Samuel Jay's Story*, David DeMeo and Reece Holman, eds. (Washington, CT: Gunn Memorial Museum, 2012), n.p.
3. Charles M. Coit to All, Deep Creek, VA, March 15, 1864, The Gilder Lehrman Collection, The Gilder Lehrman Institute of American History, New York, NY.
4. Seth F. Plumb to Friends, Deep Creek, VA, March 20, 1864, Private Collection.
5. Plumb to Brother Charlie, Deep Creek, VA, April 17, 1864, Private Collection.
6. Benjamin F. Butler, *Butler's Book* (Boston: A.M. Thayer & Co., 1862), 627–630, 638.
7. Seth F. Plumb to Friends, Yorktown, VA, April 24, 1864, Litchfield Historical Society, Litchfield, CT; and Roger M. Ford diary, April 19–21, 1864, New England Civil War Museum, Rockville, CT.
8. U.S. War Department, *The War of the Rebellion: A Compilation of the Official Records of the Union and Confederate Armies* (Washington, D.C.: U.S. Government Printing Office, 1880), Series I, Volume 33, Serial 60, 939. Special Orders No. 111, Maj. Gen. Benjamin F. Butler, April 21, 1864.
9. Butler, *Butler's Book,* 1059.
10. Coit to All, Yorktown, VA, May 1, 1864.
11. Butler, *Butler's Book*, 639–640.
12. Ford diary, May 4–5, 1864.
13. Robert J. Forman, et al., *Bermuda Hundred Campaign Tour Guide* (Chesterfield, VA: Chesterfield Historical Society, 2010), 9–13.
14. Ford diary, May 6, 1864.
15. Forman, et al., *Bermuda Hundred Campaign Tour Guide*, 13–14.
16. William G. Robertson, *Back Door to Richmond: The Bermuda Hundred Campaign April–June 1864* (Baton Rouge: Louisiana State University Press, 1987), 85.
17. U.S. War Department, *Official Records*, Series I, Volume 36, Serial 68, 132. No. 52, Report of Brig. Gen. Hiram Burnham, May 22, 1864. Note that the paragraph arrangement in the original Report has been subdivided in part here for readability purposes.
18. Henry C. Hall to Brother and Sister, Bermuda Hundred, VA, May 23, 1864, David M. Rubenstein Rare Book and Manuscript Library, Duke University, Durham, NC.
19. Ford diary, May 7, 1864.
20. Plumb to Friends, near Petersburg, VA, May 8, 1864, Private Collection.
21. Joseph R. Hawley, *History of Battle Flag Day* (Hartford, CT: Lockwood & Merritt, 1880), 118.
22. Coit to All, near Portsmouth, VA, February 28, 1864; Coit to unknown, Camp of the 8th, March 10, 1864; and Coit to George, Deep Creek, VA, April 5, 1864.
23. Coit to All, near Petersburg, VA, May 8, 1864; and Coit to All, Back at Bivouac, May 11, 1864.
24. Stephen R. Smith, et al., eds., *Record of Service of Connecticut Men in the Army and Navy of the United States During the War of the Rebellion* (Hartford, CT: Case, Lockwood, and Brainard Co., 1889), 333.
25. Forman, et al., *Bermuda Hundred Campaign Tour Guide*, 15–16.
26. 26 Robertson, *Back Door to Richmond*, 110–111.
27. Forman, et al., *Bermuda Hundred Campaign Tour Guide*, 17–18.
28. U.S. War Department, *Official Records*, Series I, Volume 36, Serial 68, 132. No. 52, Report of Brig. Gen. Hiram Burnham, May 22, 1864.
29. Ford diary, May 9–10, 1864.
30. Forman, et al., *Bermuda Hundred Campaign Tour Guide*, 22–24.
31. Butler, *Butler's Book*, 650.
32. U.S. War Department, *Official Records*,

Series I, Volume 36, Serial 68, 132. No. 52, Report of Brig. Gen. Hiram Burnham, May 22, 1864.

33. U.S. War Department, *Official Records*, Series I, Volume 36, Serial 68, 136. No. 53, Report of Lieut. Col. Martin B. Smith, May 18, 1864.

34. Plumb to Friends, near Bermuda Hundred, VA, May 25, 1864, Private Collection.

35. Ford diary, May 14, 1864.

36. Forman, et al., *Bermuda Hundred Campaign Tour Guide*, 30.

37. Robertson, *Back Door to Richmond*, 183.

38. Forman, et al., *Bermuda Hundred Campaign Tour Guide*, 30–32.

39. Forman, et al., *Bermuda Hundred Campaign Tour Guide*, 33.

40. Hall to Brother and Sister, Bermuda Hundred, VA, May 23, 1864.

41. U.S. War Department, *Official Records*, Series I, Volume 36, Serial 68, 136. No. 53, Report of Lieut. Col. Martin B. Smith, May 18, 1864.

42. Coit to All, Camp of the 8th, May 17, 1864.

43. U.S. War Department, *Official Records*, Series I, Volume 36, Serial 68, 132. No. 52, Report of Brig. Gen. Hiram Burnham, May 22, 1864.

44. U.S. War Department, *Official Records*, Series I, Volume 36, Serial 68, 126. No. 50, Report of Brig. Gen. William T. H. Brooks, May 25, 1864.

45. Croffut and Morris, *Connecticut During the War*, 547.

46. John Lovell Cunningham, *Three Years with the Adirondack Regiment* (Norwood, MA: The Plimpton Press, 1920), 114.

47. Coit to All, Camp of the 8th, May 19, 1864.

48. U.S. War Department, *Official Records*, Series I, Volume 36, Serial 68, 132. No. 52, Report of Brig. Gen. Hiram Burnham, May 22, 1864.

49. Coit to All, Camp of the 8th, May 17, 1864.

50. U.S. War Department, *Official Records*, Series I, Volume 36, Serial 68, 136. No. 53, Report of Lieut. Col. Martin B. Smith, May 18, 1864.

51. Coit to All, Camp of the 8th, May 19, 1864.

52. Plumb to Friends, near Bermuda Hundred, VA, May 25, 1864, Private Collection.

53. Coit to All, Camp of the 8th, May 19, 1864.

54. Ford diary, May 18–29, 1864.

Chapter 8

1. Gregory Jaynes and Editors of Time-Life Books, *The Killing Ground: Wilderness to Cold Harbor* (Alexandria, VA: Time-Life Books, 1986), 148, 151.

2. Ulysses S. Grant, *Personal Memoirs of Ulysses S. Grant, Volume II* (New York: Charles L. Webster & Co.,1885), 259.

3. Grant, *Personal Memoirs*, 2:254.

4. Charles Coit to Family, James River, May 29, 1864, The Gilder Lehrman Collection, The Gilder Lehrman Institute of American History, New York, NY.

5. Seth F. Plumb to Friends, Cold Harbor, Va., June 5, 1864, Private Collection.

6. Gordon C. Rhea, *Cold Harbor: Grant and Lee May 26–June 3, 1864* (Baton Rouge: Louisiana State University Press, 2002), 110.

7. Plumb to Friends, Cold Harbor, VA, June 5, 1864, Private Collection.

8. Jaynes, *The Killing Ground*, 151–152.

9. Plumb to Friends, Cold Harbor, VA, June 5, 1864, Private Collection.

10. U.S. War Dept., *Official Records*, Series 1, Volume 36, Serial 67, 1009. No. 259, Report of Capt. Charles M. Coit, June 11, 1864.

11. Grant, *Personal Memoirs*, 2:265.

12. Rhea, *Cold Harbor*, 227. See Rhea's footnote 7.

13. Rhea, *Cold Harbor*, 229.

14. U.S. War Dept., *Official Records*, Series 1, Volume 36, Serial 67, 1009. No. 259, Report of Capt. Charles M. Coit, June 11, 1864.

15. U.S. War Dept., *The War of the Rebellion: A Compilation of the Official Records of the Union and Confederate Armies* (Washington, D.C.: U.S. Government Printing Office, 1880), Series 1, Volume 51, Serial 107, 1248. Report of Brig. Gen. William T.H. Brooks, June 1864.

16. Rhea, *Cold Harbor*, 230.

17. U.S. War Dept., *Official Records*, Series 1, Volume 36, Serial 67, 1009. No. 258, Report of Brig. Gen. Hiram Burnham, June 10, 1864.

18. U.S. War Dept., *Official Records*, Series 1, Volume 36, Serial 67, 1009. No. 258, Report of Brig. Gen. Hiram Burnham, June 10, 1864.

19. Rhea, *Cold Harbor*, 251.

20. U.S. War Dept., *Official Records*, Series 1, Volume 36, Serial 67, 1009. No. 259, Report of Capt. Charles M. Coit, June 11, 1864.

21. Grant, *Personal Memoirs*, 2:266.

22. Rhea, *Cold Harbor*, 282.

23. Grant, *Personal Memoirs*, 2:271. Grant here may be mistaken about Devens supporting on the right of Martindale, because both Brooks and Devens were likely to the left of Martindale's position at that time.

24. U.S. War Dept., *Official Records*, Series 1, Volume 36, Serial 67, 1009. No. 258, Report of Brig. Gen. Hiram Burnham, June 10, 1864.

25. U.S. War Dept., *Official Records*, Series 1, Volume 36, Serial 67, 1009. No. 259, Report of Capt. Charles M. Coit, June 11, 1864.

26. Albion Brooks to Family, White House, VA, May 31, 1864, Special Collections Library, Pennsylvania State University, University Park, PA.

27. Smith to Brooks Family, Cold Harbor, VA, June 4, 1864.

28. Rhea, *Cold Harbor*, 351.

29. U.S. War Dept., *Official Records*, Series 1, Volume 36, Serial 67, 1009. No. 258, Report of Brig. Gen. Hiram Burnham, June 10, 1864.

30. U.S. War Dept., *Official Records*, Series 1, Volume 36, Serial 67, 1009. No. 258, Report of Brig. Gen. Hiram Burnham, June 10, 1864.

31. U.S. War Dept., *Official Records*, Series 1, Volume 36, Serial 67, 1009. No. 259, Report of Capt. Charles M. Coit, June 11, 1864.

32. Plumb to Friends, Cold Harbor, Va., June 5, 1864, Private Collection.
33. U.S. War Dept., *Official Records*, Series 1, Volume 36, Serial 67, 1009. No. 259, Report of Capt. Charles M. Coit, June 11, 1864.
34. Plumb to Friends, 10 Miles from Richmond, June 5, 1864, Private Collection.
35. Will Plumb to Sister Lemira, Cold Harbor, Va., June 4, 1864, Private Collection.
36. U.S. War Dept., *Official Records*, Series 1, Volume 36, Serial 67, 1009. No. 258, Report of Brig. Gen. Hiram Burnham, June 10, 1864.
37. U.S. War Dept., *Official Records*, Series 1, Volume 36, Serial 67, 1009. No. 259, Report of Capt. Charles M. Coit, June 11, 1864.
38. Coit to All, Cold Harbor, Va., June 5, 1864.
39. U.S. War Dept., *Official Records*, Series 1, Volume 36, Serial 67, 1010. No. 258, Report of Brig. Gen. Hiram Burnham, June 10, 1864.
40. Coit to All, Cold Harbor, Va., June 9, 1864.
41. U.S. War Dept., *Official Records*, Series 1, Volume 36, Serial 67, 1009. No. 259, Report of Capt. Charles M. Coit, June 11, 1864.
42. W.A. Croffut and John M. Morris, *The Military and Civil History Connecticut During the War of 1861–1865* (New York: Ledyard Bill, 1868), 528.
43. Andrew Byrne diary 1864, Manuscripts Collection, Connecticut Historical Society, Hartford, CT.
44. Grant, *Personal Memoirs*, 2:288.
45. Coit to Family, Point of Rocks, VA, June 18, 1864.
46. U.S. War Dept., *Official Records*, Series 1, Volume 40, Serial 80, 714. No. 269, Report of Capt. Charles M. Coit, June 28, 1964.
47. "William Farrar Smith," *Wikipedia*, accessed May 29, 2021, https://en.wikipedia.org/wiki/William_Farrar_Smith.
48. U.S. War Dept., *Official Records*, Series 1, Volume 40, Serial 80, 714. No. 269, Report of Capt. Charles M. Coit, June 28, 1964.
49. Moses Smith, *The Connecticut War Record*, John M. Morris, ed. (New Haven: Peck, White & Peck, 1863–1865), 234.
50. U.S. War Dept., *Official Records*, Series 1, Volume 40, Serial 80, 705. No. 262, Report of Maj. Gen. William F. Smith, June 16, 1964.
51. U.S. War Dept., *Official Records*, Series 1, Volume 40, Serial 80, 714. No. 269, Report of Capt. Charles M. Coit, June 28, 1964.
52. Coit to Family, Point of Rocks, VA, June 18, 1864.
53. Coit to Family, Petersburg, VA, June 16, 1864.
54. U.S. War Dept., *Official Records*, Series 1, Volume 40, Serial 80, 714. No. 269, Report of Capt. Charles M. Coit, June 28, 1964.
55. Croffut and Morris, *Connecticut During the War*, 605.
56. "The Second Battle of Petersburg," *Beyond the Crater*, accessed January 25, 2022, https://www.beyondthecrater.com/resources/bat-sum/first-offensive-summaries/the-second-battle-of-petersburg-summary/.
57. Grant, *Personal Memoirs*, 2:293–294.
58. Coit to Family, Henrico, VA, October 17, 1864.
59. Croffut and Morris, *Connecticut During the War*, 610.
60. Smith, *Connecticut War Record*, 234.
61. Coit to Family, Point of Rocks, VA, June 18, 1864.
62. U.S. War Dept., *Official Records*, Series I, Volume 40, Serial 81, 227. General Order of Maj. Gen. William F. Smith.
63. Coit to Family, near Petersburg, VA, June 24, 1864.
64. Coit to Family, near Petersburg, VA, June 24, 1864.
65. Croffut and Morris, *Connecticut During the War*, 619.
66. Croffut and Morris, *Connecticut During the War*, 619.
67. Plumb to sister Lemira, near Petersburg, VA, July 2 ,1864, Private Collection.
68. Plumb to sister Lemira, near Petersburg, VA, July 2, 1864, Private Collection.
69. Plumb to sister Lemira, near Petersburg, VA, July 9, 1864, Private Collection.
70. Coit to Family, Point of Rocks, VA, July 3, 1864.
71. Coit to Family, Point of Rocks, VA, July 6, 1864.
72. Coit letter, to Family, near Petersburg, VA, July 18, 1864(a).
73. Coit to Family, Point of Rocks, VA, July 23, 1864.
74. Benjamin F. Butler, *Autobiography and Personal Reminiscences of Major-General Benj. F. Butler—Butler's Book* (Boston: A. M. Thayer & Co., 1892), 692.
75. Butler, *Butler's Book*, 695.
76. William F. Smith, *From Chattanooga to Petersburg Under Generals Grant and Butler: A Contribution to the History of the War, and a Personal Vindication* (New York: Houghton, Mifflin & Company, 1893), 46.
77. Coit to Family, Point of Rocks, VA, June 18, 1864.
78. Coit to Family, Point of Rocks, VA, July 28, 1864.
79. Croffut and Morris, *Connecticut During the War*, 661.
80. Plumb to sister Lemira, near Petersburg, VA, July 22, 1864, Private Collection.
81. Plumb to sister Lemira, near Petersburg, VA, July 22, 1864, Private Collection.
82. Plumb to sister Lemira, near Petersburg, VA, July 23, 1864, Private Collection.
83. Croffut and Morris, *Connecticut During the War*, 618.
84. Croffut and Morris, *Connecticut During the War*, 625.
85. Croffut and Morris, *Connecticut During the War*, 625.

86. Coit to Family, Point of Rocks, VA, August 7, 1864.
87. Coit to Family, Point of Rocks, VA, August 7, 1864.
88. Coit to Family, Point of Rocks, VA, August 18, 1864.
89. Coit to Family, Bermuda Hundred, VA, August 28, 1864 (a).
90. Coit to Family, Bermuda Hundred, VA, August 28, 1864 (c).
91. U.S. War Dept., *Official Records*, Series I, Volume 42, Serial 88, 621.
92. Coit to Family, Bermuda Hundred, VA, August 31, 1864.
93. Coit to Family, Bermuda Hundred, VA, September 2, 1864.
94. Plumb to sister Lemira, Bermuda Hundred, VA, September 4, 1864, Private Collection.
95. Stephen R. Smith, et al., eds., *Record of Service of Connecticut Men in the Army and Navy of the United States During the War of the Rebellion* (Hartford, CT: Case, Lockwood, and Brainard Co., 1889), 327.
96. "Hampton's Beefsteak Raid," *The Siege of Petersburg Online*, accessed May 29, 2021, http://www.beyondthecrater.com/news-and-notes/siege-of-petersburg-sesquicentennial/150-years-ago-today/150-18640916-beefsteak-raid-day-3/.
97. "Beefsteak Raid," *Wikipedia*, accessed May 29, 2021, https://en.wikipedia.org/wiki/Beefsteak_Raid.
98. Smith, et al., *Connecticut Men*, 327.
99. Croffut and Morris, *Connecticut During the War*, 662.
100. Grant, *Personal Memoirs*, 2:333.
101. "Fort Harrison," *Wikipedia*, accessed May 29, 2021, https://en.wikipedia.org/wiki/Fort_Harrison.
102. U.S. War Dept., *Official Records*, Series 1, Volume 40, Serial 81, 552. Abstract of Returns, Maj. Gen. Benjamin F. Butler, June, 1864.
103. Croffut and Morris, *Connecticut During the War*, 664.
104. U.S. War Dept., *Official Records*, Series I, Volume 42, Serial 87, 794. No. 317, Report of Bvt. Maj. Gen. George Stannard Jr., April 18, 1865.
105. Douglas Crenshaw, *Fort Harrison and the Battle of Chaffin's Bluff* (Charleston, SC: History Press, 2013), 37.
106. Louis R. Manarin, *Henrico County Field of Honor Vol. 2* (Richmond: Henrico County, 2004), 606.
107. Crenshaw, *Fort Harrison*, 45.
108. U.S. War Dept., *Official Records*, Series I, Volume 42, Serial 87, 794. No. 317, Report of Bvt. Maj. Gen. George Stannard Jr., April 18, 1865.
109. Richard J. Sommers, *Richmond Redeemed: The Siege of Petersburg* (Garden City, NY: Doubleday & Co., 1981), 43.
110. Sommers, *Richmond Redeemed*, 39.
111. U.S. War Dept., *Official Records*, Series I, Volume 42, Serial 87, 794. No. 317, Report of Bvt. Maj. Gen. George Stannard, Jr., April 18, 1865.
112. Morris, *The Connecticut War Record*, 363.
113. Crenshaw, *Fort Harrison*, 38.
114. U.S. War Dept., *Official Records*, Series I, Volume 42, Serial 87, 806. No. 317, Report of Bvt. Maj. Gen. George Stannard, Jr., April 18, 1865.
115. U.S. War Dept., *Official Records*, Series I, Volume 42, Serial 87, 794. No. 317, Report of Bvt. Maj. Gen. George Stannard, Jr., April 18, 1865.
116. Croffut and Morris, *Connecticut During the War*, 664.
117. U.S. War Dept., *Official Records*, Series I, Volume 42, Serial 87, 799. No. 317, Report of Bvt. Maj. Gen. George Stannard, Jr., April 18, 1865.
118. U.S. War Dept., *Official Records*, Series I, Volume 42, Serial 87, 799. No. 317, Report of Bvt. Maj. Gen. George Stannard, Jr., April 18, 1865.
119. Sommers, *Richmond Redeemed*, 45–47.
120. John L. Cunningham, *Three Years with the Adirondack Regiment, 118th New York Volunteer Infantry* (Norwood, NY: Plimpton Press, 1920), 148.
121. Croffut and Morris, *Connecticut During the War*, 665.
122. U.S. War Dept., *Official Records*, Series I, Volume 42, Serial 87, 799. No. 317, Report of Bvt. Maj. Gen. George Stannard, Jr., April 18, 1865.
123. Sommers, *Richmond Redeemed*, 45–47.
124. U.S. War Dept., *Official Records*, Series I, Volume 42, Serial 87, 799. No. 317, Report of Bvt. Maj. Gen. George Stannard, Jr., April 18, 1865.
125. U.S. War Dept., *Official Records*, Series I, Volume 42, Serial 87, 799. No. 317, Report of Bvt. Maj. Gen. George Stannard, Jr., April 18, 1865.
126. Coit to Family, Chaffins Farm, VA, October 4, 1864.
127. U.S. War Dept., *Official Records*, Series I, Volume 42, Serial 87, 801. No. 317, Report of Bvt. Maj. Gen. George Stannard, Jr., April 18, 1865.
128. Coit to Family, Chaffins Farm, VA, October 4, 1864.
129. Grant, *Personal Memoirs*, 2:333.
130. Croffut and Morris, *Connecticut During the War*, 669.
131. Croffut and Morris, *Connecticut During the War*, 670.
132. Members, *The Story of The Twenty-first Regiment Connecticut Volunteer Infantry During the Civil War 1861–1865* (Middletown, CT: Stewart Printing Company, 1900), 294.
133. Members, *Twenty-first Regiment Connecticut*, 294.
134. U.S. War Dept., *Official Records*, Series I, Volume 42, Serial 87, 801. No. 317, Report of Bvt. Maj. Gen. George Stannard, Jr., April 18, 1865.
135. Crenshaw, *Fort Harrison*, 98.
136. U.S. War Dept., *Official Records*, Series I, Volume 42, Serial 89, 165. Circular of Maj. Gen. Benjamin F. Butler, October 11, 1864.
137. Lynita King, "Nathan Hickok A Tribute to a Civil War Hero," Nov. 27, 2006, accessed May 29, 2021, https://www.genealogy.com/forum/surnames/topics/hickok/31/.
138. U.S. War Dept., *Official Records*, Volume

24, Serial 89, 165. Circular of Maj. Gen. Benjamin F. Butler, October 11, 1864.
139. Smith, *The Connecticut War Record*, 330.
140. Smith, *The Connecticut War Record*, 330.
141. Smith, et al., *Connecticut Men*, 327.
142. Croffut and Morris, *Connecticut During the War*, 681.
143. Coit to Family, Henrico, VA, October 17, 1864.
144. Smith, *The Connecticut War Record*, 330.
145. U.S. War Dept., *Official Records*, Series I, Volume 24, Serial 89, 467. Abstract of Returns, Maj. Gen. Benjamin F. Butler, October 31, 1864.
146. U.S. War Dept., *Official Records*, Series I, Volume 42, Serial 87, 107. Itinerary of Army of the James, August–December 1864.
147. Manarin, *Field of Honor* Vol. 2, 771.
148. Manarin, *Field of Honor* Vol. 2, 771.
149. Manarin, *Field of Honor* Vol. 2, 768.
150. Manarin, *Field of Honor* Vol. 2, 774.
151. Manarin, *Field of Honor* Vol. 2, 791.
152. Croffut and Morris, *Connecticut During the War*, 676.
153. Moses Smith to Coit Family, near Richmond, VA, October 28, 1864.
154. Coit to Family, Bermuda Hundred, VA, May 2, 1865.
155. Lynita King, "Nathan Hickok A Tribute to a Civil War Hero," Nov. 27, 2006, accessed May 29, 2021, https://www.genealogy.com/forum/surnames/topics/hickok/31/.
156. Smith, *The Connecticut War Record*, 346.
157. U.S. War Dept., *Official Records*, Series 1, Volume 42, Serial 87, 150. No. 7, Return of Casualties, Fair Oaks and Darbytown, VA, October 27–28, 1864.

Chapter 9

1. Moses Smith, in *The Connecticut War Record*, John M. Morris, ed. (New Haven: Peck, White & Peck, 1863–1865), 346.
2. Smith, *The Connecticut War Record*, 346.
3. W.A. Croffut and John M. Morris, *The Military and Civil History Connecticut During the War of 1861-65* (New York: Ledyard Bill, 1868), 684.
4. Shelby Foote, *The Civil War A Narrative: Red River to Appomattox* (New York: Vintage Books, 1974), 3:739.
5. "Benjamin Butler," *Wikipedia*, accessed May 29, 2022, https://en.wikipedia.org/wiki/Benjamin_Butler, and cited there: Shelby Foote, *The Civil War: A Narrative, Red River to Appomattox* (New York: Random House, 1974), 3:739–3:740, for the first sentence; and Richard S. West, *Lincoln's Scapegoat General: A Life of Benjamin F. Butler, 1818–1893* (Boston: Houghton Mifflin, 1965), 291, for the second sentence.
6. Ulysses S. Grant, *Personal Memoirs of Ulysses S. Grant* (New York: Charles L. Webster & Co.,1885), 2:607.
7. "XXIV Corps," *Wikipedia*, accessed May 29, 2021, https://en.wikipedia.org/wiki/XXIV_Corps_(Union_Army).
8. U.S. War Department, *The War of the Rebellion: A Compilation of the Official Records of the Union and Confederate Armies* (Washington, D.C.: U.S. Government Printing Office, 1880), Series I, Volume 46, Serial 96, 319. General Orders No. 18 of Maj. Gen. John Gibbon, January 31, 1865.
9. Stephen R. Smith, et al., eds., *Record of Service of Connecticut Men in the Army and Navy of the United States During the War of the Rebellion* (Hartford, CT: Case, Lockwood, and Brainard Co., 1889), 327.
10. Croffut and Morris, *Connecticut During the War*, 757.
11. Smith, *The Connecticut War Record*, 389.
12. Croffut and Morris, *Connecticut During the War*, 780.
13. Smith, et al., *Connecticut Men*, 327.
14. Croffut and Morris, *Connecticut During the War*, 764.
15. Smith, et al., *Connecticut Men*, 327.
16. Smith, et al., *Connecticut Men*, 327.
17. U.S. War Dept., *Official Records*, Series I, Volume 46, Serial 95, 578.
18. Smith, *The Connecticut War Record*, 505.
19. Croffut and Morris, *Connecticut During the War*, 792.
20. Smith, *The Connecticut War Record*, 505.
21. Croffut and Morris, *Connecticut During the War*, 792.
22. U.S. War Dept., *Official Records*, Series I, Volume 46, Serial 97, 986. General Orders No. 51 of Maj. Gen John Gibbon, April 27, 1865.
23. Smith, *The Connecticut War Record*, 505.
24. Charles Coit to All, near Richmond, VA, May 23, 1865. The Gilder Lehrman Collection, The Gilder Lehrman Institute of American History, New York, NY.
25. Smith, et al., *Connecticut Men*, 327 and Croffut and Morris, *Connecticut During the War*, 827.
26. Coit to All, James River, VA, May 27, 1865. General Devens's troops had been the first to occupy Richmond after its fall in April 1865. Hugh Chisholm, ed. "Devens, Charles," *Encyclopaedia Britannica 11th ed.* (Boston: Cambridge University Press, 1911), 120.
27. U.S. War Dept., *Official Records*, Series I, Volume 46, Serial 97, 1314. General Orders No. 386 of Maj. Gen. A. H. Terry, July 10, 1865.
28. Smith, *The Connecticut War Record*, 515.
29. Smith, et al., *Connecticut Men*, 327.
30. Croffut and Morris, *Connecticut During the War*, 827.

Conclusion

1. *Meriden (CT) Daily Republican*, October 5, 1870, 2.
2. *The Meriden (CT) Daily Journal*, September 17, 1896, 1.

3. *The Meriden (CT) Daily Journal*, September 17, 1896, 1.
4. *Hartford (CT) Courant*, September 15, 1929, 44.
5. Joseph R. Hawley, *History of Battle Flag Day* (Hartford, CT: Lockwood & Merritt, 1880), 9.
6. Hawley, *Battle Flag Day*, 11.
7. Hawley, *Battle Flag Day*, 32.
8. Hawley, *Battle Flag Day*, 34
9. Hawley, *Battle Flag Day*, 244. In a story the following day, the *Hartford Courant* called the event a huge triumph. "[T]he walks were thronged with lookers on, and with the strains of music and the blending of colors added to the moving scene, it photographed itself on the memory, never to be obliterated." *Hartford Courant*, Sept. 18, 1879.
10. Hawley, *Battle Flag Day*, 40.
11. Hawley, *Battle Flag Day*, 65.
12. Hawley, *Battle Flag Day*, 118.
13. Walter J. Yates, *Souvenir of Excursion to Antietam* (New London, CT: Unknown, 1894), 5. In today's dollars, that $1,000 allotment would represent more than $30,000.
14. Yates, *Souvenir of Excursion to Antietam*, 6.
15. Yates, *Souvenir of Excursion to Antietam*, 7.
16. Yates, *Souvenir of Excursion to Antietam*, 9.
17. Yates, *Souvenir of Excursion to Antietam*, 20.
18. Yates, *Souvenir of Excursion to Antietam*, 30.
19. "8th Connecticut Volunteer Infantry Regiment," *Antietam Stone Sentinels*, accessed December 7, 2021, https://antietam.stonesentinels.com/monuments/connecticut/8th-connecticut/.
20. "Antietam Campaign War Department Markers," *Historical Marker Database*, accessed December 7, 2021, https://www.hmdb.org/results.asp?Search=Series&SeriesID=28.
21. Stephen Recker, "Antietam Monuments in Connecticut Park," *Virtual Antietam Blog*, accessed December 7, 2021, http://www.virtualantietam.com/blog/20141818/antietam-monuments-connecticut-park.
22. "Ninth Army Corps, Harland's Brigade, Rodman's Division," *Historical Marker Database*, accessed December 7, 2021, https://www.hmdb.org/m.asp?m=6701.

Appendix A

1. Stephen R. Smith, et al., eds., *Record of Service of Connecticut Men in the Army and Navy of the United States During the War of the Rebellion* (Hartford, CT: Case, Lockwood, and Brainard Co., 1889), 327.
2. Frederick H. Dyer, *A Compendium of the War of the Rebellion* (Des Moines: The Dyer Publishing Co., 1908), 168.
3. U.S. War Dept., *The War of the Rebellion: A Compilation of the Official Records of the Union and Confederate Armies* (Washington, D.C.: U.S. Government Printing Office, 1880), n.p. The specific volume, serial, and page citing is identified in the heading of each entry.

Appendix B

1. "LTC Hiram Appelman," *Find a Grave*, accessed 27 May 2021, https://www.findagrave.com/memorial/58768905/hiram-appelman.
2. "Connecticut Births and Christenings, 1649–1906," *FamilySearch*, accessed June 11, 2020, https://familysearch.org/ark:/61903/1:1:F74B-RJF. References Hiram Appelman, 1825.
3. "Appelman," *Find a Grave*, https://www.findagrave.com/memorial/58768905/hiram-appelman.
4. Stephen R. Smith, et al., *Record of Service of Connecticut Men in the Army and Navy of the United States During the War of the Rebellion* (Hartford, CT: Case, Lockwood, and Brainard Co., 1889), 25.
5. Smith et al., *Connecticut Men*, 329.
6. "Appelman," *Find a Grave*, https://www.findagrave.com/memorial/58768905/hiram-appelman.
7. "Appelman," *Find a Grave*, https://www.findagrave.com/memorial/58768905/hiram-appelman.
8. "United States Civil War and Later Pension Index, 1861–1917," *FamilySearch*, https://familysearch.org/ark:/61903/1:1:N4V9-W6D. References Hiram Appelman, 1863.
9. "Connecticut Marriages, 1630–1997," *FamilySearch*, accessed June 11, 2020, https://familysearch.org/ark:/61903/1:1:F7P2-JZT. References Hiram Appelman, 1866.
10. "Connecticut, Deaths, 1640–1955," *FamilySearch*, accessed June 11, 2020, https://www.familysearch.org/ark:/61903/1:1:F774-VL2. References Hiram Appelman in entry for Amelia C. Appelman, 1867.
11. "Connecticut, Deaths, 1640–1955," *FamilySearch*, accessed June 11, 2020, https://www.familysearch.org/ark:/61903/1:1:F774-LQS. References Hiram Appelman in entry for Hiram H. Appelman, 1869.
12. "Appelman," *Find a Grave*, https://www.findagrave.com/memorial/58768905/hiram-appelman.
13. "United States, Burial Registers for Military Posts, Camps, and Stations, 1768–1921," *FamilySearch*, accessed March 16, 2018, https://familysearch.org/ark:/61903/1:1:QVYT-8MC3. References Hiram Appelman, citing Death, Fort Griswold, Connecticut, United States, Volume One, p. 186, line 12, Burial Registers for Military Posts, Camps, and Stations, 1768–1921, NARA microfilm publication M2014 (Washington, D.C.: National Archives and Records Administration, n.d.), roll 1; FHL microfilm 2,155,570.
14. "Appelman," *Find a Grave*, https://www.findagrave.com/memorial/58768905/hiram-appelman.
15. Edward Thompson, descendent, to Kim Perlotto, Feb. 16, 2021. Private correspondence.
16. "Albion D. Brooks," *Find a Grave*, accessed May 27, 2021, https://www.findagrave.com/memorial/107981255/albion-d.-brooks.

17. Albion Brooks to Family, East Bridgeport, CT, August 14, 1859. Special Collections Library, Pennsylvania State University, University Park, PA.

18. Private correspondence, Ed Thompson, descendent, Feb. 16, 2021.

19. Smith et al., *Connecticut Men*, 331.

20. Moses Smith to Brooks Family, Cold Harbor, VA, June 4, 1864, Special Collections Library, Pennsylvania State University, University Park, PA.

21. Smith et al., *Connecticut Men*, 331.

22. Brooks to Family, Portsmouth, VA, November 1, 1863.

23. "Brooks," *Find a Grave*, https://www.findagrave.com/memorial/107981255/albion-d.-brooks.

24. Emily Brooks Kingman to Family Bridgeport, CT, June 11, 1864.

25. "Pvt. Oliver C. Case," *Find a Grave*, accessed May 27, 2021, https://www.findagrave.com/memorial/40098915/oliver-c.-case.

26. Smith et al., *Connecticut Men*, 335.

27. Smith et al., *Connecticut Men*, 335.

28. "Case," *Find a Grave*, https://www.findagrave.com/memorial/40098915/oliver-c.-case.

29. "Oliver Cromwell Case," *Find a Grave*, accessed May 27, 2021, https://www.findagrave.com/memorial/73007848/oliver-cromwell-case.

30. "Charles Morgan Coit Papers," Yale University Archives, Yale University, New Haven, CT, accessed May 29, 2021, https://archives.yale.edu/repositories/12/resources/3378.

31. Smith et al., *Connecticut Men*, 333.

32. "Charles M. Coit Collection," Gilder-Lehrman Collection, Gilder-Lehrman Institute of American History, New York, NY, accessed May 27, 2021, https://www.gilderlehrman.org/collection/glc03603.

33. "Charles Morgan Coit," *Find a Grave*, accessed May 27, 2021, https://www.findagrave.com/memorial/98249275/charles-morgan-coit.

34. "Capt. Roger M Ford," *Find a Grave*, accessed May 27, 2021, https://www.findagrave.com/memorial/13256378/roger-m-ford.

35. "United States Census, 1850," *FamilySearch*, accessed December 19, 2020, https://www.familysearch.org/ark:/61903/1:1:M68P. References Roger M. Ford in household of Roger W. Ford, North Haven, New Haven, Connecticut, United States; citing family NARA microfilm publication (Washington, D.C.: National Archives and Records Administration, n.d.).

36. "United States Registers of Enlistments in the U.S. Army, 1798–1914," *FamilySearch*, accessed December 27, 2020, https://www.familysearch.org/ark:/61903/1:1:QJD5-TB2T. References Roger M. Ford, 3 May 1855; citing p. 70, volume 51, New Haven, United States, NARA microfilm publication M233 (Washington, D.C.: National Archives and Records Administration, n.d.), roll 25; FHL microfilm 350, 331.

37. "United States Census, 1870," *FamilySearch*, accessed January 2, 2020, https://www.familysearch.org/ark:/61903/1:1:MN7V-7SL. References Roger M. Ford, 1870.

38. Smith et al., *Connecticut Men*, 13.

39. Smith et al., *Connecticut Men*, 342.

40. "United States Census, 1870," *FamilySearch*, accessed January 2, 2021, https://www.familysearch.org/ark:/61903/1:1:MN7V-7SL. References Roger M. Ford, 1870.

41. "United States Census, 1900," *FamilySearch*, accessed February 5, 2021, https://www.familysearch.org/ark:/61903/1:1:M973-87J. References Roger M. Ford, United States; citing enumeration district (ED) 319, sheet 8B, family 181, NARA microfilm publication T623 (Washington, D.C.: National Archives and Records Administration, 1972.); FHL microfilm 1, 240, 143.

42. "Capt. Roger M Ford," *Find a Grave*, accessed May 27, 2021, https://www.findagrave.com/memorial/13256378/roger-m-ford.

43. Barry J. Fox, descendent, to Kim Perlotto, March 16, 2001. Private correspondence. Barry donated a copy of Lucius's diary to us.

44. Smith et al., *Connecticut Men*, 354.

45. "Lucius W. Fox," Gunn Memorial Museum, Washington, CT, accessed May 29, 2021, http://washingtoncivilwarsoldiers.weebly.com/lucius-w-fox.html.

46. Barry J. Fox, descendent, to Kim Perlotto, March 16, 2001. Private correspondence.

47. "United States Census, 1880," FamilySearch, accessed February 19, 2021, https://familysearch.org/ark:/61903/1:1:MFCL-3MS. References Lucius W. Fox, Harwinton, Litchfield, Connecticut, United States; citing enumeration district ED 23, sheet 395D, NARA microfilm publication T9 (Washington, D.C.: National Archives and Records Administration, n.d.), FHL microfilm 1, 254, 101.

48. "United States Census, 1900," FamilySearch, accessed February 22, 2021, https://www.familysearch.org/ark:/61903/1:1:M9QT. References Lucius Fox, Harwinton, Litchfield, Connecticut, United States; citing enumeration district (ED) 237, sheet 7B, family 178, NARA microfilm publication T623 (Washington, D.C.: National Archives and Records Administration, 1972.); FHL microfilm 1, 240, 140.

49. Barry J. Fox, descendent, to Kim Perlotto, March 16, 2001. Private correspondence.

50. "Lucius W. Fox," Gunn Memorial Museum, Washington, CT, accessed May 29, 2021, http://washingtoncivilwarsoldiers.weebly.com/lucius-w-fox.html.

51. Barry J. Fox, descendent, to Kim Perlotto, March 16, 2001. Private correspondence.

52. "United States Census, 1920," *FamilySearch*, accessed February 1, 2021, https://www.familysearch.org/ark:/61903/1:1:MCND-3MN. References Lucius Fox, 1920.

53. "Lucius Fox," *Find a Grave*, accessed May 27, 2021, www.findagrave.com/memorial/58457545/lucius-fox.

54. "Capt. Henry C Hall," *Find a Grave*, accessed May 27, 2021, https://www.findagrave.com/memorial/46486545/henry-c-hall.
55. Smith et al., *Connecticut Men*, 344.
56. Smith et al., *Connecticut Men*, 344.
57. "Hall," *Find a Grave*, https://www.findagrave.com/memorial/46486545/henry-c-hall.
58. "Edward Harland," *Find a Grave*, accessed May 27, 2021, https://www.findagrave.com/memorial/5840312/edward-harland.
59. John D. Hoptak, "Brigadier General Edward Harland," *48th Pennsylvania Volunteer Infantry Blog*, accessed May 29, 2021, https://48thpennsylvania.blogspot.com/2009/.
60. No Author, *The Union Army; A History of Military Affairs in the Loyal States, 1861–65, Volume 8* (Madison, WI: Federal Publishing Company, 1908), 118.
61. J.P. Rogers, "Edward Harland," *Oliver Cromwell Case Blog*, accessed May 29, 2021, https://olivercromwellcase.wordpress.com/2020/02/01/edward-harland-a-man-of-great-executive-ability-and-boundless-energy-2/.
62. J.P. Rogers, "Edward Harland," *Oliver Cromwell Case Blog*, accessed May 29, 2021, https://olivercromwellcase.wordpress.com/2020/02/01/edward-harland-a-man-of-great-executive-ability-and-boundless-energy-2/.
63. J.P. Rogers, "Edward Harland," *Oliver Cromwell Case Blog*, accessed May 29, 2021, https://olivercromwellcase.wordpress.com/2020/02/01/edward-harland-a-man-of-great-executive-ability-and-boundless-energy-2/. Regarding Harland's appointment as lieutenant colonel, see *Hartford Daily Courant*, September 3, 1861; regarding Harland as colonel of the 8th Connecticut Volunteer Infantry Regiment, see *Norwich Morning Bulletin*, October 19, 1915; regarding the sword, see an article written by an unnamed private in the Third Connecticut recounting the Battle of Bull Run, *New London Daily Chronicle*, Tuesday, August 13, 1861; and regarding the field glass, see *Hartford Daily Courant*, September 5, 1861; W.C. Morris, *The Military and Civil History of Connecticut: The War of 1861–1865* (New York: Ledyard Bill, 1869); *Columbian Register*, October 5, 1861, New Haven, CT.
64. Smith et al., *Connecticut Men*, 329.
65. John D. Hoptak, "Brigadier General Edward Harland," *48th Pennsylvania Volunteer Infantry Blog*, accessed May 29, 2021, https://48thpennsylvania.blogspot.com/2009/; and "Edward Harland," *Wikipedia*, accessed May 29, 2021, https://en.wikipedia.org/wiki/Edward_Harland_(general)
66. No Author, *The Union Army; A History of Military Affairs in The Loyal States, 1861–65, Volume 8* (Madison, WI: Federal Publishing Company, 1908), 118.
67. No Author, *Journal of the Forty-ninth National Encampment Grand Army of the Republic, Washington, DC, Sept 27–Oct. 2, 1915* (Washington, D.C.: U.S. Government Printing Office, 1916), 308.
68. *Norwich (CT) Bulletin*, September 15, 1914, 5.
69. *Norwich (CT) Bulletin*, September 18, 1909, 5.
70. *Norwich (CT) Bulletin*, September 19, 1911, 5.
71. J.P. Rogers, "Edward Harland," *Oliver Cromwell Case Blog*, accessed May 29, 2021, https://olivercromwellcase.wordpress.com/2020/02/01/edward-harland-a-man-of-great-executive-ability-and-boundless-energy-2/. Regarding the W.W. Backus Hospital, see W.R. Cutter, *New England Families, Genealogical and Memorial: Volume 3* (New York: Lewis Historical Publishing, 1913).
72. John D. Hoptak, "Brigadier General Edward Harland," *48th Pennsylvania Volunteer Infantry Blog*, accessed May 29, 2021, https://48thpennsylvania.blogspot.com/2009/.
73. "Harland," *Find a Grave*, https://www.findagrave.com/memorial/5840312/edward-harland.
74. "Maj. Henry Morris Hoyt," *Find a Grave*, accessed January 11, 2021, https://www.findagrave.com/memorial/112575011/henry-morris-hoyt.
75. "United States Census, 1860," *FamilySearch*, accessed February 18, 2021, https://familysearch.org/ark:/61903/1:1:MH5T-5KY. References Henry M. Hoyt in entry for Caroline Wood, 1860.
76. Smith et al., *Connecticut Men*, 16.
77. 77 Smith et al., *Connecticut Men*, 330.
78. D. Hamilton Hurd, ed., *History of Fairfield County, Connecticut, with Illustrations and Biographical Sketches of the Prominent Men and Pioneers* (Philadelphia: J.W. Lewis & Co., 1881), 102.
79. "Hoyt," *Find a Grave*, https://www.findagrave.com/memorial/112575011/henry-morris-hoyt.
80. "Nathan E. Hickok," *Find a Grave*, accessed May 27, 2021, https://ww.findagrave.com/memorial/7834669/nathan-e.-hickok.
81. Smith et al., *Connecticut Men*, 331.
82. David Levine, *News-Times*, Danbury, CT, Nov. 11, 2009, accessed May 29, 2021, https://www.newstimes.com/news/article/A-tribute-to-a-Civil-War-hero-245824.php.
83. "Comprehensive Guide to Victoria & George Cross," accessed May 29, 2021, http://www.vconline.org.uk/nathan-e-hickok/4593320934.
84. David Levine, *News-Times*, Danbury, CT, Nov. 11, 2009, accessed May 29, 2021, https://www.newstimes.com/news/article/A-tribute-to-a-Civil-War-hero-245824.php.
85. "Hickok," *Find a Grave*, https://www.findagrave.com/memorial/7834669/nathan-e.-hickok.
86. David Levine, *News-Times*, Danbury, CT, Sep. 14, 2009, accessed May 29, 2021, https://www.newstimes.com/news/article/A-tribute-to-a-Civil-War-hero-51268.php.
87. Michael Herrick, *Historical Marker Database*, accessed May 29, 2021, https://www.hmdb.org/PhotoFullSize.asp?PhotoID=81008.
88. "Sgt. Fitz Greene Hollister," *Find a Grave*,

accessed May 27, 2021, https://www.findagrave.com/memorial/51034961/fitz-greene-hollister.

89. "United States Census, 1850," *FamilySearch*, accessed December 19, 2020, https://www.familysearch.org/ark:/61903/1:1:M682-DQ7. References Fitz G. Hollister in household of Preston N. Hollister, Washington, Litchfield, Connecticut, United States; citing family, NARA microfilm publication (Washington, D.C.: National Archives and Records Administration, n.d.).

90. Smith et al., *Connecticut Men*, 353.

91. "Fitz Greene Hollister," Gunn Memorial Museum, Washington, CT, accessed May 29, 2021, http://washingtoncivilwarsoldiers.weebly.com/fitz-greene-hollister.html.

92. "Hollister," *Find a Grave*, https://www.findagrave.com/memorial/51034961/fitz-greene-hollister.

93. "Connecticut, Vital Records, Prior to 1850," *FamilySearch*, accessed September 21, 2019, https://familysearch.org/ark:/61903/1:1:QP79-8XYK. References William L. Huntington, citing Birth, compiled by Lucius A. and Lucius B. Barbour, housed at State Library, Hartford, Connecticut; FHL microfilm 008272236.

94. "William Lyman Huntington," *Find a Grave*, accessed May 27, 2021, https://www.findagrave.com/memorial/45401797/william-lyman-huntington.

95. "Massachusetts Marriages, 1841–1915," FamilySearch, accessed January 16, 2021, https://www.familysearch.org/ark:/61903/1:1:N4ZR-SM9. References William L. Huntington and Eunice C. Perry, 18 May 1859; citing Worcester, Massachusetts, United States, State Archives, Boston; FHL microfilm 1, 433, 017.

96. Smith et al., *Connecticut Men*, 339.

97. William Huntington to sister Ellen, Lebanon, CT, February 25, 1867. Houghton Library, Harvard University, Cambridge, MA.

98. Huntington to sister Ellen, Loreto, California [Mexico], June 8, 1867.

99. Huntington to sister Ellen, Marysville, CA, October 24, 1868.

100. Huntington to sister Ellen, Marysville, CA, December 12, 1868.

101. Huntington to sister Ellen, Mammoth Mill, CA, May 24, 1869.

102. Huntington to brother Hart, San Francisco, CA, November 14, 1869.

103. "United States Census, 1880," FamilySearch, accessed November 12, 2020, https://www.familysearch.org/ark:/61903/1:1:MFZ9-RNG. References William L. Huntington, New London, Connecticut, United States; citing enumeration district ED 114, sheet 618B, NARA microfilm publication T9 (Washington, D.C.: National Archives and Records Administration, n.d.), FHL microfilm 1, 254, 108.

104. "Huntington," *Find a Grave*, https://www.findagrave.com/memorial/45401797/william-lyman-huntington.

105. William Henry Johnson, *Autobiography of Dr. William Henry Johnson* (Albany: The Argus Company Printers, 1900), 17.

106. Julie O'Connor, "John G. Stewart—Albany's First Black Newspaper Publisher," accessed January 23, 2021 https://friendsofalbanyhistory.wordpress.com/.

107. "Stewart Johnson," *Find a Grave*, accessed May 27, 2021, https://www.findagrave.com/memorial/194543121/stewart-johnson.

108. "United States Census, 1900," database with images, FamilySearch, accessed March 6, 2021, https://familysearch.org/ark:/61903/1:1:MS6M-F24. References William H. Johnson, Albany city Ward 12, Albany, New York, United States; citing enumeration district (ED) 45, sheet 5B, family 118, NARA microfilm publication T623 (Washington, D.C.: National Archives and Records Administration, 1972); FHL microfilm 1, 241, 005.

109. "William H Johnson," *Find a Grave*, accessed May 27, 2021, https://www.findagrave.com/memorial/129448737/william-h-johnson.

110. Johnson, *Autobiography*, 17.

111. Edwin S. Redkey, *A Grand Army of Black Men Letters from African-American Soldiers in the Union Army 1861–1865* (New York: Cambridge University Press, 1992), 10.

112. Johnson, *Autobiography*, 17.

113. Redkey, *Grand Army of Black Men*, 10–22.

114. Redkey, *Grand Army of Black Men*, 20.

115. Johnson, *Autobiography*, 17.

116. Johnson, *Autobiography*, 17.

117. "United States Census, 1870," *FamilySearch*, accessed January 3, 2021, https://www.familysearch.org/ark:/61903/1:1:M8JN-S74. References Wm. H. Johnson, 1870.

118. Johnson, *Autobiography*, 17.

119. Johnson, *Autobiography*, 17.

120. Johnson, *Autobiography*, 253.

121. "United States Census, 1900," *FamilySearch*, accessed March 6, 2021, https://familysearch.org/ark:/61903/1:1:MS6M-F24. References William H Johnson, Albany city Ward 12, Albany, New York, United States; citing enumeration district (ED) 45, sheet 5B, family 118, NARA microfilm publication T623 (Washington, D.C.: National Archives and Records Administration, 1972.); FHL microfilm 1, 241, 005.

122. "United States Census, 1910," *FamilySearch*, accessed March 6, 2021, https://familysearch.org/ark:/61903/1:1:M54D-PVF. References William H. Johnson in household of John W. Caldwell, Albany Ward 13, Albany, New York, United States; citing enumeration district (ED) ED 62, sheet 6A, family 89, NARA microfilm publication T624 (Washington D.C.: National Archives and Records Administration, 1982), roll 921; FHL microfilm 1, 374, 934.

123. "Sarah Ann Johnson," *Find a Grave*, accessed May 27, 2021, https://www.findagrave.com/memorial/220985776/sarah-ann-johnson.

124. "Johnson," *Find a Grave*, www.findagrave.com/memorial/129448737/william-h-johnson.

125. "United States Census, 1850," *FamilySearch*,

accessed December 19, 2020, https://www.familysearch.org/ark:/61903/1:1:M682-SCQ. References Wolcott P. Marsh in household of Edward Marsh, New Hartford, Litchfield, Connecticut, United States; citing family, NARA microfilm publication (Washington, D.C.: National Archives and Records Administration, n.d.).

126. "Wolcott P. Marsh Family Papers," Clements Library, University of Michigan, accessed May 29, 2021, https://quod.lib.umich.edu/c/clementsead/umich-wcl-M-2662a.3mar?view=text.

127. Sandra Marsh Mercer and Jerry Mercer, eds., *Letters to a Civil War Bride* (Westminster, MD: Heritage Books, Inc., 2006), 3.

128. Smith et al., *Connecticut Men*, 4.

129. Smith et al., *Connecticut Men*, 330.

130. Sandra Mercer and Jerry Mercer, eds., *Letters to a Civil War Bride: Captain Wolcott P. Marsh* (Westminster, MD: Heritage Books, 2006), 525.

131. "United States Census, 1870," *FamilySearch*, accessed January 2, 2021, https://www.familysearch.org/ark:/61903/1:1:MD3W-GWT. References Wolcott Marsh, 1870.

132. Mercer and Mercer, eds., *Letters to a Civil War Bride*, 526.

133. Mercer and Mercer, eds., *Letters to a Civil War Bride*, 526.

134. "California Deaths and Burials, 1776–2000," *FamilySearch*, accessed February 4, 2020, https://familysearch.org/ark:/61903/1:1:HGH9-L7ZM. References Woolcott P. Marsh, 1894.

135. "W P Marsh," *Find a Grave*, accessed May 27, 2021, https://www.findagrave.com/memorial/20881358/w-p-marsh.

136. "United States General Index to Pension Files, 1861–1934," *FamilySearch*, accessed November 24, 2020, https://www.familysearch.org/ark:/61903/1:1:KDBD-CK5. References Wolcott P. Marsh, 1893.

137. Mercer and Mercer, eds., *Letters to a Civil War Bride*, 526.

138. "Connecticut Births and Christenings, 1649–1906," *FamilySearch*, accessed January 7, 2020, https://familysearch.org/ark:/61903/1:1:F74Q-39N. References Samuel Jay Nettleton, 1832.

139. "United States Census, 1860," *FamilySearch*. Accessed November 10, 2020, https://www.familysearch.org/ark:/61903/1:1:MH51-WNT. References Samuel J. Nettleton in entry for Sarah Nettleton, 1860, and "Samuel Jay Nettleton," *Find a Grave*, accessed May 27, 2021, https://www.findagrave.com/memorial/170013185/samuel-jay-nettleton.

140. Smith et al., *Connecticut Men*, 353.

141. "Samuel Jay Nettleton," Gunn Memorial Museum, Washington, CT, accessed May 29, 2021, http://washingtoncivilwarsoldiers.weebly.com/samuel-jay-nettleton.html.

142. "United States Census, 1880," *FamilySearch*, accessed November 12, 2020, https://www.familysearch.org/ark:/61903/1:1:MFCL-M91. References Samuel J. Nettleton, Litchfield, Connecticut, United States; citing enumeration district ED 19, sheet 339B, NARA microfilm publication T9 (Washington, D.C.: National Archives and Records Administration, n.d.), FHL microfilm 1,254,101.

143. "Samuel Jay Nettleton," Gunn Memorial Museum, Washington, CT, accessed May 29, 2021, http://washingtoncivilwarsoldiers.weebly.com/samuel-jay-nettleton.html.

144. "United States Census, 1910," database with images, FamilySearch, accessed February 9, 2021, https://familysearch.org/ark:/61903/1:1:MK2H-J1N. References Samuel J Nettleton, Washington, Litchfield, Connecticut, United States; citing enumeration district (ED) ED 282, sheet 7A, family 166, NARA microfilm publication T624 (Washington D.C.: National Archives and Records Administration, 1982), roll 135; FHL microfilm 1, 374, 148.

145. "Nettleton," *Find a Grave*, www.findagrave.com/memorial/170013185/samuel-jay-nettleton.

146. "United States General Index to Pension Files, 1861–1934," *FamilySearch*, accessed November 24, 2020, https://www.familysearch.org/ark:/61903/1:1:QJDG-N7JJ. References Samuel J. Nettleton, 1890.

147. "United States Census, 1850," *FamilySearch*, accessed December 19, 2020, https://www.familysearch.org/ark:/61903/1:1:M682-675. References Seth F Plumb in household of Frederick W. Plumb, Litchfield, Litchfield, Connecticut, United States; citing family, NARA microfilm publication (Washington, D.C.: National Archives and Records Administration, n.d.).

148. Plumb family oral history.

149. "United States Census, 1860," *FamilySearch*, accessed November 10, 2020, https://www.familysearch.org/ark:/61903/1:1:MH5Y-TCK. References Seth Plumb in entry for John S. Plumb, 1860.

150. Smith et al., *Connecticut Men*, 346.

151. "Seth F. Plumb," *Find a Grave*, accessed May 27, 2021, https://www.findagrave.com/memorial/127928584/seth-f.-plumb.

152. "GAR Post No. 80 Records," Helga J. Ingraham Memorial Library, Litchfield Historical Society, Litchfield, CT.

153. Smith et al., *Connecticut Men*, 331.

154. "United States City and Business Directories, ca. 1749–ca. 1990," *FamilySearch*, accessed April 29, 2021, https://www.familysearch.org/ark:/61903/1:1:6Z83-CKZW. References Joseph E. Shadek, 1856–1858.

"United States City and Business Directories, ca. 1749–ca. 1990," *FamilySearch*, accessed April 13, 2021, https://www.familysearch.org/ark:/61903/1:1:6ZMT-PVQX. References Joseph E. Shadek, 1869–1872.

"United States City and Business Directories, ca. 1749–ca. 1990," *FamilySearch*, accessed March 8, 2021, https://www.familysearch.org/ark:/61903/1:1:6CBL-YHW9. References Joseph E. Shadek, 1873–1875.

"New York, County Naturalization Records, 1791–1980," *FamilySearch*, accessed March 2,

2021, https://familysearch.org/ark:/61903/1:1:-QP48-7F76. References Joseph E Shadek, 1864; citing Naturalization, New York, United States, citing multiple County Clerk offices of New York; FHL microfilm 005394930.

155. Mercer and Mercer, eds., *Letters to a Civil War Bride*, 278, 282.

156. Mercer and Mercer, eds., *Letters to a Civil War Bride*, 333, 334.

157. *Frank Leslie's Illustrated Newspaper*, May 24, 1862.

158. Smith et al., *Connecticut Men*, 331.

159. Smith et al., *Connecticut Men*, 344.

160. "United States Veterans Administration Pension Payment Cards, 1907–1933," *FamilySearch*, accessed February 19, 2021, https://familysearch.org/ark:/61903/1:1:QJDQ-C7CB. References Joseph E. Shadek, 1907–1933; citing NARA microfilm publication M850 (Washington, D.C.: National Archives and Records Administration, n.d.); FHL microfilm 1, 636, 014.

161. "United States Census, 1850," *FamilySearch*, accessed December 19, 2020, https://www.familysearch.org/ark:/61903/1:1:M682-2R2. References Martin B. Smith in household of Silas Frost, Plymouth, Litchfield, Connecticut, United States; citing family, NARA microfilm publication (Washington, D.C.: National Archives and Records Administration, n.d.).

162. "United States Census, 1860," *Family Search*, accessed February 18, 2021, https://familysearch.org/ark:/61903/1:1:MHRH-NTQ. References Martin B. Smith, 1860.

163. Smith et al., *Connecticut Men*, 329.

164. "Ohio, County Death Records, 1840–2001," *FamilySearch*, accessed December 14, 2020, https://www.familysearch.org/ark:/61903/1:1:-F6KR-5PV. References Martin B. Smith, 25 Oct. 1899; citing Death, Townsend Township, Huron, Ohio, United States, source ID v 2 p. 188, County courthouses, Ohio; FHL microfilm 410, 483.

165. "Connecticut, Charles R. Hale Collection, Vital Records, 1640–1955," *FamilySearch*, accessed September 16, 2020, https://www.familysearch.org/ark:/61903/1:1:F7VJ-F3N. References Polly C. Smith, 1879.

166. "Ohio, County Death Records, 1840–2001," *FamilySearch*, accessed December 14, 2020, https://www.familysearch.org/ark:/61903/1:1:-F6KR-5PV. References Martin B. Smith, 25 Oct. 1899; citing Death, Townsend Township, Huron, Ohio, United States, source ID v 2 p 188, County courthouses, Ohio; FHL microfilm 410, 483.

167. "Bright's Disease," *Wikipedia*, accessed May 29, 2021, https://en.wikipedia.org/wiki/Bright%27s_disease.

168. "LTC Martin B Smith," *Find a Grave*, accessed May 27, 2021, https://www.findagrave.com/memorial/29181343/martin-b-smith.

169. Smith et al., *Connecticut Men*, 41.

170. Smith et al., *Connecticut Men*, 329.

171. "United States Census, 1870," *FamilySearch*, accessed January 2, 2021, https://www.familysearch.org/ark:/61903/1:1:MN7L-X6B. References John E Ward in entry for J Woodmansee, 1870.

172. "United States Civil War and Later Pension Index, 1861–1917," *FamilySearch*, accessed March 24, 2016, https://familysearch.org/ark:/61903/1:1:-N4V9-FMF. References John E. Ward, 1883.

173. "Col. John E Ward," *Find a Grave*, accessed May 27, 2021, https://www.findagrave.com/memorial/132678194/john-e-ward.

174. "Connecticut Births and Christenings, 1649–1906," *FamilySearch*, accessed January 7, 2020, familysearch.org/ark:/61903/1:1:F74Z-ZHY. References Marvin Wait, 1843.

175. "United States Census, 1860," *FamilySearch*, accessed February 18, 2021, https://familysearch.org/ark:/61903/1:1:MHRW-55M. References Marvin Wait in entry for John T. Wait, 1860.

176. Smith et al., *Connecticut Men*, 330.

177. Smith et al., *Connecticut Men*, 327.

178. "Lieut. Marvin Wait," *Find a Grave*, accessed May 27, 2021, https://www.findagrave.com/memorial/80232736/marvin-wait.

Appendix C

1. Geraldine S. Caughman, *Qui Transtulit Sustinet: Connecticut Battle Flag Collection Vol. I* (Wethersfield, CT: Caughman Associates, 2006), xi.

2. "Visual Flag Survey" (Hartford, CT: Connecticut State Capitol, December 26, 1990), accession #1990-000-081-A.

3. "Visual Flag Survey" (Hartford, CT: Connecticut State Capitol, December 26, 1990), accession #1990-000-081-A.

4. Caughman, *Qui Transtulit Sustinet Vol. I*, 57.

5. "Visual Flag Survey," (Hartford, CT: Connecticut State Capitol, December 17, 1990), accession #1990-000-080-A.

6. Caughman, *Qui Transtulit Sustinet Vol. I*, 58.

7. Caughman, *Qui Transtulit Sustinet Vol. I*, 59.

8. Caughman, *Qui Transtulit Sustinet Vol. I*, 60.

9. "Visual Flag Survey" (Hartford, CT: Connecticut State Capitol, January 1991), accession #1990-000-082-A.

10. "Visual Flag Survey" (Hartford, CT: Connecticut State Capitol, January 1991), accession #1990-000-083-A.

11. Caughman, *Qui Transtulit Sustinet Vol. I*, 37.

12. Wolcott P. Marsh to Wife, near Fredericksburg, November 27, 1862, in Sandra Marsh Mercer and Jerry Mercer, eds., *Letters to a Civil War Bride* (Westminster, MD: Heritage Books, 2006), 494.

13. Allen Dauchy to cousin MaryLib, Suffolk, VA, May 28, 1863, Lewis Leigh Collection, U.S. Army Heritage and Education Center, Carlisle, PA.; and Caughman, *Qui Transtulit Sustinet Vol. I*, 59.

14. Charles M. Coit to All, Portsmouth, VA,

June 21, 1863, The Gilder Lehrman Collection, The Gilder Lehrman Institute of American History, New York, NY.

Appendix D

1. Editors of Time-Life Books, *Echoes of Glory, Arms and Equipment of the Union* (Alexandria, VA, 1991), 114, 121.
2. John L. Merriam to Friend, November 12, 1861, Lincoln Memorial Shrine. A.K. Smiley Library, Redlands, CA.
3. Seth F. Plumb to Friends, Beaufort, NC, April 23, 1862, Private Collection.
4. *Echoes of Glory*, 184.
5. "Slouch Hat," *Wikipedia*, accessed June 28, 2021, https://en.wikipedia.org/wiki/Slouch_hat.
6. Charles M. Coit to All, Falmouth, VA, December 8, 1862, The Gilder Lehrman Collection. The Gilder Lehrman Institute of American History, New York, NY.
7. Picture Group. The Andrew M. Morgan Collection (RG:081), Box 3, Connecticut State Library, Hartford, CT.
8. Joseph E. Shadek, Civil War Sketchbook (BHC-MSS 0063) Bridgeport History Center, Bridgeport, CT.
9. W.A. Croffut and J. M. Morris, *The Military and Civil History Connecticut During the War of 1861-1865* (New York: Ledyard Bill, 1868), 167.
10. Oliver C. Case to Sister, Newbern, NC, March 15,1862, Simsbury Historical Society, Simsbury, CT.
11. Warren K. Tice, *Uniform Buttons of the United States 1776-1865* (Gettysburg, PA: Thomas Publications, 1997), 255.
12. "Records of the Office of the Chief of Ordnance—Summary Statements of Ordnance and Ordnance Stores on Hand in Regular and Volunteer Army Organizations, 1862-1867, 1870-1876," National Archives and Records Administration, Washington, D.C. (Record Group 156, M1281).
13. Howard Michael Madaus, "The Percussion Martial Longarms of Eli Whitney, Jr.," *ARMAX* Volume II, Number I (1988): 7-8.
14. David James Naumec, "The Connecticut Contracted '61 Springfield: The Special Model to the 'Good and Serviceable' Arm," *American Society of Arms Collectors Bulletin* 90 (2004):10.
15. Naumec, "The Connecticut Contracted '61 Springfield," 10, and Madaus, "The Percussion Martial Longarms of Eli Whitney, Jr.," 24–31.
16. The Andrew M. Morgan Collection (RG:081), Box 2, Connecticut State Library, Hartford, CT.
17. "M1841 Mississippi Rifle," *Wikipedia*, accessed June 28, 2021, https://en.wikipedia.org/wiki/M1841_Mississippi_rifle.
18. Madaus, "The Percussion Martial Longarms of Eli Whitney, Jr.," 8–11.
19. Coit to Brother and Faithful Correspondent, Newport News VA, July 18, 1862.
20. Coit to unknown, location unknown, November 29, 1861.
21. Samuel Jay Nettleton to Friends at Home, Jamaica, L.I., NY, October 22, 1861, in *Life Through Letters: Samuel Jay's Story*, David DeMeo and Reece Holman, eds. (Washington, CT: Gunn Memorial Museum, 2012), n.p.
22. Records of the Office of the Chief of Ordnance—Summary Statements of Ordnance and Ordnance Stores (Record Group 156, M1281).
23. Madaus, "The Percussion Martial Longarms of Eli Whitney, Jr.," 31.
24. Naumec, "The Connecticut Contracted '61 Springfield," 10–11.
25. Records of the Office of the Chief of Ordnance—Summary Statements of Ordnance and Ordnance Stores (Record Group 156, M1281).
26. Earl J. Coates and John D. McAulay, *Civil War Sharps Carbines & Rifles* (Gettysburg, PA: Thomas Publications, 1996), 13.
27. Coit to All, Annapolis, MD, December 26, 1861.
28. "Invoice of Camp & Garrison Equipage for Company B," dated July 22, 1863, The Andrew M. Morgan Collection (RG:081), Box 2, Connecticut State Library, Hartford, CT.
29. Joseph E. Shadek Civil War Sketchbook (BHC-MSS 0063), Bridgeport History Center, Bridgeport, CT.
30. Case to Sister, Newbern, NC, May 8, 1862.
31. Coit to Home, near Newbern, NC, May 8, 1862.
32. Coit to Home, near New Berne, May 20, 1862.
33. Roger M. Ford, diary, September 8, 1862, New England Civil War Museum, Rockville, CT.
34. "Account Book of Company F, 8th Regiment Conn. Volunteers," The Andrew M. Morgan Collection (RG:081), Box 3, Connecticut State Library, Hartford, CT.

Appendix E

1. "Eighth Conn. Vols., Co. A, Inc.," accessed May 31, 2021, http://www.8cv.org.
2. "United States Volunteers," accessed May 31, 2021, http://www.usvolunteers.org.
3. "New England Brigade," accessed May 31, 2021, http://m1020.wixsite.com/newenglandbrigade.

Bibliography

Primary Sources

Brooks, Albion D., Papers (HCLA9616). Special Collections Library, Pennsylvania State University, University Park, PA.

Byrne, Andrew, Diary (MS45302). Manuscripts Collection, Connecticut Historical Society, Hartford, CT.

Case, Oliver C., Papers. Simsbury Historical Society, Simsbury, CT.

Coit, Charles M., Papers (GLC03603). The Gilder Lehrman Collection, The Gilder Lehrman Institute of American History, New York, NY.

Dauchy, Allen, Correspondence (Box 16, Folder 11, Book 34, Number 19). Lewis Leigh Collection, U.S. Army Heritage and Education Center, Carlisle, PA.

Eaton, Jacob, Papers (MS100799). Manuscripts Collection, Connecticut Historical Society, Hartford, CT.

Ferris, Hilliard B., Papers (973.78 F417). Classified Archives Collection, Connecticut State Library, Hartford, CT.

Ford, Roger M., Diary. New England Civil War Museum, Vernon, CT.

Fox, Lucius W., Diary. New England Civil War Museum, Vernon, CT.

Hall, Henry C., Papers (OCLC:19657410)(ID: 000857304). David M. Rubenstein Rare Book and Manuscript Library, Duke University, Durham, NC.

Hollister, Seth (from Fitz G.), Letters (OCLC: 19793265)(ID:000861198). David M. Rubenstein Rare Book and Manuscript Library, Duke University, Durham, NC.

Huntington, William L., Papers (HOLLIS: 990006025370203941). Houghton Library, Harvard University, Cambridge, MA.

Huntington, William L., Papers (MS74023). Manuscripts Collection, Connecticut Historical Society, Hartford, CT.

Marsh, Wolcott P., Papers (1991. M-2662a3). William L. Clements Library, University of Michigan, Ann Arbor, MI.

Marsh, Wolcott P., in *Letters to a Civil War Bride: Captain Wolcott P. Marsh*. Sandra Marsh Mercer and Jerry Mercer, eds. Westminster, MD: Heritage Books, 2006.

Merriam, John L., Papers. Lincoln Memorial Shrine, A.K. Smiley Public Library, Redlands, CA.

Nettleton, Samuel Jay, in *Life Through Letters: Samuel Jay's Story*. David DeMeo and Reece Holman, eds. Washington, CT: Gunn Memorial Museum, 2012.

Plumb, Seth F., Family Correspondence (1975-50-0). Helga J. Ingraham Memorial Library, Litchfield Historical Society, Litchfield, CT.

Plumb, Seth F., Letters. Private Collection.

Shadek Joseph E., Civil War Sketchbook (BHC-MSS 0063), Burroughs-Saden Library, Bridgeport History Center, Bridgeport, CT.

Stone, Alva, Letters (1899-02-0). Helga J. Ingraham Memorial Library, Litchfield Historical Society, Litchfield, CT.

Contemporary Sources

Brainerd, Wesley. "The Pontoniers at Fredericksburg" in *Battles and Leaders of the Civil War*, 4 vols., Clarence C. Buel and Robert U. Johnson, eds. New York: Century Co., 1884–1888.

Burnside, Ambrose E. *The Burnside Expedition*. Providence, RI: N. Bangs Williams & Company, 1882.

Butler, Benjamin Franklin. *Autobiography and Personal Reminiscences of Major-General Benj. F. Butler: Butler's Book*. Boston: A.M. Thayer & Co., 1892.

Carman, Ezra A. *The Maryland Campaign of September 1862: Volume 2, Antietam*. Thomas G. Clemens, ed. El Dorado Hills, CA: Savas Beatie LLC, 2012.

Croffut, W.A., and John M. Morris. *The Military and Civil History Connecticut During the War Of 1861-65*. New York: Ledyard Bill, 1868.

Cunningham, John L. *Three Years with The Adirondack Regiment, 118th New York Volunteer Infantry*. Norwood, NY: Plimpton Press, 1920.

Dyer, Frederick H. *A Compendium of the War of the Rebellion*. Des Moines: The Dyer Publishing Co., 1908.

Eaton, Jacob. *Memorial of Marvin Wait*, New Haven, CT: Thomas J. Stafford, Printer, 1863.

Grant, Ulysses S. *Personal Memoirs of Ulysses S. Grant, Volume II*. New York: Charles L. Webster & Company, 1886.

Hawley, Joseph R. *History of Battle Flag Day: September 17, 1879.* Hartford, CT: Lockwood & Merritt, 1880.

History of Litchfield County, Connecticut, with Illustrations and Biographical Sketches of Its Prominent Men and Pioneers. Philadelphia: J.W. Lewis & Co., 1881.

Hurd, D. Hamilton, ed. *History of Fairfield County, Connecticut, with Illustrations and Biographical Sketches of the Prominent Men and Pioneers.* Philadelphia: J.W. Lewis & Co., 1881.

Hurd, D. Hamilton, ed. *History of New London County, Connecticut, With Biographical Sketches of Many of Its Pioneers and Prominent Men.* Philadelphia: J.W. Lewis & Co., 1882.

Johnson, William Henry. *Autobiography of Dr. William Henry Johnson.* Albany: The Argus Company Printers, 1900.

Malles, Edward. *Bridge Building in Wartime, Colonel Wesley Brainerd's Memoir of the 50th New York Volunteer Engineers.* Knoxville: University of Tennessee Press, 1997.

McClellan, George B. *McClellan's Own Story.* New York: Charles L. Webster & Company, 1887.

Members. *The Story of The Twenty-first Regiment Connecticut Volunteer Infantry During the Civil War, 1861–1865.* Middletown, CT: Stewart Printing Company, 1900.

Morris, John M., ed. *The Connecticut War Record.* New Haven, CT: Peck, White & Peck, 1863–1865.

Smith, Stephen R., Frederick E. Camp, Lucius A. Barbour, George M. White, eds. *Record of Service of Connecticut Men in the Army and Navy of the United States During the War of the Rebellion.* Hartford, CT: Case, Lockwood, and Brainard Co., 1889.

Smith, William Farrar. *From Chattanooga to Petersburg Under Generals Grant and Butler—A Contribution to The History of The War, And A Personal Vindication.* New York: Houghton, Mifflin & Company, 1893.

Thompson, S. Millett. *Thirteenth Regiment Of New Hampshire Volunteer Infantry in The War of the Rebellion, 1861–1865.* Cambridge, MA: Riverside Press, 1888.

U.S. War Department, Robert N. Scott, H.M. Lazelle, George B. Davis, Leslie J. Perry, Joseph W. Kirkley, Fred C. Ainsworth, et al. *The War of the Rebellion: A Compilation of the Official Records of the Union and Confederate Armies.* Washington, D.C.: U.S. Government Printing Office, 1880–1901.

Yates, Walter J. *Souvenir of Excursion to Antietam.* New London, CT: Unknown, 1894.

Modern References

Bailey, Ronald H., and Editors of Time-Life Books. *The Bloodiest Day.* Alexandria, VA: Time-Life Books, 1984.

Bailey, Ronald H., and Editors of Time-Life Books. *Forward to Richmond.* Alexandria, VA: Time-Life Books, 1983.

Barrett, John G. *The Civil War In North Carolina.* Chapel Hill: University of North Carolina Press, 1963.

Boatner, Mark Mayo, III. *The Civil War Dictionary.* New York: David McKay Company, Inc., 1959.

Branch, Paul, Jr. *The Siege of Fort Macon.* Morehead City, NC. Herald Printing Company, 1982.

Caughman, Geraldine S. *Qui Transtulit Sustinet: Connecticut Battle Flag Collection, Volume I.* Wethersfield, CT: Caughman Associates, 2006.

Close, F. Perry. *The History of Hartford Streets.* Hartford, CT: Connecticut Historical Society, 1969.

Coates, Earl J., and John D. McAulay. *Civil War Sharps Carbines & Rifles.* Gettysburg, PA: Thomas Publications, 1996.

Cormier, Steven A. *The Siege of Suffolk: The Forgotten Campaign, April 11–May 4, 1863.* Lynchburg, VA: H.E. Howard, Inc., 1989.

Crenshaw, Douglas. *Fort Harrison and the Battle of Chaffin's Bluff.* Charleston, SC: History Press, 2013.

Foote, Shelby. *The Civil War a Narrative: Red River to Appomattox.* New York: Vintage Books, 1974.

Forman, Robert J., et al. *Bermuda Hundred Campaign Tour Guide.* Chesterfield, VA: The Chesterfield Historical Society, 2010.

Goolrick, William K., and Editors of Time-Life Books. *Rebels Resurgent Fredericksburg to Chancellorsville.* Alexandria, VA: Time-Life Books, 1985.

Hewett, Janet B. *Supplement to the Official Records of the Union and Confederate Armies.* Wilmington, NC: Broadfoot Publishing Co., 1994–2001. FHL US/CAN Book 973 M29u ser. 1 supp. pt. 2 v. 4 Record of Events—Connecticut troops (Union, 1st–8th Regiments)—v. 4. (serial no. 16) Connecticut troops (Union, 9th–28th Regiments).

Hill, Steven W. *Connecticut Battle Flags: The Civil War.* Hamden, CT: League of Women Voters of Connecticut Education Fund, 1986.

Jaynes, Gregory, and Editors of Time-Life Books. *The Killing Ground: Wilderness to Cold Harbor.* Alexandria, VA: Time-Life Books, 1986.

Johnson, Curt, and Richard C. Anderson, Jr. *Artillery Hell.* College Station, TX: Texas A&M University Press, 1995.

Madaus, Howard Michael. "The Percussion Martial Longarm of Eli Whitney, Jr," *ARMAX* Volume II, Number I (1988).

Manarin, Louis R. *Henrico County Field of Honor, Volume 2.* Richmond: Henrico County, 2004.

Marvel, William *Burnside,* Chapel Hill: University of North Carolina Press, 1991.

Naumec, David James. "The Connecticut Contracted '61 Springfield: The Special Model to the 'Good and Serviceable' Arm." *American Society of Arms Collectors Bulletin* 90 (2004), https://americansocietyofarmscollectors.org/wp-content/uploads/2019/06/2004-B90-The-Connecticut-Contracted-61-Springfiel.pdf.

Niven, John. *Connecticut for the Union: The Role of the State in the Civil War*. New Haven: Yale University Press, 1965.

O'Reilly, Francis A. *The Fredericksburg Campaign: Winter on the Rappahannock*. Baton Rouge: Louisiana State University Press, 2003.

Redkey, Edwin S. *A Grand Army of Black Men: Letters from African-American Soldiers in the Union Army, 1861–1865*. New York: Cambridge University Press, 1992.

Rhea, Gordon C. *Cold Harbor: Grant and Lee May 26-June 3, 1864*. Baton Rouge: Louisiana State University Press, 2002.

Robertson, William G. *Back Door to Richmond: The Bermuda Hundred Campaign April–June 1864*. Baton Rouge: Louisiana State University Press, 1987.

Salmon, John S. *The Official Virginia Civil War Battlefield Guide*. Mechanicsburg, VA: Stackpole Books, 2001.

Sauers, Richard A. *A Succession of Honorable Victories: The Burnside Expedition in North Carolina*. Dayton, OH: Morningside House, 1996.

Sommers, Richard J. *Richmond Redeemed: The Siege of Petersburg*. Garden City, NJ: Doubleday & Co., 1981.

Tice, Warren K. *Uniform Buttons of the United States 1776–1865*. Gettysburg, PA: Thomas Publications, 1997.

Time-Life Books Editors. *Echoes of Glory: Illustrated Atlas of The Civil War*. Alexandria, VA: Time-Life Books, 1991.

Todd, Frederick P. *American Military Equipage, 1851–1872*. Westbrook, CT: The Company of Military Historians, 1978.

Trotter, William R. *Ironclads and Columbiads: The Civil War in North Carolina, The Coast*. Winston-Salem, NC: John F. Blair Publisher, 1989.

Trudeau, Noah Andre. *Like Men of War: Black Troops in the Civil War, 1862–1865*. New York: Little, Brown, 1998.

Index

An * beside a name denotes an 8th Conn. Vols. member.

Acquia Creek, VA 65, 104
Alabama Infantry: 44th Regiment 113; 48th Regiment 115
Alexander, Joseph H. (J.H.)* 55
Alice Price (steamer) 40, 49, 55, 57, 62
Allen, Cornelius (Lunenburg Artillery, VA) 178
Andrews, Gov. Charles B. 195
Annapolis, MD 16–18, 21–24, 29, 30, 140, 201, 202, 211, 242
Antietam Creek 73–75, 77, 84, 88
Antietam Iron Works, MD 88
Appelman, Hiram* 10, 38, 53, 55, 60, 61, 67, 81–84, 120, 195, 204, 209, 210
Appomattox River 138, 141, 164–166, 170, 172–174, 176
Army Corps (Federal): Second Corps 164, 184; Fifth Corps 157; Sixth Corps 157, 161, 162, 166, 168; Seventh Corps 107, 109, 110, 122, 127, 204, 205; Ninth Corps 6, 63, 66, 68, 72, 78, 88, 89, 91, 98, 99, 101, 102, 106–109, 120, 173, 174, 204; Tenth Corps 141, 142, 149, 184; Eighteenth Corps 127, 140–142, 147, 149, 151, 154, 156, 157, 160, 162–164, 166, 168, 171–173, 175–178, 184–186, 205–207; Twenty-fourth Corps 187–189, 207, 208
Army of the James 140, 146, 149, 156, 164, 171, 176, 182, 186–188, 205–207
Army of the Potomac 6, 7, 61, 63, 66–68, 90, 91, 104, 106, 119, 127, 134, 140, 156, 160, 162, 163, 171, 175, 201, 204
Arnold, Charles* 22
Ashby's Landing, NC 33, 35

Baltimore & Ohio Railroad 70
Barton, Clara 102
Bartram, Ashbel E.* 192, 197
baseball 105, 106
Battle Flag Day 146, 194–196, 218, 219
Bealeton, VA 90, 92

Beaufort, NC 24, 39, 40, 48, 50–52, 60
Beeman, Charles N.* 85
Benning, Henry L. 82, 83, 178
Bermuda Hundred, VA 138, 140, 141, 147, 155–157, 162–164, 168, 174, 175, 177, 203
Bigelow, James A.* 188
Bingham, Levi C.* 136, 145
Bingham, Seth D.* 83
Bishop, Jacob* 182, 183
Bishop, Thomas W. 194
Blackford's Ford, MD 79
Bogue Banks, NC 48, 52, 53, 55, 56, 59
Boonsboro, MD 69, 70, 72, 73
Booth, George F.* 7, 60, 85, 86, 130
Boteler's Ford, MD *see* Blackford's Ford, MD
Bragg, Braxton 178
Brainerd, Wesley 96, 97, 99
Branch, Lawrence O. 79, 82
Breed, Charles* 62
Brookman, H.D. (bark) 26, 27, 29–31
Brooks, Albion D.* 109, 129, 131, 160, 161, 210–212
Brooks, William T.H. 140, 142, 145, 147, 148, 151–154, 158–161, 166–168, 206
Brookville, MD 69, 70
Brown, Duwaine* 22
Brown, James S. (Wise Artillery, VA) 77, 79
Brunswick, MD 90
Buckingham, Gov. William A. 9, 10, 12, 13, 110–112, 134, 173, 218
Burnham, Hiram 140, 142, 143, 147–154, 158–162, 165–168, 176–181 206, 207
Burnside, Ambrose E. 7, 13, 16, 18, 21, 24–28, 31, 32, 34–43, 46, 48, 55, 57, 58, 60–66, 71, 72, 74, 75, 77, 78, 88–92, 94, 96, 97, 102–104, 106–110, 120, 135, 160, 172, 173, 199, 201–204
Burnside Bridge *see* Burnside, Ambrose E.
Burnside Expedition *see* Burnside, Ambrose E.

Butler, Benjamin F. 132, 133, 138, 140, 142, 147, 149, 156, 163, 164, 171, 176, 182–184, 186, 187, 203, 205–207
Byrne, Andrew* 163

Camp Buckingham 11–13, 18, 218
Camp Burnside *see* Camp Hicks
Camp Hicks 18, 22
Carey, Dwight* 86
Carolina City, NC 50–52
Carr, Joseph B. 175, 207
Case, Oliver C.* 13, 14, 16, 18–22, 40, 41, 43, 44, 46, 59, 60, 63, 69, 86, 212
Catoctin Mountain 69, 70
Chapin, Harlow* 193, 196
Chasseur (steam-transport/gunboat) 26, 27, 29–31, 33, 35, 36, 38, 39, 49, 50
Chatham Manor *see* Lacy House
Chickahominy River 157
City of New York (propeller ship) 29
City Point, VA 138, 140, 141, 164, 172, 176, 203
Clark, Joseph C., Jr. (Battery E, 4th U.S. Artillery) 77
Clark, Lemuel B.* 86
Clift, Amos* 55
Coit, Charles M.* 12, 15, 17–19, 22, 23, 26, 27, 29–32, 37–40, 43–45, 49–54, 58–65, 68, 82, 84, 87–89, 91, 92, 95, 98, 102–106, 110–112, 115–122, 125, 128, 137, 140, 145, 146, 152–157, 159–164, 166–175, 180, 181, 183–185, 188–190, 206, 207, 213, 236, 238, 239, 242, 244, 246
Cold Harbor, VA 156–158, 162–164, 168, 171, 203, 211, 212
Columbia (steamer) 63
Cone, William H.* 195
Connecticut Artillery: 1st Conn. Heavy Artillery 9, 95; 1st Light Battery 189; 2nd Conn. Heavy Artillery 157, 161
Connecticut Infantry: 1st Regiment 9, 16, 66, 214, 219, 225; 2nd Regiment 9, 66,

210, 223, 245; 3rd Regiment 9, 11, 66, 217, 218, 230; 4th Regiment 9; 5th Regiment 9; 6th Regiment 9; 7th Regiment 9; 8th Regiment (Company A 10, 14, 16, 18, 21, 22, 27, 36, 40, 43, 52, 54, 55, 57, 59, 60, 62, 74, 85, 86, 114, 134, 183, 185, 211, 212, 219, 220, 225, 228, 229, 231, 232, 242, 246; Company B 10, 11, 43, 52, 59, 114, 115, 163, 169, 189, 212, 213, 244, 245; Company C 10, 39, 86, 97, 114, 115, 188, 195, 245; Company D 10, 52, 62, 114, 115, 195, 221, 230, 231, 242, 245; Company E 7, 10, 17, 21, 27, 29, 39, 50, 52, 54, 59, 60, 65, 85, 101, 103, 105, 111, 114, 115, 120, 145, 154, 214, 228, 229; Company F 10, 36, 59, 60, 62, 82, 114, 144, 169, 214, 217, 225, 244, 247; Company G 10-12, 36, 43, 54, 55, 114, 130, 145, 148, 154, 166, 169, 178, 188, 210, 214, 245; Company H 10, 39, 54, 59, 71, 97, 111, 114, 115, 169, 173; Company I 11-15, 17, 18, 33, 49, 54, 78, 83, 85, 102, 105, 115, 165, 170, 185, 188, 215, 216, 221, 226, 245; Company K 11, 12, 20, 30, 36, 39, 43, 52, 53, 68, 74, 80, 83, 86, 112, 114, 130, 132, 148, 154, 166, 188, 214, 245); 9th Regiment 9; 10th Regiment 11, 12, 17, 25, 36; 11th Regiment 11, 21, 22, 25, 27, 31, 41, 42, 45, 61, 62, 65-67, 72, 74, 101, 102, 105, 108, 134-137, 188, 190, 199, 244, 245; 14th Regiment 12; 15th Regiment 101, 102, 108, 112, 117, 130-132, 136; 16th Regiment 6, 7, 12, 67, 69, 73-79, 86, 101, 102, 108, 117, 128, 196, 197, 199; 21st Regiment 101, 102, 131, 158, 161, 178, 182, 188, 189; 29th Regiment 188
Cook, Roger W.* 145
Cox, Jacob D. 67, 71, 72, 78, 204
Cullen, Edgar M. 175, 207

Damascus, MD 68, 70
Darby, William* 163
Dauchy, Allen* 120, 239
Deep Creek, VA 119, 120, 128-130, 137, 140, 154, 203
Dept. of Virginia and North Carolina 107, 138, 171, 186, 187, 205-207
Devens, Charles, Jr. 158, 160, 188, 190, 207, 208
Diederich, Otto, (Battery A, 1st NY Light Artillery) 101
Dismal Swamp see Great Dismal Swamp
Dismal Swamp Canal 128, 129, 137
Dix, John A. 109, 110, 122, 124, 127, 202, 204, 205
Dixon, John A.* 88

Donelson (steamer) 62
Donohue, Michael T. 178, 179, 188, 208
Dougherty, Ambrose M.* 184
Douglass, Frederick 223, 224
Drayton, Thomas F. 81-83
Durell, George W. (Battery D, PA Light Artillery) 77
Durfee, William H.* 181

Elizabeth City, NC 37, 39, 128, 129
Elizabeth River 62, 122, 137
Elmore, Harvey E* 86
Elwood, Cornelius* 18
Escort (transport) 140
Eshleman, Benjamin F. (Washington Artillery, LA) 76
Eubank, John L. (Bath Artillery, VA) 74
Evans, Jerome* 145
Ewell, Richard S. 178

Fairchild, Harrison S. 67, 74, 75, 77, 78, 81-83, 87
Falmouth, VA 63, 64, 89, 91-94, 104, 202
Farnham, George W.* 132, 188
Ferris, Hilliard B.* 12, 13
Ferris, Robert* 85
Flagler, Daniel W. 53
flags 12, 15, 27, 35, 37, 39, 44, 45, 51, 55-58, 71, 83, 84, 92, 103, 105, 112, 115, 116, 118, 120, 134, 135, 146, 180, 183, 185, 194-196, 218-220, 233-240
Ford, Roger M.* 68-71, 80, 83, 91, 92, 98, 103, 129, 133, 135, 140, 141, 145, 148, 149, 151, 154, 169, 188, 214, 215
Fort Bartow 32-35, 38
Fort Burnham 182, 184, 190
Fort Clark 27
Fort Darling 151, 154, 203
Fort Harrison 112, 176, 177, 179-185, 187, 190, 203, 220, 228, 229, 253
Fort Hatteras 27
Fort Huger 32, 112, 113, 115, 116, 202, 236
Fort Macon 39, 48, 49, 51-55, 58-60, 73, 92, 202, 210, 234, 235, 238
Fort Monroe see Fortress Monroe
Fort Powhatan 141, 176
Fort Stevens 151, 153
Fortress Monroe 21, 24-27, 62, 63, 104, 117, 122, 127, 135-138, 140, 141, 146, 155, 171, 183, 185
Foss, Samuel S.* 111, 112, 119, 175, 180, 181, 188
Foster, John G. 21, 24, 37, 40-43, 45, 46, 63, 127, 205
Fowler, Douglas* 10
Fox, Lucius* 35, 215, 216
Frederick, MD 69-71, 202
Fredericksburg, VA 7, 63-66, 89, 90-93, 95, 96, 100-103, 118, 119, 202, 225, 234, 235, 238
Friend House 154, 166

Galena (ironclad) 104
Gallup, Frederick* 192, 196, 197
Garrigus, Horace* 145, 193
Garrigus, J. Henry* 192
Gaskins Mill, VA 89-92
Gates, Horace P.* 108
George Washington (steamer) 141
Georgia Infantry: 11th Regiment 82; 17th Regiment 178
Getty, George W. 91, 92, 98, 101, 102, 107-109, 113-116, 118, 120, 122, 124, 127, 202, 204, 205, 238
Gibbon, John 187-189, 207, 208
Gillmore, Quincy A. 142
Glenn (bark) 51
Glover, Joseph* 169, 170
Goddard, Alfred M.* 108, 148
Godfrey, Sylvester* 97
Goldsborough, Louis M. 24, 25, 32, 33
Goodrich, Elam T.* 111, 128, 133, 169, 170, 184
Gordon, Andrew* 163, 193
Granite State 13
Grant, Ulysses S. 121, 133, 138, 140, 156, 157, 160, 161, 163, 164, 167, 171, 173, 176, 181, 184, 186-188, 190, 208, 224
Great Dismal Swamp 108-110, 117, 120-122, 129
Guerrant, John (Goochland Light Artillery, VA) 178
Guide (steamer) 61, 62

Hagadon, William* 192
Hagood, Johnson 142, 147, 151
Half-Way House 149, 154
Hall, Henry C.* 14, 15, 18, 78, 79, 81-83, 94, 95, 132, 144, 152, 169, 216, 217
Halleck, Henry 63, 64, 103, 110, 156
Hancock, Winfield S. 164, 171, 172
Harland, Edward* 11, 13, 15, 17, 18, 22, 23, 26, 31, 32, 37, 38, 40, 43-45, 49, 52, 53, 55, 61, 62, 67, 68, 73-75, 77-79, 81, 83-88, 91, 100-102, 104, 108-110, 118, 124, 127, 128, 134, 192-194, 199, 203-206, 217, 218
Hartford, CT 5, 9-16, 84, 108, 122, 133, 134, 136, 183, 191, 192, 194-196, 201, 218, 224, 225, 228, 235, 239, 241
Hatteras, NC 25, 27-31, 35, 40, 135, 202
Havelock Station, NC 48-50
Hawkins, Rush C. 36, 37, 39, 81, 101
Hawley, Joseph R. 146, 194-196
Hawley, Timothy E.* 83, 193
Heckman, Charles A. 141, 142, 147, 153, 179, 181, 206
Henagan, John W. 159

Index

Henry, Guy V. 158–162
Hickok, Nathan E.* 183, 185, 220
Highland Light (steamer) 59
Hill, Ambrose P. 7, 79, 82, 87, 199
Hill, A.P. *see* Hill, Ambrose P.
Hill's Point *see* Fort Huger
Hincks, Edward W. *see* Hinks, Edward W.
Hinks, Edward W. 165
Hoke, Robert 151, 152, 156
Hollister, Fitz G.* 168, 221
Hooker, Joseph 104, 119, 122, 204
Hotchkiss, Philo D.* 145
Hoyt, Henry M.* 10, 18, 60, 82, 98, 130, 132, 136, 168, 175, 180, 184, 192, 194, 204, 206, 219
Hubbard, Thomas J.* 146, 194, 195
Hubbell, William S. 182
Humphrey, Benjamin G. 159
Huntington, William L.* 107, 108, 115, 116, 127, 128, 131, 133, 134, 221, 222

Irwin, Charles N.* 105, 181
Ives, Heber S.* 194
Ives, Noah P.* 30, 108

Jackson, Charles* 197
Jackson, Frederick W.* 11, 193
Jamaica, LI, NY 14–16, 120
James River 24, 25, 61, 62, 104, 112, 122, 127, 138, 140, 141, 151, 156, 163, 175–177, 179, 180, 182, 184, 188, 189, 203
Jericho Canal 117, 120, 121
Jerome, Francis D.* 115, 116
Jewett, Joseph H.* 192
John Brooks (steamer) 104
John Haswell (transport barge) 155
Johnson, Bushrod 147, 151
Johnson, William H.* 53
Johnson, William Henry* 222–224
Jones, David R. 77, 79, 81, 82
Jones, Henry R.* 194, 196, 197

Kanawha Division 67, 71, 78
Keables, Amos L.* 181
Keedysville, MD 69, 70, 73
Keeler, Silas P.* 145
Kemper, James L. 79, 81–83
Kershaw, Joseph B. 159
Kilbourne, James B.* 181
Kingman, Emily Brooks 210, 211

Lacy House 64, 93–100, 102, 103
Lamson, Roswell 108, 113, 114
Lane, John S.* 184, 192, 196, 197
Lathrop, Dr. DeWitt C.* 26, 53
Laytonsville, MD 70
Lee, Robert E. 7, 61, 68, 107, 122, 124, 125, 140, 156, 164, 176, 178, 181, 189
Leesborough, MD 68, 69, 70
Lewis, Charles E.* 86
Liberty, VA 92

Lincoln, Pres. Abraham 5, 9, 61, 63, 66, 88, 94, 103, 171, 186, 187, 217
Lion, Thomas W. 78, 80
Long, William* 163
Longstreet, James 81, 107, 111, 118, 184, 185
Lord, Orton L.* 86
Lovettsville, VA 89, 90
Lynchburg, VA 190, 203

Mann, Peter* 88
Marsh, Wolcott P.* 16, 18, 20, 27–39, 41, 45–47, 50–60, 62, 64, 65, 69, 70–74, 76, 77, 82, 85, 86, 92, 95, 98, 102, 224–226, 228
Marston, Gilman 147, 148, 159, 161, 162
Martin, John H. 178
Martindale, John H. 160–162, 167
Mary Benton 13
Maryland Infantry: 5th Regiment 188
Mason, Thomas* 85
Massachusetts Infantry: 21st Regiment 17, 25, 41, 42, 44; 23rd Regiment 24; 24th Regiment 24, 36; 25th Regiment 17, 24, 36, 38, 147, 161; 27th Regiment 17, 24, 36, 43, 138, 147; 28th Regiment 138; 40th Regiment 158, 160
Matson, Philo* 43
Mattaponi River 124, 126
McCall, John* 84, 148, 154
McCann, Norton O.* 163
McCarty, William H.* 192
McClellan, George B. 24, 25, 61, 63–66, 68, 75, 78, 88, 89, 91, 110, 111, 124, 126, 176, 204
McIntosh, David G. (Pee Dee Artillery, SC) 79–83
Meade, George 125, 160, 161, 164, 171
Merriam, John, L.* 20, 133, 241, 242
Middletown, MD 70, 72
Mississippi Infantry: 13th Regiment 159; 17th Regiment 159; 18th Regiment 159; 21st Regiment 159
Moore, George (sutler) 31
Moore, James R.* 242
Morehead City, NC 48, 50–53, 55, 59, 61, 62, 202
Morgan, Andrew M.* 98, 186, 216, 219, 230, 244
Morgan, Henry E.* 55, 84
Morris, John M.* 10, 84, 85, 97, 116, 122, 124, 126, 127, 129–131, 153, 163, 187, 191, 217
Morris, Lewis O. 53
Mosquito Fleet 33, 37

Nansemond River 109–113, 118, 121, 138, 202
Nash, Charles W.* 10
National Road 70–72

Neff, Henry H.* 86
Nettleton, Samuel Jay* 13–15, 17, 19, 21, 25, 33–38, 49–51, 64, 65, 68, 69, 71, 73, 79, 81, 84, 86, 88, 91, 96, 104, 105, 111, 121, 125, 126, 132, 133, 137, 192, 197, 226, 227, 242, 245
Neuse River 39–41, 48, 49, 59
New Bern, NC 24, 39, 40, 42, 44–50, 52, 53, 55, 59, 61, 106, 202
New Hampshire Infantry: 2nd Regiment 162; 6th Regiment 25, 39; 10th Regiment 111, 115, 132, 142, 147, 152, 154, 159–161, 163, 178, 188; 12th Regiment 188; 13th Regiment 138, 140, 142, 154, 159, 162, 166
New Hartford, CT 10, 97, 224
New Haven, CT 5, 97, 130, 131, 134, 136, 214, 243
New Jersey Infantry: 9th Regiment 25, 36; 24th Regiment 36
New York (steamer) 39, 62
New York, NY 13–15, 18, 24, 40, 136, 228, 237
New York, Artillery: 1st Battalion Light Artillery 101; 1st Regiment Marine Artillery 35
New York Engineers: 15th Regiment 96; 50th Regiment 96–99;
New York Infantry: 1st Mounted Rifles 142; 9th Regiment (Hawkin's Zouaves) 35–37, 39, 67, 75, 81, 101, 103, 198; 51st Regiment 18, 25; 53rd Regiment (D'Epineuil's Zouaves) 22, 25, 27; 81st Regiment 190; 89th Regiment 25, 39, 67, 77, 113–116; 92nd Regiment 159, 163; 96th Regiment 178, 179, 183, 188; 98th Regiment 190; 103rd Regiment 67, 81; 117th Regiment 115; 118th Regiment 131, 140, 142, 150–153, 159, 160, 162, 166, 178, 188; 139th Regiment 162, 163
Newcomb, Franklin A.* 60
Newport News, VA 62, 63, 104–107, 110–112, 140, 141, 202
Newport River 48, 50, 51
Nichols, George F. 178
Nichols, Jerome* 85
Norfolk, VA 24, 62, 104, 108, 110, 119–122, 131, 175, 252
Norfolk & Petersburg Railroad 117, 119, 120
Norfolk & Weldon Railroad 121
North Carolina Infantry: 7th Regiment 78, 79, 81, 82; 37th Regiment 78, 79, 81–83; 55th Regiment 115; 66th Regiment 130
Northerner (steamer) 39
Norwich, CT 10, 11, 62, 84, 85, 108, 112, 146, 154, 173, 192, 193, 213, 217, 218, 223, 230–232, 237

Index

Ord, Edward O.C. 171, 172, 175–181, 187, 188, 207
Orleans, VA 89–91

Pamunkey River 123, 124, 156, 157, 162
Parke, John G. 21, 22, 25, 37, 40–46, 48, 51, 53, 55, 57, 58, 63, 64, 66, 201, 203, 204
Peck, John J. 107–109, 111, 115, 117–119
Pelham, Marcus L.* 188
Pelton, Edward E.* 193
Pennsylvania, Infantry: 48th Regiment 95; 51st Regiment 25, 40, 41; 53rd Regiment 36; 58th Regiment 158, 159, 190; 188th Regiment 158, 190
Peters, James T.* 85
Petersburg, VA 7, 11, 139, 141, 144, 146, 147, 149, 151, 163, 164, 166–168, 171–176, 178, 184, 188, 192, 203, 214, 217, 221
Peterson, William H.* 181
Phelps, Howes* 43
Philomont, VA 89–91
Phoenix (steamer) 36
Pickett, George 146
Pioneer Corps 137, 138, 146, 154
Pleasant Valley, MD 88–90, 202
Plumb, Seth F.* 7, 17–21, 27, 29, 59, 60, 62, 64–66, 85, 86, 88, 95, 97, 99–106, 110, 114, 116, 118–122, 125–133, 137, 138, 140, 145, 151, 154, 157, 161, 162, 169, 170, 172, 173, 175, 182, 227, 228, 241, 248
Plumb, William H. 161, 162
Point of Rocks, VA 141, 164–166, 168
Port Walthall Junction, VA 141–144, 146, 147, 168, 188, 195, 203, 222, 230
Portsmouth, VA 108, 110, 117, 119, 121–130, 132, 134–137, 140, 202, 205, 236, 239
Potomac River 63, 79, 88–91
Pratt, William M.* 188, 208

Ransom, Robert 151
Rappahannock River 64, 65, 91–93, 96, 99, 101–103, 119
Rathbun, John A.* 181, 192
Recruit (hospital ship) 22
Reilly, James (Rowan Artillery, NC) 77
Reno, Jesse 25, 37, 40–42, 45, 46, 63, 64, 66, 68, 71, 72, 78, 204
Reynolds, Gilbert G.* 181
Rhode Island Infantry: 4th Regiment 25, 37, 42–45, 48, 50–53, 55, 57, 61, 64–67, 74–79, 86, 101, 102, 131, 199; 5th Regiment 25, 42, 44, 45, 48, 51, 53, 54, 57, 58
Rice, F.F. 235
Rice, Robert* 97
Richardson, John B. (Washington Artillery, LA) 77, 82

Richmond, VA 7, 24, 26, 39, 61, 63, 68, 107, 120, 122, 124, 125, 138–140, 144, 149, 151, 156, 157, 159, 162, 175, 176, 182, 184, 188–190, 192, 203
Richmond & Petersburg Railroad 117, 119, 120, 141, 142, 145, 147
Richmond Turnpike 147, 149, 151
Ridgeville, MD 68, 70
Ripley, Eleazer H.* 84, 128, 129, 189
Roanoke Island, NC 25, 32–35, 37, 39, 92, 129, 135, 202, 223, 229, 234, 235, 238, 246
Roberts, Samuel H. 177, 179, 180
Roberts, William J.* 102, 165, 188
Rodman, Isaac P. 37, 43, 44, 66–68, 71, 72, 74, 75, 77–79, 83, 86, 87, 204
Rohrbach, Henry R. 73, 74
Root, Orlow* 146, 194, 195
Rouse, Horace G.* 86
Russell, Charles L. 11
Russell, James L. * 54, 84, 192
Ruth, Patrick K.* 10, 11

St. John's College 17
Sanders, Horace T. 149
Scammon, Eliakim P. 72, 78
Second Independent Brigade 190
Sentinel (gunboat) 31, 32, 38–40, 49
Sexton, Henry D.* 22
Seymour, Thomas H. 110, 111
Shadek, Joseph E.* 23, 30, 34, 46, 56, 58, 228, 229, 242, 246
Sharpsburg, MD 7, 69, 70, 72, 73, 77, 78, 82, 85, 92, 197–199, 212
Shedek, Joseph E. *see* Shadek, Joseph E.
Sheffield, Thomas* 54, 194
Shippen House 147, 148
Simmons, William S.* 182, 183
Simons, John H. 86
Slaughter, Montgomery 102
Slocum's Creek, NC 40, 48–50
Smith, Caleb 18
Smith, Elijah Y.* 10
Smith, Martin B.* 10, 95, 111, 117, 120, 132, 150, 152–154, 168, 169, 180, 181, 187, 188, 229, 230
Smith, Moses* 134, 153, 161, 168, 169, 175, 181, 183–186, 188–190
Smith, William A.* 181
Smith, William F. 140, 142, 149, 156–158, 160, 161, 164–168, 171, 172, 206
Smithson, Walter* 163
Snavely's Ford, MD 75, 77, 199
Sons of Connecticut 15, 194, 235
South Carolina Infantry: 2nd Regiment 159; 3rd Regiment 159; 7th Regiment 159; 8th Regiment 159; 11th Regiment 147; 12th Regiment 79; 15th Regiment 159; 20th Regiment 159; 25th Regiment 142, 145, 151; 27th Regiment 142

South Mills, NC 128–130, 202
South Mountain, MD 70, 72, 88, 92, 135, 202, 234, 235, 238
Spaulding, Ira 96, 98, 99
Stannard, George J. 161, 168, 169, 176–183, 206
State of Georgia (cruiser) 52
Stedman, Griffin A. 11, 161, 162, 173
Steele, Henry* 189
Stepping Stones (gunboat) 114–116
Stevens, Aaron F. 142, 168, 177–179, 181
Stevens, Emerson R.* 184
Stevens, Isaac I. 63, 64
Stocking, Sabin* 124, 129
Storrs, Dr. Melanethon* 26, 38, 53, 55, 108, 119, 183, 184, 192, 194
Stribling, Robert M. (Fauquier Battery, VA) 112, 113
Strickland, Henry E.* 44, 86, 195
Suffolk, VA 7, 106–108, 110–113, 117–122, 127, 128, 138, 202, 235
Sumner, Edwin V. 91, 92, 238
Sweet, William A.* 86
Swift Creek, VA 147–149, 154, 203

Taylor, George 124, 125, 127
Taylor, Richard C. 178
Tennessee Infantry: 17th Regiment 178; 23rd Regiment 178
Terry, Alfred H. 184, 190
Terry, Andrew* 22, 26
Thomas, Albert H.* 20, 193
Toombs, Robert A. 82, 83
Trask, Frank* 86
Trent River 39, 45, 46, 60
Tucker, George H.* 111

Union (tugboat) 31, 59
United States Colored Troops 141, 183
Upham, Charles L.* 11, 43, 52, 75, 80, 81, 83, 102, 112, 130, 193
Utica (transport) 122

Vandall, Mitchell* 132
Vermont Infantry: 3rd Regiment 166; 9th Regiment 115, 117, 188, 190, 208
Virginia Cavalry: 24th Regiment 185
Virginia Infantry: 7th Regiment 81
Vorra, John H.* 188

Wadhams, Edward* 105, 154
Wadhams, Martin L.* 86
Wait, Marvin* 84–86, 135, 217, 231, 232
Wales, Francis* 132
Walker, Charles H.* 84, 195
Ward, John E.* 10, 18, 45, 52, 55, 60, 61, 81, 83, 84, 97, 108, 109, 111, 112, 114–116, 117, 119, 120, 126, 128, 143, 144, 150, 153, 157, 168,

169, 170, 175, 184, 188, 204–207, 230, 231
Warner, Patrick* 185
Warrenton, VA 91
Washington, D.C. 5, 7, 16–18, 66, 68, 70, 73, 89, 91, 104, 112, 119, 129, 140, 156, 171, 173, 183, 186, 187, 189, 197, 202, 222, 223
Waterford, VA 90
Waterloo, VA 91
Weed, Thomas S.* 181, 184
Weitzel, Godfrey 149, 151, 181, 184, 185, 187, 207
West Branch Battery see Fort Huger

Wheatland, VA 89–91
Wheel Barrow see *Union*
Wheeler, Lucius* 86
White, Moses J. 48, 55, 57
White House, VA 123, 124, 126, 127, 156, 157, 162, 164, 168, 184, 202, 203
Whiting, James R. (9th NY Howitzers) 75–77
Whitman, Walt 102
Whitney, Eli, Jr. 243–245
Wiard, Norman (Wiard gun) 35
Wilcox, Whiting 84, 86
Willcox, Orlando B. 66, 72, 77, 78, 91, 98, 101, 204

Williams, Isaac* 192, 196
Williamson, Robert S. 53
Woodbury, Daniel P. 96–99
Wright, Dr. David M. 131, 132
Wright, Horatio G. 157, 158, 160

Yorktown, VA 122–124, 126, 127, 135, 140, 141, 168, 203

Zouave (gunboat) 35

www.ingramcontent.com/pod-product-compliance
Lightning Source LLC
Chambersburg PA
CBHW080801300426
44114CB00020B/2784